BUTLER'S LIVES OF THE

THE LIVES OF THE SAINTS

led by the

REV. ALBAN BUTLER

Now Edited, Revised, and Copiously Supplemented by

HERBERT THURSTON, S.J.

AND

DONALD ATTWATER

VOL. VIII
AUGUST

LONDON
BURNS OATES & WASHBOURNE LTD.
PUBLISHERS TO THE HOLY SEE

NIHIL OBSTAT:

EDUARDUS J. MAHONEY, S.TH.D.,
Censor deputatus.

IMPRIMATUR:

✠ JOSEPHUS BUTT,
Vicarius generalis.

WESTMONASTERII,
die 7a Februarii, 1933.

Made and Printed in Great Britain
1933

PREFACE

IN publishing an extensive work of the Lives of the Saints to divide it into twelve volumes of more or less uniform length, each devoted to one month of the year, is an obvious measure of suitability and convenience. But it has the practical objection that the number of saints and *beati* whose feasts occur in any one month is by no means constant; there is a very notable increase during the summer and autumn. In this August volume it will be found, nevertheless, that the number of saints dealt with is somewhat less than in any of the preceding volumes yet published, for the reason that there occurs a number of feasts of saints of importance and interest of whom a great deal is known. Some of these were dealt with at considerable length by Alban Butler; *e.g.* our Blessed Lady, St Dominic, St Clare, St Helen, St Bernard, St Jane Frances de Chantal, St Louis of France, and St Augustine of Hippo. Others have been canonised or beatified only since his time: such are St Alphonsus Liguori (who was a contemporary of Butler), Blessed Peter-Julian Eymard, the Curé of Ars, Blessed Peter Faber, St John Eudes, Blessed Juvenal Ancina, and several outstanding figures among the English and Welsh martyrs. Among other additions to Butler's text, notable in interest if not in length, are St Tarsicius, whose *cultus* has been so widely spread by the greatly increased frequency of holy Communion among the laity since the eighteenth century, and St Philomena, the popular devotion to whom was so much extended by the influence of St John Vianney.

In this volume English saints and *beati* are well represented. In addition to SS. Ethelwold, Waltheof, Ebba, and the post-Reformation martyrs, room has been found for SS. Oswald, Oswin, Sebbe, and others. In this there has been no thought of favouring nationalist particularism, but it is right and proper that recognition should be given to St Oswald, who was formerly regarded as a great national hero, and St Sebbe, the sanctity of both of whom is approved by mention in the Roman Martyrology, as well as to those who, like St Oswin and St Thomas of Dover, have now an interest that is almost entirely historical. Ireland also is well represented (notably by St Aidan, though his importance is primarily English) and in

PREFACE

a lesser degree Scotland; in both cases there is the standing difficulty of lack of really reliable information about the early Celtic saints.

DONALD ATTWATER.

I have only to add that, as in the July volume, the biographies have either been entirely written by Mr. Attwater (with the exceptions of BB. Michael Carvalho, Mary Michaela, and Timothy of Montecchio, which I have written myself) or adapted by him from Butler's text, while I have contributed the bibliographical notes.

HERBERT THURSTON, S.J.

CONTENTS OF VOLUME VIII

(The entries marked with an asterisk are additions to Butler's text. A few of his notices have been discarded and written anew; many have been supplemented, and all have been revised.)

AUGUST 1

	PAGE
St Peter in Chains	1
The Holy Machabees, marts.	3
SS. Faith, Hope, Charity, and Wisdom, marts.	8
St Ethelwold, bp. and conf.	8

AUGUST 2

*St Alphonsus Liguori, bp. and conf.	11
St Stephen I, pope and mart.	24
*St Theodota, mart.	27
*The Portiuncula Indulgence	28

AUGUST 3

The Finding of St Stephen	32
*Bd. Benno, bp. and conf.	35
*Bd. Augustine Gazotich, bp. and conf.	36
*Bd. Peter Julian Eymard, conf.	38

AUGUST 4

St Dominic, conf.	43
*SS. Ia and her Comps., marts.	55
St Molua, abbot and conf.	56
St Waltheof, abbot and conf.	57

AUGUST 5

Our Lady of the Snow	61
*SS. Addai and Mari, bps. and confs.	62
St Afra, mart.	65
*St Nonna, matron	67
*St Thomas of Dover, mart.	68

AUGUST 6

The Transfiguration of our Lord	69
SS. Sixtus, Felicissimus, and Agapitus, marts.	71
SS. Justus and Pastor, marts.	73
*St Hormisdas, pope and conf.	74

CONTENTS OF VOLUME VIII

AUGUST 7

St Cajetan, conf.	77
*St Claudia, matron	83
*St Dometius the Illustrious, mart.	83
*St Victricius, bp. and conf.	84
*St Albert of Trapani, conf.	86
*BB. Agathangelo and Cassian, marts.	87

AUGUST 8

SS. Cyriacus, Largus, and Smaragdus, marts.	94
St Hormisdas, mart.	95
*The Fourteen Holy Helpers	96
*Bd. Altmann, bp. and conf.	97
*Bd. Joan of Aza, matron	99
*Bd. John Felton, mart.	100

AUGUST 9

*St John Mary Vianney, conf.	103
St Romanus, mart.	113
SS. Nathy and Phelim, confs.	114
St Oswald, king and mart.	115
*Bd. John of Salerno, conf.	118
*Bd. John of Alvernia, conf.	120
*Bd. John of Rieti, conf.	121

AUGUST 10

St Laurence, mart.	123
*Bd. Amadeus of Portugal, conf.	126

AUGUST 11

SS. Tiburtius, mart., and Chromatius, conf.	128
*St Philomena, virg. and mart.	129
*St Alexander the Charcoal-burner, bp. and mart.	132
St Susanna, virg. and mart.	133
*St Attracta, virg.	134
St Equitius, abbot and conf.	135
St Blaan, bp. and conf.	136
St Gaugericus or Gery, bp. and conf.	137
*Bd. Peter Faber, conf.	138

AUGUST 12

St Clare, virg. and abbess	142
St Euplius, mart.	149
St Muredach, bp. and conf.	150
*SS. Porcarius and his Comps., marts.	151

CONTENTS OF VOLUME VIII

August 13

	PAGE
St Hippolytus, mart.	152
St Cassian, mart.	155
*St Simplician, bp. and conf.	156
St Radegunde, queen	157
*St Maximus Homologetes, abbot and mart.	161
St Wigbert, abbot and conf.	163
*St Nerses Glaiëtsi, bp. and conf.	164
*Bd. Gertrude of Altenberg, virg.	165
*Bd. Francis of Pesaro, conf.	166
*Bd. William Freeman, mart.	167

August 14

St Eusebius, conf.	169
St Eusebius, mart.	170
*St Marcellus of Apamæa, bp. and mart.	172
*St Fachanan, bp. and conf.	173
*St Athanasia, matron	174
*Bd. Eberhard, abbot and conf.	175
*BB. Antony Primaldi and his Comps., marts.	176

August 15

The Blessed Virgin Mary	177
*St Tarsicius, mart.	183
St Arnulfus of Soissons, bp. and conf.	184

August 16

St Joachim, conf.	186
*St Arsacius, hermit	188
*St Armel, abbot and conf.	189
*Bd. Laurence Loricatus, hermit	189
St Roch, conf.	190

August 17

St Hyacinth, conf.	192
St Mamas, mart.	195
SS. Liberatus and his Comps., marts.	196
St Clare of Montefalco, virg.	197

August 18

St Agapitus, mart.	199
*SS. Florus and Lorus, marts.	199
St Helen, empress	201
St Alipius, bp. and conf.	205
Little St. Hugh, mart.	208
*Bd. Angelo Augustine Mazzinghi, conf.	209
*Bd. Beatrice da Silva, virg.	210
*Bd. Aimo Taparelli, conf.	211

CONTENTS OF VOLUME VIII

August 19
	PAGE
*St John Eudes, conf.	213
*St Andrew the Tribune, mart.	219
SS. Timothy, Agapius, and Thecla, marts.	220
St Sixtus III, pope and conf.	221
St Mochta, bp. and conf.	222
*St Bertulf, abbot and conf.	223
*St Sebald, conf.	224
St Louis of Anjou, bp. and conf.	225
Bd. Emily Bicchieri, virg.	228

August 20
St Bernard, abbot and doctor	230
*St Amadour, hermit	247
St Oswin, king and mart.	248
St Philibert, abbot and conf.	249

August 21
St Jane-Frances de Chantal, widow and abbess	251
*St Anastasius Cornicularius, mart.	258
*SS. Luxorius, Cisellus, and Camerinus, marts.	259
SS. Bonosus and Maximian, marts.	260
St Sidonius Apollinaris, bp. and conf.	261
*Bd. Humbeline, matron and abbess	265
Bd. Bernard Tolomeo, conf.	266

August 22
SS. Timothy, Hippolytus, and Symphorian, marts.	268
*St Sigfrid, abbot and conf.	270
St Andrew, conf.	271
*BB. William Lacey and Richard Kirkman, marts.	271
*Bd. John Wall, mart.	274
*Bd. John Kemble, mart.	275

August 23
St Philip Benizi, conf.	278
SS. Claudius, Asterius, and others, marts.	283
St Eugene, bp. and conf.	286
*Bd. James of Mevania, conf	287

August 24
St Bartholomew, apostle	289
The Martyrs of Utica	291
St Audoenus or Ouen, bp. and conf.	292

CONTENTS OF VOLUME VIII

August 25

	PAGE
St Louis, king and conf.	294
St Genesius the Comedian, mart.	303
St Genesius of Arles, mart.	305
*St Mennas, bp. and conf.	306
St Ebba, virg. and abbess	308
St Gregory of Utrecht, abbot	309
*Bd. Michael Carvalho, mart.	311
*Bd. Joan Antide Thouret, virg.	312
*Bd. Mary Michaela, virg.	314

August 26

St Zephyrinus, pope and mart.	316
*SS. Secundus and Alexander, marts.	317
*St Adrian, mart.	318
*Bd. Herluin, abbot and conf.	319
*Bd. Timothy of Montecchio, conf.	320
*Bd. Thomas Percy, mart.	320

August 27

St Joseph Calasanctius, conf.	324
*St Marcellus and his Comps., marts.	330
St Pœmen, abbot and conf.	331
St Cæsarius of Arles, bp. and conf.	333
St Syagrius, bp. and conf.	339
*Bd Amadeus of Lausanne, bp. and conf.	339
*Bd. Angelo of Foligno, conf.	340
*St Margaret the Barefooted, widow	341
*Bd. Gabriel Mary, conf.	341
*Bd. David Lewis, mart.	343

August 28

St Augustine of Hippo, bp. and doctor	346
St Hermes, mart.	363
St Julian of Brioude, mart.	363
*SS. Alexander, John III, and Paul IV, bps. and confs.	364
*St Moses the Black, mart.	366
*St Rumon, conf.	367
*The London Martyrs of 1588	368
*Bd. Edmund Arrowsmith, mart.	371

August 29

The Beheading of St John the Baptist	373
St Sabina, mart.	377
St Sebbe, king and conf.	377
St Medericus or Merry, abbot and conf.	378
*Bd. Richard Herst, mart.	379

CONTENTS OF VOLUME VIII

August 30

	PAGE
St Rose of Lima, virg.	381
SS. Felix and Adauctus, marts.	383
St Pammachius, conf.	384
St Fiacre, conf.	386
*St Fantinus, abbot and conf.	388
*Bd. Bronislava, virg.	388

August 31

St Raymund Nonnatus, card. and conf.	390
*St Paulinus of Trier, bp. and conf.	393
St Aidan, bp. and conf.	394
St Cuthburga, queen and abbess	396
*The Servite Martyrs of Prague	396
*Bd. Juvenal Ancina, bp. and conf.	397

THE LIVES OF THE SAINTS

AUGUST 1

ST PETER IN CHAINS
c. A.D. 42

THE chains and prisons of the martyrs were their joy and glory, and the source of their grace and crown, and God honoured them in the Prince of the Apostles with miracles. It has been related in the life of St James the Great that Herod Agrippa, having put to death that apostle, in order to please his people by an action still more agreeable to them caused St Peter to be cast into prison. It was his intention to put him publicly to death after Easter. The whole church at Jerusalem sent up its prayers and cries to God without ceasing for the deliverance of the chief pastor of His flock. The King took all precautions possible to prevent the escape of his prisoner, as he and the other apostles had once before been delivered out of prison by an angel (Acts v 18, 19). St Peter, in complete tranquillity of mind and entire resignation of himself, lay fast asleep on the very night before the day on which he was to be brought before the people, when it pleased God to deliver him out of the hands of his enemies. He was guarded by sixteen soldiers, four of whom always kept sentry in their turns : two in the same dungeon with him, and two at the gate. He was fastened to the ground by two chains, and slept between the two soldiers. In the middle of the night a bright light shone in the prison and an angel appeared near him and, striking him on the side, awaked him out of his sleep, and bade him instantly arise, gird his coat about him, put on his sandals and his cloak, and follow him. The chains dropped off from his hands, and Peter rose up and went after the angel, thinking that he was in a vision. He passed after him through the first and second ward, and through the iron gate which led into the city, which opened to them of its own accord. The angel conducted him through one street ; then suddenly disappeared, leaving him to seek some shelter. Till then the Apostle still doubted whether the whole thing was not a dream, but now he knew in very deed that the Lord had sent His angel and delivered him from Herod and from the expectation of the Jews. He went directly to the house of Mary the mother of John, surnamed Mark, where several disciples were together, praying for his deliverance. As he stood knocking, a young woman came to the door, and, perceiving it was his voice, ran in and told the others that Peter was outside; and when she persisted, they thought it must be his angel sent by God, until, being let in, he told them the whole manner of his escape. And having enjoined them to tell what had happened to St James and the rest of the brethren, he withdrew to a place of more security. The next day, when he was not to be found, Agrippa commanded the keepers to be put to death, supposing them to be, either by connivance or carelessness, accessory to St Peter's escape.

The Western Church has long kept this festival on August 1, either as the day of the dedication of the church of the Holy Apostles at Rome, built on the Esquiline Hill in the fourth century, or of the consecration of its rebuilding by Pope St Sixtus III about 440, when it received the chain which had bound the Apostle, sent by the Empress Eudocia, wife of Theodosius II, from Jerusalem; whence it came to be known as the church of St Peter in Chains (San Pietro in Vincoli). The other chain was given to Constantinople, where a church was built to receive it and dedicated on January 16, the date on which the Byzantines keep the feast of St Peter's escape from chains. The Roman chain is still treasured in the church on the Esquiline and the popes were accustomed to send filings of these chains to devout princes, and they were often instruments of miracles. The Pope himself rasped off the filings, which he enclosed in a cross or in a golden key, as appears from St Gregory who says in his letter to King Childebert, to whom he sent one of these keys, that many persons out of devotion hung them about their necks. St Caesarius says that the chains also with which this Apostle was bound in his last imprisonment before his martyrdom were preserved by the faithful and honoured at Rome in his time. Thus, as the same saint says, we may see that the iron chains of St Peter have been esteemed as more precious and valuable than gold. Pagan Rome never derived so much honour from the spoils and trophies of a conquered world as Christian Rome receives from the corporeal remains of the two glorious Apostles, before which the greatest emperors laid down their diadems and prostrated themselves, as St Chrysostom and St Augustine observe. August 1 was formerly called in England Lammas-day, *i.e.* Loaf-Mass, from Old English *hláfmæsse*, it being a sort of early harvest-thanksgiving, at which a

Mass of thanksgiving for the first-fruits of the earth, or of the corn, was celebrated. It was kept with a solemn procession and was also called the Guild of August. The solemn blessing of new grapes was performed both among the Greeks and Latins, in some places on the 1st, in others on the 6th day of August, and is expressly mentioned in ancient liturgical books.

The latest pronouncement upon this feast is to be found in the volume issued in 1932 by the Bollandists—the *Acta Sanctorum* for November, vol. ii, part 2, pp. 409–410. This volume is a commentary upon the " Hieronymianum," the ancient martyrology which for some reason bears this misleading name. The notice in this early compilation runs thus : " At Rome the dedication of the first church which was built and consecrated by St Peter." This is, of course, a misconception. The " titulus apostolorum," the earliest name by which the parish was known, possibly came into existence at the end of the fourth century, and it had reference to the two apostles Peter and Paul, as inscriptions prove. But after the new church had been consecrated by Sixtus III it was called the " titulus Eudoxiae," and it is only somewhat later, under Pope Symmachus (498–514), that we find any reference to the " chains." See H. Grisar, *History of Rome and the Popes* (Eng. Ed.), i, p. 190 ; also H. Grisar in the *Civiltà Cattolica*, 1898, vol. iii, pp. 204–221 ; *Dictionnaire d'Archéologie*, vol. iii, cc. 3–19 ; J. P. Kirsch, *Die römischen Titelkirchen*, pp. 45–52. Formerly in the apse of St Peter's ad Vincula there was an inscription with this distich :

Inlaesas olim servant hæc tecta cathenas
Vincla sacrata Petri, ferrum pretiosius auro.

If Cæsarius really wrote as Butler reports, the idea may have been suggested by these lines.

THE HOLY MACHABEES, Marts.

166 B.C.

Machabee (probably meaning " the hammer ") was the surname of Judas, the third son of that Mathathias who was the first leader of the Jews in their revolt against Antiochus IV Epiphanes ; the name was afterwards extended to the whole family and descendants of Mathathias, and was applied to those who followed them in their rising against the King of Syria, among them the martyrs who are celebrated on the first day of August. These Machabean martyrs are the only saints of the Old Law who are commemorated liturgically throughout the Universal Church, and the only ones to figure in the general calendar of the Western Church ; feasts of Old Testament saints are common in the East, but, apart from the Machabees, are unknown in the West, except for a few proper to religious orders or places, *e.g.* SS. Elias and Eliseus among the Carmelites, and others in the Latin province of Jerusalem.

The cause of the rebellion of the Jews was the efforts of Antiochus to impose Greek paganism upon them, in which he was assisted by the intruded high priest Josue (Jason) and his simoniacal successor Onias (Menelaus); but the occasion of the first actual outbreak was a persecution of the Jews undertaken by Antiochus in rage and mortification when his second campaign against Egypt was stopped by the Roman senate in 168 B.C. He sent a general, Apollonius, with twenty-two thousand men to Jerusalem, whose orders were to hellenise the city by killing the Jews and importing foreigners in their place. Apollonius concealed his design under a show of peace, but on the next Sabbath day, when all was quiet, he commanded his soldiers to go through the streets and massacre all persons they should meet, which they did without the least resistance from the Jews, who suffered themselves to be butchered for fear of violating the Sabbath. About ten thousand persons who escaped the slaughter were carried away captives, and others fled. Apollonius then ordered the city to be plundered, and afterwards set on fire. The walls were demolished, the service of the Temple abandoned, and the holy place polluted. The Temple itself was dedicated to Jupiter Olympius, and his statue was erected on the altar of burnt-offerings. Many of the Jews apostatised under this persecution, but others courageously sealed their fidelity to the law of God with their blood. Altars and statues were set up in every town of Judæa, and groves were consecrated to idolatrous mysteries; and the Jews were compelled to offer sacrifice to idols. It was made immediate death to be caught observing the Sabbath, the rite of circumcision, or any other part of the Mosaic law.

Among the martyrs who preferred torments and death to violation of the divine law one of the most eminent was St Eleazar. He was one of the chief among the Scribes or doctors of the law, a man ninety years old, and of a comely aspect. His countenance inspired all with veneration for his person and confidence in his virtue. The persecutors thought that they could gain all the rest if they succeeded in perverting this holy man, whose example held many others steadfast. They therefore tried by bribery, threats, and violence to make him commit an act of apostasy, but he remained firm. Certain Gentiles and apostates were moved with pity for the old man, and, taking him aside, desired that flesh might be brought which it was lawful for him to eat, that the people might believe that he had eaten swine's flesh, and the King be satisfied by such a pretended obedience. He rejected the subterfuge, saying that by such dissimulation the young men would be tempted to transgress the law, thinking that Eleazar, at the age of fourscore and ten years, had gone over to the rites of the heathens, and that if he should be guilty of such a crime he could not escape the hand of the Almighty, either alive or dead. He was forthwith carried to execution, and as he was dying under the stripes he exclaimed, "O Lord, whose holy light pierces the most secret recesses of our hearts, Thou seest the pains I endure; but my soul feels joy in suffering these things for the sake of Thy law, because I fear Thee." With these words the holy man gave up the ghost, leaving by his death an example of courage and a memorial of virtue to his whole nation.

The confession of St Eleazar was followed by the martyrdom of seven brothers, who suffered tortures one after another with invincible courage, whilst their heroic mother stood by, encouraging and strengthening them, and last of all died herself with the same cheerfulness and intrepidity. By an order of Antiochus, these brothers were apprehended with their mother, and tormented with whips in order to compel them to eat swine's flesh, against their law. The eldest said to the King, "We are ready to die rather than to transgress the laws of God." The King, being provoked at this resolute answer, commanded vessels to be made hot; the tongue of him that had spoken to be cut out, and the skin of his head to be flayed, and his hands and feet to be chopped off, his mother and the rest of his brothers looking on. When he was thus maimed, the tyrant commanded him to be brought to the fire and to be fried in a great pan. The first having thus ended his life, the guards advanced with the second brother. The executioner having flayed off all the hair and skin of his beard, face, and head, inflicted on him the same torments. When he was at the last gasp he said to the King, with a courage and strength which God alone can inspire in such moments, "You destroy our mortal life; but the King of the world, for whose law we suffer, will raise us up in the resurrection of eternal life." After him the third was made a laughing-stock; and when he was commanded he put forth his tongue and courageously stretched out his hands, saying with confidence, "These have I received from Heaven, and with pleasure resign them, to bear testimony to the law of God; and I shall one day receive them again from the hand of Him that gave them." The King was amazed at his courage, not understanding how religion could inspire such greatness of soul, by which a youth despised the most frightful agony; and seeing his power set at nought he grew more enraged than ever, and without putting any questions to the fourth he commanded him to be flayed, his hands and feet maimed, and his body thrown into the burning pan; but he, looking at the King, said, "It is good for us to be put to death by men, for we meet it with an assured hope in God that He will raise us up again. As for you, you will have no share in the resurrection to life." No sooner had this brother finished his course than the fifth was brought forth to be butchered in the same way. He told the King that he must not imagine God had entirely forsaken His people, but rather he had reason to tremble, for he should very soon find himself and his family overtaken by divine wrath. When he was dead, the sixth youth was brought forward, and on his refusal to comply with the King's orders they immediately fell to work, cutting, slashing, and burning him without being able to shake his constancy. To the barbarous King he also said, " Do not deceive yourself ; for though we suffer these things because we have offended God, you will not escape unpunished, for you have attempted to fight against God."

The mother saw her seven sons slain, one after another, by these barbarous torments in one day. Filled with more than heroic courage, she overcame the weakness of her nature, and did not shed one tear, which might have discouraged her children ; she thought of nothing but of securing their victory, saying to them, joining a man's heart to a woman's thought, " I know not how you were formed in my womb. You received neither a soul nor life from me ; nor did I frame your limbs. God, the Creator of the world, gave you all this ; it is easy to Him to repair His own work, and He will restore to you in His mercy that breath and life which you now despise for the sake of His laws." The vanity of the King was yet more wounded at this continued public defiance of his power, and he turned to the youngest brother, trying to cajole him into submission. He called himself his master, his king, and his father, and promised upon his oath that, if he would comply and turn to his religion, he would make him rich, happy, and powerful. The youth not being moved, the King then addressed himself to the mother, with a seeming compassion, and entreated her to prevail upon her only surviving child, to spare this small remnant of the family. She leaned towards him, speaking in her own tongue very different words from those for which the King hoped. " My dear child, now my only one, have pity on me, who bore you nine months in my womb, and gave you suck three years, and nourished you, and brought you up to this age. Do not afflict me by infidelity and cowardice. Look up to the heavens, behold the earth, and all that is in them, and remember that God made them all out of nothing by His almighty power. This is the God whom we worship. Have Him before your eyes, and fear not this executioner. Show yourself worthy of your brothers, and receive death without fear ; so shall I see you all joined in martyrdom, and meet you in the place of eternal mercy and repose." The young martyr cried out to his executioners, "For whom do you wait? I do not obey the command of the King, but the command of the divine law given us by Moses." Then to the King he said, "You, the author of so much malice and evil against the Hebrews, shall not escape the hand of God. We suffer thus for our sins, yet God will be again reconciled to His servants. My brothers have undergone a short pain and are under the covenant of eternal life. Like them I offer up my life and my body for the holy law of our fathers, begging God to be speedily merciful to our people. In me and in my brothers the wrath of the Almighty, which has been justly brought upon our nation, shall cease." The youngest brother therefore was likewise put to death, with yet more cruelty than the others, and last of all their noble mother, having given the lives of all her children, yielded up her own rather than desert the law of the Most High.

The place of martyrdom of the Holy Machabees was probably Antioch; there is no evidence that King Antiochus was at Jerusalem during the suppression of Jewish worship there, and their relics were venerated at Antioch from the fourth century; some have rested in the church of San Pietro in Vincoli at Rome since the sixth century, brought there from Constantinople whither they had been early translated. The names of the brothers and their mother are not known; the Syrian tradition calls her Samona (S'muni), and Eastern liturgical books call the sons Machabee, Abel, Machir, Judas, Achaz, Areth, and Jacob, with variations; but the attribution of these names is worthless.

Presumably because they typified and in some sense were taken to represent the vast army of Christian martyrs who amid similar torments were to follow their example, the Machabees seem to have been honoured in every part of the Church at a very early date. We find them mentioned and connected with Antioch in the Syriac "breviarium" of the first years of the fifth century. They are also in the Fasti of Polemius Sylvius, in the Carthaginian calendar and in the "Hieronymianum." See the *Acta Sanctorum*, Nov., vol. ii, part 2, p. 409. It is curious that in the church of St Peter ad Vincula, just mentioned, there should be preserved a great stone sarcophagus divided into seven compartments and bearing an inscription which attests that the bones and ashes of the seven brothers with their parents had been buried therein. See the *Dictionnaire d'Archéologie*, vol. iii, cc. 12–13, where an engraving is given. It should be noted also that St Leo the Great preaching on August 1, probably in that church, mentions the double celebration of the dedication of the building and the passion of the seven brothers. One difficulty which defies solution is that raised by St Jerome himself. He had seen the relics of the Machabees at Modeim, and he asks how they could be exposed for veneration at Antioch. See Delehaye, *Les Origines du Culte des Martyrs*, pp. 233–234.

SS. FAITH, HOPE, AND CHARITY, AND THEIR MOTHER WISDOM, MARTS.

SECOND CENTURY (?)

The Roman widow St Wisdom and her three daughters suffered for the faith under the Emperor Hadrian. According to a spurious legend St Faith, aged twelve, was scourged, thrown into boiling pitch, taken out alive, and beheaded; St Hope, aged ten, and St Charity, aged nine, being unhurt in a furnace, were also beheaded; and their mother suffered while praying over the bodies of her children. Some have maintained that the whole story is a myth, but the universality of their *cultus* both in the East and the West suggests that there may have been early martyrs of these names. Indeed, there is reference to two groups of them; a family martyred under Hadrian and buried on the Aurelian Way, where their tomb under the church of St Pancras was afterwards resorted to : their names were Greek, Sophia, Pistis, Elpis, and Agape; and another group of martyrs of an unknown date, Sapientia, Fides, Spes, and Caritas, buried in the cemetery of St Callistus on the Appian Way. The Roman Martyrology names Faith, Hope, and Charity on August 1, and their mother (of whose martyrdom it says nothing) on September 30. The great church of St Sophia at Constantinople has nothing to do with this saint or with any other of her name; it is dedicated in honour of the Holy Wisdom ($\dot{\eta}$ $\dot{\alpha}\gamma\dot{\iota}\alpha$ $\sigma o\phi\dot{\iota}\alpha$), that is, to Christ as the Word of God.

Father Delehaye, commenting upon these supposed martyrs, remarks : "Every one will agree that it would need very strong evidence to lend verisimilitude to even a single group of this kind, but no such evidence is here forthcoming." *Les Origines du Culte des Martyrs*, pp. 326–327. J. P. Kirsch also, in the *Lexikon für Theologie und Kirche*, iii, 1035-6, seems to concur in this verdict. The cult cannot be called ancient. No earlier evidence has been adduced than the *Index oleorum* which dates only from the end of the sixth century.

ST ETHELWOLD, BP. OF WINCHESTER, CONF.

A.D. 984

This saint was well born, and a native of Winchester. Being moved in his youth with an ardent desire to devote himself to the divine service, he submitted himself to St Elphege the Bald, bishop of his native city, who gave him the tonsure and in due course the priesthood, at the same time as St Dunstan, who was about his equal in age. When Dunstan became abbot of Glastonbury in 944 and introduced strict Benedictine observance there, Ethelwold took the habit and was made one of the deans of the house. He was a practitioner of the servile arts, especially bell-founding, and at the same time his zeal for knowledge made him study also the sacred sciences, with so much the greater ardour as these studies had become his duty. In 947 King Edred rebuilt and endowed the abbey of Abingdon in Berkshire, which had been founded by King Cissa in 675. In 955 Ethelwold was appointed abbot of this monastery, which with the help of five monks from Glastonbury he rendered a model of regular discipline and a nursery of good monks. He procured from Corbie a master of church music, and sent Osgar to Fleury, a monastery which at that time surpassed all others in the reputation of strict observance, to learn its discipline for the benefit of Abingdon. The Danes had made such havoc of religious houses that practically no monks were then left in all England except in the two monasteries of Glastonbury and Abingdon; and the education of youth, and every other support of learning and virtue, was almost banished by the ravages of the barbarians. These deplorable circumstances awaked the zeal especially of St Dunstan, St Ethelwold, and St Oswald of York, and these three set themselves with great industry to restore monasticism and studies.

St Ethelwold was consecrated bishop of Winchester by St Dunstan in 963. The disorders and ignorance which reigned among many of the clergy of England had produced some very scandalous states of affairs, and Ethelwold found these evils obstinate and past recovery among the secular canons of the cathedral of Winchester. He therefore expelled them, allotting to each a part of their prebends for their subsistence and placing monks from Abingdon in their room, with whom he kept choir as their bishop and abbot. Three of the former canons took the monastic habit and continued to serve God in that church. The year following, St Ethelwold expelled the seculars out of the Newminster monastery at Winchester, and placed there Benedictine monks under an abbot, and was the means of peopling Chertsey and Milton Abbas with monks also. He repaired the nunnery dedicated in honour of our Lady in his cathedral city, and bought of the King the lands and ruins of the great nunnery of St Etheldreda in the isle of Ely, which had been burnt by the Danes a hundred years before, and he established on the same spot an abbey of monks, which King Edgar enriched. He likewise purchased the ruins of Thorney in Cambridgeshire, which he restored in like manner about the year 970. He directed and assisted Adulf to buy the ruins of Peterborough Abbey, and rebuilt and peopled it as well; this monastery, after having flourished two hundred years, was destroyed by the Danes in 870. Adulf, chancellor to King Edgar, having buried his only son who died in his infancy in 960, gave his whole estate to this house, took the monastic habit in it, and was chosen the first abbot. St Ethelwold also rebuilt and consecrated his cathedral and enshrined the relics of St Swithin therein.

His reforming activities, in particular the displacing of slack canons by strict monks, met with a deal of opposition, but to malcontents he was "terrible as a lion," while the good-willed and persevering found in him a benevolent shepherd, "more gentle than a dove." He who was fittingly called "the father of monks" and who laboured so strenuously for the divine honour and the sanctification of others, was always solicitous first to adorn his own soul with all virtues, and to make himself a sacrifice agreeable to God; for it is only the humility and charity of the heart that give a value to exterior actions : without these, to give our goods to the poor and our bodies to the flames would not avail us. The fervour of devotion and compunction must be always nourished and increased, or it grows lukewarm ; in this great bishop interior devotion and exterior actions of virtue mutually supported and gave strength to each other. He rested from his labours on August 1, 984, and was buried in the cathedral of Winchester, on the south side of the high altar. Authentic proofs of miracles wrought through his intercession having been made, his body was taken up and solemnly deposited under the altar by St Elphege, his immediate successor, afterward archbishop of Canterbury and martyr. Several written works are credited to St Ethelwold, of which the most important was a translation into English of the Rule of St Benedict.

There is a fair amount of historical material for the Life of St Ethelwold. One biography by a certain Alfric has been printed in part by Mabillon, *Acta Sanctorum O.S.B.*, but fully by Stevenson in the *Chronicon de Abingdon* (Rolls Series) ; another, attributed to Wolstan, has been more often printed, but Dean Armitage Robinson is inclined to question the authorship and early date. There are also references in the *Historia Eliensis*, William of Malmesbury, etc. Ethelwold is now generally recognised as the author of the *Concordia Regularis* which was formerly assigned to St Dunstan. See H. W. Keim, "Ethelwold und die Mönchsreform in England" in *Anglia*, vol. 39 (1917), pp. 405–443 ; Dean Armitage Robinson, *The Times of St Dunstan* (1923) ; Stanton's *Menology*, pp. 375–377.

AUGUST 2

ST ALPHONSUS LIGUORI, Doctor of the Church, Bp. of Sant' Agata de' Goti

A.D. 1787

ST ALPHONSUS was born at Marianella, near Naples, on September 27, 1696; his parents were Don Joseph de Liguori, captain of the royal gallies, and Donna Anna Cavalieri, whose elder brother became bishop of Troia and was a friend of St Paul-of-the-Cross : both people of virtuous and distinguished life. The boy was baptised Alphonsus Mary Antony John Francis Cosmas Damian Michael Gaspar, but preferred in afterlife to call himself simply Alfonso Maria; the use of the Latin form of his name has become usual in English. Don Joseph was determined that his first-born should have every advantage that formal education could give him, and he was early put under tutors. He learned Greek, Latin, and French, the rudiments of mathematics, physical science and architecture, drawing and painting, riding and swordsmanship, and became an accomplished musician, especially as a player of the harpsichord. At thirteen he began the study of jurisprudence, and when sixteen he was allowed, by dispensation of four years, to present himself before the university of Naples for examination for the doctor's degree in both laws (civil and canon); it was granted him with acclamation. For two years Alphonsus was the pupil of two distinguished Neapolitan lawyers, Perrone and Jovene, and in 1715 he was called to the Bar. In the same year he was admitted to the spiritual confraternity of the Doctors, which was directed by the Oratorians. His reputation as a barrister is testified by the tradition (not certainly true) that in eight years of practice he never lost a case. In 1717 Don Joseph arranged a marriage for his son, but it came to nothing and Alphonsus continued to work diligently and quietly; for a year or two some slackness in religious care was observable, coupled with and perhaps due to an affection for "society life" and fashionable amusements, but he had the will to avoid serious sin. He was very fond of the music of the theatre, but music was not the only thing on the Neapolitan stage of the eighteenth century; however, Alphonsus was very short-sighted and when the curtain went up his spectacles came off, and so he was able to enjoy the good without receiving harm from the dangerous. A retreat with the Lazarists during the Lent of 1722 and reception of the sacrament of Confirmation in the following autumn steadied him and revived his fervour, and at the next Lent he made a private resolution not to marry and to continue in his profession only until it should appear that God wished him to abandon it. What he took to be a clear indication of the divine will was shown him only a few months later.

A certain Neapolitan nobleman (whose name has not come down to us) was suing the Grand Duke of Tuscany for possession of an estate valued at over £100,000. Alphonsus was briefed in the case, for which side we do not now know, but probably for his countryman, and made a great speech on his client's behalf which much impressed the court. When he sat down opposing counsel coolly remarked, "You have wasted your breath. You have disregarded the evidence on which the whole case depends." "What do you mean ? Where ? How ? " asked Alphonsus. He was handed a document which he had read through several times, but with a passage marked that had entirely escaped his notice. The point at issue was whether the estate was held under Lombard law or under the Angevin capitularies : this clause made the point clear, and decided against the client of Alphonsus. For a moment he was silent. Then he said, "I have made a mistake. The case is yours," and left the court, murmuring to himself, "Now I know you, O world ! These courts shall not see me again ! " He was as good as his word, and, braving the fiery indignation of his father, refused either to go on with his profession or to entertain a second project for his marriage. While visiting the sick in the hospital for incurables he twice heard as it were an interior voice, saying, "Leave the world, and give yourself to me " ; he went straight to the church of our Lady of Ransom, laid his sword on her altar, and then offered himself to the priests of the Oratory. Don Joseph tried every way to dissuade his son, but was at last constrained to agree to his being a priest, provided that, instead of joining the Oratory, he should stay at home. On the advice of his director, Father Pagano, himself an Oratorian, Alphonsus accepted this condition.

He began his theological studies at home, and at the end of 1724 received minor orders. He thereupon was admitted to the Society of Propaganda, a local missionary-training congregation, and also joined the society called White Fathers whose particular work was ministering to criminals condemned to death. After being ordained deacon the Archbishop of Naples licensed him to preach in any church of the city, and in 1726 he was advanced to the priesthood. For the two following years he was engaged in missionary work throughout the kingdom of Naples, and at once made his mark. The early eighteenth century was a time of pompous oratory and florid verbosity in the pulpit—a fruit of the Renaissance out of control,—and of rigorism in the confessional—a fruit of Jansenism; Don Alphonsus repudiated both these characteristics. He preached simply and without affectation : " It is a pleasure to listen to your sermons ; you forget yourself and preach Jesus Christ," somebody said to him, and he afterwards instructed his missioners : " Your style must be simple, but the sermon must be skilfully constructed. If skill is lacking it is unconnected and tasteless ; if it be bombastic, the simple cannot understand it. I have never preached a sermon which the poorest old woman in the congregation could not understand." He treated his penitents as souls to be saved rather than as criminals to be punished or frightened into better ways ; he is said never to have refused absolution to a penitent. This was not pleasing to everybody, and some looked with suspicion on Don Alphonsus. He organised the *lazzaroni* of Naples into groups which met for instruction in Christian doctrine and virtue ; one of the members was reproved by Don Alphonsus for his imprudent fasting, and another priest added, " It is God's will that we should eat in order to live. If you are given cutlets, eat them and be thankful. They will do you good." The remark was taken up and twisted into a matter of offence : the clubs were secret societies of Epicureans, of Quietists, of some other heresy, there was a new sect, of Cutlets. The solemn wiseacres of Church and State took the matter up, arrests were made, and Don Alphonsus had to make explanations. The Archbishop counselled him to be more careful, the " Cutlet clubs " continued undisturbed, and developed into the great Association of the Chapels which numbers thousands of working-men who meet daily for prayer and instruction in the confraternity chapels. In 1729, being then thirty-three years old, Alphonsus left his father's house to become chaplain to the College of the Holy Family, recently founded by Don Matthew Ripa for the training of missionaries to China. Here he met Thomas Falcoia, and became friendly with him ; he was a priest twice his own age, whose life had been devoted to trying to establish a new religious institute in accordance with a vision he claimed to have had in Rome. All he had succeeded in doing was to establish a convent of nuns at Scala, near Amalfi, to whom he had given a version of the rule of the Visitandines. One of the nuns, however, Sister Mary Celeste, alleged that she had received a revelation of the rule which the nuns were to follow, and when Father Falcoia discovered that its provisions tallied with those intimated to him twenty years before he was naturally impressed. In 1724 he proposed that this new rule should be adopted by the community, but there was a minority strongly opposed to it. This minority appealed to Father Falcoia's superior (he was a member of the congregation of *Pii Operarii*), who ruled that Sister Mary Celeste had been deceived, that no alteration in their life should be made, and that Father Falcoia should cease to direct the convent. This was the position when, six years later, Falcoia got St Alphonsus interested in the matter. About the same time an unexpected turn was given to events by his appointment to the see of Castellamare; this left him free to associate himself with the convent of Scala again, and one of his first episcopal acts was to invite Alphonsus to give a retreat to the nuns, a step that had far-reaching consequences for everybody concerned.

With his two friends John Mazzini and Vincent Mannarini, St Alphonsus went to Scala in September 1730, and after conducting a novena in the cathedral, betook himself to the convent; in addition to giving the retreat he investigated, with a lawyer's precision, the matter of Sister Mary Celeste's revelation, and came to the conclusion that it was from God and not an hallucination. He therefore recommended, and the nuns agreed, that the convent should be re-organized in accordance with the vision, and the Bishop of Scala gave his consent; there were still difficulties to be overcome, but on the feast of the Transfiguration 1731 the nuns put on their new habit, of red and blue, and entered upon their strictly enclosed and penitential life. Thus began the Redemptoristines, who still flourish in several lands. The new rule had been expanded and made more explicit by St Alphonsus himself, who took over responsibility for their direction from the aged Mgr. Falcoia. No sooner was this brought about than the Bishop of Castellamare intimated to Don Alphonsus that he should now undertake the establishment of a new congregation of missionaries to work especially among the peasants of the country districts: his own original vision had included an institute of men and further revelations to that effect were attributed to Sister Mary Celeste. Alphonsus knew there was room for much work, but he was already committed to the Society of Propaganda and so referred the question to his director; rather unexpectedly Father Pagano approved of the Bishop's project and told Alphonsus to undertake it. The next twelve months were given over to facing a storm of opposition: his colleagues of the Propaganda Society and even his friends, Father Ripa and Canon Gizzio, violently objected to the scheme, while, in addition to Father Pagano, the Jesuit provincial, Manulio, the Lazarist superior, Cutica, and a learned Dominican, Fiorillo, supported it. At last, after a long and painful leave-taking with his father, St Alphonsus left Naples in November 1732 and went to Scala. There the Congregation of the Most Holy Redeemer (which for its first seventeen years was known as " of the Most Holy Saviour ") was born on the 9th of that month, and its first home was in a small house belonging to the convent of nuns. There were seven postulants under Alphonsus, with Mgr. Falcoia as informal superior general, and dissensions began at once, centring chiefly in this very matter of who was in supreme authority ; a party opposed the Bishop, and consequently Alphonsus, and a schism was formed in both houses. Sister Mary Celeste went off to found a convent at Foggia, and at the end of five months St Alphonsus was alone but for one lay-brother. But other subjects came, a larger house became necessary, and in the autumn of 1733 successful missions were given in the diocese of Amalfi. In the following January a second foundation was made, at the request of the Bishop of Cajazzo, at Villa degli Schiavi, and here Alphonsus went to reside, and conducted missions. The saint is so well known as a moral theologian, for his writings, and for his efforts in founding the Redemptorists, that his eminence as a missioner has been overshadowed ; but from 1726 till 1752 he was preaching up and down the kingdom of Naples, especially in villages and rural settlements, and with the greatest success. His confessional was crowded, hardened sinners returned to the healing sacraments in great numbers, enemies were reconciled, family feuds healed, and he established the practice, characteristic of the method of his followers, of returning some months after a mission was closed in order to confirm and consolidate the work.

But the troubles of the young Redemptorists were not over : indeed they had hardly begun. In the same year as the foundation at Villa degli Schiavi, Spain re-asserted its authority over Naples, the absolutist Charles III was in power, and he had as his prime minister the Marquis Bernard Tanucci, who was to be the lifelong opponent of the new congregation. A third house was started at Ciorani, between Salerno and Avellino, but in 1737 a priest of bad character spread evil reports about the establishment at Villa, the community was attacked by armed men, and it was deemed wise to close the house ; in the following year troubles caused Scala too to be abandoned. On the other hand Cardinal Spinelli, Archbishop of Naples, put St Alphonsus at the head of a general mission throughout his diocese, and for two years the saint organized and conducted this, until the death of Mgr. Falcoia in 1743 recalled him to the work of the congregation. A general chapter was held, at which St Alphonsus was elected rector major (*i.e.*, superior general), vows were taken, and rules and constitutions were drawn up. They were now constituted as a religious institute and proceeded in the following years to make foundations at Nocera de' Pagani, Deliceto, and Caposele, all under great difficulties of local and official opposition; " regalism " was in the ascendant and the implacable anti-clericalism of Tanucci was a sword at all times threatening the existence of the congregation. There was no question of getting the royal approbation for it, in spite of the efforts of Alphonsus, and when in 1749 Pope Benedict XIV approved the constitutions of the new institute the *exequatur* to the papal brief was refused by the King of the Two Sicilies, who only a short time before had wished to make its founder archbishop of Palermo.

The first edition of the *Moral Theology* of St Alphonsus, in the form of annotations to the work of Busembaum, a Jesuit theologian, was published at Naples in 1748, with the *imprimatur* of both the King and the Archbishop;* and the second edition, which is properly the first of his own complete work, in 1753–5. It was approved by Pope Benedict XIV and had an immediate success, for with consummate wisdom it steered a middle course between the rigorism of Jansenism and an improper laxity; seven more editions were called for in the author's lifetime. There is no need here to follow the controversy concerning " probabilism," with which the name of St Alphonsus is associated. Probabilism is the system in moral theology which holds that, if of two opinions one insists that in certain circumstances a law binds, while the other holds that in these circumstances it does not, one is allowed to follow an opinion favouring liberty provided it be truly and solidly probable, even though the opinion favouring the law be more probable. St Alphonsus eventually favoured what he called Aequiprobabilism, which insists that the law must be obeyed unless the opinion favouring liberty is at least nearly equally probable with that favouring the law, though there would appear to be little practical difference between the two systems. The Church permits the application of either, but the reader may be reminded that Probabilism is primarily a principle for the moral theologian and is not put forward as an ideal of Christian life; often the more perfect and therefore more desirable course of action is to follow the more

* The royal censor, a Dominican, noted with evident satisfaction that the author had not failed to provide for the rendering to Cæsar of the things that are Cæsar's!

probable opinion according to which the law is binding. Attempts have been made to impugn the morality of the teaching of St Alphonsus about lying: his was the ordinary teaching of the Church, namely, that all lies are intrinsically wrong and illicit. The Holy See's estimate of him as a moral theologian is shown by a decree of the Sacred Penitentiary in 1831 which allows confessors to follow any of his opinions, without considering the grounds on which they are based. Among the consequences of the teachings of the Jansenists was that holy Communion can be received worthily only very rarely and that devotion to our Lady is a useless superstition; St Alphonsus vigorously attacked both these errors, the last-named particularly by the publication in 1750 of *The Glories of Mary*. To many readers this famous book has seemed in parts exaggerated, but it must be borne in mind that it was written in answer to certain people who were trying to "regulate" devotion to our Lady in such a way as to do away with it altogether; and that it was intended for people who were sufficiently intelligent to distinguish between metaphorical and literal language, and who were well enough instructed in their religion to know that all the glories of Mary are "for the sake of her Son." Among his numerous other works for which he was recognized as a doctor of the Church are *The True Spouse of Jesus Christ*, *The Great Means of Prayer*, *The Way of Salvation*, *The Admirable Workings of Divine Providence*, and a history of the Council of Trent.

From the time of the death of Mgr. Falcoia, St Alphonsus led a life of extraordinary industry: guiding and fostering his new congregation through troubles both external and internal, trying to get it authorized by the King, ministering to individual souls, conducting missions all over Naples and Sicily, even finding time to write hymns, compose music, and paint pictures. After 1752 his health was failing, his missionary vigour decreased, and he devoted much more time to writing. The general opinion of him was voiced by a prebendary of Naples, "If I were the Pope I would canonize him without process." "He fulfilled in a most perfect way," said Father Mazzini, "the divine precept of loving God above all things, with his whole heart and with all his strength, as all might have seen and as I saw better than anyone during the long years I spent with him. The love of God shone forth in all his acts and words, in his devout manner of speaking of Him, his recollection, his deep devotion before the Blessed Sacrament, and his continual exercise of the divine presence." He was strict, but tender and compassionate, and, often suffering acutely from scrupulosity himself, was particularly pitiful to others afflicted in the same way. His one remedy was implicit obedience to one's confessor, as is shown clearly in his letters to Father Rizzi, a priest of knowledge and good judgement who was, nevertheless, tormented by distressing scruples (this unfortunate man once wrote to a bishop, who was his penitent, advising him on a dispute that he had with his diocese. The bishop threatened to imprison him!). Father Cajone testified during the process of beatification of St Alphonsus that " His special and characteristic virtue seemed to me to be purity of intention. In all things and at all times he acted for God without any admixture of self. He said to us one day, ' By the grace of God I have never confessed having acted from passion. It may be that I have not noticed what was passing in me, but I have not remarked it so as to confess it.' " This is the more remarkable when it is considered that Alphonsus was a Neapolitan, and by nature passionate and precipitate, easily moved by anger, pride, or a sudden resolve.

When he was sixty-six years old St Alphonsus was made by Pope Clement XIII Bishop of Sant' Agata de' Goti, between Benevento and Capua. It was an honour entirely unexpected and unwanted: when the messenger of the nuncio apostolic presented himself at Nocera, greeted him as " Most Illustrious Lord," and handed over the letter announcing the appointment, Alphonsus read it through and handed it back, saying, " Please do not come back again with any more of your ' Most Illustrious '; it would be the death of me." But the Pope would take no refusal, and he was consecrated in the church of the Minerva at Rome. Sant' Agata was only a small diocese, but that was about all that could be said in its favour; it numbered 30,000 souls with 17 religious houses and 400 secular priests, of whom some did no pastoral work at all, living on the proceeds of an easy benefice, and others were not only slack but positively evil-living. The laity were to match, and rapidly getting worse; the results of nearly thirty years of neglect were apparent on all sides. After having established his own modest household, the new Bishop sent out a band of priests to conduct a general mission throughout the diocese: they were recruited from all orders and institutes in Naples except, for reasons of tact and prudence, his own congregation of Redemptorists. Alphonsus recommended two things only to these missioners, simplicity in the pulpit, charity in the confessional, and after hearing one of the priests neglect his advice he said to him, " Your sermon kept me awake all night.... If you wanted to preach only yourself, rather than Jesus Christ, why come all the way from Naples to Ariola to do it ? " At the same time he set about a reform of the seminary, which had plenty of candidates but many of doubtful character, was housed in an unhealthy building, and suffered under a rector far too old for the post. " The Church," said St Francis de Sales, " does not need many priests, but she must have good ones," and St Alphonsus would not ordain anyone of whose good character and dispositions he was not personally satisfied. There were numerous benefices without cure of souls in the diocese, and he had to exercise an unremitting vigilance that personal influence was not brought to bear in granting them, and lest they were given to men of poor qualification on the plea that they were needy and could not do much harm. Some priests were in the habit of saying Mass in fifteen minutes or less; these were suspended *ipso facto* until they amended their ways, and the Bishop wrote a moving treatise on the subject : " ' The priest at the altar,' says St Cyprian, ' represents the person of Jesus Christ.' But whom do so many priests to-day represent ? They represent only mountebanks earning their livelihood by their antics. Most lamentable of all is it to see religious, and some even of reformed orders, say Mass with such haste and such mutilation of the rite as would scandalize even the heathen. . . . ' Truly the sight of a Mass celebrated in this way is enough to make one lose the Faith.' " After he had been ten months at Sant' Agata St Alphonsus set out on a visitation of his diocese, during which he instructed, catechized and heard confessions in person, and insisted that scandals be put down firmly, whether arising from dirty and unkempt churches or from public wickedness and disorder. He was taken seriously ill at Ariola, and almost immediately after his return a famine broke out, with its usual accompaniment of plague. Alphonsus had foreseen and prophesied this calamity several times in the previous two years, but nothing had been done to avert it. Thousands were literally starving, and he sold everything to buy food for distribution among the sufferers, down to his carriage and mules and his uncle's episcopal ring ; the Holy See authorized him to make use of the property of the endowment of the see for the same purpose, and he contracted debts right and left in his efforts at relief. When the mob clamoured for the life of the mayor of Sant' Agata, who was wrongfully accused of withholding food, Alphonsus braved their fury, offered his own life for that of the mayor, and finally distracted them by distributing the rations of the next two days. The Bishop was most vigorous in his concern for public morality ; he always began with kindness, but when amendment was not promised or relapse occurred he took strong measures, invoking the help of the civil authorities. This made him many enemies, and several times his life was in danger from people of rank and others against whom he instituted proceedings. The custom of the courts of banishing hardened offenders, whether public vagabonds or private sinners, must have pressed somewhat hardly on the districts to which they went, and the bishops of neighbouring dioceses probably found scant consolation in the observation of the Bishop of Sant' Agata that, " Each must look after his own flock. When these people find themselves turned out everywhere, in disgrace and without food or shelter, they will come to their senses and give up their sinful lives."

Just before the suppression of the Jesuits in the Spanish dominions in 1767 a determined effort was made to disperse the still struggling Redemptorists. It was led by the powerful Don Francis Maffei, who had a grudge against the fathers at Deliceto because they remained neutral in a dispute he had with the local municipality, and Baron Sarnelli, who also had a personal grievance. The religious were denounced to the King as " degenerated . . . dominated by a spirit of greed. . . . They multiply properties and build magnificent monasteries. They eclipse even the Jesuits in their luxury and ostentation . . . they excite the people to rebel against their lords." Other charges and claims were added to this nonsensical indictment, and St Alphonsus went to Naples to defend his brethren. This was more than his opponents had bargained for, and when the case at last came on in the royal court the plaintiffs did not appear. But the judge would not enter judgement for the Redemptorists ; instead he adjourned the case *sine die*, and Alphonsus returned to Arienzo, where he was living. He now set himself to answer the writings of Mgr. von Hontheim (" Febronius "), a German bishop who taught an exaggerated Gallicanism, opposing the authority of princes, bishops and councils to that of the Holy See. In the circumstances the *Vindication of the Supreme Power of the Roman Pontiff* had to be printed secretly in Naples, published privately and anonymously, and a few copies smuggled out of the country, even though Febronianism had already been condemned by the Pope. In June 1767 St Alphonsus was attacked by terrible rheumatic pains which developed into an illness from which he was not expected to recover : not only did he receive the last sacraments but preparations were begun for his funeral. After twelve months his life was saved, but he was left with a permanent and incurable bending of the neck, familiar from the portraits of him ; until the surgeons had succeeded in straightening it a little the pressure of the chin caused a raw wound in his chest and he was unable to celebrate Mass, which afterwards he could do with the aid of a chair at the communion. In addition to attacks on his moral theology, he had to face an accusation against the Redemptorists of carrying on the Society of Jesus under another name, and in 1770 the Sarnelli action came on again; this time the prime minister, Tanucci, intervened and appointed a commission to draw up a report. The case dragged on for another thirteen years before it was decided in favour of Alphonsus on all counts. Pope Clement XIV died on September 22, 1774,* and St Alphonsus in the following year petitioned his successor, Pius VI, for permission to resign his see. Similar petitions had been refused by Clement XIII and XIV, but the effects of his rheumatic fever were now taken into consideration; permission was granted, and the aged Bishop retired to his Redemptorist's cell at Nocera, hoping to end his days in peace.

But it was not to be. In 1777 the procurator in the Sarnelli case issued his report, a vicious document in which Alphonsus was not only charged with having illegally founded a religious body but with undermining Christian morality by his impious doctrines, "built up entirely from Jesuit authors"; Probabilism must be destroyed and the Redemptorists should be suppressed as simply Jesuits in disguise.† St Alphonsus at once applied himself to drawing up a detailed refutation. In 1778 Maffei died, ruined by the litigation in which he had deliberately involved himself; he left six children and large debts. These debts were liquidated and these orphans provided for by the efforts of Father Antony Tannoia, C.SS.R., with the assistance and encouragement of Alphonsus Liguori. Shortly after, Ferdinand di Leon, the procurator, died also, and taking advantage of the resentment which his report on the Redemptorists had aroused among many in Naples, St Alphonsus addressed a brief memoir to the King in defence of the exterior government of his congregation; as a result the established houses, with their superiors and novitiate, were approved. Thus encouraged he determined to make another effort to get the royal sanction for his rule (it was as religious rather than as priests that the congregation was objected to); in addition to the four houses in Naples and one in Sicily, it had now four others in the Papal States, at Scifelli, Frosinone, Sant' Angelo a Cupolo, and Benevento.

* After saying Mass on the 21st, Alphonsus became unconscious and so remained for twenty-four hours. On coming round he announced that "I have been assisting the Pope, who has just died." This incident is sometimes put forward as an example of bilocation, but seems simply to have been a clairvoyant trance. It was referred to, but no great importance was attached to it in the process of beatification.

† This report was drawn up by the supporters of royal supremacy in religious affairs, under the influence of Jansenists. But an orthodox Catholic can sympathize with their point that there was no need for a new congregation in a country that already had 65,000 priests, which on the basis of England to-day would give the Two Sicilies a population of 44 millions.

What followed was nothing less than tragic. Alphonsus agreed with the royal almoner, Mgr. Testa, to waive any request to be allowed to hold property in common, but otherwise to submit the rule unchanged, and the almoner would put it before the King. Then Testa betrayed him. He altered the rule in many respects, even to the extent of abolishing the vows of religion; he won over to his plot one of the consultors of the congregation, Father Majone, and this altered rule (*regolamento*) was presented to Alphonsus, written in a small hand and with many erasures. He was old, crippled, deaf, his sight was bad: he read over the familiar opening lines of the document—and signed it. Even his vicar general, Father Andrew Villani, connived at the cruel deception, probably through fear of the others. The King approved the *regolamento*, it became legally binding, and its provisions were made known to the Redemptorists—and to their founder. The storm broke on him: "You have founded the congregation and you have destroyed it," he was told. For a moment he was indignant with Father Villani: "I never thought I could be so deceived by you, Don Andrew," and then he overwhelmed himself with reproaches for his infirmity and his remissness. "It was my duty to read it myself, but you know I find it difficult to read even a few lines." To refuse to accept the *regolamento* now would mean suppression of the Redemptorists by the King; to accept it would mean suppression by the Pope, for the Holy See had already approved the original rule. Alphonsus cast about in every direction to save a *débâcle*, but in vain; he would consult the Pope, but the Redemptorists in the Papal States had forestalled him, for they had at once denounced the new rule and put themselves under the protection of the Holy See. Pius VI forbade them to accept the *regolamento*, and withdrew them from the jurisdiction of St Alphonsus; he provisionally recognized those of the Papal States as the only true Redemptorists, and named Father Francis de Paula their superior general. In 1781 the fathers of Naples accepted the *regolamento*, with a slight modification which the King had accepted; but this was not acceptable at Rome and the provisional decree was made final. Thus was St Alphonsus excluded from the order which he had founded.

He bore the humiliation, inflicted by the authority he so loved and respected, with the utmost patience, and without murmuring accepted the apparent end of all his hopes as the will of God. Some followers deserted him and the remaining fathers in the Neapolitan kingdom were reduced to great want and distress, and by some of the bishops were looked on with suspicion and distrust; but in 1783 these same bishops, feeling the effect on their flocks of the loss of the missioners, whose mission faculties had been withdrawn by the Holy See, petitioned for their restoration, which was granted. This was a great consolation to St Alphonsus, who also had the happiness of seeing Father de Paula repentant for the separatist part which he had played. But there was still one more bitter trial for the saint: during the years 1784-85 he went through a terrible "dark night of the soul." He was assailed by temptations against every article of faith and against every virtue, prostrated by scruples and vain fears, and visited by diabolical illusions. For eighteen months this torment lasted, with intervals of light and relief, and was followed by a period when ecstasies were frequent, and prophecy and miracles took the place of interior trials. The end came peacefully on the night of July 31-August 1, 1787, when he was within two months of his ninety-first birthday. Pius VI, the pope who had condemned him under a misapprehension, in 1796 recognized Alphonsus Liguori as a venerable servant of God, in 1816 he was beatified, in 1839 canonized, and in 1871 declared by Pope Pius IX a Doctor of the Church. After the affair of the *regolamento* St Alphonsus predicted that the separated houses in the Papal States would prosper and spread the Redemptorist congregation and that those who had favoured division would become the advocates of reunion, but that this reunion would not come about till after his death. These predictions were verified; St Clement Hofbauer from Frosinone in 1785 first established the congregation beyond the Alps, and in 1793 the Neapolitan government recognized the original rule and the Redemptorists were again united, with Father Blasucci as rector major. To-day they are established as missioners throughout Europe and America, and in several other parts of the world.

The first considerable biography of St Alphonsus was that of his devoted friend and religious son Father Tannoja which appeared at Naples in three volumes (1798-1802). It was long ago translated into English in the Oratorian Series of Lives of the Saints. For a very valuable criticism of Tannoja see Father Castle's book, vol. ii, pp. 904-905, a note strangely incorporated in the Index of the work. The Lives of Alphonsus by Cardinal Villecourt (1864) and Cardinal Capecelatro (1892) do not offer much that is new, but the German Life by Father K. Dilgskron, C.SS.R. (1887), was to a considerable extent based on unpublished material and corrected many previous misconceptions. The most exhaustive biography, however, is that compiled in French by Père Berthe, C.SS.R. (1900), but it has been greatly improved, and in many points corrected, by the late Father Harold Castle, C.SS.R., in his English Translation, published in two bulky volumes in 1905. Many minor publications exist, studying particular aspects of the life and work of St Alphonsus. On the question of Probabilism and Æquiprobabilism reference ought to be made to the books *Vindiciæ Alphonsianæ*, 1873, and *Vindiciæ Ballerinianæ*, 1873.

ST STEPHEN I, POPE AND MART.

A.D. 257

St Stephen was by birth a Roman of the *gens Julia*, and being promoted to holy orders was made archdeacon under the holy popes and martyrs St Cornelius and St Lucius. The latter going to martyrdom recommended him to his clergy for his successor. He was accordingly chosen pope on May 3, 254. Immediately after his election, he was called to put a stop to the havoc threatened in the churches of Gaul and Spain. Marcian, Bishop of Arles, embraced the error of Novatian and refused absolution to many penitents even at death. Faustinus, Bishop of Lyons, and other Gaulish prelates sent information and complaint against him to St Stephen and St Cyprian: to the first, on account of the superior authority and jurisdiction of his see; to the other, on account of the great reputation of his sanctity, eloquence, and zeal against the Novatians. St Cyprian, having no jurisdiction over Arles, could do no more than join the Gaulish Catholics in stirring up St Stephen to exert his authority, and not suffer an obstinate heretic to disturb the peace of those churches to the destruction of souls. This he did by a letter to St Stephen, in which he says, " It is necessary that you despatch ample letters to our fellow-bishops in Gaul, that they no longer suffer the obstinate Marcian to insult our college. Write to that province and to the people of Arles that, Marcian being excommunicated, a successor may be provided for his see. Acquaint us, if you please, who is made bishop of Arles in the room of Marcian, that we may know to whom we are to send letters of communion, and to direct our brethren." Though the replies of St Stephen have not reached us, we cannot doubt but by his order everything here mentioned was done; in an ancient list of the bishops of Arles, published by Mabillon, the name of Marcian does not occur. In Spain, Basilides, Bishop of Merida, and Martial, Bishop of Leon and Astorga, had fallen into the crime of the *libellatici*, that is, to save their lives in the persecution had purchased for money letters of safety from the persecutors, as if they had sacrificed to idols. For this Martial was deposed in a synod, and Basilides voluntarily resigned his see. Basilides soon after repented of what he had done, went to Rome and, imposing upon St Stephen, was admitted by him to communion as a colleague in the episcopal order: which was the more easy as no sentence of deposition had passed in his case. Returning into Spain with letters of the Pope in his favour he was received in the same rank by some of the bishops; and Martial, encouraged by his example, presumed to claim the same privilege. The Spanish bishops consulted St Cyprian what they ought to do, and he answered that persons notoriously guilty of such crimes were, by the canons, utterly disqualified for presiding in the Church of Christ and offering sacrifice to God ; that the election and ordination of their two successors having been regular and valid, they could not be rescinded or made null ; and lastly, that the Pope's letters were obtained by fraud and a suppression of the truth. " Basilides, going to Rome, there imposed upon our colleague Stephen, living at a distance and ignorant of the truth that was concealed from him. All this only tends to accumulate the crimes of Basilides, rather than to abolish the remembrance of them ; since to his former account is hereby added the guilt of endeavouring to circumvent the pastors of the Church." He lays the blame not on him who had been imposed upon, but Basilides who fraudulently gained access to him. We know no more of this affair either, but doubtless the Pope (whose jurisdiction none of the parties disclaimed) was better informed, and the proceedings of the Spanish bishops confirmed.

The controversy concerning the rebaptising of heretics gave St Stephen much more trouble. It is the constant doctrine of the Catholic Church that Baptism given in the evangelical words, that is, in the name of the three persons of the Holy Trinity, is valid even if it be conferred by an heretic. This was the practice even of the African church till Agrippinus, Bishop of Carthage at the close of the second century, changed it. St Cyprian, in three African councils, decreed, according to this principle, that Baptism given by an heretic is always null and invalid ; which decision he founds on this false premise, that no one can receive the Holy Ghost by the hands of one who does not himself possess Him in his soul. This reasoning would equally prove that no one in mortal sin can validly administer any sacrament ; but Christ is the principal, though invisible, minister in the administration of the sacraments ; and though both faith and the state of grace be required in him who confers any sacrament, lest he incur the guilt of sacrilege, yet neither is required for the validity. Many bishops of Cilicia, Cappadocia, and Phrygia, having at their head Firmilian, the learned bishop of Cæsarea, fell in with the Africans and maintained the same error. All the partisans of this practice falsely imagined it to be a point, not of faith, which is everywhere invariable, but of mere discipline, in which every church might be allowed to follow its own rule or law. St Cyprian and Firmilian carried on the dispute with too great warmth, the latter especially, who spoke of St Stephen in an unbecoming manner; and the Pope himself wrote with very great severity of St Cyprian. If such great and holy men could be betrayed into anger, and biased by prepossession, how much ought we sinners to watch over our hearts against passion and mistrust our own judgement! The Pope, who saw the danger which threatened the Church, opposed himself immovably, declaring that no innovation is to be allowed, but that the tradition of the Church, derived from the Apostles, is to be inviolably maintained. When in the year 256 a synod of seventy-one African bishops met at Carthage and agreed with St Cyprian, St Stephen refused to see the delegates they sent to Rome and even refused them any hospitality in the city. On the other hand, he suffered himself patiently to be traduced as a favourer of heresy in approving heretical baptism, being insensible to all personal insults (such as Firmilian hurled at him), not doubting that those great men, who by a mistaken zeal were led astray, would, when the heat of disputing should have subsided, calmly open their eyes to the truth. Thus by his zeal he preserved the integrity of faith and by his forbearance saved many souls from the danger of shipwreck. "Stephen," says St Augustine, "thought of excommunicating them; but being endued with the pity of holy charity, he judged it better to abide in union. The peace of Christ triumphed in their hearts." St Vincent of Lérins said of this unhappy controversy: "When all cried out against the innovation, and the clergy everywhere opposed it in proportion to each one's zeal, then Pope Stephen, of blessed memory, bishop of the Apostolic See, stood up with his other colleagues against it, but he in a signal manner above the rest, thinking it fitting, I believe, that he should go beyond them as much by the ardour of his faith as he was raised above them by the authority of his see. In his letter to the church of Africa he thus decrees: 'Let no innovation be introduced, but let that be observed which is handed down to us by tradition.' The prudent and holy man understood that the rule of true religion admits nothing new, but that all things are to be delivered to our posterity with the same fidelity with which they were received; and that it is our duty to follow religion, and not make religion follow us; for the proper characteristic of a modest and sober Christian is, not to impose his own conceits upon those who come after, but to make his own ideas conform to the wisdom of those that went before him. What then was the issue of this grand affair but that which is usual?—antiquity kept possession and novelty was exploded."

Pope St Stephen sent material succour to all the faithful in the provinces of Syria and Arabia, and the *Liber Pontificalis* states that he decreed that clothes worn by clerics at the services of the Church were to be kept for that purpose, and not taken into daily use or worn by lay people. In 257 the persecution of Valerian broke out, and St Stephen is traditionally said to have been put to death while sitting in his throne behind the altar after celebrating Mass. But, though he is venerated liturgically as a martyr, the fact of his martyrdom is doubtful.

Not only bishops but all superiors are Christ's vicegerents, and are bound to be mindful of their charge, of which they will be demanded to give a rigorous account. How many such live as if they had only their own souls to take care of, and yet think themselves good Christians? Few have the light, the courage, the charity, and the zeal necessary for such responsibility; and many through laziness, self-love, or a passion for pleasure, company, and the world, neglect various obligations of their state. It will be a false plea for such to allege, at the last day, that they have kept well their own vineyard, whilst they have suffered others under their care to be overgrown with briers and weeds.

Mgr. Duchesne in his edition of the *Liber Pontificalis* (i, p. 154) and in his *Histoire ancienne de l'Église* (vol. i, pp. 419–432) has called attention to the main points of interest. Our other authorities are Eusebius, *Ecc. Hist.*, Bk. vii, and the letters of St Cyprian, Firmilian, and St Dionysius of Alexandria. A larger fragment of a letter of Dionysius to this Pope has been recovered from an Armenian source by F. C. Conybeare and printed in the *English Historical Review*, xxv (1910), pp. 111–113. See also the *Dictionnaire de Théologie*, vol. v, cc. 970–973.

ST THEODOTA, Mart.
A.D. 304

St Theodota, named in the Roman Martyrology on this day, was a noble lady of Nicæa. According to the *acta*, which are of little value, she was sought by the prefect Leucatius, and when she refused to have anything to do with him he denounced her and her three children to Nicetius, proconsul in Bithynia, as Christians. It was at the time of the persecution of Diocletian, and when they were brought before Nicetius he asked Theodota if it were she who had taught her children the new-fangled impiety which they believed. She retorted that they had been taught nothing new, but rather the age-old law. "What!" asked her questioner, "Did your ancestors know these doctrines?" At this the eldest boy, Evodius, spoke up and said, "If our ancestors have been in error it is not because God has hidden the truth from them. Rather they were blind, and wandered into untruth through their blindness. But we are going to follow our mother." " Your mother is going to sacrifice to the gods, whether she likes it or not," replied Nicetius, and then, blaming Theodota for the offensive candour of her son's words, urged her to sacrifice that they might follow her example and be saved. But when he could in no way move either her or them, he ordered them to be all burned together. Which was done.

Although the so-called " Acts " both in the Greek and Latin recensions are worthless, there is good reason to believe that the martyrdom of St Theodota at Nicæa with her three sons is an authentic fact. "The sons of Theodota" are mentioned in the Syriac " breviarium " at the beginning of the fifth century, and it is probable that September 2, the date there assigned them, is the true anniversary, though in the " Hieronymianum," from which our Roman Martyrology derives, August 2 has been erroneously indicated. See the full discussion in the *Acta Sanctorum*, Nov., vol. ii, part 2 (1932), pp. 412-414.

THE PORTIUNCULA INDULGENCE
OR PARDON OF ASSISI

This, August 2nd, is the day appointed for gaining the great indulgence or, to use the more happy word again coming into use in English, the pardon of the Portiuncula. Its name is taken from that of a little ruined chapel rebuilt and opened for worship again by St Francis of Assisi in 1209, Santa Maria della Porziuncola; the origin of the chapel's peculiar title, " of the Little Piece," is uncertain : probably it was so called because of the smallness of the piece of ground on which it was originally built. The important part which this tiny building (now entirely enclosed within the great church of Santa Maria degli Angeli) played in the history of St Francis and his friars is referred to on his feast-day, October 4th ; we are here concerned only with the indulgence that bears its name. During a summer night in the year 1216 St Francis went into the Portiuncula chapel to pray, and as he prayed he had a vision of our Lord, who told him to go to the Pope and ask that whosoever should visit that chapel, being truly sorry for his sins and having already confessed them and had absolution, should receive a plenary indulgence.*

* It may be explained for the benefit of non-Catholic readers that an *indulgence*, or *pardon*, is the remission, not of the guilt, but of the temporal punishment due to those sins of which the guilt has already been forgiven (normally by confession and absolution), granted by the Church and ratified by God ; the amount of the remission is expressed in terms of time, of which the significance is only relative. A *plenary indulgence* is such a remission of *all* temporal punishment hitherto incurred.

Accordingly, St Francis made his way to Honorius III, who was only recently elected, and preferred his request for an indulgence to be attached to devoutly visiting the Portiuncula, and that without requiring any offering to be made. The Pope pointed out that it was not usual to grant an indulgence without an offering, as it was only fitting that those who desired the favour should make some sacrifice for it; anyway, how long an indulgence did he ask for? "May it please your Holiness," replied Francis, "to grant not years but souls." Honorius was puzzled. "How would you have souls?" he asked. "Holy Father, by giving a complete remission of all penalty, from the day of baptism till the moment of their coming into that church." "You are asking a lot," said the Pope, "it is not the custom of the Church to grant such an indulgence." "No, holy Father," replied St Francis, "but I ask not of myself but from the Lord Jesus Christ who sent me." "It is my will that you have what you ask for," said Honorius. At once some of the cardinals present remonstrated and urged the Pope to reconsider his decision: for such an indulgence would make all others, even those for the Crusades and the tombs of the Apostles, worthless in the estimation of the people. The Pope listened and weighed their objections; finally, he refused to withdraw the concession but limited its exercise to one day in the year, namely, the anniversary of the date on which the Portiuncula chapel should be consecrated. As Francis was leaving the Pope reminded him that he had no evidence for the grant just made. "Holy Father," answered the saint, "Your word is enough. If this is the work of God it is for Him to make it manifest. I want no other document. Our Lady shall be the charter, Christ the notary, and the angels witnesses." The chapel of the Portiuncula was consecrated on August 2nd, and St Francis published the indulgence for that day and all succeeding anniversaries. Beyond this announcement he did nothing to make the granting of the indulgence more generally known.

Such, in brief, is the story of the original grant of the Portiuncula indulgence as it is now accepted—by those who do accept it. But the fact of the indulgence having been originally granted to St Francis personally has been seriously questioned, because for sixty-one years after the alleged event there is no documentary reference to it, either in the "lives" by Thomas of Celano and St Bonaventure, in the *Speculum Perfectionis*, or in any of the early legends. In the year 1277 Friar Angelo, the minister provincial of Umbria, collected together what evidence he could concerning the grant of the indulgence, which included written declarations by Bd. Benedict of Arezzo that he had been told of the grant by Brother

Masseo who was with St Francis when he interviewed Honorius III, and by Peter Zalfani, who said he was present when the indulgence was published at the Portiuncula. This collection of Friar Angelo and a good deal of secondary evidence is put forward by those who support the indulgence; and they explain the long silence of sixty-one years as a deliberate policy of St Francis and his friars, who did not wish to " broadcast " the indulgence in the face of the known opposition of some of the cardinals: to do so might cause breaches of charity and perhaps the withdrawal of the grant. According to Giacomo Coppoli, a friend of Brother Leo, St Francis distinctly said of the grant to Leo, " Keep this secret until the day of my death," meaning that, in view of the opposition that the grant and its first promulgation had aroused, no more should be said about it until things had settled down. It is objected on the other side that the grounds of the cardinals' opposition to such an indulgence had been removed long before 1277, and that the attestations from personal knowledge attributed to that date are a forgery: a statement that the opponents of the authenticity of the indulgence cannot be said to have substantiated. It is sufficient to quote here the words of Father Cuthbert, O.S.F.C., in his *Life of St Francis of Assisi* (London, 1917): " The toleration of the indulgence by the Holy See towards the end of the thirteenth century suggests that the indulgence must have been long in existence and that its authenticity was then unquestioned by the highest authorities."

The Portiuncula indulgence could at first be gained only in that chapel, between Vespers on August 1st and sunset on the following day. In 1480 Pope Sixtus IV extended it to all Franciscans in any church of the Friars Minor or Poor Clares, and in 1622 Pope Gregory XV granted it to any of the faithful visiting such churches on the appointed day. During the same century it was further extended to all churches of the Capuchins, of the Third Order Regular, and of the Conventuals, and in time to all churches whatsoever in any way associated with the Franciscan order (*e.g.*, parish churches wherein the Third Order Secular was erected). In 1911 the Holy See renewed a decree by which bishops may appoint any public church for the gaining of the Portiuncula indulgence, either on August 2nd or the following Sunday. A similar indulgence has been granted to the churches of several religious orders, *e.g.*, Benedictine, Dominican, Carmelite, Servite, Minim, on various dates. Plenary indulgences are very much more common now than they were in 1216, but the Portiuncula is distinguished as being one of the few plenary indulgences that may be gained *toties quoties*, that is, not only once but so often as the conditions are fulfilled within the prescribed time : in the present case, having been absolved and re-received holy Communion, to visit the designated church and say there at least six Our Fathers, Hail Marys, and *Glorias* for the Pope's intentions. It may, of course, be applied each time for the advantage of the souls in Purgatory; but it may also be applied more than once for the benefit of the person making the exercise. Now no one can profit by an indulgence in a greater proportion than the state of his soul requires, and having gained for himself one plenary indulgence there can be no object in trying to gain another, unless and until he has again fallen into sin and been absolved. The Church therefore by this permission means to increase the opportunities of the living to obtain this indulgence for themselves: for it requires some hardihood to have so much confidence in the perfection of one's dispositions that one can feel certain of having gained a plenary indulgence on any given occasion. So important is the original Portiuncula indulgence in the eyes of the Church that its concession in the church at Assisi was one of the few indulgences not suspended during the holy year of Jubilee, 1925.

In the course of centuries this Indulgence has been much discussed, and in particular it has been very seriously doubted whether St Francis did himself obtain such a grant from Pope Honorius. M. Paul Sabatier, who in his Life of St Francis (1894) rejected the evidence, subsequently changed his mind (see his *Nouveau Chapitre*, 1896, and his preface and notes to F. Bartholi, *Tractatus de Indulgentia S. Mariæ de Portiuncula*, 1900). Similarly J. Jörgensen, who at first disputed, came afterwards to defend, the historic fact. On the other hand, Dr. N. Paulus, who has given his best years to a study of the history of Indulgences, has recanted in the contrary sense. Though he at first accepted the authenticity of the story, he ended by very positively rejecting it for good reasons assigned (see his *Geschichte des Ablasses im Mittelalter*, 1922, vol. ii, pp. 312–322; where many bibliographical references are supplied), and he is supported by such authorities as Père Van Ortroy (in the *Analecta Bollandiana*, xxi, 372 seq., and xxvi, 140 seq.), and P. A. Kirsch in the *Theologische Quartalschrift* for 1906. On the other hand, many Franciscan scholars support the traditional story, see *e.g.* Lemmens in *Der Katholik* for 1908 and Holzapfel in *Archivum Franciscanum Historicum*, i (1908), pp. 31–45. Perhaps the most complete work is that of Fierens, 1910, but it is written in Flemish. See also two books published to commemorate the seventh centenary of the Indulgence—Spader-Giusto, *Archivum Portiunculæ*, 1916; and *L'Oriente Serafico, nel VII centenario*, etc., 1917. Whether the grant was made to St Francis or not, one thing is quite certain that the gaining of the Indulgence over and over again by going in at one door and out at another was not dreamed of in his day. This would be *magis derisorium quam devotum*, wrote Nicholas de Lyra; and other medieval theologians speak in the same sense.

AUGUST 3

THE FINDING OF ST STEPHEN
A.D. 415

THIS second festival in honour of the protomartyr St Stephen was instituted by the Church on the occasion of the discovery of his relics. His body long lay concealed, whilst the glory of his sanctity shone both in Heaven and on earth; the very remembrance of the place of his burial had been blotted out of the minds of men, and his relics lay covered under the ruins of an old tomb, in a place twenty miles from Jerusalem, called Kafr Gamala, that is, "the village of Gamaliel," where stood a church which was served by a priest named Lucian. In the year 415, on Friday, December 3rd, about nine o'clock at night, Lucian was sleeping in the baptistery, where he commonly lay in order to guard the sacred vessels of the church. Being half awake, he saw a tall old man of venerable aspect, with a long white beard, clothed in a white garment edged with small plates of gold marked with crosses, and holding a golden wand in his hand. This person approached Lucian and, calling him thrice by his name, bid him go to Jerusalem, and tell John the bishop to come and open the tombs in which his remains and those of other servants of Christ lay, that they might be given more honourable burial and the glory and mercy of God by their means shown yet more among men. Lucian asked his name. "I am," said he, "Gamaliel, who instructed Paul the Apostle in the law. On the east side of the monument lies Stephen, who was stoned by the Jews outside the north gate. His body was left there a day and a night, but was not touched by birds or beasts. I urged the faithful to carry it off in the night and then had it carried secretly to my house in the country, where I celebrated his funeral rites forty days. I then laid him in my own tomb. Nicodemus, who came to Jesus by night, lies there in another tomb. He was excommunicated by the Jews for following Christ, and banished out of Jerusalem. I received him into my house and maintained him to the end of his life; after his death I buried him honourably near Stephen. I likewise buried there my son Abibo, who died before me at the age of twenty years. His body is in the third tomb, which stands higher up, where I myself was also interred after my death.

My wife Ethna, and my eldest son Semelias, who were not willing to confess the faith of Christ, were buried in another place." Lucian, fearing to be taken for an impostor, prayed that if the vision was from God he might be favoured with it a second and a third time ; and he fasted on bread and water. On the Friday following Gamaliel appeared again to him as before, and repeated his directions. As emblems of the relics he showed Lucian four baskets, three of gold and one of silver. The golden baskets were full of roses, two of white and one of red, and the silver basket of saffron. The priest asked what these were. Gamaliel said, " They are our relics. The red roses represent Stephen, who lies at the entrance of the sepulchre : the second basket Nicodemus, who is near the door ; the silver basket my son Abibo, who departed this life without stain ; his basket is next to mine." Lucian then awaked, gave thanks to God, and continued his fast. In the third week, on the same day and at the same hour, Gamaliel appeared again and upbraided him with his neglect, saying that the drought which then afflicted the country would be removed only by his obedience and the discovery of their relics. Lucian promised he would no longer delay, and he went to Jerusalem and laid the whole affair before bishop John, who bid him go and search for the relics. As Lucian was going the morning following to see a field near his church dug up, he was met by Migetius, a monk, who told him that Gamaliel had appeared to him and bade him inform Lucian that they laboured in vain in that place, "We were laid there," said he, " at the time of our funeral, according to the ancient custom ; and that heap of stones was a mark of the mourning of our friends. Search elsewhere, in a place called Debatalia." " Then," continued the monk, " I found myself in the same field, where I saw a neglected ruinous tomb, and in it three beds, adorned with gold : in the highest lay two men, an old and a young, and one in each of the other beds." Lucian praised God for having another witness of his revelation, and went to the other place. In digging up the earth here three coffins or chests were found, whereon were engraved these words in very large characters : Cheliel, Nasuam, Gamaliel, Abibo. The first are the Syriac names of Stephen, or " crowned," and Nicodemus, or " victory of the people." Lucian sent immediately to tell the Bishop of Jerusalem of his discovery, and he came from the Synod of Lydda, bringing with him Eutonius, Bishop of Sebaste, and Eleutherius, Bishop of Jericho. Upon opening St Stephen's coffin there came out an agreeable odour, the like of which no one had ever smelled before, and numbers of those present were cured of their sicknesses on invoking the saint. His body was reduced to dust excepting the bones, which were whole and in their natural positions. The bishop consented to leave a small portion of them at Kafr Gamala and the rest were carried with singing of psalms and hymns to an oratory, built by a senator, Alexander, near the church of Zion at Jerusalem. At the time of this translation there fell a great deal of rain, which refreshed the country after a long drought. The history of this miraculous discovery and translation was written by Lucian himself, and translated into Latin by Avitus, a Spanish priest then living at Jerusalem, an intimate friend of St Jerome. St Stephen's body remained at the church of Zion till the Empress Eudocia, wife of Theodosius the Younger, going a second time to Jerusalem in 455, built a church to God in his honour, outside the city on the north, at a place which since the twelfth century has been mistakenly supposed to be the scene of his martyrdom. To this his remains were translated in 460.

Relics of St Stephen were soon taken to many other places, and God was pleased to glorify His divine name by numerous miracles wrought through their means and the intercession of His first martyr. Many of them were described by Evodius, Bishop of Uzalium, and by St Augustine, who said of them to his flock, " Let us so desire to obtain temporal blessings by his intercession, that we may by imitating him deserve those which are eternal." Our corporal necessities were not the motive which drew our divine Physician down from Heaven, but the spiritual miseries of our souls. In His mortal life He restored many sick to health, and delivered demoniacs, to give men a sensible proof of His divine power, and as a sign that He came to relieve spiritual disease and to put an end to the empire of the Devil over our souls. In the same way, when He has bestowed temporal blessings on men through His servants, He raises our confidence in His mercy to ask through their intercession His invisible graces. We ought to pray for our daily bread and all our bodily necessities; but we should make these petitions subordinate to the great end of our sanctification and His honour, making them under this condition, as we know not what is most expedient for us in temporal blessings. God offers us His grace, His love, Himself: Him we must make the great and ultimate end of all our requests to Him. If some prince should promise to grant us whatever we should ask, it would be discourteous to him if we confined our request to pins or such trifles, as St Teresa remarks.

The most trustworthy text of Lucian's narrative is the Latin translation by Avitus, which is printed, for example, in the works of St Augustine (see Migne, *P.L.*, vol. xli, cc. 805–816), but there are also versions in Greek, Syriac, Armenian, and Old-Slavonic. The story of the discovery of the relics as narrated by Lucian and its bearing upon certain traditional sites in Jerusalem, led in the years 1900–1908 to a good deal of lively controversy. For this see especially the *Revue de l'Orient chrétien* (1907–1908) and the article of Père Peeters in the *Analecta Bollandiana*, vol. xxvii (1908), pp. 359–368. Père Delehaye, the colleague of Père Peeters, does not suppose that there was really any supernatural revelation made to Lucian or Megetius. He, with not a few other critics, suggests that the discovery was accidental, but that a few years afterwards the incident was " dramatised " by Lucian in accord with the hagiographical precedents of that age. See Delehaye, *Origines du Culte des Martyrs* (1912), pp. 96–98. Upon the miracles at Uzalum, etc., see the same writer's *Recueils antiques des Miracles des Saints* (1925), pp. 74–85, and upon the surprising fact that the " inventio b. Stephani " is commemorated on August 3, see the *Analecta Bollandiana*, vol. xlix (1931), pp. 22–30. A very full article on the " inventio," with copious references, has been contributed by Dom H. Leclercq to the *Dictionnaire d'Archéologie*, vol. v, cc. 624–671.

BD. BENNO, Bp. OF METZ, CONF.

A.D. 940

Was born in the second half of the ninth century, a Suabian and nearly related to Raoul, Duke of Burgundy. About the year 906 he resigned his canonry of the cathedral of Strasburg in order to become a hermit. Some seventy-five years previously St Meinrad, a monk of Reichenau, had retired to a forest at mount Etzel, taking with him a wonder-working statue of our Lady ; Meinrad had been murdered by robbers in 861, and Bd. Benno now took over his abandoned hermitage and chapel, rebuilt them, and re-established the shrine. He lived here with a few disciples until 927, when he was appointed by the Emperor, Henry I the Fowler, to be bishop of Metz. His predecessor, Witger of Lorraine, had been an unworthy prelate and the unruly diocese was too much for Bd. Benno ; he strove earnestly to bring it to order, to remove abuses and reform the lives of his flock, but the chief result was to kindle their anger and discontent. He made powerful and unscrupulous enemies, and in the second year of his episcopate he was seized by them and blinded, out of hatred and revenge ; these scoundrels were excommunicated at a synod at Duisburg and the Emperor condemned the ringleaders to death, but Benno asked leave to resign his see and return to his cell. He lived there for about another ten years, during which the number of his followers increased, forming a little community of hermits under his direction ; from it sprang the great Swiss abbey of Einsiedeln, with its pilgrim-shrine of Our Lady of the Hermits—St Meinrad's statue, still miraculous and sought by large numbers of pilgrims every year. When Bd. Benno died in 940 he was buried by his companion, Eberhard, who had given up the provostship of the chapter of Strasburg to join his friend; Bd. Eberhard, whose feast is observed on the 14th of this month, was the actual founder of the monastery of Einsiedeln and is reckoned its first abbot.

A short notice is in Mabillon, *Acta Sanctorum, O.S.B.*, vol. v, pp. 122–4. See also the Chronicle of Hermann Contractus in Pertz, *Monumenta Germaniæ, Scriptores*, vol. iii, pp. 113–114; and F. A. Weyland, *Vies des Saints du diocêse de Metz* (1910), pp. 303–313. There seems to be very little, if any, trace of *cultus*, and the Bollandists for this reason say nothing of Benno.

BD. AUGUSTINE GAZOTICH, BP. OF LUCERA, CONF.

A.D. 1323

Was born at Trau (Trogir) in Dalmatia about the year 1260 and before he was twenty received the habit of the Friars Preachers. After profession he was sent into Italy and then to Paris, to study at the university, and on his way thither nearly came to an untimely end: while passing through the district of Pavia with a fellow-Dominican, Brother James, they were set on by footpads; James was killed and Brother Augustine recovered only after some weeks' nursing in a near-by country-house. After completing his course at Paris, and being ordained, he preached fruitfully in his own country and established several new houses of his order, to which he gave as their motto the words of his patron, St Augustine of Hippo, " Since I began to serve God, as I have hardly ever seen better men than those who live a holy life in monasteries, so I have never seen worse than those in monasteries who live not as they should." After missions in Italy and Bosnia, missions wherein he confirmed his reputation for great charity and prudence, Bd. Augustine was sent to Hungary, where the people had been reduced to a bad state of misery and irreligion by continual civil wars on account of disputed succession to the throne. Here he met the Dominican Cardinal Nicholas Boccasini, the papal legate, who was to become Bd. Benedict XI, and attracted his favourable notice, and when Cardinal Boccasini became pope in 1303 he sent for Bd. Augustine and consecrated him bishop of Zagreb (Agram) in Croatia. His clergy, and in consequence the whole diocese, was badly in need of reform, and he held disciplinary synods whose canons he enforced and supported in frequent visitations, and he encouraged learning and the study of the Scriptures by establishing a Dominican priory in his cathedral city. He was present at the general council at Vienne in 1311-12, when the suppression of the Knights Templars was decided on; on his return he suffered persecution at the hands of Miladin, governor of Dalmatia, against whose tyranny and exactions he had protested. Bd. Augustine had in a marked degree the gift of healing (he had cured of rheumatism the hands that gave him episcopal anointing) and there is a pleasant story told of how he rebuked those who flocked to him for this reason: he planted a lime tree, and humbly suggested to them that its leaves would be more efficacious than his hands. God and the people took him at his word, and even the invading Turks respected the wonder-working tree.

After ruling the diocese of Zagreb for fourteen years Bd. Augustine was translated to the see of Lucera or Nocera in the province of Benevento by Pope John XXII at the request of Robert the Wise, King of Naples, who required the restoration of religion in his distracted kingdom. On his way to Italy he passed through Trau, where he in vain tried to persuade his countrymen to withdraw their support from the tyrant Miladin; he left them with a prophecy that they would regret their obstinacy, which indeed they did. His great task at Lucera was to eradicate the semi-Mohammedanism and the complete corruption of morals which the Saracens had left behind them; the remainder of the Moslems had been more or less converted in a body in 1300. He immediately ordered, as a sign and portent, that the city should again be known by its old name of Santa Maria della Vittoria, in whose honour the new cathedral, built on the ruins of the chief mosque, was dedicated, and he proceeded to take the diocese in hand. King Robert gave him the fullest support and endowed a monastery of Dominicans who zealously assisted their bishop in his holy work, and within five years the face of the country was changed. Bd. Augustine was venerated by all, from the royal family downwards, and when he died on August 3, 1323, a *cultus* began which was approved by the reigning Pontiff at the request of Charles, Duke of Calabria, and formally confirmed by Pope Clement XI.

The principal source seems to be a Latin Life written as late as the seventeenth century by Thomas Marnavich, Bishop of Bosnia. In this the family name figures as Gozottus. It is printed in the *Acta Sanctorum*, August, vol. i. See also Taurisano, *Catalogus Hagiographicus O.P.*, pp. 27–28; in which *inter alia* a reference is given to Mortier, *Maîtres Généraux O.P.*, iv, 461–467. The pages in question, however, have nothing to do with the Bishop, Blessed Augustine, but with another Augustine of Zagreb, who lived a century later.

BD. PETER JULIAN EYMARD, Conf.
Founder of the Priests of the Blessed Sacrament
a.d. 1868

He was born in 1811 at La Mure d'Isère, a small town in the diocese of Grenoble, the son of Jules Eymard and his second wife, Marie Madeleine Pelorce, both devout folk. M. Eymard was a cutler and, though he showed strong signs of a vocation to the priesthood, Peter Julian worked at his father's trade, and in an oil-press, until he was eighteen; in his spare hours he studied Latin and had some instruction from a priest at Grenoble for whom he worked for a time, and in 1829 he was accepted by the superior of the Society of Mary at Marseilles. His health broke down ten months later and when he was recovered he went to the seminary of Grenoble. He was ordained there in 1834 and for the five following years ministered in the parishes of Chatte and Monteynard. What they thought of him there was expressed in the words of his bishop, Mgr. de Bruillard, when the Abbé Eymard asked for permission to rejoin the Marists : " I show my esteem for that congregation by allowing such a priest as yourself to enter it." After his novitiate he was appointed rector of the junior seminary at Belley, and in 1845 provincial of his congregation at Lyons. Always the Blessed Sacrament had been the centre round which his life revolved, " without It I should have been lost," and on a certain Corpus Christi Sunday, while carrying the Host in procession, he had an overwhelming experience : " My soul was flooded with faith and love for Jesus in the Blessed Sacrament. Those two hours seemed but a moment. I laid at the feet of our Lord the Church in France and throughout the world, everybody, myself. My eyes were filled with tears : it was as though my heart were under the wine-press. I longed at that moment for all hearts to have been within my own and to have been fired with the zeal of St Paul." In 1851 Père Eymard made a pilgrimage to Notre Dame de Fourvières : " One idea haunted me, and it was this : that Jesus in the Blessed Sacrament had no religious institute to glorify His mystery of love, whose only object was entire consecration to Its service. There ought to be one. . . . I promised Mary to devote myself to this end. It was still all very vague, and I had no idea of leaving the Society. . . . What hours I spent there ! " His superiors advised him to defer his plans till they were more mature, and he spent four years at La Seyne, where he instituted a day of adoration once a month in the community chapel. During this time he received encouragement from Pope

Pius IX and from the Ven. John Colin, founder of the Marists, and he determined to sacrifice his vocation with the Society of Mary and to devote himself to a new society; " I promised God that nothing should deter me, even if I had to endure the greatest misery and die in a poorhouse. And I asked Him for the grace to work without any human consolation—perhaps this was rash of me. But that grace has upheld me in all my trials—and they have not been small." In 1856 he was verbally dispensed from his vows by Père Favre and went to make a retreat with a community in Paris, and during the course of it, after a severe struggle, he made up his mind to take the crucial step. He submitted his scheme for an institute of priest-adorers of the Blessed Sacrament to Mgr. de Sibour, Archbishop of Paris, who referred it to the Bishops of Carcassonne and Tripoli, and at the end of twelve anxious days it was approved. Mgr. de Sibour put a large house at his disposal, wherein Père Eymard took up his residence with one companion, and on January 6, 1857, the Blessed Sacrament was exposed in its chapel for the first time, and Père Eymard preached to a large assembly.

The first members of the Congregation of Priests of the Most Blessed Sacrament were Père de Cuers and Père Champion, and they began with exposition three times a week. Vocations were slow: many were called but few chosen; and the difficulties were great. They had to leave their first house, and in 1858 they obtained a small chapel in the Faubourg Saint Jacques, where during nine years the grace of God was poured out so abundantly that Père Eymard called it the " chapel of miracles." In the following year Pope Pius IX gave the congregation a laudatory brief and a second house was opened, at Marseilles, and in 1862 a third, at Angers. By this time there were enough members to establish a regular novitiate, and the congregation rapidly expanded; to-day it has houses in France, Italy, Belgium, Czechoslovakia, Germany, Holland, Spain, and the Americas. The priests recite the Divine Office in choir and perform all other duties of the clergy, subordinate to their chief business of maintaining perpetual adoration of the Blessed Sacrament exposed, in which they are assisted by the lay-brothers; every hour of the day, at the sound of a bell, all kneel and say prayers in honour of the Eucharist and of our Lady. In 1858, with Mère Marguerite-du-Saint-Sacrement, Père Eymard established the Servants of the Blessed Sacrament, sisters who are also engaged in perpetual adoration and spreading the love of our Lord; and he founded the Priests' Eucharistic League, whose members pledge themselves to spend so far as possible about an hour a day in prayer before the Tabernacle. But Père Eymard did not confine his labours to the clergy and religious; in his Work for Poor Adults he put before his congregation the necessity for preparing for first Communion all adults who are no longer of an age to attend the parish catechism classes, or who are unable to go to these classes. This work was particularly dear to his heart and he would often give the instructions himself; " I would not give it up for anything in the world.... A youth who has never made his first Communion may be looked on as lost to the Church. He usually follows his evil inclinations, and the only aim of his life is to make a living. He knows neither God nor his Saviour Jesus Christ. He is a barbarian with the vices of civilization." Père Eymard also organized the Archconfraternity of the Blessed Sacrament, whose value is so highly regarded by the Church that by canon law a branch should be erected in every parish, and wrote a number of books on the Eucharist which have been translated into several languages.

Of the difficulties which beset Père Eymard in making his new foundation one of the most trying was the adverse criticism he was subjected to at its very inception, because he had left the Oblates of Mary. " I have received some very painful letters," he wrote, " I have seen all that they think, and I know all that they say. God knows it, He wills it for the best, and I say to myself: May He be blessed. And I think I have answered calmly and charitably." And detractors of the work were not wanting, when it was started. He excused them: " They do not understand it, and each one who thinks to oppose it does it a service. For I know well it must be persecuted. Was not our Lord persecuted throughout His life?" His project to found a house at Jerusalem failed, with considerable unpleasantness for himself, and the Nemours house had to be given up after two years, with the defection of several of his subjects. " One must be humiliated, crushed, and destroyed to become good fertilizing soil for God's glory. Is our Lord served, His ministry extended? Yes! Then the rest is nothing. The poor *ego* must be the oil of the sanctuary lamp.... Let God be praised! We must be ready to suffer and to forgive, without bitterness and without recrimination." But in spite of all the congregation was approved by the Holy See, as has been said, in his lifetime, and was finally confirmed *in perpetuum* in 1895. He had an engaging spirit of *pietas:* whenever he visited his home at La Mure he regularly made three " stations ": at the font at which he was baptized, at the altar where he received his first Communion, and at the tomb of his parents; and again, in 1867, " For how long have I wanted to see again the dear country of Chatte and Saint-Romans," scenes of his earliest ministry.

Père Eymard had been looked on as a saint even in those days, and throughout his life the impression of his holiness was recognized more and more, in his daily life and virtues, in his works, and in his supernatural gifts : several times he knew the thoughts of persons absent, he read souls, and more than once had prophetic prevision. Thus he had a premonition of his death when in Rome in 1865, and made a long retreat, when God withdrew from him all sensible consolation—not for the first time : " For four or five years the good God pursued me with His sweetness, His tenderest encouragements —and then He treated me rather differently. May He be praised ! . . . I, who am generally so sensitive and weep so easily, am now cold, dry, insensible. So He wishes me to give myself entirely to Him, a complete sacrifice—*non tua volo, sed te!* He makes me understand that by a personal act of humility or poverty I honour Him more than by all the acts of virtue I could obtain for Him from others. This last is external, the first is in my own soul." St John-Baptist Vianney, who knew Père Eymard personally, said of him, " He is a *saint*. The world hinders his work, but not knowingly, and it will do great things for the glory of God. Adoration *by priests!* How fine ! . . . Tell the good Père Eymard I will pray for the work every day."

During the last four years of his life Père Eymard suffered from rheumatic gout and insomnia, and his sufferings were added to by saddening difficulties. One of his houses got into trouble with its bishop ; a person was going around raising scandals against him and another was pushing ridicule to the verge of slander ; a sum of sixty thousand francs was lost just when it was required for the congregation. For once he allowed his discouragement to be seen. " He opened his heart to us," wrote Père Mayet in 1868, " ' This time,' he said, ' I am crushed under the cross, fallen, annihilated.' His heart felt the need of seeking relief from a friend, because, as he explained, ' I am obliged to bear my cross alone, so as not to frighten or discourage my *confrères*.' " The presentiment of approaching death was stronger than ever. " I shall return sooner than you think," was his reply when his sister urged him to visit La Mure more often. This was in February, and he began to go around visiting his penitents and others who looked to him, speaking to them as one who spoke for the last time. In July he broke down and his doctor ordered him to leave Paris at once. On the 17th he said farewell to his brethren, and on the 21st, after saying Mass, left Grenoble by coach for La Mure ; it was very hot and he arrived in a state of collapse and partial paralysis. On August 1 he died. Miracles took place at his tomb before the end of that year, and in the Holy Year of Jubilee 1925 Peter Julian Eymard was beatified by Pope Pius XI.

A summary of the depositions of witnesses is printed in the process of beatification, and the various decrees of the Cong. of Sacred Rites, culminating in the beatification brief (*Acta Apostolicæ Sedis*, xvii, 1925, pp. 370–374) contain a good deal of biographical matter. There is a short sketch by Lady Herbert, *The Priest of the Eucharist* (1898); an excellent Life by J. M. Lambert in the series " Les Saints," 1925; and a fuller Italian biography by Paolo Fossati, 1925. See also A Bettinger, *Pierre-Julien Eymard et sa méthode d'Adoration*, 1927, and Kempf, *The Holiness of the Church in the 19th Century*, pp. 176–179. The work of Blessed Eymard has frequently formed the subject of discussion at the great Eucharistic Congresses.

AUGUST 4

ST DOMINIC, Conf.
Founder of the Friars Preachers
A.D. 1221

ST DOMINIC was born in the year 1170 at Calaruega, then Calaroga, in Castile, of which village his father, Felix de Guzman, was royal warden. Practically nothing is known with certainty of Don Felix, though the Guzmans were a noble family, with illustrious connections; his wife was Bd. Joan of Aza, and the few authentic particulars recorded of Dominic's birth and childhood are mentioned in these pages under the 8th day of this month, which is her feast-day. When he was fourteen years old he left the care of his uncle, who was the archpriest of Gumiel d'Izan, and was entered at the school of Palencia. For six years he followed the arts course, and then for four he studied theology, being while still a student made a canon of the cathedral of Osma by his bishop, Martin de Bazan; the stipend of this benefice enabled him to carry out his theological studies to their conclusion, and in 1195 he was ordained priest. After his ordination Dominic went to Osma and took up his duties as a canon. The chapter lived a community life under the Rule of St Augustine with constitutions provided by Martin de Bazan, and their regularity of observance was such as to provide an admirable school for the young priest. His life there was, so far as is known, undistinguished by outward event, a gathering of strength and exercising of virtues for the labours that were to come; he seldom left the canons' house and spent much time in church, "weeping for the sins of others, and reading and putting into practice the *Conferences* of Cassian." Bd. Jordan of Saxony learned from those who had known the holy canon during this time that he appeared " as a bright ray of sunshine, in his own humble estimation the least among his brethren, in holiness the first, shedding around himself the fragrance of quickening life, like the sweet smell of pine-woods on a hot summer's day. He went on from strength to strength, like the wide-spreading olive and the slender tall cypress. . . . A special grace had been given him by God, of experiencing sorrow for sinners, for those in trouble of any kind, and the thought of their misery wrung his heart with a grief that expressed itself outwardly in tears. . . . He especially asked God that true charity should help him in the effective salvation of souls, for he could not regard himself as a real member of the mystical body of Christ until his whole time should be spent in gaining men, as his Lord had spent Himself for them on the cross." It is not surprising then that he was soon made subprior, and when Diego d'Azevedo became bishop of Osma about 1201 he succeeded him as prior of the chapter. He was then thirty-one years old, and had been leading this contemplative life for six or seven years; it at last came to an end, and Dominic began his work in the world in unexpected fashion in 1203.

In that year Alfonso IX, King of Castile, chose the Bishop of Osma to go as ambassador to the Lord of the Marches to negotiate a match between the daughter of that prince and his son, Prince Ferdinand. Which "Marches" were in question is not known. Some take it for a province in the north of Germany or in Sweden; others for a territory of that name in Limousin in France. The bishop took Dominic with him. On their way they passed through Languedoc, which was then filled with the heresy of the Albigenses. He in whose house they lodged at Toulouse professed it, and St Dominic, pierced to the heart with compassion for the man, spent the whole night in discussion with him, and with such effect that with the light of morning came the light of faith, and the man abjured his errors. It is generally supposed that from this moment Dominic knew what work God required of him. They proceeded on their journey, the treaty of marriage was concluded, and the ambassadors returned to Spain; then they were sent back with a suitable retinue to conduct the princess thither. They arrived at her father's house only to assist at her funeral, so they sent back their equipage into Spain, and went themselves to Rome to ask of Pope Innocent III leave to go to preach the Gospel to the infidels in the East. The Pope at once appreciated their zeal and virtue, but exhorted them rather to choose the neighbouring harvest and to oppose a heresy which threatened the Church at home. The bishop begged that he might be allowed to resign his episcopal see in Spain. This his Holiness would not consent to, but gave him leave to stay two years in Languedoc. On their return they made a visit to Citeaux, whose monks were the officially appointed organizers and preachers against the Albigenses; here Don Diego received the Cistercian habit, and almost at once set out for his diocese with St Dominic and a band of missioners. But at Montpellier they met the Abbot of Citeaux, together with two monks, Peter of Castelnau and Raoul of Fontefroide, who had been in charge of the missions in Languedoc, and Diego and Dominic confirmed their observations of why all these efforts against the heresy were fruitless. The Albigensian system was based on the dualism of two opposing principles, good and evil, and all matter was regarded as in itself evil; therefore the reality of the Incarnation was denied and all the sacraments rejected: human perfection, so far as it was attainable, required complete abstinence from procreation and the minimum of eating and drinking; suicide was, indeed, a most praiseworthy act. The rank and file of the Albigensians did not attempt any such austerity of life, but the inner circle of the "Perfect" maintained an heroic standard of purity and asceticism, against which the rather easy-going observance of the Cistercian monks looked mediocre. In the circumstances a reasonable use of material things was the wrong weapon for Christian orthodoxy to use: the good common people followed those who were obviously leading an heroic life for Christ—and these were not the Cistercian preachers. When they saw this, St Dominic and the Bishop of Osma invited these preachers to follow more closely the example of their opponents: to give up travelling with horses and retinues and staying at the best inns, with servants to wait on them. Then, when they had shown themselves worthy of being listened to, to use persuasion and peaceful discussion, rather than threats and overbearingness. The task was the more difficult and dangerous in that Albigensianism was a different religion rather than an heresy from Christianity, and in its more fanatical forms threatened human society as such. Dominic maintained that its spreading torrent could be stemmed, and God was pleased to make his preaching the instrument of His grace to open the ears and to soften the hearts of many. And the example he urged others to give he was the first to give himself: except out of consideration for others he rarely ate more than bread and soup, his wine was two-thirds water, he slept on the floor unless, tired out with walking and talking, he lay down by the side of the road.

The first conference of the missionaries with the heretics was held at Servian in 1206 and lasted eight days, during which several remarkable conversions were wrought. They preached after this eight days at Béziers, where the far greater number shut their ears against the Catholic faith. Diego and Dominic proceeded thence to Carcassonne, Verfeuil, Fanjeaux, Pamiers, and Montréal, but nowhere did they have any startling success. At one public debate the judges submitted St Dominic's statement of the Catholic faith to the ordeal by fire, and three times the written parchment was rejected unharmed by the flames. But the hold of the heresy, supported for their own reasons by the great lords, temporal and spiritual, was too strong, and neither right-living, exposition, nor miracles could move the people. The beginning of the mission was a failure, and the disappointed Diego returned to Osma, leaving his companion in France. But before he went St Dominic had already taken that step which was the first in the definite foundation of his order, by which the tide of Albigensianism began to be stayed. He was greatly concerned by the activities of women in the propagation of Albigensianism (the " ordinary woman " had more intellectual influence in the Middle Ages than she has now), and also by the fact that many Catholic girls of good family were, on the one hand, exposed to evil influences in their homes and, on the other, were sent to Albigensian convents to be educated. On the feast of St Mary Magdalen, 1206, he had a sign from Heaven, and in consequence of it within six months he had founded at Prouille, near Fanjeaux, a monastery of our Lady to shelter nine nuns, all of whom were converts from the heresy. " He put these servants of Christ under the protection of wonderful observance, of strict silence, and permanent enclosure. He gave them the spinning of wool as their manual work to occupy them in the intervals of their religious exercises. He entrusted the care of their souls to the brothers of his order established outside the cloister, keeping for himself with the title of prior the spiritual administration of the convent," wrote Humbert de Romans. It would appear that a house of the " brothers " referred to was founded at the same time and place. Thus St Dominic began to provide for a supply of trained and virtuous preachers, for a shelter for converted ladies, for the education of girls, and for a permanent house of prayer.

The murder of the Pope's legate, Peter of Castelnau, who was assassinated by a servant of the Count of Toulouse and another ruffian, on January 15, 1208, and other outrages committed by the heretics, let loose a crusade, with all the attendant horrors of civil war. The Albigensians were led by Raymund, Count of Toulouse, the Catholics by Simon de Montfort, *de iure* Earl of Leicester, who captured Fanjeaux in 1209, Lavaur in 1211, La Penne d'Ajen in 1212. Béziers was sacked and the population decimated, and the victories of Montfort were everywhere accompanied by harsh and cruel severity. In this St Dominic had no share, and made use of no other arms to repulse injuries than those of meekness and patience. He never complained of insults or wrongs which he received, courageously encountered every danger wherever the good of souls called him, and sought only all the good in his power for those who hated and persecuted him. When a guide deliberately led him out of his way, through briery thickets and over rocks, Dominic smilingly thanked him for showing him a short cut; when he had escaped from assassins, he replied to a heretic who asked what he would do if he were caught, that, " I would ask you to kill me slowly and painfully, a little at a time, and so earn a more glorious crown in Heaven." All this was very different from the methods of the official converters. When the army of the crusade approached the saint redoubled his earnestness among the people, and saved many. When he went among the crusaders, the disorders, vices, and ignorance of the mysteries of faith and duties of a Christian life which he found in many, who had joined that army merely for the sake of plunder, moved his compassion and zeal, and he laboured among them with no less diligence than among the Albigenses. The military power of the heretics, under Peter of Aragon, was finally crushed at the battle of Muret in 1213, a remarkable victory which Simon de Montfort attributed to the prayers of St Dominic, on his knees in the church of St James. But to the sorrow of the saint, who was the more distressed at the Earl's excesses because they were personal friends of one another, the war was unjustly carried on for aggression and conquest till Montfort was killed in battle in 1218. Dominic himself had no illusions as to the efficacy or propriety of inducing Christian orthodoxy by military activity nor, as is sometimes alleged, had he anything to do with the establishment of inquisitions in concert with the civil power, which was done in the Midi from the end of the twelfth century.* He never appears to have in any way concurred in the execution of any of those unhappy persons that then suffered. The authors of his life mention, that by his entreaties he saved the life of a young man who was going to the place where he was to be burnt, the saint assuring the judges that he would die in the Catholic faith ; which was verified when, some years after, he became a Catholic and made a happy end in St Dominic's own order. The original historians mention no other arms to have been used by him against the heretics than those of instruction, patience, penance, fasting, tears, and prayer ; and he rebuked his ex-troubadour supporter, Foulques, Bishop of Toulouse, when he went on a visitation accompanied by soldiers, servants, and sumter-mules, with the words, " The enemies of the Faith cannot be overcome like that. Arm yourself with prayer,

---

* The Dominican order later received charge of the Inquisition with unwillingness. In 1243 they asked to be relieved of the commission, but Pope Innocent IV refused the petition. The provincial chapter of Cahors in the next year forbade the acceptance of any monies accruing from its work. The fifth master general, Blessed Humbert de Romans, instructed the friars to avoid its duties whenever possible. Only two of the inquisitors general of Spain were Dominicans : the notorious and somewhat maligned Torquemada was one of them.

rather than a sword; wear humility rather than fine clothes." Three times efforts were made to raise him to the episcopate, of Béziers in 1212, of Comminges in 1213, of Navarre in 1215: each time he refused firmly. He was called to another work.

St Dominic had now spent nearly ten years preaching in Languedoc, and as leader, though with no canonical status, of a small band of special preachers, whom he had given a headquarters at Prouille. All this time he had worn the habit of a regular canon of St Augustine, and followed that rule. But he earnestly desired to revive an apostolic spirit in the ministers of the altar, the want of which in many was a subject of great scandal to the people, and a great source of the overflowing of vice and heresy. This spirit is founded on a sincere contempt of the world and a perfect disinterestedness; for so long as the love of the world and attachment to its vanity, delights, and riches, keeps possession of a heart there can be no room for the Holy Ghost. The fences by which this spirit had been formerly maintained in the clergy were then by custom easily broken through by many without scruple, and he designed to raise others that might be stronger. With this view, he projected an order of religious men, not like the monks who were contemplatives and not necessarily priests, but who to retirement and exercises of contemplation should join a close application to sacred studies and all the functions of a pastoral life, especially that of preaching. He wished to prescribe perpetual abstinence from flesh meat and severe poverty, that his friars should receive their subsistence from the alms of the faithful, and that they should be organized in such a way that their activities could be extended under central control from one diocese to any part of the Church, forming an institution of a sort new in Christian history. The principal aim of the saint was to multiply in the Church zealous preachers, whose spirit and example might be a means more easily to spread the light of faith and the fire of divine charity, and to assist the pastors in healing the wounds which the Church had received from false doctrine and ill-living. In order that he might have means at his disposal Foulques of Toulouse in 1214 gave him a benefice at Fanjeaux and extended his episcopal approval to the embryonic order in the following year. A few months later Dominic accompanied Foulques to the Fourth Lateran Council as his theologian.

Pope Innocent III, who had then governed the Church eighteen years, received the saint with great kindness and gave his approbation of the nunnery of Prouille. Moreover, he drew up a decree, which he inserted as the tenth canon of the council, to enforce the obligation of preaching, and the necessity of choosing for pastors men who are powerful in words and works, who will instruct and edify their flocks both by example and preaching, a neglect of which was the source of the ignorance, disorders, and heresies that then reigned in several provinces, and ordering that fit men be selected specially for this office of preaching. But to get approval for Dominic's great project was no easy matter : it contained too many innovations for permission to be given hurriedly, especially as that very Council had legislated against the multiplication of new religious orders. It is said that Innocent had decided to refuse but that, the night following, the Pope dreamed he saw the Lateran church in danger of falling, and that St Dominic stepped in and supported it with his shoulders. Be that as it may, the Pope at last gave a guarded approval of the new order by word of mouth, bidding the founder return to his brethren and select which of the already approved rules they would follow. They met at Prouille in August, 1216, and after consultation with his sixteen colleagues, of whom eight were Frenchmen, seven Spaniards, and one Englishman, he made choice of the rule of St Augustine, the oldest and least detailed of the existing rules, written for priests by a priest, who was himself an eminent preacher. St Dominic added certain particular constitutions, some borrowed from the order of Prémontré. Pope Innocent III died on July 18, 1216, and Honorius III was chosen in his place. This change retarded St Dominic's second journey to Rome ; and in the meantime he finished his first friary at Toulouse, to which the bishop gave the church of St Romain, and wherein the first community of Dominicans under the rule of St Augustine assembled and began community life under vows.

St Dominic arrived at Rome with a copy of his constitutions in October 1216. He found access to his Holiness difficult for some time, but eventually Honorius III confirmed his order and its constitutions by two bulls, dated 22nd and 23rd December, the same year : " Considering that the religious of your order will be champions of the faith and a true light of the world, we confirm your order." Instead of returning at once to Toulouse, St Dominic remained in Rome till after Easter, preaching with great effect. He pointed out to the Pope that many of the clerics attached to his court could not attend outside lectures and courses of instruction, and therefore a domestic master of sacred studies in his residence would be of great advantage. His Holiness thereupon created the office of Master of the Sacred Palace, who by his place is the Pope's personal canonist and theologian, assists at consistories, and nominates the Pope's preachers. Pope Honorius obliged St Dominic to take upon himself that charge, which has been ever since committed to one of his order. The saint wrote at Rome a commentary on the epistles of St Paul, much commended by writers of that age, but now lost; he had learned what an inexhaustible treasure of piety and spiritual knowledge a Christian preacher will draw from the inspired writings of this apostle. It was during this time that he formed his friendships with Cardinal Ugolino, afterwards Pope Gregory IX, and St Francis of Assisi. The story goes that Dominic saw in a vision the sinful world threatened by the divine anger but saved by the intercession of our Lady, who pointed out to her Son two figures, in one of whom St Dominic recognized himself, but the other was a stranger. Next day while at prayer in a church he saw a ragged beggar come in, and recognized him at once as the man of his dream; going up to him therefore, he embraced him and said, "You are my companion and must walk with me. For if we hold together no earthly power can withstand us." This meeting of the two founders of the friars is commemorated twice a year, when on their respective feast-days the brethren of the two orders sing Mass in each other's churches, and afterwards sit at the same table "to eat that bread which for seven centuries has never been wanting." The character of St Dominic is sometimes assumed to suffer by comparison with St Francis. The comparison is a meaningless one, for actually the two men complete and are complementary to one another, the one corrects and fills out the other: they meet on the common ground of the Faith, tenderness, and love.

On August 13, 1217, the Friars Preachers met under their leader at Prouille. He instructed them on their method of preaching and teaching and exhorted them to unremitting study, but in particular reminded them that their first business was their own sanctification, that they were to be the successors of the Apostles in establishing the kingdom of Christ. He added instructions on humility, distrust of themselves and an entire confidence in God alone, by which they were to stand invincible under afflictions and persecutions, and courageously to carry on the war against the world and the powers of Hell. Then, on the feast of the Assumption, to the surprise of all, for heresy was again gaining ground in all the neighbourhood, St Dominic broke up his band of friars and dispersed them in all directions. "We must sow the seed," he said, "not hoard it. You shall no longer live together in this house." Four were sent to Spain, seven to Paris, two returned to Toulouse, two remained at Prouille, and the founder himself in the following December went back to Rome. He wished that he might now resign his part in the nascent order and go into the East to evangelize the Cuman Tartars; but this was not to be.

On his arrival in Rome the Pope gave him the church of St Sixtus (San Sisto Vecchio), and while making a foundation there the saint lectured on theology, both in the Palace and in the City, and preached in St Peter's with such eloquence as to draw the attention and admiration of the whole city. Theodoric relates that a certain gentlewoman named Gutadona, coming home one day from hearing his sermon, found her little child dead. In her grief she took him in her arms out of the cradle, and carrying him to St Sixtus's, laid him at the feet of the saint. He was moved to compassion and, after saying a fervent prayer, made the sign of the cross on the child, and restored him to life. The Pope would have published this miracle in the pulpit, but the entreaties of Dominic prevented him. He likewise raised, whole and sound, a mason who had been crushed by the fall of a vault in building the convent of St Sixtus, and restored to health a religious man, whilst his brethren were reciting by his bedside the prayers appointed for one dying.

At this time a large number of nuns lived in Rome without keeping enclosure, and almost without regularity, some dispersed in small monasteries, others in the houses of their parents or friends. Pope Innocent III had made several attempts to assemble all such nuns into one enclosed house, but had not been able, with all his authority, to compass it. Honorius III committed the management of this reformation to St Dominic. The saint desired that three cardinals should be nominated commissaries with him, and his Holiness appointed Ugolino, Dean of the Sacred College, Nicholas, Bishop of Tusculum, and Stephen of Fossa Nuova. St Dominic, in order to remove several difficulties, offered to leave to these nuns his own monastery of St Sixtus, which was built and then ready to receive them, and which Innocent III had formerly offered them ; and he received for his friars a house of the Savelli, on the Aventine, with the church of St Sabina. The monastery of St Mary, beyond the Tiber, was the principal and most obstinate of those that were to be thus reformed. The saint went there with the three cardinals, and exhorted the nuns with such force of reasoning and so much charity that he overcame their objections. The abbess first of all, then all the nuns, except one, agreed to obey, but no sooner were the commissaries gone than the parents, friends, and protectors of the nuns ran thither, and buzzed it in their ears that they would repent at leisure of so hasty a step, which could never be recalled ; that their house was too ancient and noble, their conduct too virtuous and irreproachable, their privileges of too old a standing to be abrogated, and that no authority could submit them to rules to which they had never engaged themselves, and under which they would never have taken up that manner of life. Accordingly the whole community changed their former mind and determined not to comply. St Dominic gave them some days to reflect, and prevented the Pope from having recourse to strong measures, which never gain the heart and are seldom expedient in duties which must be voluntary; in the meantime he fasted and prayed, recommending the matter to God. After some days he went again to St Mary's, said Mass there, and afterwards spoke to the nuns, reproaching them for their reluctance, saying, " Can you then repent of a promise you have made to God ? Can you refuse to give yourselves up to Him without reserve, and to serve Him with your whole hearts ? " His natural sweetness was hard for anyone to resist, and his exhortation was so strong and affecting that at the end of it the abbess and all her nuns confirmed their readiness to comply in all things with the Pope's wishes. They moreover asked that the saint himself would be their director and give them his own rule ; to which he agreed. It is related that when, on Ash Wednesday in 1218, the abbess and some of her nuns went to their new monastery of St Sixtus, and were in the chapter house with St Dominic and the three cardinals, a messenger ran in to say that the young Napoleon, Cardinal Stephen's nephew, was thrown from his horse and killed. At this news the saint endeavoured first to alleviate Stephen's grief ; then ordered the body of Napoleon to be brought into the house, and bid Brother Tancred make an altar ready that he might say Mass. When he had prepared himself, the cardinals with their attendants, the abbess with her nuns, the friars, and a great concourse of people went to the church. The Sacrifice being ended, Dominic, standing by the body, disposed the bruised limbs in their proper places, prayed, rose from his knees, and made the sign of the cross over the corpse ; then, lifting up his hands to Heaven, he cried out with a loud voice, " Napoleon, I say to you in the name of our Lord Jesus Christ, arise." That instant, in the sight of all, the young man arose sound and whole.

A foundation having been successfully made by Friar Matthew of France at the University of Paris, St Dominic sent some brethren to the University of Bologna, where, under the guidance of Bd. Reginald of Orleans, one of the most famous of Dominican establishments was set on foot. In 1218 he took a journey through Languedoc into Spain, and founded a friary at Segovia, and another at Madrid, with a convent of nuns directed by his brother, Bd. Manes. He returned to Toulouse in April 1219, and from thence went to Paris, the first and only visit he made to that city. After two months he left Paris, and having founded convents on his road at Avignon, Asti, and Bergamo, arrived at Bologna, about the end of summer in 1219, which city he made his ordinary residence to the end of his life. In 1220 Pope Honorius III officially confirmed Dominic's title and office as master general, and at Pentecost was held the first general chapter of the order, at Bologna, at which were drawn up the final constitutions which made the organization of the Friars Preachers " the most perfect of all the monastic organizations produced by the Middle Ages " (Hauck). In the same year the Pope ordered the Dominicans to undertake a preaching crusade in Lombardy, in company with certain monks. St Dominic took the field, but the mission was abortive, although 100,000 heretics are said to have been reconciled.

Wherever the saint travelled, he preached ; and he never ceased to pray for the conversion of infidels and sinners. It was his earnest desire, if it had been God's will, to shed his blood for Christ, and to travel among the barbarous nations of the earth to announce to them the good news of eternal life. Therefore did he make the ministry of the word the chief end of his institute : he would have all his religious to be applied to it, every one according to his capacity, and those who had particular talents for it never to discontinue the office of preaching, except in intervals allotted to retirement that they might preach to themselves in silence. The vocation of his friars is " to hand on to others the fruits of contemplation," and for this high work he prepares the religious by long habits of virtue, especially of prayer, humility, self-denial, and obedience. It was a saying which he frequently repeated to them, " That a man who governs his passions is master of the world. We must either rule them, or be ruled by them. It is better to be the hammer than the anvil." He taught his missionaries the art of preaching to the heart by animating them with charity. Being once asked after preaching in what book he had studied his sermon, " In no other," said he, " than in that of love." Learning, study of the Bible, and teaching were from the beginning of first importance in the order : some of its chief achievements have been in intellectual work and the founder has been called " the first minister of public instruction in modern Europe." But an eminent spirit of prayer and recollection has at all times been the characteristic of the Dominicans, as it was of St Dominic. A great figure in the order, Bartholomew de Martyribus, Archbishop of Braga, addresses himself to all pastors on this subject : " Woe to you, ministers of the Lord, if the source of religion be dried up in your souls. This tender and sincere spirit of piety is the spring of living water which gives fertility to all our virtues and sanctifies all our actions, which without it are dry and barren. This is the heavenly wine which fortifies our hearts with a joy altogether divine. This is the balsam which mollifies our passions. It is the tongue with which we speak to God, and without which our souls are dumb before Him. It is this that draws down upon us the heavenly dew that strengthens our hearts; it is the spiritual nourishment which enables us to labour with fruit in the vineyard of the Lord."

St Dominic was inflexible in maintaining the severe discipline he had established. Coming back to Bologna in 1220, after seeing the poverty of St Francis at Cremona, he was so much offended to find the convent of his friars in that city being built in a stately manner, not consistent with his idea of the austere poverty and penance which he professed by his rule, that he would not allow the work to be continued. This was the discipline and strength that was behind the rapid spread of his order; by the second general chapter in 1221 it had some sixty friaries divided into eight provinces; friars had already got to Poland, Scandinavia, and Palestine, and Brother Gilbert with twelve others had established monasteries in Canterbury, London, and Oxford. The Order of Preachers is still world-wide.

After the second general chapter, which was held at Bologna, Dominic visited Cardinal Ugolino at Venice. On his return he was ill, and he was taken to a country place for the better air. But he knew he was dying. To his brethren he spoke of the beauty of chastity, and, having no temporal goods, made his last testament in these words: "These, my much-loved ones, are the bequests which I leave to you as my sons: have charity among you; hold to humility; keep willing poverty." He spoke more at length on this subject of poverty, and then at his request was carried back to Bologna that he might be buried " under the feet of his brethren." Gathered round him, they said the prayers for the dying; at the *Subvenite* St Dominic repeated those great words, and died. It was the evening of 6th August, 1221; he was fifty-one years old; and he died in that poverty of which he had so lately spoken: " in Brother Moneta's bed because he had none of his own; in Brother Moneta's habit, because he had not another to replace the one he had long been wearing." It may be said of him after death what Bd. Jordan of Saxony wrote of him in life: " Nothing disturbed the even temper of his soul except his quick sympathy with every sort of suffering. And as a man's face shows whether his heart is happy or not, it was easy to see from his friendly and joyous countenance that he was at peace inwardly. In spite of his unfailing gentleness and readiness to help, no one could ever despise his radiant nature, which won all who met him and made him attract people from the first." When he signed the decree of canonization of his friend in 1234 Pope Gregory IX (Cardinal Ugolino) said that he no more doubted the sanctity of Dominic than he did that of St Peter or St Paul.

Beginning with the Life written by Blessed Jordan of Saxony, the successor of St Dominic in the generalship of the Order, there is a good deal of biographical material of relatively early date. Without particularising, it may be sufficient to say that the more important elements will be found in the *Acta Sanctorum*, Aug., vol. i; in the *Scriptores O.P.* by Quétif and Echard; and in sundry issues of the *Analecta Fratrum Prædicatorum*. Perhaps, however, the most generally useful contribution to the study of the history of the Saint is the work in three volumes which PP. Balme and Lelaidier have published under the name of *Cartulaire de Saint Dominique* (1893–1901), consisting largely of extracts and documents with pictorial illustrations. Unfortunately, however, the collection stops short at his death, and the evidence given in the process of canonization by the Fathers who had lived with him is not included. These testimonies which reveal so much of his interior spirit are printed in the *Acta Sanctorum* and elsewhere. Among modern Lives that of Mother Frances Raphael (Drane) is still perhaps the best in English. There are also good German biographies by M. Rings (1920), B. Altaner (1922), and H. C. Scheeben (1927). The excellent sketch contributed by Jean Guiraud to the series " Les Saints " has also been translated into English. See further B. Jarrett, *The Life of St Dominic* (1924) and Mortier, *Histoire des Maîtres Généraux O.P.*, vol. i. The institution of the devotion of the Rosary which some years ago was so vehemently claimed for St Dominic is now, and with good reason, no longer insisted upon.

SS. IA AND HER COMPANIONS, Marts.
A.D. 360

In the worst times of Roman persecution of Christians there was never a more cruel and bloody period than that of from about 314 until 379, during which King Sapor II persecuted in Persia; in proportion to the numbers involved and its duration, this persecution had more victims than any other. Among them was St Ia and those that suffered with her. She was a Greek, a captive, who made many converts among the Persian women so that she was denounced by the Mazdæan priests and ordered to be put to the most fiendish tortures. Her passion is chiefly a record of the cruelties which she suffered. Her limbs were first stretched apart and she was remorselessly beaten, at which she only prayed aloud, " O Lord Jesus Christ, Son of the living God, strengthen thy handmaiden and save me from the wolves that rend me." She was put back into prison until she had recovered and then offered her life if she would apostatize. She again refused, and was beaten as before, by forty men with apple-rods, till she could neither speak nor move. After another six months her tormentors stuck slips of bamboo all over her body and wound her round with ropes, so as to press them into her flesh ; then each was sharply pulled out again. She nearly died from loss of blood, but after another ten days was brought out of prison, hung up by her hands, and lashed until her bones were bare and life was extinct. Then her head was struck off and her body thrown away. The Roman Martyrology records the tradition that those who suffered death with her numbered nine thousand. This St Ia must not be confounded with the Irish maiden Ia who gives her name to the town of Saint Ives in Cornwall.

The best text of the Passio is that edited by Père Delehaye in the *Patrologia Orientalis*, vol. ii, pp. 453-473, fasc. 4 ; but it is also printed in the *Acta Sanctorum*, August, vol. i. The martyr's Syriac name simply meant " violet " (ιον), as Peeters had shown (*Analecta Bollandiana*, xxv, (1906), p. 340). It has nothing to do with Εὐδοκία.

ST MOLUA or LUGHAEDH, Abbot and Conf.

A.D. 605

Molua (Lugid, Luanus, and other forms) was the son of Carthach, of a family in the Hy-Fidhginte district of Limerick county, and his mother came from Ossory. When a lad he was employed as a herd-boy till, as his late " life " tells us, having distinguished himself by miracles he was sent to be a monk under St Comgall at Bangor. There were already fifty Lughaedhs there, so he was distinguished as Lughaedh Maccan. He was ordained priest and in time sent by his abbot to establish monasteries elsewhere, which he did to the number of over one hundred, according to St Bernard who refers to him in his " life " of St Malachy. The most important of them was at Clonfert Molua, now called Kyle, in the Slievebloom mountains between Leix and Offaly, which had a very large community. He was taken to Rome by St Dagan, and took the opportunity to submit to Pope St Gregory the Great the rule he had drawn up for his monasteries ; it was, like all Celtic monastic rules, extremely arduous and the Pope said of it that, " The holy man who drew up this rule has laid a hedge round his family which reaches to Heaven." On his death-bed St Molua addressed his monks and said, " Dearest brethren, cultivate your land industriously, that you may have a sufficiency of food, drink and clothing ; for where there is sufficient, there is stability ; where is stability, there is true religion ; and the end of true religion is life everlasting ": *Rerum novarum* and *Quadragesimo anno* in a nut-shell.

There is some confusion between this Molua and other saints of the same name. Killaloe (Kill da Lua) may get its name from this Molua or from another who was called " the Leper," or they may both be the same person. In Scotland a St Molua, also said to be a disciple of St Comgall and who preached in Rosshire and the Isles, was venerated on June 25th; his crozier (*bachal*) is still in the possession of the Dukes of Argyll, having been for generations hereditary in the family of Livingstone of Lismore.

There are three Latin recensions of the Life of St Molua; one has been printed in the *Acta Sanctorum*, Aug., vol. i; another in De Smedt's edition of the Codex Salmanticensis, and the third by C. Plummer in his *Vitae Sanctorum Hiberniae*, ii, pp. 206-225. *Cf.* Forbes, *Kalendars of Scottish Saints* (pp. 409-411), who repudiates any identity between St Molocus and St Molua. See also Ryan, *Irish Monasticism*, pp. 128-9 and *passim*.

ST WALTHEOF OR WALTHEN, ABBOT OF MELROSE, CONF.

A.D. 1160

He was second son of Simon, Earl of Huntingdon, and Maud, daughter to Judith, the niece of William the Conqueror who was married to Waltheof, Earl of Northumberland. His elder brother was called Simon, and in their childhood it was the pastime of this Simon to build castles and play at soldiers, but Waltheof's to build churches and monasteries of stones and wood. When grown up, the elder inherited his father's martial disposition together with his title; but Waltheof had a strong inclination for the religious life and was mild and peace-loving. Their mother Maud, after the death of her first husband, was given in marriage by King Henry I to David I, King of Scotland, the worthy son of St Margaret, and Waltheof followed his mother to that court, where he formed an intimate friendship with St Aelred, who was master of the royal household at that time. The king was charmed with his stepson, gave him marks of his particular affection, and took great delight in his company, but the young nobleman was too steadfast to be led away by the flatteries of the world, and they served only to make him the more careful of its dangers. For, loving and valuing only heavenly things, whatever he did he used to say to himself, " What will this avail me to eternal life ? " When he went out hunting with the king he would give his bow and quiver to some servant or other person and, withdrawing from the company into the wood, used to hide himself in some thicket and there employ the day in meditation or reading. The king, having one day surprised him at this, told the queen that her son was not a man of this world, for he could find no amusement or satisfaction in any of its diversions. Only once did it look as if his vocation might be lost; he had attracted the attention of one of the ladies of the court and accepted from her a ring, which he wore on his finger. Such gages commonly have more serious developments, but when a courtier, noticing the ring, said, " Ha ! At last Waltheof begins to take some notice of women," he pulled himself together, snatched off the ring, and threw it into the fire. Soon after he decided to avoid the life of a court cleric and become a religious. To be free from distracting visits and from the neighbourhood of the court he left Scotland, and made his profession among the regular canons of St Augustine in St Oswald's monastery at Nostell, near Pontefract in Yorkshire. Here he lived in the company of his crucified Jesus, humbling himself so much the lower in proportion as he had been exalted in the world. His former companions were astonished, but his fellow-religious were more surprised to see one come out of a court already advanced in the life of the spirit. He was promoted to the priesthood, and was appointed sacristan. He was soon after chosen prior of Kirkham, a house of the order in the same county, and, realising the obligations he now lay under for the sanctification of others as well as for his own, he redoubled his austerity and regularity of observance. In saying Mass one Christmas Day, after the consecration of the bread he was ravished in the contemplation of that divine mystery of God made man, and was favoured with a wonderful vision. The divine Word, who on that day had made Himself visible to mankind by His birth, was pleased to manifest Himself not only to the eyes of faith but also to the bodily eyes of His servant. Waltheof saw in his hands, not the form of bread, but the radiant form of the child Jesus. When he had laid the Host on the altar he saw only the sacramental form. He disclosed this marvel only to his confessor, Everard, who after his death told it to several others and confirmed his testimony, that he received the account from the saint himself, with an oath. The author of his " life," Jordan, a monk of Furness, says he himself heard it from the mouth of this confessor, and also from several Cistercian monks, both at Melrose and at Holm Cultram. Whilst a canon of Kirkham was saying Mass, a spider fell into the chalice. The prior being called made the sign of the cross over the chalice, then bid the priest drink it, which he did without any harm or feeling any repugnance. In those days it was commonly believed that any spider was virulently poisonous.

Waltheof, impressed by the life and vigour of the Cistercian order, was very anxious to join it, and naturally he was encouraged by the advice of his friend St Aelred, then abbot of Rievaulx. Accordingly he took the habit at Wardon, a Cistercian convent in Bedfordshire. The canons, who loved and honoured him, used all endeavours to keep him among them, and Earl Simon, his brother, employed both secular and ecclesiastical influence to make him leave Wardon, and even threatened to destroy the monastery if he remained in it. The monks therefore sent their postulant back to Rievaulx. Four years after his profession St Waltheof was chosen abbot of Melrose, on the river Tweed, a Cistercian abbey recently founded by King David. In correcting his monks he tempered severity with sweetness, so as to make them love the correction itself and to gain their heart to their duty. After the person had done penance for a fault, he would never suffer it to be mentioned again, for even the evil spirits forget our sins when they have been wiped away by sincere repentance. Whenever he fell into the smallest failing of inadvertence he had recourse immediately to confession and accused himself of it with many tears, a practice of perfection which his confessors found rather trying, as one of them admitted to Dom Jordan. By these frequent exercises of penance he sought to obtain the grace by which his soul might be cleansed more and more perfectly, that he might at the last present himself without spot before God, who is infinite purity and infinite sanctity and whose eyes cannot bear the least uncleanness. Yet cheerfulness and spiritual joy always shone in his face, and his words were animated with a fire which penetrated the hearts of those that heard him; his voice was sweet and soft, but feeble and low owing to weakness of body and continual psalmody. His alms supported the poor of the whole country round his abbey, and in a famine which happened in 1154 some four thousand poor strangers came and settled around Melrose, for whom he provided for several months; he sometimes asked his monks to content themselves with half their pittances of bread, in order to supply the poor. He is said to have twice multiplied bread miraculously, and to have given away all the cattle and sheep that belonged to his monastery. In travelling he would carry the gear of his companions, and sometimes that of servants; he once went to King Stephen in England, about affairs of his community, carrying a bundle on his back. His brother Simon, who was present, was very annoyed and said to the king, " See how this brother of mine, and cousin of yours, disgraces his family." " Not so," said the king. " If we understand what the grace of God is, he does honour to us and all his kindred." He readily granted all the saint desired, begged his blessing, and after his departure expressed how much he was moved by his example to a contempt of the world for the love of God. In 1154 Waltheof was chosen archbishop of Saint Andrews; but by his repeated assurances that the weight of such a burden would put an end to his life he prevailed on St Aelred to oppose the election and not to oblige him to accept it. Once when giving a conference to his community he had occasion to refer to a vision of the glory of Heaven which had been vouchsafed to him, but he spoke in the third person as of another; but at last by inadvertence he spoke in the first person: he no sooner realized it than, cutting his discourse short, he withdrew in tears, much afflicted for the word which had escaped him. The contemplation of that day which would drown him in the ocean of eternal joy was the comfort and support of his soul during his last lingering illness, in which he bore terrible pain with silence and patience. Having exhorted his brethren to charity and regular discipline and received the last Sacraments, lying on sackcloth and ashes he died at a great age on August 3rd, 1160.

Under the Latin form "Walthenus," a long Life, attributed to Joscelin, or Jordan, a monk of Furness (*c.* 1210), is printed in the *Acta Sanctorum,* Aug., vol. i. Though prolix, the narrative may be considered fairly reliable. See also T. D. Hardy, *Descriptive Catalogue of MSS.* (Rolls Series), vol. ii, p. 285. Although his feast may have been kept on other days of August, Waltheof's biographer is precise in saying that he died on August 3, on the feast of the finding of St Stephen.

AUGUST 5

THE DEDICATION OF OUR LADY OF THE SNOW
c. A.D. 435

THIS feast celebrates the dedication of the third of the patriarchal basilicas within the walls of Rome, to which at first the name of " Liberian Basilica " was given, because it was founded in the time of Pope Liberius, in the middle of the fourth century; it was restored and consecrated under the title of the Virgin Mary by Sixtus III, about the year 435, and is now generally known as St Mary Major (Santa Maria Maggiore), because it is in both age and dignity the first church of the City among those dedicated to God in honour of our Lady. In the liturgical books it is called St Mary *ad Nives*, or " of the Snow," from a popular tradition that the Mother of God chose this place for a church under her invocation by a miraculous fall of snow upon this spot in summer, and by a vision in which she appeared to a patrician named John, who munificently founded and endowed this church in the pontificate of Liberius at the site thus indicated on the Esquiline Hill. No mention is found of this miracle until some hundreds of years later, and it is now everywhere recognized as a myth. A commission for the reform of the Breviary recommended to Pope Benedict XIV in 1742 that its old name of " Dedication of St Mary " should be restored to the feast; this has not been done yet, except in the new Benedictine calendar (1915). This basilica has sometimes also been known by the name of St Mary *ad Præsepe*, from the alleged relic of the crib or manger of Bethlehem, in which Christ was laid at His birth.

The church is one of the most famous in the whole world for the devotion of the faithful to the Mother of God. They here assemble from all parts of Christendom, to unite together in praising God for the mercies He has shown to this holy Virgin, and through her to the whole world, and in imploring her intercession. Supplications which are public and general are most honourable to God and powerful in obtaining His graces. To say nothing of the precious relics of many saints which are there deposited, and the many mercies which by the prayers of the faithful have been there obtained for the whole Church, these Christian gatherings alone suffice to recommend the sanctity of this and other such venerable churches beyond all the glory of the temple of Solomon in the Jewish law. The Church, which is always solicitous to instruct her children in the most powerful means of attaining to salvation, never ceases from the primitive ages strongly to urge them to make their devotions to the Mother of God, as a most efficacious means of sanctifying themselves. She teaches us earnestly to implore Him who is the author of our being and of our salvation to listen to her prayers for us; and humbly to remind Him that through her He bestowed Himself upon us, and that for love of us He vouchsafed to be born of her. The Church teaches us to see in her " the mother of grace and pity," and to place a confidence in her mediation, that by it we shall more easily obtain from her Son, and through His merits, all graces. That Christian neglects a great means of succour who does not every day most earnestly recommend himself and his particular difficulties and necessities to her intercession. To make our supplications the more worthy, we ought to unite them in spirit to those of all fervent penitents and devout souls in invoking this advocate for sinners. We ought to be ashamed if we do not appear among the foremost and most ardent in our devotion, in proportion to our necessities and obligations.

See H. Grisar, *Analecta Romana* (1900), p. 70, and the same writer's *Geschichte Roms und der Päpste* (1901), p. 153, note 1; as well as Duchesne, *Liber Pontificalis*, i, p. 235. Stress is rightly laid upon the fact that no mention is made of any miraculous fall of snow in Sixtus III's inscription for the dedication of the basilica. Though the original has now perished, its text is quite well known, and has been reprinted, for example, from De Rossi's *Inscriptiones Christianæ*, vol. ii, pp. 71, 98, 139, in Duchesne's footnote.

SS. ADDAI AND MARI, Bps and Confs.
Apostles of East Syria and Persia
c. A.D. 150 (?)

There were inhabitants of Mesopotamia present when St Peter and his companions preached at Pentecost, and for all that we know the first East Syrian Christians were made at that time, but the actual date of the introduction of Christianity into those parts, among the Edessene Jews, is unknown. There is evidence of a Christian colony at Edessa in the second century, but it was probably not till the coming of the Sassanid dynasty that the Faith began to spread from there over Mesopotamia, Adiabene, and Persia.

Local ecclesiastical tradition, however, attributes their evangelization to the apostle St Thomas, and more particularly to St Addai, St Aggai, and St Mari. The story of how they came to Edessa, combined from the narratives of Eusebius and of a Syriac document called *The Doctrine of Addai* (written *c.* 375–400), is as follows. At the time when our Lord was still incarnate upon earth there reigned in Osroene a king called Abgar the Black, who lived at Edessa. He suffered from some apparently incurable disease and, having heard from legates whom he had sent into Palestine of the miracles of healing of our Lord, he sent to Him a letter by the hand of his secretary, Hannan. In it he addresses Christ as "the good Physician" and asks Him to come to Edessa and heal him, professing to believe, in consequence of the reported wonders, that, "either Thou art God, who hast come down from Heaven, or else the Son of God, who brings all these things to pass." Hannan found our Lord in the house of Gamaliel, "Chief of the Jews," and He replied to Abgar that, "Happy art thou who hast believed in Me without having seen Me, for it is written that they who see Me shall not believe and they who see Me not shall believe. As for My coming to you, I am about to return to My Father, all for which I was sent into the world being finished. But when I shall have ascended to Him I will send thee one of My disciples, who shall heal thee of thy sickness and bring thee and thine to eternal life. Thy city shall be blessed for ever and no enemy shall overcome it." According to Eusebius our Lord wrote out this message Himself and it was accordingly greatly reverenced throughout Christendom during the Middle Ages; it was used as an amulet in England before the eleventh century. The statement about the inviolability of the city is regarded as evidence for the antiquity of the story, as Edessa was occupied by the Romans in 116 and again captured by them a hundred years later. The Syriac document states that Hannan also brought back to Abgar a portrait of our Lord which he had painted, and which as the Holy Mandeylion is famous in Christian iconography. After the Ascension, "Judas Thomas" accordingly sent one of the seventy-two disciples, Addai (Thaddeus), to the court of King Abgar. He lodged at the house of a Jew, Tobias, and when he was brought before the king he healed him of his disease, and spoke to him of the faith of Christ, incidentally telling him of the finding of the true cross, in which Protonice, wife of the Emperor Claudius, plays the part of St Helen. Addai converted Abgar and multitudes of his people, among others the royal jeweller, Aggai, whom he made bishop and his successor, and Palut, whom he ordained priest on his death-bed. In due course St Aggai was martyred and Palut had to go to Antioch to be consecrated by Serapion, who in his turn had been made bishop by Pope St Zephyrinus at Rome. Quite apart from any other consideration, this last statement throws the whole of the legend into confusion, for it is known that there was a Serapion, Bishop of Antioch, who was at least contemporary with St Zephyrinus, and was, moreover, contemporary with Abgar IX, who was certainly a Christian king of Edessa between about 176 and 213, and was probably the first; so Serapion could not possibly have consecrated a convert of one of the Seventy-two.

The most, then, that can be said of St Addai is that he was probably a missionary in Edessa, before the end of the second century; the first known bishop there was Kona, who built a church in 313. St Mari is an even less satisfactory person, for there are serious doubts of his existence at all. According to his sixth-century "acts" he was a disciple of St Addai, who sent him to Nisibis; he preached there and took up the work of Jonas the prophet at Ninive, then he went down the Tigris, until he began "to smell the smell of the apostle Thomas," and died near Seleucia-Ctesiphon, after consecrating as its bishop Papa bar Aggai, another certainly historical personage, the first katholikos of the East Syrian churches—but at the beginning of the fourth century. Wherever he went St Mari made numerous converts, destroyed temples, built churches, and founded monasteries, on a scale familiar in spurious legends but rarely, if ever, found in sober history. Nevertheless, SS. Addai and Mari, nebulous as they now are, have from early ages been venerated as the evangelists of the lands around the Tigris and Euphrates, and still are by their successors, the Catholic Chaldeans and the Nestorians of Iraq and Kurdistan; they are referred to as "the Holy Apostles," and the principal *anaphora* of the Liturgy of those Christians bears their name.

The two primary sources are Eusebius' *Ecclesiastical History*, Bk. i, ch. 13; and the *Doctrine of Addai* (Syriac text with Eng. trans.), edited by G. Phillips, 1876. Some years ago the authenticity of the letters exchanged between Abgar and our Saviour was still very warmly defended, *e.g.* by the Abbé Paulin Martin in the *Revue des Sciences Ecclésiastiques* for 1888–1889 (several articles), as against Tixeront, Rubens Duval, R. Lipsius, and others. On the Armenian version and its bearings on the controversy, consult P. J. Dashian, "Zur Abgar Sage," three articles in the *Vienna Oriental Journal* for 1890. Modern opinion tends strongly to regard the whole incident as apocryphal, see *e.g.* Bardenhewer, *Geschichte der altkirchlichen Literatur*, vol. i, pp. 569 seq. and p. 443; and *Dictionnaire de la Bible : Supplément*, cc. 540–542. *Cf.*, however, Casartelli in *The Dublin Review* for April 1889, and *The Month*, September 1892, pp. 39–61.

ST AFRA, Mart.
A.D. 304

The persecution of Diocletian was carried on with great cruelty by his colleague Maximian in those provinces which fell to his share in the division of the empire. At Augsburg, in Rhætia, the officers apprehended a woman called Afra, known to have formerly been a common prostitute. St Narcissus, Bishop of Gerona, having been driven from his see during the persecution, lodged in her mother's house, converted them both, and ordained her uncle Dionysius. Afra was a true penitent and had her sins always before her eyes; persuaded she never could do enough to efface them, she never dwelt on what she had already done for that end; immediately upon her conversion she gave what she possessed to the poor, led a most penitential life, and she rejoiced to suffer in order to atone for her former crimes. When she was brought to trial the judge, by name Gaius, who knew who she was, said, " Sacrifice to the gods; it is better to live than to die in torments." Afra replied, " I was a great sinner before I knew God; but I will not add new crimes, or do what you command me." Gaius said, " Go to the capitol, and sacrifice." Afra answered, " My capitol is Jesus Christ, whom I have always before my eyes. I every day confess my sins; and because I am unworthy to offer Him any sacrifice, I desire to sacrifice myself for His name, that this body in which I have sinned may be purified and offered up to Him." " I am informed," said Gaius, " that you are a prostitute. Sacrifice therefore, as you are a stranger to the God of the Christians and cannot be accepted by Him." Afra replied, " My Lord Jesus Christ has said that He came down from Heaven to save sinners. The Gospel says that a sinful woman washed His feet with her tears and obtained pardon, and that He never rejected the outcasts but welcomed them to eat with Him." The judge said, " Sacrifice, that your paramours may come to you again and make you rich." Afra answered, " I will have no more of those wicked wages. I have thrown away what I had by me of such ill-gotten money. Even our poor brethren would not accept it." Gaius said, " Your Christ will have nothing to do with you. It is in vain for you to call Him your God: a harlot can never be called a Christian." Afra replied, " It is true, I am unworthy to bear the name of Christian; but Christ has admitted me to be one." " How do you know?" " He has not rejected me but has allowed me to confess Him before you; and I hope that my confession will earn forgiveness of my sins." " That is nonsense. Sacrifice to the gods and you will be safe." The martyr replied, " My saviour is Jesus Christ, who upon the cross promised paradise to the thief that confessed Him." The judge said, " Sacrifice, lest I order you to be whipped in the presence of your lovers." Afra replied, " Do what you like. Only the memory of my sins can cause me confusion and grief now." " I am ashamed," exclaimed Gaius, " that I have disputed so long with you. If you do not comply, you shall die." Afra replied, " That is what I desire, if I am not unworthy to find rest by martyrdom." The judge said, " Sacrifice, or I will order you to be tortured and then burnt alive." Afra answered, " Let the body which has sinned suffer ; but I will not ruin my soul by false worship." Then the judge passed sentence upon her. The executioners immediately seized her, and carried her to an island in the river Lech. There they stripped her and tied her to a stake. She lifted up her eyes to Heaven, and prayed with tears, saying, " O Lord Jesus Christ, almighty God, who camest to call, not the righteous, but sinners to repentance, accept the penance of my sufferings and by this passing fire deliver me from the everlasting fire which burns both body and soul." Whilst the executioners were heaping a pile of vine branches about her and setting fire to them, she was heard to say, " I thank Thee, O Lord Jesus Christ, for Thy goodness in receiving me, a holocaust for Thy name's sake : Thou who didst offer Thyself upon the altar of the cross as a sacrifice for the sins of the whole world, the just for the unjust, the sinless for sinners. I offer myself a victim to Thee, who livest and reignest with the Father and the Holy Ghost world without end. Amen." Having spoken these words she gave up her spirit, being suffocated by the smoke.

Three servants of the martyr, Digna, Eunomia, and Eutropia, who had lived disorderly lives with their mistress, but were converted and baptised at the same time by the holy bishop Narcissus, stood all the while on the banks of the river, and watched her triumph. After the execution they went to the island, and found the body of Afra entire. Hilaria, the martyr's mother, came in the night with some priests and carried away the body, which she buried in a sepulchre she had built for herself and family, two miles from the city. Whilst Hilaria and her attendants were still within the tomb, Gaius was informed of what they had done. He therefore dispatched soldiers with an order to persuade the whole company to offer sacrifice, and if they refused to burn them alive without any other formality. The soldiers used both mild words and threats ; but finding all to no purpose they filled the vault of the sepulchre with dry thorns and vine branches, shut the door upon them, and having set fire to the sticks, went away. Thus St Afra, her mother, and three servants were honoured with the crown of martyrdom on the same day.

The existence of a martyr called Afra, who suffered at Augsburg and was venerated there from early times, is firmly established. The *Acta* from which the above relation is taken is a document of two distinct parts; that which narrates her trial and martyrdom is probably a "touched-up" version of an earlier narrative. The separate story of her being a harlot from Cyprus, her conversion, and the execution of her mother and servants, is an invention of the Carlovingian era. St Afra is referred to by Venantius Fortunatus and named in the Roman Martyrology, and is still venerated in southern Germany.

The two Latin texts of most importance have both been edited by Bruno Krusch in the *Monumenta Germaniae; Scriptores rerum Meroving.*; the one in vol. iii, pp. 55–64; the other in vol. vii, pp. 192–204. The Armenian version on which H. Goussen in *Theologie und Glaube*, i, pp. 791–794, laid great stress, proves to be of no importance. Much discussion has centred round the question whether the original text of the *Acta* is really a Merovingian document as Duchesne contended, or, as Krusch believed, was only elaborated out of the notice in the "Hieronymianum"—"In Provincia Retia, civitate Augusta, Afrae veneriae." A. Bigelmair, Albert Poncelet, and O. Riedner support Krusch, but in the latest volume of the *Acta Sanctorum*, Nov., vol. ii, part 2, p. 423, an opposite view is taken. See the same notice for fuller bibliographical references. Künstle's *Ikonographie*, vol. ii, pp. 35–36, deals with St Afra in art; and Bächtold-Stäubli, *Handwörterbuch*, vol. i, pp. 207–209, gives information as to the folk-lore of the *cultus* of St Afra.

ST NONNA, MATRON

A.D. 374

Nonna was born towards the end of the third century and, although she was brought up a Christian, married Gregory, the magistrate of Nazianzus in Cappadocia, who was a member of a Judaic-pagan sect called the Hypsistarians. However, this was a case of a "mixed marriage" turning out, by the grace of God, for the very best, and the resulting family was one of the most famous and brilliant saintly families of Christian history. By her shining example St Nonna converted her husband, and he became a priest, and then a bishop: in those days the now universal law that a bishop must be single or a widower was not yet everywhere in force; he is moreover venerated as a saint and is known as St Gregory Nazianzen the Elder. They had three children, all of them saints, and the eldest, St Gregory Nazianzen the Divine, became one of the greatest of the Doctors of the Church ; he is one of the four chief Greek doctors, and in his writings often refers to the devoted and virtuous life of his mother Nonna. The next child was a girl, St Gorgonia, who married and had three children. The third was St Cæsarius, a physician by profession. St Nonna outlived two of her children : Gorgonia died in her arms, and she heard the funeral sermons preached for her and Cæsarius by Gregory the Younger which have continued to be the admiration of succeeding ages. She survived her husband only a few months and died at a considerable age in 374 : a valiant woman, whose children rose up and called her blessed, whose husband praised her. St Nonna is named in the Roman Martyrology and her feast is kept by the Greek monks of Grottaferrata, near Rome.

A sufficient account of St Nonna is given in the *Acta Sanctorum*, August, vol. ii, and in the *Dictionary of Christian Biography*.

ST THOMAS OF DOVER, Mart.

A.D. 1295

Among the English saints of the Middle Ages who have quite dropped out of memory is Thomas of Hales, a monk of the Benedictine Priory of St Martin at Dover, a cell of Christ Church, Canterbury. On August 5, 1295, a French raid descended on Dover from the sea, and the monks of the priory fled with the exception of this venerable old man, who was too infirm to get away. When the raiders invaded the monastery they found him in bed and told him to disclose where the church plate and other valuables had been hidden ; he refused and was at once put to death. Miracles were recorded at his tomb and Simon Simeon, an Irish friar who made a pilgrimage to the Holy Land about 1322, mentions the honour given to him as a martyr " at the Black Monks, under Dover Castle." King Richard II asked Pope Urban VI to canonize Thomas, and a process was begun in 1382 but never carried out ; nevertheless there was certainly an altar dedicated in honour of Thomas of Hales in Dover priory-church in 1500. From the fact that he was represented among the paintings of saints in the English College of Rome it may be judged that his *cultus* was considerable.

See Stanton's *Menology of England and Wales*, pp. 605 and 665, and T. D. Hardy, *Catalogue of British History* (Rolls Series), vol. iii, p. 247.

AUGUST 6

THE TRANSFIGURATION OF OUR LORD

OUR divine Redeemer, in order to show us that the sufferings of His servants are usually intermingled with spiritual comforts and to give us a sensible demonstration of the truth of His promises of an eternal glory reserved for us in the world to come, was pleased to manifest His majesty in the mystery of the Transfiguration. Being in Galilee about a year before His passion, He chose to be witnesses of His glory the same three beloved disciples who were afterward to be witnesses of His agony in the garden, namely St Peter, and the two sons of Zebedee, SS. James and John. He took three, that their evidence might be unexceptionable; but He would not publicly show His glory, to teach His followers to love the closest secrecy in all spiritual graces and favours. Practices contrary to this are suggested by self-love, not by the spirit of God; they are a disguised pride and a dangerous illusion. Every true servant of God loves to be hidden; his motto, even when he most warmly invites all creatures to magnify the Lord with him for all His unspeakable mercies, is: " My secret to myself, my secret to myself " (Isaias xxiv 16). He fears lest he should be at all considered or thought of in what belongs purely to God alone. Jesus therefore showed this miracle in retirement, and He led these three apostles to a lonely mountain, as He was accustomed to go often to some solitude to pray. The tradition of the Christians in Palestine, of which St Cyril of Jerusalem, St John Damascene, and other fathers speak, assures us that this was Mount Thabor, which is high and beautiful and covered with green trees and shrubs, and was very fruitful. It rises, something like a sugar-loaf, in a vast plain in the middle of Galilee. This was the place in which the Man-God appeared in His glory. He was transfigured whilst at prayer, because it is usually then that the soul receives the dew of divine consolations, and tastes how infinitely sweet and good God is to those who sincerely seek Him. Many Christians indeed are strangers to this effect of prayer because they do not apply themselves to it with perseverance and fervour, or neglect to disengage their affections from creatures by humility, self-denial, and mortification of the senses. Without purity of heart no man shall see God. A little lime entangles the feathers of a bird, and holds down the strongest pinion from being able to raise the body in the air. So the least earthly dust clogs the wings of the soul, the least inordinate attachment is a weight which hinders the perfect union of her affections with God, and the full flow of His graces upon her ; but a Christian worthily disposed and fitted by the Holy Ghost to receive the spirit of prayer purifies his love more and more, transforms his affections, and renders them ever more spiritual and heavenly. Of this, the Transfiguration of our Lord was, among other transcending prerogatives, a most noble and supereminent prototype.

Whilst Jesus prayed He allowed that glory which was always due to His sacred humility, and of which for our sake He deprived it, to diffuse a brightness over His whole body. His face was altered and shone as the sun, and His garments became white as snow. By this glorious transfiguration of His flesh He has confirmed our hope that even our bodies will share with our immortal souls in the bliss which He has promised us, and will inherit His glory. From the contemplation of this glorious mystery we ought to gain a true idea of future happiness ; if this once possesses our souls, it will make us indifferent to any difficulties or troubles we can meet with here and regard with great indifference all the goods and evils of this life, provided we can but attain our place in the kingdom of God's glory. Thabor is our encouragement by setting that beatitude before our eyes, but Calvary is the way that leads to it. When Christ admits us to the secrets of His love and the cross, and makes us taste that interior sweetness and secure peace which He has hidden therein and which the world knows not, then we find a comfort and joy in our sufferings themselves, and with St Paul we think of nothing but of loving and suffering in whatever manner it shall please God : treading in the footsteps of His divine Son and desiring only to walk in the continual exercise of pure love.

In the East the tendency to commemorate incidents of the gospel history by special feasts is more pronounced than in the Western Church, and it is probable that we must look to the Oriental rites for the earliest traces of such a celebration as the present. What is certain is that the Transfiguration was widely and very solemnly honoured in the Byzantine Church on August 6 before the year 1000. See the *Synaxarium Cp.*, edited by Père Delehaye, p. 897, and Nilles, *Kalendarium Manuale*, vol. i, pp. 235–238. The feast seems to have been adopted sporadically and on different days by certain local churches in the West, but it did not become of general observance until Pope Callistus III, to commemorate the victory gained over the Turks in 1456 by G. Hunyady and St John of Capistrano, required the Transfiguration to be everywhere honoured on this day. See Holweck, *Calendarium Liturgicum* (1925), pp. 258–259.

SS. SIXTUS II, Pope, FELICISSIMUS AND AGAPITUS, Deacons, and their Comps., Marts.

A.D. 258

Sixtus according to tradition was a native of Athens, but this is probably a mistake. He succeeded Pope St Stephen I in the year 257 and was the first pope to bear the same name as a predecessor. In continuation of a dispute begun under Stephen immediately after his election St Dionysius of Alexandria consulted him by three letters on certain difficulties, and recommended him to bear a little while with the Africans and some among the Asiatics with regard to their error concerning the validity of baptism given by heretics. Accordingly this Pope was indulgent towards them, contenting himself with strongly recommending the truth ; his successors pursued the same conduct till the error that heretical baptisms are invalid was condemned in the plenary council mentioned by St Augustine. St Sixtus is referred to by Pontius, the biographer of St Cyprian, as a " good and peaceable priest." The Emperor Valerian published his first decree against the Christians in April 257, which was followed by the martyrdom of Pope Stephen and many others. The persecution grew more fierce in the following year when, Valerian marching into the east against the Persians, sent a new rescript to the senate to be passed into law, the effect of which St Cyprian notified to his fellow-bishops in Africa : " Valerian has sent an order to the senate, importing that bishops, priests, and deacons should forthwith die " (even although they should be willing to conform), " but that senators, persons of quality, and Roman knights should lose their honours, have their estates forfeited and, if they still refuse to sacrifice, lose their heads : that matrons should have their goods seized, and be banished : that any of Cæsar's officers or domestics who have already confessed the Christian faith, or should now confess it, should forfeit their estates to the exchequer, and should be sent in chains to work in Cæsar's farms. To this order the Emperor joined a copy of the letters which he has despatched to the presidents of the several provinces concerning us : which letter I expect and hope will soon be brought hither. . . . You are to understand that Sixtus (Bishop of Rome) suffered in a cemetery upon the sixth day of August, and with him Quartus. The officers of Rome are very keen upon this persecution ; and the persons who are brought before them are sure to suffer, and to forfeit their estates to the exchequer. Pray notify these particulars to my colleagues, that so our brethren may everywhere be prepared for their great conflict : that we may all think rather of immortality than death, and derive more joy than fear or terror from this confession, in which we know that the soldiers of Christ are properly not killed but crowned."

St Sixtus suffered in a cemetery, for the Christians in times of persecution resorted to those subterranean caverns to celebrate the divine Mysteries. Here they met, though Valerian had forbidden them to hold assemblies, and here they were hunted out. Sixtus was seized while seated in his chair, addressing the assembly, and was either beheaded immediately or hurried off to a court for sentence and then brought back for execution. He was buried in the cemetery of St Callistus on the Appian Way, across the road from the cemetery of Prætextatus in which he was taken, and a hundred years later Pope St Damasus wrote an inscription for his tomb. St Sixtus was the most highly venerated among the popes martyred after St Peter, and he is named in the canon of the Mass.

The Quartus to whom St Cyprian refers is probably a slip of the copiers, and should be read "with four deacons"; for there were four deacons, SS. Januarius, Vincent, Magnus, and Stephen, who were seized with St Sixtus and suffered with him; two others, SS. Felicissimus and Agapitus, were martyred on the same day. The last two were buried in the cemetery of Prætextatus. The seventh deacon of the City, St Laurence, followed them three days later; of whom an apocryphal story tells that he, seeing the Pope led to execution, expostulated with him, lamenting to be left behind. St Sixtus replied that " he should follow him within three days, by a more glorious triumph ; himself being spared because of his old age."

The body of evidence which attests the fact that St Sixtus suffered on August 6 and was buried in the catacomb of Callistus is remarkably early and conclusive. In the recently published volume of the *Acta Sanctorum* (1932, November, vol. ii, part 2, pp. 420–421) this evidence has been most effectively summarised. The letter of St Cyprian, referred to above, must have been written within a month or two, and in Hartel's critical text of the letter (Cypriani, *Opera*, p. 840) there is no reference to any " Quartus," but simply a mention of " diacones quattuor," four deacons. A misunderstood phrase in one of Damasus's inscriptions apparently led Prudentius into the erroneous belief that Sixtus was crucified; but he was put to death by the sword. Further, the *Liber Pontificalis* is wrong in stating that the " four deacons " as well as Felicissimus and Agapitus were buried in St Prætextatus ; see Duchesne's notes (vol. i, pp. 155–156), and P. Franchi de' Cavalieri in *Studi e Testi*, vol. vi, pp. 147–178. On the other hand, the supposed " Passio S. Sixti," in all its recensions, is a historically worthless document.

SS. JUSTUS AND PASTOR, Marts.

A.D. 304

They were two brothers who, while still schoolboys, overcame with heroic courage the rage and power of Dacian, armed with all the instruments of cruelty. This judge was governor of Spain under Diocletian and Maximian, and one of the most furious ministers of their cruelty in persecuting the Christians. In his progress through his province in search of the servants of God, he arrived at Complutum, now called Alcalá de Henares, and having caused the edicts to be read in the market-place, began to put to the torture the Christians that were brought before him. Justus and Pastor, children who were then learning their elements in the public school of that city (the one being thirteen, the other only seven years old), hearing of the torments which were inflicted on the followers of Christ, were fired to have a share in their triumphs. They threw down their books, ran to the place where the governor was interrogating the confessors, and by their behaviour showed the holy faith which they professed. They were soon taken notice of and presented to the judge. He, instead of being touched, was furious to see children brave his power and authority and, not doubting that a little correction would dispel their courage, commanded them to be severely whipped. This was executed in the most barbarous manner; but He who makes the tongues of infants eloquent in His praise, gave them strength to defy their tormentors. The soldiers and spectators were filled with astonishment to see the constancy with which in their turn they encouraged each other to be brave for Christ and for an eternal crown; and the patience with which they suffered the torture. The judge, being informed that their resolution was not overcome, to cover his shame gave an order that they should be secretly beheaded. This sentence was executed in a field near the town, and their bodies were buried by the Christians on that very spot which their blood had sanctified. A chapel was afterwards built on the place. Their relics are enshrined under the high altar of the collegiate church at Alcalá, of which city and Madrid they are the patrons.

Whatever may be thought of the value of the reputed "Acts," printed by the Bollandists under August 6, there can be no question as to the genuiness and antiquity of the *cultus* of these saints. St Paulinus of Nola had his little son buried close beside them at Alcalá. Prudentius numbers them among the most glorious martyrs of Spain. Their names also are recorded in the "Hieronymianum," though the notice there occurs on August 25. See the *Acta Sanctorum*, August, vol. ii, and Delehaye, *Culte des Martyrs*, pp. 417–418.

ST HORMISDAS, Pope and Conf.

a.d. 523

Hormisdas was the son of Justus, a man of consideration, who lived at Frosinone in the Campagna. On the death of his wife (their son St Silverius became Pope in 536), Hormisdas received holy orders and was a deacon of St Symmachus during that pontiff's trouble with the antipope Laurence. He was notary of the synod that met in Rome, subsequent to the Palmary Synod of 502, to legislate regarding the administration of ecclesiastical property, and earned the high opinion of St Ennodius, who prophesied that he would become pope. Two days after the death of Symmachus in 514 the prediction was fulfilled; Hormisdas was elected without a voice dissenting, and he proceeded at once to clear up the remains of the Laurentian schism. This Pope is famous in ecclesiastical history as the author of the confession of faith which bears his name (the Formula of Hormisdas), and practically the whole of his pontificate was devoted to dealing with the delicate and complex situation brought about in the East by Monophysism. At the time of his accession the heresy had a firm hold and every one of the four Eastern patriarchs professed it: it was the period of the Acacian Schism. Almost immediately the Emperor Anastasius II, himself a Monophysite, was forced by a revolting general, Vitalian, as part of the price of his good behaviour, to propose to the Pope the convening of a council with the object of restoring unity to the Church, which could only be by universal acceptance of the Council of Chalcedon. Hormisdas sent a legation to Constantinople to discuss the matter, armed with a profession of faith for the dissident Eastern bishops. It was led by St Ennodius, now bishop of Pavia, but accomplished nothing; the Emperor shuffled and did not do anything but send two officials to Rome, who vainly tried to pervert the Senate from support of the Pope. Encouraged by the submission of a number of bishops of Scythia, Illyria and Greece, who accepted the condemnation of Acacius of Constantinople and subscribed the new formula, St Hormisdas sent another legation to the imperial court; Anastasius tried to bribe the legates, and when he found that he could not and that they were circulating a letter calling on the people to re-unite with the Holy See, he quietly deported them, with a message that "the Emperor was not at the beck and call of pontiffs and priests." He was proceeding to more open defiance when he died suddenly in 518 during a violent thunder-storm; the orthodox said he was struck by lightning. His successor, Justin I, was a good Catholic, and joined the people of Constantinople in calling on their new patriarch, John II, to accept Chalcedon and to anathematize Severus, the intruded patriarch of Antioch, who in addition was persecuting the orthodox. The Emperor, Patriarch, and the Emperor's nephew, Justinian, together asked the Pope to come to Constantinople and restore ecclesiastical order. St Hormisdas sent a third legation, with strict instructions as to what was required, particularly the repudiation of the names of Acacius, Zeno, and Anastasius from the liturgical prayers and the acceptance of his profession of faith. This famous document, which has been cited in the deliberations of the Church so lately as at the Vatican Council, is one of the most important pieces of evidence of the recognition of papal authority in the first six centuries; it was made œcumenical by the signatures of all the fathers of the eighth general council (Constantinople iv) and was confirmed at Lyons in 1274 and Florence in 1439. Its opening words are: " The first safeguard is to guard the rule of right faith and to deviate in no whit from what the Fathers have laid down; for the words of our Lord Jesus Christ, ' Thou art Peter, and upon this rock I will build My Church,' cannot be set aside. These words which were said have been proved by events, for the Catholic religion has always been preserved in all its purity in the Apostolic See." It affirms clearly that the perfection and wholeness of the Catholic religion lies in communion with that see, and that those are out of its communion who do not agree with it; it insists on the "tome" of Pope St Leo I and the definitions of Chalcedon, and condemns Nestorius, and Eutyches, Dioscoros, Acacius and other Monophysite leaders by name. A few bishops from Thessaly wanted to alter its wording; the papal legates replied, " You cannot. If you will sign, thank God. If not, we have come here and greeted you and we will go away again." In the cathedral of Constantinople at Easter 519 all the Eastern patriarchs and bishops (except Timothy III of Alexandria and his followers), together with the Emperor, signed this document and East and West were once again in communion. It was not the end of Monophysism but it was a most important moment in Christian history and the exterior event for which Pope St Hormisdas is remembered.

In the same year some Scythian monks caused fresh trouble by making use of the formula: " One of the Trinity suffered," and were accused of the Theopaschite heresy of Peter the Fuller. St Hormisdas in 521 refused to sanction it, as it is capable of an heretical as well as an orthodox interpretation; he suggested as an unambiguous substitute: " One of the three divine Persons suffered in the flesh." Nothing is known of the private life of this Pope, but it is clear from what has gone before that he was a man of peace, and he severely rebuked some African monks for their quarrelsomeness, they having accused a Provençal bishop of Semipelagian teaching; he refused to condemn the offending works *in toto*. He was particularly impressed and pleased by the foundation and rule of St Caesaria's nunnery at Arles, and joyfully confirmed it at the request of her brother St Caesarius, exempting it from episcopal jurisdiction and otherwise providing for its complete autonomy. A record is preserved of the gifts which he received on behalf of the Roman church, including precious fabrics and books of the Gospels ornamented with gold and jewels for the shrine of St Peter from the Emperor Justin, two silver candlesticks from King Theodoric, and a crown of gold set with gems from Clovis, King of the Franks. Pope St Hormisdas died on August 6th, 523, and was buried in St Peter's; his last days were made happy by the news of the cessation of Arian persecution in Africa, consequent on the death of the Vandal king, Thrasamund.

Save for the succinct account given in the *Liber Pontificalis*, there is nothing in the nature of a biography of Pope Hormisdas. A fairly full discussion of his public activities will be found in the *Acta Sanctorum*, August, vol. ii. See also Mgr. Duchesne's notes to the *Liber Pontificalis*, vol. i, pp. 272-274; and H. Grisar, *Geschichte Roms und der Päpste*, i, pp. 478-481, and *passim*.

AUGUST 7

ST CAJETAN or GAETANO, Conf.
Founder of the Clerks Regular
A.D. 1547

ST CAJETAN was son of Gaspar, Count of Thienna (Tiene), and Mary di Porto, of the nobility of Vicenza, where he was born in 1480. Two years later his father was killed, fighting for the Venetians against King Ferdinand of Naples, and his widow was appointed guardian of Cajetan and his two brothers. The admirable example and teaching she gave her sons bore quick and abundant fruit, and Cajetan in particular was soon known for his unusual goodness. His love of prayer taught a constant recollection, and the application of his mind to eternal truths made him shun all loss of time in amusements or idle conversation : for no talk was interesting to him, unless it tended to raise the mind to God. His affections were accordingly sweetened into a loving charity towards all men, particularly the poor and all that were in affliction. He went for four years to the University of Padua where the long exercises of devotion which he daily practised were no hindrance to his studies, but sanctified them and purified his understanding, enabling him the better to judge of truth. He distinguished himself in theology, and brilliantly took the degree of doctor in civil and canon law in 1504. He then returned to his native town, of which he was made a senator, and in pursuance of his resolve to serve God as a priest he received the tonsure from the Bishop of Vicenza. Out of his own patrimony he built and founded a chapel-of-ease at Rampazzo, for the instruction and benefit of many on his mother's estate there who lived at a considerable distance from the parish-church. In 1506 he went to Rome, not in quest of preferment or to live at court, but because of a strong inward conviction that he was needed for some great work there. Soon after his arrival Pope Julius II conferred on him the office of protonotary in his court, with a benefice attached. Happily the saint had the art to join interior recollection with public employments, and to live retired among distractions, for his office was no sinecure. He became, unconsciously, an expert consultor for the ecclesiastical authorities, who often confidently referred disputed questions to him, so wide and exact was his knowledge. Moreover, Venice having been attacked by the League of Cambrai on behalf of the Pope, he was active and successful in negotiating for reconciliation and peace. A contemporary, the Archbishop of Taranto, wrote: " It is impossible to tell the difficulties, contradictions and tiresome obstacles which Cajetan had to meet and overcome. . . . The arduousness of the business was beyond description. . . . The Venetian ambassadors found in him great prudence, strong and impressive authority, opportune and wise counsels. . . ." On the death of Julius II in 1513 he refused his successor's request to continue in his office, and devoted three years to preparing himself for the priesthood, for he was still only a cleric in minor orders; he was ordained in 1516, being thirty-three years old, and was in retreat for three months before celebrating his first Mass, at St Mary Major on Christmas day. He returned to Vicenza in 1518 to visit his dying mother.

Cajetan had joined, and perhaps founded, a confraternity in Rome, called " of the Divine Love," which was an association of zealous and devout clerics who devoted themselves by pious exercises and regulations to labour with all their power to promote God's honour and the welfare of souls. At Vicenza he now entered himself in the Oratory of St Jerome, which was instituted upon the plan of that of the Divine Love but consisted only of men in the lowest stations of life. This circumstance gave great offence to his friends, who thought it a reflection on the honour of his family. He persisted, however, and exerted his zeal with wonderful fruit. He sought out the most distressed persons among the sick and the poor over the whole town and served them with his own hands, and cared for those who suffered from the most loathsome diseases in the hospital of the incurables, the revenues of which he greatly increased. But his primary concern was for the spiritual life of the members of his Oratory; he gave them frequent conferences and encouraged them to frequent Communion, then not at all customary. He set them on fire with divine love and his fellow-citizens were proud to follow where he led. " In this Oratory," he said, " we try to serve God by worship; in our hospital we may say that we actually find Him." He founded a similar Oratory at Verona and then, in obedience to the advice of his confessor, John-Baptist of Crema, a Dominican friar of great prudence, learning, and piety, Cajetan went in 1520 to Venice, and taking up his lodgings in the new hospital of that city, pursued his former manner of life there. He was so great a benefactor to that house as to be regarded as its principal founder, though his chief care was to provide the sick with every spiritual help possible. It was the common saying at Rome, Vicenza, and Venice, that Cajetan was an angel at the altar and an apostle in the pulpit. He remained in Venice three years, and introduced exposition of the Blessed Sacrament in that city, as well as continuing the promotion of frequent Communion; "I shall never be content till I see Christians flocking like little children to the priest to feed on the Bread of Life, and with eagerness and delight, not with fear and false shame," he wrote.

The state of Christendom at this time was not less than shocking. The general corruption weakened the Church before the assaults of Protestantism and provided an apparent excuse for that revolt, and the decay of religion with its accompaniment of moral wickedness was not checked by the clergy, many of whom, high and low, secular and regular, were themselves sunk in iniquity and indifference. The Church was " sick in head and members." The obscure friar John-Baptist of Crema saw this and was distressed; then he had an inspiration from God: he told his holy penitent Cajetan to go back to Rome and once again to associate himself with the Oratory of Divine Love there, the principal members of which were no less eminent for their learning and prudence than for their goodness. This he obediently did in 1523 and he deliberated with them on some effectual means for the reformation of life among Christians, grieving that the sanctity of religion should be so little known and practised by the greatest part of those that professed it. All agreed that this could not possibly be done otherwise than by reviving in the clergy the spirit and zeal of those holy pastors who first planted the Faith, and to put them in mind what this spirit ought to be, and what it obliges them to, a plan was formed for instituting an order of regular clergy upon the model of the lives of the Apostles. The first associates of St Cajetan in this design were John Peter Caraffa, afterwards pope under the name of Paul IV but at that time bishop of Theate (Chieti); Paul Consiglieri, of the family of Ghislieri; and Boniface da Colle, a gentleman of Milan. Those among them who had ecclesiastical livings asked Pope Clement VII for leave to resign them with a view of making such an establishment. His Holiness made great difficulties with regard to the Bishop, but at length gave his consent. The plan of the new institute was drawn up, laid before the Pope, and examined in a consistory of cardinals in 1524. In order to break down and avoid avarice, always fatal to the ecclesiastical order where it gets footing, and to establish in the hearts of those engaged in that state a spirit of disinterestedness and entire disengagement from the world, the founders wished it to be observed, not as a precept but as a counsel, that this regular clergy should not only possess no property but also should be forbidden to beg, content to receive the voluntary contributions of the faithful and relying entirely upon Providence. The cardinals objected, not unnaturally thinking it inconsistent with prudence. But their opposition was overcome by Cajetan, who urged that Christ and His apostles having observed this manner of life, it could be followed by those who were their successors in the ministry of the altar and of the word. But a clause was added, that if a community should be reduced to extreme necessity they should give public notice of their distress by tolling a bell. The institute therefore was approved by Clement VII and Caraffa was chosen the first provost general. From his episcopal name of Theatensis these clerks regular came to be distinguished from others as Theatines. On September 14, feast of the Exaltation of the Holy Cross, the four original members laid aside their prelatical robes and made their profession in St Peter's in the presence of the papal delegate Mgr. Bonziano, Bishop of Caserta. The principal ends which they proposed to themselves were to preach sound doctrine to the people, assist the sick, oppose errors in faith, restore the devout and frequent use of the sacraments, and re-establish in the clergy disinterestedness, regularity of life, sacred studies (especially of the Bible), preaching and pastoral care, and the fitting conduct of divine worship.

They lived at first in a house in the Campo Marzio, which belonged to Boniface da Colle, but soon moved to another, on the Pincian, where their life and work attracted the attention of many visitors and several religious works were entrusted to them. But the success of the new congregation was not immediate, and in 1527, when it still numbered only a dozen members, a calamity happened which might well have put an end to it. The army of the Emperor Charles V, which was commanded by the Constable of France, marched from Milan to Rome, and took it by assault on May 6, 1527. The Pope and cardinals retired into the castle of Sant' Angelo, while the German and other Catholic and Lutheran mercenaries plundered the city and were guilty of greater cruelties and excesses than had been committed by the Huns and Goths a thousand years before. The house of the Theatines was rifled, and almost demolished, and a soldier who had known St Cajetan at Vicenza as a member of a rich family, gave information to his officer to that effect; whereupon he was barbarously abused to extort from him the wealth which he had not got. After all had suffered great hardships he and his companions left Rome, with nothing but their breviaries and their clothes, and escaped to Venice, where they were kindly received and settled in the convent of St Nicholas of Tolentino. Caraffa's term as general expired in 1530, and St Cajetan was chosen in his place. He accepted the office with reluctance, but did not let its cares abate the energy with which he worked to inspire the clergy with his own fervour and devotion, and his charity was made most conspicuous during a plague which was brought to Venice from the Levant, and followed by a dreadful famine. Moved by his example, St Jerome Æmilian founded another congregation of regular clerks, called Somaschi, from the place where they lived between Milan and Bergamo, the object of which was to bring up orphans and such children as were destitute of means of education, and Cajetan himself helped Jerome in his foundation. He was at this time also at work with Caraffa and others on the revision of the Divine Office, whose length and complication was a serious tax on busy priests.

At the end of the three years of office, Caraffa was made general a second time, and Cajetan was sent to Verona, where both the clergy and laity were tumultuously opposing the reformation of discipline which their bishop was endeavouring to introduce among them. He induced the people to see that the proposed reform was one of which they themselves would reap the advantage. Shortly after, he was called to Naples to establish the clerks regular there. The Count of Oppido gave him a large house for that purpose, and tried to prevail upon him to accept an estate in lands ; but this he refused. In vain the Count, backed by the religious of the city, pointed out that the Neapolitans were neither so rich nor so generous as the Venetians. "That may be true," replied Cajetan, "but God is the same in both cities." A general improvement at Naples both in the clergy and laity was the fruit of his example, preaching, and labours, and he was foremost in the successful opposition to the activities of three apostates, a layman, an Augustinian, and a Franciscan, who, respectively Socinian, Calvinist, and Lutheran, were corrupting the religion of the people. In 1536 Caraffa was created cardinal by Paul III, and in 1540 Cajetan went back to Venice, being made general a second time ; here he had again to cope with the Lutheran friar Ochino, whose errors were for a long time not recognized by the authorities. Then in 1543, at the request of its citizens, he returned to Naples, and governed the house of his order in that city until his death. During the last years of his life he established with Bd. John Marinoni the benevolent pawnshops (*montes pietatis*) sanctioned some time before by the Fifth Lateran Council. Worn out with trying to appease a civil strife which had broken out in Naples, and disappointed by the suspension of the Council of Trent from which he hoped so much for the Church's good, Cajetan had to take to his bed in the summer of 1547. When his physicians advised him not to lie on the hard boards but to use a mattress in his sickness, his answer was : " My Saviour died on a cross, allow me at least to die on wood." He lingered for a week, the end coming on Sunday, August 7. Many miracles wrought by his intercession were approved at Rome after a rigorous scrutiny, and he was beatified by Urban VIII in 1629 and canonized by Clement X in 1671.

St Cajetan was one of the most outstanding figures among the pre-Tridentine Catholic reformers, and his institution of clerks regular, priests bound by vow and living in community but engaged in active pastoral work, played a very great part in the Counter-Reformation. To-day, with the one tremendous exception of the Jesuits, all their congregations have been reduced to small bodies, but continuing their original life and work. Thomas Goldwell, Bishop of Saint Asaph and last survivor of the old hierarchy of England and Wales, was a Theatine, who entered their house of St Paul at Naples in the year of St Cajetan's death.

The example of this saint displays that disinterestedness which Christ has laid down in His gospel. He teaches us that all inordinate desire or care for the goods of this world is a grievous evil prejudicial to Christian virtue ; he impressed upon his followers in the strongest terms the duty of fighting against it, showing them how avarice steels the heart against charity and even common humanity, and excludes all true ideas of spiritual and heavenly things. Disinterestedness and contempt of the world, necessary in all Christians, is more essentially the virtue of the ministers of the altar : it formed the character of every holy priest. But it is not unknown for the idol of covetousness to find a place even in the sanctuary itself, to the scandal of the faithful and profanation of all that is sacred or good. New barriers have been often set up against this evil, but all become useless for those who do not try to ground their souls in the true spirit of the opposite virtue.

No biography of this Saint has been left us by anyone who actually knew him. The Life which is printed in the *Acta Sanctorum*, August, vol. ii, compiled by Antonio Caracciolo, a Theatine, was not written until some sixty years after the holy priest's death. Probably St Cajetan's close association with Caraffa, and the extreme unpopularity of the latter's pontificate—he became Pope, as Paul IV, eight years after the former went to Heaven—rendered the early history of the Theatines a delicate subject to handle. It is only in recent times that Pastor, G. M. Monti, O. Premoli, and other conscientious investigators have thrown light upon many matters formerly buried in obscurity. Though only a slight sketch, the booklet of O. Premoli, *S. Gaetano Thiene*, 1910, perhaps offers the most reliable picture of the Saint ; but for the earlier portion of his career, Pio Paschini, *S. Gaetano Thiene, Gian Pietro Carafa e le origini dei Chierici Regolari Teatini*

(1926), has provided a study of great value, largely based upon unpublished letters. The Life by R. de Maulde la Clavière, which having been translated into English is the most easily accessible, cannot be recommended without reserves. See the reviews of both the original and the revised edition in the *Analecta Bollandiana*, vol. xxii, p. 119, and vol. xxiv, p. 419.

ST CLAUDIA, Matron
First Century

In his second letter to St Timothy (2 Tim. iv 21), St Paul says, " Eubulus and Pudens and Linus and *Claudia* and all the brethren salute thee." She was evidently a lady of considerable importance: the *Apostolic Constitutions* (fourth century) state that Claudia was the mother of Linus, and St Irenæus says that the Linus mentioned by St Paul was he who succeeded St Peter in the supreme pontificate. The poet Martial mentions in his *Epigrams* a British lady, Claudia Rufina, who was the wife of his friend Aulus Pudens, and by some this man has been identified with the Pudens of St Paul. That St Claudia was a Briton is maintained independently by a tradition that she was a daughter of the British King Caractacus, who was defeated by the Roman general Aulus Plautius and sent with his family in chains to Rome in the year 51. They were released by the Emperor Claudius, but one of the daughters remained in Rome, was baptized, and took the name of Claudia, and is the lady whom St Paul mentions. Others think she was the daughter, not of Caractacus, but of Cogidubnus, a British ally of Claudius who adopted the Emperor's name. None of these theories have more than the weight of not-impossible suppositions; it is not even certain that St Claudia was the wife of St Pudens.

Bishop Lightfoot (*Apostolic Fathers*, i, part 1, pp. 76–79), who discusses these identifications in connection with St Clement and Pudens, finds nothing which can lend them any probability.

ST DOMETIUS THE ILLUSTRIOUS, Mart.
c. A.D. 362

Was a Persian convert who became a monk first at Nisibis and then at Rhesæna, where he was ordained deacon. He then went to live in a cave on the banks of the river Marsyas in Syria, and converted many of the pagans of the country round about. Having reproached Julian the Apostate for his impiety, he was by the

Emperor's orders walled up in his cave, with two of his followers, and there left to die of starvation. This is the Dometius referred to by the Roman Martyrology on this day as having been stoned to death at Nisibis, and is probably identical with the Domitius named on July 5, a martyr in Syria, "who by his power affords many benefits to the dwellers in those parts." St Dometius has a great reputation in the East as an ascete and wonder-worker, and is invoked as the "healer of paralysis."

The Greek Acts have been printed in the *Analecta Bollandiana*, vol. xix (1900), pp. 285–320. They agree with the Syriac recension edited by Bedjan (though the whole narrative of this last has been transformed in a variety of details), as to the manner of the martyrdom. Dometius, they assert, was not walled up, but was stoned to death in the cave in which he had taken refuge. We have evidence that the martyr was honoured both in Cyprus and in southern Italy, and we find him referred to in the Syriac martyrology of Rabban Sliba as "healer of paralysis" (*Analecta Bollandiana*, xxvii, p. 164). See also Delehaye, *Les Origines du Culte des Martyrs*, p. 223

ST VICTRICIUS, ABP. OF ROUEN, CONF.

c. A.D. 409

Among the many great bishops of the Western Church during the fourth century three stand out conspicuously in Gaul, namely, Hilary of Poitiers, Martin of Tours, and Victricius of Rouen. Of these the last-named is the least well known to fame because we have less information about his career, whereas the other two are pretty well documented. It has been attempted to prove that he was born in Britain, but it is more likely that his birthplace was somewhere not far from the Scheldt, that he was born about the year 330, and that his father or near ancestor was a soldier in one of the Roman legions called *Victrix*. Nothing is known of his early years, but at the age of seventeen he became a soldier and not long afterwards a Christian. At this time the lawfulness of the military profession for a Christian had not yet been decided in the Church; there were not wanting learned and good men, Tertullian among them, who denied that a Christian could bear arms without blame; and St Victricius, laying down his weapons one day on parade, asked for his discharge (*cf.*, the action of St Martin of Tours in similar circumstances). His period of service was not yet expired, so his tribune treated the request as a breach of discipline and ordered him to be flogged. Unable to move him, the tribune referred the matter to the *comes*, who sentenced Victricius to death for desertion. St Paulinus of Nola says in one of his letters that miraculous intervention prevented the sentence from being carried out : the executioner was smitten with blindness and his assistants were converted by the sight of Victricius's chains falling off him ; he and some Christian comrades were released and discharged.

Then follows a blank in the history of Victricius, and when next heard of he is bishop of Rouen, to which see he must have been elected about the year 380. Within his diocese there were still many pagans and the Christians included a number of Arians ; to the conversion of both groups the bishop applied himself with zeal, and he introduced monasticism into Rouen in the loose unorganized form that it had in Gaul at that time. He refers to his " flock of ascetes, thin with fasting " and to his " choir of maidens," whose " life is even more splendid than it is, in the world's eyes, hard." The number of Christians so increased that he had to build a larger cathedral, and obtained for it numerous relics of the saints, including some of John the Baptist, Thomas and Andrew the Apostles, Luke the Evangelist, and Gervase and Protase from Milan ; these relics were received by all the people in solemn procession and duly enshrined. In connection with these translations he preached or wrote his work *On the Praise of the Saints*, which partakes of the nature both of a panegyric and of a thesis on the *cultus* of the saints ; as a piece of literature it is particularly valuable for the study of the rhythmical *cursus*. Victricius established a number of rural parishes, which in those days were still rare, but progress against paganism was slow among the country people, and it was destined to linger on for another couple of hundred years. About the year 386 he went on a journey with St Hilary of Poitiers to Vienne, and it has been speculated that this visit had something to do with the loose surveillance which the Bishop of Rouen began to exercise over his neighbouring bishops, which causes him to be regarded as the first metropolitan of Rouen. It was somewhat in this capacity that St Victricius received from Pope St Innocent I in 404 or 405 a famous decretal on disciplinary matters, including the reference of *causae maiores* from the local bishops to the Holy See. He undertook missionary work far beyond the bounds of his own diocese and preached himself in Artois, western Flanders, Hainault, and Brabant ; but his work was largely undone and the religious centres he established destroyed by the barbarian invasions early in the fifth century. His reputation for wisdom and holiness had meanwhile crossed the Channel, and sometime between 394 and 410 he came over at the request of the British bishops to settle some differences that had arisen amongst them. Their nature is not known, but a passage in Gildas hints that Arianism was the trouble. Whatever it was, Victricius, in his own words, " did all he could, even if he did not do all that wanted doing. . . . I inspired the wise with love of peace, I taught it to the teachable, I explained it to the ignorant, I imposed it on the obstinate, insisting on it in season and out of season. . . ."

Towards the end of his life St Victricius came under suspicion of the Apollinarist heresy, and he went to Rome to clear himself, which he had no difficulty in doing. While there the Emperor Honorius arrived in the city, and Victricius was present when the Pope appealed to the Emperor for a reform of the law governing the admission of citizens from the higher ranks into the clergy; this was one of the matters referred to in St Innocent's letter, *Liber Regularum*, to Victricius. The exact date of the death of St Victricius is not known; his name does not appear in a letter of St Paulinus giving a list of the principal Gaulish bishops in 409.

Considering the important position claimed for St Victricius it is curious that we possess no early Life of him. We have to be content for the most part with such information as may be gleaned from the letters of St Paulinus of Nola. There is an excellent study of all that is known of Victricius by G. Vacandard published in the series " Les Saints " (1903). *Cf.* also Duchesne, *Fastes Épiscopaux*, vol. ii, p. 205.

ST ALBERT OF TRAPANI, Conf.

A.D. 1306

St Albert, also called " of Sicily," was born at Trapani in that island about the year 1240. It is said that his parents were Benedict Adalberti and Joan of Palizze and that, having been long without issue, they vowed that if they had a male child he should be dedicated to our Lady of Mount Carmel in her order. At any rate, the young Albert became a Carmelite, and after he had been ordained was sent to the priory of Messina, where he preached with much success, especially among the Jews. He added many voluntary austerities to those of his rule, among them the custom of repeating the whole Psalter on his knees before a crucifix every night before he went to bed. Unfortunately this and other particulars given by his biographer were written long after he was dead and are far from reliable. He tells us that when the King of Naples was besieging Messina and had blockaded it so effectually that the city was in imminent danger of starvation, Frederick III of Sicily contemplated burning it down to keep it out of the enemy's hands; certain of the citizens came to St Albert in great distress about this, and the sudden arrival of three food ships that had successfully run the blockade was attributed to his prayers. After having been prior at Trapani he was made provincial of the order in Sicily, and he was present at the general chapter held at Bruges in 1297; he made all his visitations on foot, and refused to take any other food but bread and water. His biographer records that St Albert made a pilgrimage to Palestine to the cradle of his order, where he became as famous for his miracles as he was at home; but in fact this journey was never undertaken, and the miracles must be regarded as probably equally apocryphal. During the last years of his life he lived as a hermit near Messina. When, three hundred years later, St Mary Magdalen of Pazzi was violently tempted to leave the Carmel at Florence and return to the world, she asked the prayers of St Albert in Heaven; the temptation left her, and she was confirmed in her good resolution by a vision of the saint. He was never formally canonized, but his feast was introduced among the Carmelites in 1411, and in 1453 Bd. John Soreth had permission from Pope Callistus III for churches and altars to be dedicated in his honour.

The Latin Life upon which all the others of more recent date are directly or indirectly founded, has been printed in the *Analecta Bollandiana*, vol. xvii (1898), pp. 317–366. It was only written at the beginning of the fifteenth century. See also Fr. Benedict Zimmerman, *Monumenta Historica Carmelitana*, pp. 259, 422, etc.

BB. AGATHANGELO AND CASSIAN, MARTS.

A.D. 1638

The foundation and first direction of the Capuchin missions in the Levant in the seventeenth century was the work of Father Joseph of Paris (Joseph Leclerc du Tremblay), known on account of his influence with Richelieu and Louis XIII as "the Grey Cardinal." Early in 1629 five Capuchins landed at Alexandretta, among them Father Agathangelo of Vendôme.

He had been born in that town in 1598, the son of Francis Noury and Margaret Bégon, people of good birth and position, and at the age of twenty-one entered the Capuchin friary of Le Mans, the novitiate house for Touraine and Brittany. After his profession he was sent to the Poitiers house and three years later to Rennes, to study theology. During this time he did not attract attention to himself in any way; he was just a satisfactory religious and, as his biographer says, common life under a rule faithfully followed is alone enough to make a saint. He was ordained priest in 1625 and was a preacher in his own country until he was asked if he were willing to go to Syria. He spent two hours in prayer and reflection before the Blessed Sacrament; then said, " Send me "; and set out at once. At Aleppo he ministered to the French and Italian traders and others while he was learning Arabic, and soon mastered that language sufficiently well to talk and preach; he cultivated the society of Moslems and the schismatical Christians, winning the goodwill of such notables as the *imam* of the principal mosque and the superior of the Dervishes, and even explained Christianity to the Turks in spite of the forbiddance by the Congregation of Propaganda of any public preaching among Mohammedans. The fruit of this work was to induce an atmosphere of tolerance and interest : Father Agathangelo was too good a missionary to look for any more tangible results before due time. Among the Christians he reconciled a dissident Orthodox bishop and a number of Armenians and Jacobites, but his work was cut short by an ill-timed act of the Custodian of the Holy Land, as a result of which Father Agathangelo was sent by his superiors to work for a time among the Catholic Maronites. He was welcomed by their Patriarch at Deir-Kanobin, and for over a year preached in the Lebanese villages with such success that it was said that " the fruits of his missions are greater than the mountains of Lebanon." Ten Christians, French or Maltese, having been captured by corsairs, were imprisoned at Aleppo and an exorbitant ransom demanded; the European merchants were unable or unwilling to raise the sum, and the prisoners were about to alleviate their hardships by apostasy to Islam. Whereupon Father Agathangelo and some other friars offered to take the place of the captives, but the slave-trader could see no profit in the exchange and refused it. So for twenty-one months Father Agathangelo and his companions took turns of a week in rotation to minister to both the spiritual and bodily needs of the ten unfortunates, till at last the Turk, despairing of getting what he asked and perhaps somewhat touched by the charity of the Christians, agreed to accept one-eighth of the original ransom.

In 1630 a Capuchin mission was established at Cairo which did not prosper, and at the end of 1633 Father Agathangelo was sent there to take charge. He was joined by three new missionaries from Marseilles, one of them being Father Cassian of Nantes, a Frenchman by birth but Portuguese by parentage. He was born in 1607, with a twin sister, of John Lopez-Netto and Guyomart d'Almeras, and at the age of sixteen became a Capuchin at Angers. After his profession and ordination he was stationed at the friary of Rennes, distinguishing himself by his heroism during the plague of 1631–32, until he offered himself for the Eastern missions. After his arrival in Cairo he soon became the right-hand man of Father Agathangelo and entered whole-heartedly into his efforts to bring about a reunion with the Holy See of the Coptic or native Egyptian Monophysite church. Their first success, however, was among the Syrian Jacobites of the Nile delta, whose bishop put himself at the disposal of the Capuchins in all their undertakings among the local Christians. Father Agathangelo got into personal touch with the Coptic bishops, and their Patriarch of Alexandria, Matthew, opened all the dissident churches to him; using powers granted by Rome, he said Mass, preached, and catechized therein and reconciled a number of individual Copts. But the support of the Patriarch was of only limited value; he was an old and cowed man, vacillating and weak, dependent on the alms of wealthy merchants and afraid of the Turks. Agathangelo and Cassian therefore determined to try and gain the influence of the monks, from among whom the Coptic bishops were chosen, and in company with the Syrian bishop made several visits to the monastery of St Macarius in the Nitrian desert. In 1636 Father Agathangelo took with him Father Benedict of Dijon and made the long journey to the monastery of St Antony in the Lower Thebaïd. They were well received by the fifteen monks and made a stay of four months, Father Agathangelo conducting doctrinal discussions and giving spiritual conferences; of the two books which he used for the last purpose one was the treatise *On the Holy Will of God*, written by the English Father Benedict of Canfield (William Fitch), the first Capuchin missionary in England in penal times. Two of the community were reconciled to the Church, and Father Agathangelo left them at the monastery in the hope that they would draw their brethren after them. This was his deliberate policy in Egypt, especially as there were no Catholic churches of the Coptic rite for reconciled dissidents to attend: priests were allowed to celebrate the Liturgy in, and lay-people to frequent, the schismatic churches whose schism they had repudiated; thus they were not left without ministration and they might in time leaven the whole. Then the Congregation of Propaganda declared the practice illicit. Father Agathangelo asked the opinion of the Custodian of the Holy Land. "I think," replied the Recollect, "that if those eminent Lords had known the conditions in this country they would never have come to such a decision, and that is the opinion of all my friars as well." All the missionaries of Palestine and Egypt agreed, and Father Agathangelo wrote a long letter to the Cardinal Prefect giving theological, canonical, and practical reasons for a withdrawal of the decree. The matter was referred to the Holy Office; there is no record of its reply, but it was probably favourable, for the successors of Father Agathangelo at Cairo followed his policy without hindrance.

Unhappily, and not for the only time in history, the great obstacle to Coptic reunion in a body was the Latin Catholics themselves. Some years before encouraging negotiations had taken place between the Coptic Patriarch and the consuls of France and Venice, and the French friars did not hesitate to make the renown and power of his Most Christian Majesty a *point d'appui* of their undertaking. Or rather, they wished to. But the parties to the previous conversations were all dead, and the then consul of France was a man of such shocking life that his house deserved the name given to it by Father Agathangelo, " a synagogue of Satan." Moreover, the general life of Europeans in Cairo was such that he had to write to his superiors that the public scandals made the Church " so great an object of abomination among the Copts, Greeks, and other Christians that it will be very difficult to overcome their aversion for the Latins." Even the appointment of a new and virtuous consul in 1637 did not mend matters. When the synod of the Coptic patriarch met in the same year to discuss the possibility of reunion, one of his councillors denounced the proposal because of the scandalous lives of the Catholics of Cairo, which Coptic priests could not tolerate as the Latin clergy did ; " the Roman Church is in this country a brothel," he exclaimed. Father Agathangelo was present, but could not deny the truth of what was said ; after gently urging that the sins of individuals, however terrible, could not alter the fact of the truth and holiness of the Church, he left the assembly and wrote a letter to the Cardinal Prefect of Propaganda. After pointing out that for three years he had asked in vain for authority publicly to excommunicate the worst offenders, he said he had done his best and could do no more ; " I have appealed, I have reproved, I have threatened. . . . Now my enthusiasm, whether reasonable or indiscreet, can no longer tolerate that those who have authority should not use it. They are dumb dogs, who are afraid to bite. Your Eminence will do whatever your good zeal for God's glory may suggest to you. . . . For the love of our crucified Lord and His holy Mother may your Lordships find a cure for these enormous scandals. As for myself, I shall not be held responsible for them before the judgement-seat of Christ who will judge us all. . . ." A few days later he left Egypt for Abyssinia with Father Cassian.

In the middle of the sixteenth century the Negus of Abyssinia, or Ethiopia as it was called then, had expressed a wish to the King of Portugal of submitting himself and his people to the Holy See, but when Susneyos died in 1632 his successor, Basilides, led a reaction against Catholicism. From early times the Church of Abyssinia has depended on that of Egypt, the Patriarch of Alexandria appointing a Coptic monk as its primate (*abuna*), and in 1634 Father Agathangelo used his influence with the patriarch Matthew to get named to this dignity the monk Ariminios: he was the abbot of Deir-Amba-Antonios, whom the Capuchin had met in Cairo and found well disposed towards the Holy See. He was duly consecrated bishop, taking the name of Mark, and despatched to Abyssinia, with a letter of recommendation to any Jesuits he might meet—and secretly accompanied by a German Lutheran physician, one Peter Heyling, who had already been a cause of trouble for the Capuchins. On the way this man stopped at a monastery and made a profession of Coptic Christianity, even to the extent of submitting to circumcision; he then rejoined the archbishop, Abuna Mark, and by playing on his personal ambition successfully poisoned his mind against the Catholic Church. He then set himself to gain the favour of the Negus and popularity among the people by conducting a school and by the free exercise of his medical skill, and at length with the help of Mark prevailed on him to promulgate a law decreeing death for any Catholic priest who should enter the country.

A Capuchin mission had been erected in Abyssinia in 1637, and at the time of the Coptic synod mentioned above Fathers Agathangelo and Cassian were awaiting orders to go and establish it, in complete ignorance of the results of Peter Heyling's activities. They eventually arrived at Girgeh on January 7, 1638, carrying letters from the Coptic Patriarch to the Negus and Abuna of Abyssinia, visiting with excommunication all who should in any way molest Catholics. For some years Father Cassian had been destined for Abyssinia, and with this in view had set himself while in Cairo to learn Amharic, the principal dialect in use among the Ethiopians; he now therefore took the leading place before Father Agathangelo, who knew little of the language. After a month's travelling across desert with a caravan the friars arrived at Suakim, where they were entertained by a Greek Catholic, Constantine, and eventually came to Dibarua, a place which has not been certainly identified. Hitherto the Coptic monastic habit which they wore and their facility in Arabic had sheltered them from interference, but now they were brought before the governor and questioned by the archiepiscopal vicar: "Who are you? Where do you come from? Why are you dressed like Egyptian monks?" "We have come from Amba Matthew, Patriarch of the Copts," replied Father Cassian, "and we have letters from him to the Negus, to the Archbishop, and to the people of Ethiopia." The vicar guessed they were Catholic priests and ordered their baggage to be searched, wherein Roman vestments and altar vessels were at once found. The governor ordered the friars to be put in prison, to await orders from the Negus. As manacles were fastened on them, Bd. Cassian exclaimed in Amharic, " These are the treasures and jewels which we are looking for and which we have left our homes and families to find ! " During the month which they were detained at Dibarua they were visited and their needs supplied by an Abyssinian Christian, Monica, sister of the governor, who served them with fearless devotion.* They were then taken to Gondar, a slow and painful journey which took three weeks, on foot and in chains. The day after their arrival they were brought, chained and in muddy and torn Franciscan habits, before Basilides and his court. In reply to his questions Bd. Cassian replied, " We are Catholics and religious, natives of France. We have come to invite you to reunion with the Roman Church. We are well known to Abuna Mark, who has had a letter from the Patriarch of Alexandria, and we should like to speak with him." But Peter Heyling, who was active all the time but took care not to show himself, had told Mark that Father Agathangelo intended to supplant him as archbishop, and so he refused to see the friars, saying, " I indeed knew this Agathangelo in Egypt and he is an evil and dangerous man. He tried to draw the people there to his religion and has come to do the same here. I do not wish to see him. I recommend you to hang them both." A Mohammedan remonstrated with the archbishop, but he repeated his words, with abuse. The Negus Basilides was inclined to banish the friars, but Peter Heyling with Mark and the King's mother worked on the mob to demand their death, and so they were sentenced after they had been given the opportunity to save themselves by abjuring the Catholic faith in favour of that of Dioscoros of Alexandria.

When the two martyrs were brought beneath the trees from which they were to be hung there was some delay. " Why are you so slow ? What are we waiting for ? " asked Bd. Cassian. " We have had to send for ropes," answered the executioner. " But have we not ropes round our clothes ? " And so they were hung with the cords of their Franciscan habits. But before they were dead the traitor Mark appeared before the crowd, crying out, " Stone these enemies of the faith of Alexandria, or I will excommunicate you ! " Volleys of stones were immediately flung at the swinging bodies, and thus Blessed Agathangelo and Blessed Cassian died, the one being

* She afterwards renounced her schism, and had a vision of the martyrs in glory on the day of their passion, as she related at the time to a Portuguese priest.

forty years old, the other thirty. For four nights miraculous lights were reported to be seen above the bodies, and Basilides in terror ordered them to be buried; but some Catholics took them away by stealth and their resting-place is to this day unknown. The cause of their beatification was begun in 1665, but was interrupted for two hundred years until in 1887 it was taken up again by Cardinal Massaïa, who worked for thirty-five years in Abyssinia; eventually, on January 1, 1905, Agathangelo of Vendôme, one of the most remarkable missionaries of the seventeenth century, and his faithful companion, Cassian of Nantes, were declared blessed by Pope Pius X.

The decree of beatification may be read in the *Analecta Ecclesiastica*, vol. xiii (1905), pp. 6 and 7. A sufficient account of these martyrs—the second of whom was presumably of Portuguese descent, since his name was Gonsalues Vaz Lopez Netto—is provided in Ladislas de Vannes, *Deux Martyrs Capucins* (1905); and Antonio da Pontedera, *Vita e Martinio dei BB. Agatangelo da Vendôme e Cassiano da Nantes* (1904).

AUGUST 8

SS. CYRIACUS, LARGUS, SMARAGDUS, AND THEIR COMPS., MARTS.

A.D. 304

ST CYRIACUS was a deacon at Rome, under Pope St Marcellus. In the persecution of Diocletian he was crowned with martyrdom in that city on March 16. With him suffered also Largus and Smaragdus, and twenty others. Their bodies were first buried near the place of their execution on the Salarian Way, by John the priest; but were soon after translated to a farm of the devout lady Lucina, on the Ostian road, on this eighth day of August, as is recorded in the ancient Liberian calendar and others. The *passio* of St Cyriacus is a worthless document apparently written as propaganda against the Manichæans.

To honour the martyrs and duly celebrate their festivals, we must learn their spirit and study to imitate them according to the circumstances of our state. We must, like them, resist evil unto blood, must subdue our passions, suffer afflictions with patience, and bear with others without murmuring or complaining. Some people practise voluntary austerities cheerfully because they are of their own choice. But true patience requires, in the first place, that we bear all afflictions and contradictions from whatever quarter they come; and in this consists true virtue. Though we pray for Heaven our prayers will not avail unless we make use of the means which God sends to bring us thither. The cross is the ladder by which we must ascend.

That Cyriacus was an authentic martyr, honoured on this day in Rome from an early date, is proved from the " Depositio Martyrum " of 354. Therein he is said to rest close beside the seventh milestone on the road to Ostia in company with Largus, " Ixmaracdus," and three others, who are named. Père Delehaye shows that this Cyriacus has been confused with another Cyriacus, the founder of the " Titulus Cyriaci," and that a fictitious story was later evolved which is best known to us as an episode in the (spurious) Acts of Pope St Marcellus. See on the whole question Delehaye in the *Acta Sanctorum*, November, vol. ii, part 2, p. 425 (with which *cf. ibidem* pp. 190 and 431–433); and also Duchesne in *Mélanges d'Archéologie et d'Histoire*, vol. xxxvi, pp. 49–56; with Delehaye in *Les Origines du Culte des Martyrs*, pp. 328–329. Thus the burial by John the priest on the Salarian Way and the subsequent translation to the farm of the devout lady Lucina, as mentioned by Butler, have no basis in historical fact.

ST HORMISDAS, Mart.
c. A.D. 420

The shocking persecution of Christians carried on by Sapor II, King of Persia, was renewed by Yazdagird I, the occasion being the burning down of a Mazdæan temple by a priest. This unhappy man, who brought so much distress on the Faithful, was constrained to admit that persuasion and not violence is the only Christian method, but this did not mollify the anger of the King. It is not easy, says Theodoret, to describe or express the cruelties which were then invented against the disciples of Christ. Some were flayed alive, others had the skin torn from off their backs only, others off their faces from the forehead to the chin. Some were stuck all over with reeds split in two, and looked like porcupines; then these reeds were forcibly pulled out, so as to bring off the skin with them. Some were bound hand and foot, and thrown into pits which were filled with hungry rats and other vermin, which gnawed and devoured them by degrees, without their being able to defend themselves. On the death of Yazdagird the persecution was carried on by his son Bahram; and Hormisdas (Hurmizd) was one of the chief victims. He was of the nobility among the Persians, son to the governor of a province, and of the race of the Achæmenides. Bahram sent for him, and commanded him to renounce Jesus Christ. Hormisdas answered him, "Nay! This would offend God, and be against charity and justice; whoever dares to violate the supreme law of the sovereign Lord of all would easily betray his king, who is only a mortal man. If that be a crime deserving death, what must it be to renounce the God and King of the universe?" The King at this answer caused him to be deprived of his rank, honours, and goods, and even stripped of his clothes to his loin-cloth, and ordered him in this state to drive and look after the camels of the army. A long time after the King, looking out of a window, saw Hormisdas all sunburnt and covered with dust, and calling to mind his former position and the high office of his father, he was filled with pity; so he sent for him, ordered a shirt to be given him, and said, "Now lay aside your obstinacy, and renounce the carpenter's Son." The saint pulled off the shirt and threw it away, saying, "Why should you have thought that I should so easily be tempted to abandon the law of God? Take back your present." The King, incensed at his boldness, sent him back to his camels. It is not known when and how St Hormisdas suffered martyrdom; he is not named in any of the old martyrologies and his *cultus* is unknown in the East.

See the *Acta Sanctorum*, August, vol. ii, where the passage of Theodoret, Bk. v, ch. 39, is quoted at length. See also Assemani, *Bibliotheca Orientalis*, vol. iii, part 2, p. 384. There seems to be a reference to this St Hormisdas in the Martyrology of Rabban Sliba on September 1; for which *cf.* the *Analecta Bollandiana*, vol. xxvii (1908), p. 193. The Syriac " breviarium " also mentions a Hormuzd among the Persian confessors; but Bahram V, son of Yezdegerd I, only came to power in 420, and the " breviarium " was apparently written or copied in 412.

THE FOURTEEN HOLY HELPERS

This name represents a group of saints, devotion to whom as a body was German in origin and largely German in diffusion. The idea behind the devotion is sufficiently indicated by its name, and the theoretical qualification for inclusion in the group was a real or alleged divine promise to the saint during life that he or she would have particular intercessory power to help men in need. The usual fourteen names are ACHATIUS (22nd June); BARBARA (4th December; invoked against lightning, fire, explosion, sudden and unprepared death); BLAISE (3rd February; invoked against all throat troubles); CATHERINE (25th November; invoked by philosophers, students, wheelers, and others); CHRISTOPHER (25th July; invoked by travellers in difficulties); CYRIACUS (8th August); DENIS (9th October; invoked against headache and rabies); ERASMUS (2nd June; against colic, cramp, *etc.*); EUSTACE (20th September; invoked by hunters); GEORGE (23rd April; protector of soldiers); GILES (1st September; invoked against epilepsy, insanity, and sterility); MARGARET (20th July; invoked against possession and by pregnant women); PANTALEON (27th July; invoked against phthisis); and VITUS (15th June; invoked against epilepsy and his " dance ").

It will be noticed that all these saints except one (Giles) were martyrs. Among the other saints included in the group locally were Dorothy (6th February), Leonard of Noblac (6th November), Magnus of Füssen and Magnus of Altino (6th October), Oswald (5th August), and Nicholas of Myra (" Santa Klaus "; 6th December). All the above will be found referred to herein under their dates. In France the Helpers are fifteen, the extra one being our Lady.

The earliest known reference to this devotion is in the title of an altar at Krems in Austria in 1284, and the various ravages of the " black death " did much to encourage it. But the height of its popularity came after the years 1445 and 1446, when a shepherd-boy of the Cistercian abbey of Langheim at Frankenthal in Bavaria claimed to have been commanded in visions to build a church in honour of the XIV Helpers. This was done and in 1448 it was solemnly consecrated under that title and became a place of pilgrimage. A confraternity devoted to the propagation of the devotion was established a few years later and approved by Pope Paul V in 1618. In the meantime the *cultus*, which had hitherto been unknown outside the Germanies, spread to Bohemia, Moravia, Galicia, Hungary, Italy, and France; it does not seem to have reached England. A feast with proper Mass and Office was permitted in various places, and churches, hospitals, and shrines named after them. The feast was celebrated on 8th August at Hildesheim and Hamburg; it is still observed at Alstadt and Frankenthal (4th Sunday after Easter) and at Gonsenheim and Hammelburg, the chief modern centre of the devotion, on the 3rd Sunday after Pentecost. There is a church dedicated in honour of the Holy Helpers at Baltimore.

The book of H. Weber, *Die Verehrung der hl. vierzehn Nothhelfer*, 1886, supplies abundant information. The Bollandists touch upon the subject in dealing with St George, *Acta Sanctorum*, April, vol. iii, pp. 149-150. See also A Franz, *Die Messe im deutschen Mittelalter* and Zöckler in the *Realencyklopädie für protestantische Theologie*, vol. xiv, pp. 217-218.

BD. ALTMANN, CONF. BISHOP OF PASSAU,

A.D. 1091

Was born at Paderborn during the first quarter of the eleventh century, and studied at Paris, where he formed friendships with St Adalberon and Bd. Gebhardt, both afterwards bishops. After being ordained he was appointed canon and master of the cathedral-school at Paderborn, then provost of the chapter of Aix-la-Chapelle and chaplain to the Emperor Henry III at Goslar, and confessor and councillor of the Dowager Empress Agnes. In 1064 he took part in a pilgrimage to the Holy Land, which numbered seven thousand persons (according to a monk who was there) and was led by several archbishops and bishops, and the adventure was a most unhappy one. Having safely traversed Europe and Asia Minor with no more than the misfortunes inevitable to so long a journey on horseback, they were attacked by Saracens in Palestine and sustained a siege of three days in an abandoned village; lack of food forced them to surrender, and they might all have been massacred but for the intervention of a friendly emir. Though they eventually reached Jerusalem they were not able to visit many of the other holy places because of the enmity of the Saracens, and by the time the pilgrimage reached home again it had lost nearly half of its members, dead from hardship, sickness, and murder. It was happenings of this sort which contributed, thirty years later, to the institution of the crusades. Immediately on his return Bd. Altmann was nominated to the see of Passau, and was consecrated by his friend Bd. Gebhardt, now Archbishop of Salzburg; and he set himself energetically to govern a large and deteriorated diocese. For the increase of learning, the care of the poor, and proper carrying out of divine worship he looked particularly to the regular clergy; at Göttweig he founded an abbey of Augustinian canons, put the same order at Sankt Pölten in the place of secular canons, and introduced the Cluniac reform at Kremsmünster. In these works he had the help of the Empresses Agnes and Bertha, and the Emperor Henry IV was a benefactor of the see; but Bd. Altmann soon found himself in conflict with that monarch. When in 1074 Pope St Gregory VII renewed the pontifical decrees against simony and married clergy, Bd. Altmann read out the letter in his cathedral. It was very ill received, he had to escape from the ensuing uproar, and found himself opposed in the matter of celibacy by a strong party led by his own provost. The bishop's chief supporters were the Augustinian canons, but the rebels invoked the help of the Emperor; Altmann did his best to enforce the decree, excommunicated the provost, and, when in the following year the Pope forbade lay investiture, definitely ranged himself against Henry. He was one of the only four South German bishops who refused to take part in the Diet of Worms which pretended to depose the Pope. He was driven from his see, Hermann of Carinthia was intruded in his place, and Altmann went to Rome. He had some scruples as to whether he held his own see simoniacally, as he had received it by favour of the Empress Agnes; but St Gregory VII confirmed him in it and appointed him delegate apostolic for Germany. On the death of Hermann, repentant for his intrusion, Bd. Altmann returned to his see in 1081, but was turned out again almost at once; he spent the remaining years of his life in exile but maintained a footing in the eastern part of his diocese, from whence he exercised a great influence. He had lost all his revenues and was in great poverty, but for all that his charity to the poor did not abate, and in a time of famine he sold his furniture to relieve the suffering. Nor did the disturbance of his rule and his long banishment entirely spoil his work; a canon of Göttweig who wrote an account of him not long after his death says that when he was appointed bishop many of his churches were of wood, and so were his priests; he had stone churches built and, though it was more difficult to reform the clergy than their buildings, he had inspired many priests with an enthusiasm for celibacy and a contempt for riches. Bd. Altmann died at Zeiselmauer in 1091, and his ancient *cultus* was confirmed by Pope Leo XIII.

There are two Lives printed in the *Acta Sanctorum*. The older of these (re-edited in Pertz, *Monumenta Germaniæ ; Scriptores*, vol. xii, pp. 226–243) was written some fifty years after Altmann's death by a monk of Göttweig. The second for the greater part adds no new facts, but fills some *lacunæ* in the narrative towards the end. An excellent German translation of the earlier document, with abundant notes, has recently been published by A. Fuchs, *Der heilige Altmann* (1929). See also Hans Hirsch " Die Vita Altmanni " in *Jahrbuch für Landeskunde von Nieder-oesterreich*, N.F., vols. xv and xvi, pp. 348–366.

BD. JOAN OF AZA, Matron
End of Twelfth Century

Of the descent of this lady we have no certain information, except that it was noble ; by some she is claimed to have been of the house of the Dukes of Brittany, by others of the Spanish family of Garciez, and so a kinswoman of St Louis IX and St Ferdinand III. She was born in the castle of Aza, near Aranda in Old Castile ; nothing is known of her childhood, but doubtless her marriage took place when she was very young, according to the custom of the time and country. Her husband was Don Felix de Guzman, who was royal warden of the small town of Calaruega in the province of Burgos, of which Dante writes in speaking of St Dominic : " Happy Calaroga ! there where the gentle breeze whispers and wanders among the young flowers that bloom over the garden of Europe, near that shore where the waves break and behind which the great sun sinks at evening." Here they lived and here were born to them four children, Antony, who became a canon of St James and sold all that he had that he might serve the poor and sick in a hospital ; Bd. Mannes, who followed his younger brother, St Dominic ; and an unknown daugher, whose two sons became preaching friars. The greatest of these children was a child of promise, for when Antony and Mannes were already grown up and clerics, Doña Joan wished for another son and prayed to that end in the abbey-church of Silos ; and a vision of St Dominic of Silos appeared to her in sleep, telling her that a son would be born to her and that he would be a shining light to the Church : and she in thankfulness determined that he should be baptized Dominic.

While the child was yet unborn Bd. Joan dreamed "that she bore a dog in her womb and that it broke away from her with a burning torch in its mouth wherewith it set the world aflame"; this dog became a symbol of the Dominican order and in later ages gave rise to the pun *Domini canes*, "the watch-dogs of the Lord." His godmother at his baptism (or, as some say, Bd. Joan again) likewise had a dream in which the babe appeared with a shining star upon his forehead, enlightening the whole world : wherefore is a star often shown upon images of the saint. Dominic remained under the care of his mother till he was seven years old, and then was sent to school with his uncle, the parish priest of Gumiel d'Izan. Other stories are told, but by later writers, about the saint's infancy : for example, that when the Abbot of Silos was saying a Mass of thanksgiving for Bd. Joan's safe delivery, as he turned to say "Dominus vobiscum," his eyes lighted on the child and he said instead, "Ecce reparator Ecclesiae"; nor could he correct the words, though he tried three times.

It has not been given to many mothers of saints to be themselves beatified, and Joan achieved this distinction by her own virtues and not by those of her children : it is not unusual for hagiographers to praise the parents of their heroes, but to the mother of St Dominic such praise is due in her own right ; to beauty of soul she added beauty of body, and both were handed on to the greatest of her sons. Her *cultus* dates from the moment of her death ; a hermitage at Uclés, where she would go to visit the commandery of the Knights of St James of the Sword, was called after her, and likewise a chapel in the cemetery at Calaruega ; her body was soon translated thence to her husband's grave in the church of Gumiel d'Izan and then, about 1350 by the Prince John Emmanuel who had a great devotion to her, to the Dominican church which he had endowed at Peñafiel. At the request of King Ferdinand VII this *cultus* was confirmed by Pope Leo XII in 1828.

It is to be feared that the little we are told concerning Blessed Joan does not rest upon a very sound basis of evidence. See, however, Ganay, *Les Bienheureuses Dominicaines*, pp. 13 seq. ; R. Castaño, *Monografia de Santa Joanna*, 1900 ; Procter, *Dominican Saints*, pp. 215-219.

BD. JOHN FELTON, Mart.

A.D. 1570

On the 25th February, 1569-70, Pope St Pius V published a bull, *Regnans in excelsis*, directed against Queen Elizabeth, who was at the time ostensibly a Catholic. By it she was declared excommunicate, deprived of the kingdom which she claimed, and all her subjects discharged from their allegiance, because she claimed headship of the Church in England, sheltered heretics, oppressed Catholics, and coerced her subjects into heresy and repudiation of the Holy See, contrary to her coronation oath. On the following 25th May, being the feast of Corpus Christi, the citizens of London woke up to find a copy of this bull of excommunication of their sovereign fastened to the door of the Bishop of London's house, adjoining St Paul's cathedral; it had been put there late on the previous night by Mr. John Felton, a gentleman of a Norfolk family who lived in Southwark, at a mansion built on the site of the Cluniac Abbey of Bermondsey. His daughter, Frances Salisbury, tells us that, " the danger of such an employment, which [my father] took for an act of virtue, daunted him no whit. Whereupon promising his best endeavours in that behalf, he had the bull delivered him at Calais, and after the receipt thereof came presently to London, where being assisted with one Lawrence Webb, doctor of the civil and canon laws," he displayed it as above. Dr. Webb at once made his way out of the country, but Mr. Felton would not stir, and it was not long before it was discovered who had done the deed. Searchers in the chambers of a well-known Catholic lawyer in Lincoln's Inn found a copy of the bull, arrested the lawyer, and racked him, whereupon he confessed that he had had it from Felton. He was at once seized at Bermondsey but, although he at once admitted what he had done, he was not brought to trial for three months; he was kept in prison, Newgate and the Tower, and was three times racked, in the hope that he would confess to some political intrigue with the Spaniards. But there had been none on his part: he had published the bull as a legitimate pontifical censure for the Queen's religious offences. When brought to trial at the Guildhall on 4th August, he pleaded guilty and openly declared the supremacy of the Holy See. Four days later he was dragged to St Paul's churchyard, reciting the penitential psalms on the way; the scaffold was set up opposite the door on which the bull had been posted, and at the sight of the barbarous paraphernalia of execution the martyr was seized with a violent spasm of fear. By an effort of will more violent he overcame it: he pointed at the bishop's door, saying, " The Supreme Pontiff's letters against the pretended Queen were by me exhibited there. Now I am ready to die for the Catholic faith "; to that queen, as a token of good-will, he sent a valuable ring off his finger; then he knelt and said the *Miserere*, commended his soul to God, and was cast off. The executioner would in pity have let him hang, but the sheriff ordered that he be cut down alive, and as his heart was torn out Mrs. Salisbury heard him utter the name of Jesus twice.

The wife of Bd. John Felton had been a personal friend of the Queen, who after her husband's death licensed her to have a priest as chaplain in her house : there are few enough acts of this sort to Elizabeth's credit to make this one worth recording, and the circumstance doubtless had its effect in determining the career of her son, Bd. Thomas Felton, then a babe of two, who eighteen years later followed his father to martyrdom. Bd. John was equivalently beatified in the decree of 1886. There is no need here to discuss the question of the bull *Regnans in excelsis* ; Bd. John suffered for publishing a canonical act of the Holy See against a supporter of heresy and a persecutor, who proceeded against him for supporting papal ecclesiastical jurisdiction. Whether that act was opportune or justifiable under the circumstances is beside the point. Popes, even when they are saints, as Pius V was, are not immune from errors of judgement, and it is now the general opinion of Catholics that *Regnans in excelsis* was a belated attempt to exercise a deposing power already in fact a dead letter. For the rest, we have the words of another Pope Pius, to the Academy of the Catholic Religion, in 1871 : " Though certain popes have sometimes exercised this deposing power in extreme cases, they did so in accordance with the public law of the time and by the agreement of Christian nations, whose reverence for the Pope as the supreme judge for Christ extended to his passing even civil judgement on princes and nations. But the present state of affairs is entirely different. . . . No one now thinks any more of the right of deposing princes which the Holy See formerly exercised ; and the Supreme Pontiff even less than anyone."

A full acount is given by Father Keogh in B. Camm, *Lives of the English Martyrs*, vol. ii (1905), pp. 1–13 ; *cf.* also the Introduction, pp. xviii–xx ; and see further J. H. Pollen in *The Month*, February 1902.

AUGUST 9

ST JOHN MARY BAPTIST VIANNEY, Conf.
A.D. 1859

AMONG the interesting, and at first sight surprising, phenomena of our time is the interest shown in and affection expressed for two newly canonized saints by many non-Catholics: not that non-Catholics are usually unconcerned about sanctity (far from it), but the "Protestant tradition" tends consciously or unconsciously to view with suspicion or indifference any example of holiness which too obviously is stamped with the hallmark of Rome. But the beauty of holiness will not be gainsaid, and from time to time some more than usually resplendent example forces the admiration of the whole world. Such were "the Little Flower" and "the holy Curé of Ars." And of these two the popularity of M. Vianney is the more remarkable, because the halo of sentimentality, with which undisciplined devotees or unscrupulous exploiters can so easily surround Sœur Thérèse, is far less easily fitted to *his* head. His face alone is a difficulty, for little can be done by way of getting superficial "appeal" out of a man whose exterior appearance is that of a sanctified Voltaire. And the life of a country *curé* in France is no less, even if no more, unfamiliar to the average Englishman or American than the inside of a Carmelite convent. The world into which Jean-Marie Vianney was born, at Dardilly, near Lyons, on May 8, 1786, was not an undisturbed one. When he was three the Revolution began and two years later Dardilly found itself saddled with a "constitutional priest," so the little John and his parents had to hear in secret the Mass of any fugitive loyal priest who came to the neighbourhood. While the Terror was going on, no less at Lyons than at Paris and elsewhere, he was learning to be a herd-boy, shepherding the cattle and sheep of Matthieu Vianney's farm in the meadows on either side of the little river Planches. He was a quiet, well-behaved and religious child, who urged his companions to be good and would always rather "play at church" than at games, though he had skill at quoits, which they played for *sous*. He made his first Communion, in secret, when he was thirteen, and very shortly after Mass could be said again in public at Dardilly. Five years later he broached to his father his project of becoming a priest. But the good man was unwilling; he could not afford to educate his son, having already had to provide for other members of the family, and could not spare him from the work of the farm, and it was not till he was twenty that Jean-Marie could get permission to leave home for the neighbouring village of Ecully, where the Abbé Balley had established a "presbytery-school."

His studies were a source of great trouble to him; he had little natural aptitude and his only schooling had been a brief period at the village school opened at Dardilly when he was nine. Latin above all he found such difficulty in mastering that for a time he and his teacher were discouraged. In the summer of 1806 he made a pilgrimage on foot, over sixty miles and begging his food and shelter on the way there, to the shrine of St John Francis Regis at La Louvesc, to implore God's assistance in this unforeseen obstacle. On his return he found his studies no easier, but the deadly spiritual disease of discouragement was gone, and in the following year he was further strengthened by the sacrament of Confirmation, received at the hands of Cardinal Fesch, Archbishop of Lyons. On this occasion he added the name of Baptiste to Jean-Marie. And this grace came at the right moment, for another and very serious trial was at hand. Through his name not having been entered on the roll of exempt ecclesiastical students, Jean-Marie Vianney was conscripted for the Army. In vain M. Balley tried to get the matter put right, in vain Matthieu Vianney tried to get a substitute for his son; he had to report at the depôt in Lyons on October 26, 1809. Two days later he was taken ill and sent to hospital, and his draft for the army in Spain left without him. On January 5, being barely convalescent, he was ordered to report at Roanne for another draft on the morrow, and, having gone into a church to pray, arrived only after it had gone. However, he was given his movement-order and set out to catch up the draft at Renaison, having still no military accoutrements but his knapsack (it carried the saint's halo rather than the marshal's baton). Jean-Marie made but poor progress and while he was resting at the approach to the mountains of Le Forez a stranger suddenly appeared, picked up the knapsack, and peremptorily ordered him to follow; he was too tired to do aught but obey, and presently found himself in a hut near the remote mountain-village of Les Noës. He now learned that the stranger was a deserter from the army, and that many more such were hiding in the woods and hills around. Jean-Marie did not know what to do; he saw at once that his situation was compromising, and after a few days reported himself to the mayor of the commune. M. Fayot was an humane official and a sensible man; he pointed out to Jean-Marie that he was already technically a deserter, and that of two evils the lesser was to remain in refuge where he was; and found him a lodging in the house of his own cousin. His hiding-place was in a stable under a hay-loft. For fourteen months Jean-Marie (known as Jerome Vincent) was at Les Noës, persevering with his Latin, teaching the children of his hosts and working on their farm, and earning their love and respect; several times he was nearly taken by gendarmes, once feeling the point of a sword between his ribs as it was thrust about in the hay of the loft. In March, 1810, the Emperor, on the occasion of his marriage with the Archduchess Marie-Louise, had proclaimed an amnesty for all defaulters, and early in the following year, on his brother volunteering to join up before his time as a substitute, Jean-Marie was able to return home, a free man.

In 1811 Jean-Marie received the tonsure and at the end of the following year was sent for a year's philosophy to the *petit séminaire* at Verrières. His career there was anything but distinguished, but he plodded on humbly and doggedly, and in the autumn of 1813 went to the *grand séminaire* of St Irenæus at Lyons. Here all the instruction and studies were in Latin and, although the authorities recognized his quality and made special provision and allowances for him, Jean-Marie made no headway at all. At the end of the first term he left the seminary to be coached privately by M. Balley at Ecully, and after three months presented himself at St Irenæus again for examination. In his *viva* he lost his head and broke down; the examiners could not accept him for ordination but recommended him to try another diocese. M. Balley went off at once to see the Abbé Bochard, one of the examiners, and he agreed to come with the rector of the seminary and interview Vianney privately. After this interview, which was satisfactory, they went to put the case of " the most unlearned but the most devout seminarian in Lyons " before the vicar general, who was governing the diocese in the archbishop's absence. M. Courbon asked one question : " Is M. Vianney good ? Has he devotion to our Lady ? Does he know how to say his rosary ? " " He is a model of goodness," was the reply. " Very well. Then let him be ordained. The grace of God will do the rest." On July 2, 1814, Jean-Marie Vianney received the minor orders and sub-diaconate from the Bishop of Grenoble, and returned to Ecully to continue his studies with M. Balley. In June 1815 he received the diaconate (five days after the battle of Waterloo), and on August 12 the priesthood. He said his first Mass the following day, and was appointed curate to M. Balley, to whose clear-sightedness and perseverance is due, under God, the fact that St John-Mary Vianney ever attained to the priesthood.

"The Church wants not only learned priests but, even more, holy ones," the Vicar General of Lyons had said at his ordination, and Mgr. Simon, Bishop of Grenoble, had seen in the Abbé Vianney a " good priest." The things that a priest must know he did know : but not necessarily from text-books. Moral theology, for example. When M. Bochard cross-examined him on difficult " cases," his replies were explicit and accurate : for the Abbé Vianney was a saint and he had common sense ; and moral casuistry is sanctified common sense. A few months after his appointment to Ecully he received his faculties to hear confessions ; his first penitent was his own rector, and very soon the " run " on his confessional was noticeable. Later on the hearing of confessions was to take up three-quarters of his time. Quietly, rector and curate began to have a holy competition in austerity, rather after the manner of monks in the Thebaïd ; the *curé* denounced his *vicaire* to the Vicar General for " exceeding all bounds," while M. Vianney retorted by accusing the rector of excessive mortifications. M. Courbon laughed, and said the people of Ecully were lucky to have two such priests to do penance for them. In 1817 to the infinite sorrow of his pupil M. Balley died, and early in the following year the Abbé Vianney was made parish-priest of Ars-en-Dombes, a remote and neglected place of 230 souls, " in every sense of the word ' a hole.' "

There has been a good deal of exaggeration of the debased spiritual state of Ars at the time when M. Vianney took it in hand (just as there has been of the " ignorance " of the good man himself). It seems to have been in just about the same state as most English villages in the second quarter of the twentieth century : little definite immorality and malicious wickedness, but even less true religion and love of God ; the greatest scandal at Ars was probably the " deadly scandal of ordinary life." For the rest, there were several exemplary Christian families, including that of the mayor, and the " lady of the manor," Mlle M. A. C. Garnier des Garets (" Mlle d'Ars "), was sincerely, if rather fussily, pious. The new *curé* (he was really at that time only a chaplain to a sort of chapel-of-ease) not only continued but redoubled his austerities, especially the use of a cruel " discipline," and for the first six years of his incumbency lived on practically nothing but potatoes, seeking to make of himself a sacrifice for the shortcomings of his " feeble flock." The evil spirits of impurity and drunkenness and dishonesty and indifference are " not cast out but by prayer and fasting," and if the people of Ars would not pray and fast for themselves, well, then their pastor must do so for them.

When he had personally visited every household under his care and provided a regular catechism-class for the children, he set to work in earnest to make a real conversion of Ars, by personal intercourse, in the confessional, and by laboriously and carefully prepared sermons which he delivered naturally, but not quietly.* The people were too sunk in religious indifference and material preoccupations to be amenable to quietness and moderation ; moreover, in those days Jansenism was still something more than a memory and had left its backwash in the methods and teaching of orthodox but rigorist directors and theologians. Consequently it is not surprising to find that the Curé of Ars was very strict indeed. There were too many taverns in the village, where money was wasted, drunkenness encouraged, evil talk not reprehended : first the two near the church were shut, for lack of enough business ; then two more ; seven new ones were opened in succession, but each one had to close down. He waged relentless war against blasphemy, profanity, and obscenity, and was not afraid to utter from the pulpit the words and expressions that offended God, so there should be no mistake as to what he was talking about. For eight years and more he struggled for a proper observance of Sunday : not merely to get everybody to Mass and Vespers, but to abolish work which at harvest and other times was done on Sunday without a shadow of necessity. Above all he set his face against dancing, maintaining that it was of necessity an occasion of sin to those who took part, and even to those who only looked on ; to those who took part in it, whether publicly or privately, he was merciless : they must give it up entirely and keep to their resolution, or absolution was refused them. M. le Curé waged this battle, and the associated engagement of modesty in clothes, for twenty-five years ; but he won in the end.†

In 1821 the district of Ars was, by the good offices of the Vicomte des Garets, made into a succursal parish, and in 1823 it was separated from the archdiocese of Lyons to become part of the revived diocese of Belley. This was an occasion for slanderous attacks on M. Vianney (whose reforming zeal naturally made enemies for him) and his new bishop, Mgr. Devie, sent the dean to enquire what it was all about ; but the bishop soon learned to have confidence in the Curé of Ars and later offered him an important parish elsewhere which he refused only after a good deal of hesitation. In the meanwhile

* " Did M. le Curé preach long sermons ? " asked Mgr. Convert of gaffer Drémieux. " Yes, long ones, and always on Hell. . . . There are some who say there is no Hell. Ah, well ! He believed in it."

† Over the arch of the chapel of St John the Baptist in the parish-church he had painted the words : " Sa tête fut le prix d'une danse ! "

the reputation of his holiness and achievements was also becoming known, and he was asked to give several parochial missions, when his confessional was always besieged. In 1824 there was opened at Ars by the enterprise of the Curé a free school for girls, run by Catherine Lassagne and Benoîte Lardet, two young women of the village whom he had sent away to a convent to be trained; neighbouring parishes took advantage of this, and soon they had sixteen free boarders on their hands as well. From this school sprang, some three years later, the famous institution of *La Providence*. M. Vianney enlarged the school-house, the pupils were confined to day-girls, and the room thus gained was made into a shelter for orphans and other homeless or deserted children, neither babies on the one hand nor adolescent girls on the other being turned away. Not a halfpenny was accepted from the inmates, even from girls who could pay, and neither Mlle Lassagne, Mlle Lardet, nor any other helper received any salary; it was a charity, run on alms, and its final end the saving of souls. At times there were sixty people thus being provided for, and the *curé* was hard put to it to support such a family. On one occasion the loft was found full of wheat under circumstances that clearly indicate a miracle, and on another occasion the cook testified to making ten 20 lb. loaves from a few pounds of flour, at the prayer of M. Vianney. Such works as these slowly and surely brought about a change of heart among his parishioners, and visitors noticed and commented on their orderly appearance and good behaviour; and it was the personal influence and example of the man himself that moved them in the first place: " Our *curé* is a saint and we must obey him." " We are no better than other people, but we live close to a saint." Some of them doubtless never got beyond that, to " It is the will of God, we must obey Him," but that is neither here nor there so long as they persevered in obeying the *curé* precisely because he was a good man.

And he, while his people were slowly and painfully coming back to a Christian life, was being the object of manifestations which would appear to be nothing less than a persecution by the Devil himself, as M. Vianney believed them to be. There is in history no other record of seemingly diabolical " infestation " so long, so varied, and so cogent; the phenomena ranged from noises and voices to personal violence and the unexplained burning of the saint's bed, and continued intermittently from 1824 for over thirty years, both by day and night, sometimes under conditions in which they were observed by others beside the sufferer. It is not an exaggeration to say he took it as all part of the day's work. " You must get very frightened," the Abbé Toccanier said to him. " One gets used to everything, my friend," was the reply, " The *grappin* and I are almost comrades." Not only was the Curé of Ars subjected to supernatural persecution but he also suffered from attacks which were it not for the fallen state of human nature would be labelled unnatural. Some of the less worthy and less discerning among his brother-priests, remembering only his lack of education and formal training, listening perhaps to idle gossip, certainly unable to recognize sanctity when they saw it, criticized his " ill-judged zeal," his " ambition," his " presumption " ; he was even a " quack " and an " impostor." " Poor little Curé of Ars ! " he commented, " What don't they make him do and say ! They are preaching on him now and no longer on the gospel." But they did not stop at verbal criticism and sacristy tittle-tattle : they delated him to the Bishop of Belley ! The *curé* refused to take any action, nor after enquiry did Mgr. Devie ; but having heard a priest apply the adjective " mad " to M. Vianney, he referred to it before his clergy assembled at their annual retreat and added, " Gentlemen, I wish that all my clergy had a small grain of the same madness." In 1832 the Bishop gave him faculties to absolve reserved sins throughout the diocese.

Another of the astonishing circumstances of the Abbé Vianney's incumbency of Ars was its becoming a place of pilgrimage even during his lifetime : and that not to the shrine of " his dear little St Philomena," which he had set up, but to himself. No doubt curiosity had its share in starting it, for miracles of loaves and visits of the Devil cannot be kept quiet, but it gathered strength and volume and continued because people wanted the spiritual direction of the village priest in his confessional. This steady stream of penitents, "the pilgrimage," was what chiefly upset his myopic clerical critics : some of them even forbade their people to go to him. People from afar began to consult him so early as 1827 ; from 1830 to 1845 the daily visitors averaged over three hundred ; at Lyons a special booking-office was opened for Ars, and 8-day return tickets issued—one could hardly hope to get a word with the *curé* in less. For him this meant not less than eleven or twelve hours every day in the confessional in winter, and anything up to sixteen in summer ; nor was he content with that : for the last fifteen years of his life he gave a catechism-instruction every day in the church at eleven o'clock. Simple discourses, unprepared—he had no chance to prepare them—which went to the hearts of the most learned and the most hardened. Rich and poor, learned and simple, good and bad, lay and cleric, bishops, priests, religious, all came to Ars, to kneel in the confessional and sit before the " catechism-stall." M. Vianney did not give long instructions and directions to his penitents ; a few words, a sentence even, but it had the authority of holiness and not infrequently was accompanied by supernatural knowledge of the penitent's life: how many times, for example, he was able to correct the number of years since a penitent had last been to confession, or remind him of a sin which he had forgotten. " 'Love your clergy very much,' was all he said to me," said the Archbishop of Auch; "Love the good God very much," to the superior general of a teaching institute; "What a pity! What a pity!" he would murmur at each accusation, and weep at the tale of sin: for this people came hundreds of miles and waited sometimes twelve hours on end, or had to attend in the church day after day, before they could be heard; by these simple means numberless conversions were made. At first the rigour with which the *curé* treated his own flock was extended to outsiders; but with advancing years came greater experience of the needs and capabilities of souls and deeper insight into moral theology, and pity, kindness, and tenderness modified his severity. He discouraged people from encumbering themselves with a multiplicity of little "devotions." The rosary, the *Angelus*, ejaculatory prayer, above all, the Church's liturgy, these he recommended. "Private prayer," he would say, "is like straw scattered here and there: if you set it on fire it makes a lot of little flames. But gather these straws into a bundle and light them, and you get a mighty fire, rising like a column into the sky: public prayer is like that." "There were no affected attitudes, no ' ohs ! ' and ' ahs ! ', no sighs and transports about M. Vianney; when most interiorly moved he simply smiled—or wept." Reference has been made to his power of reading souls, and his knowledge of the hidden past and of future events was no less remarkable than his more formal miracles. None of these things can be brought within the charge of "uselessness," a sneer so easily and so thoughtlessly made at the marvels attributed to some of the saints; but the Abbé Vianney's prophecies did not relate to public affairs but to the lives of individuals and were directed to their personal help and consolation. On one occasion he made the interesting admission that hidden things seemed to come to him by way of memory. He told the Abbé Toccanier that, " I once said to a certain woman, ' So it is you who have left your husband in hospital and who refuse to join him.' ' How do you know that ? ' she asked, ' I've not mentioned it to a soul.' I was more surprised than she was; I imagined that she had already told me the whole story." The Baronne de Lacomble, a widow, was troubled by the determination of her eighteen-year-old son to marry a girl of fifteen. She determined to consult the Curé of Ars, whom she had never met. When she went into the church it was crowded to the doors and she despaired of ever getting a word with him; suddenly he came out of his confessional, went straight up to her and whispered, "Let them marry. They will be very happy!" A servant-girl was warned by him that a great peril awaited her in Lyons; a few days later the memory of this warning enabled her to escape from the hands of a notorious murderer of girls, at whose trial she subsequently gave evidence. To Mgr. Ullathorne, Bishop of Birmingham, he in 1854 said with great conviction, "I believe that the Church in England will recover her former greatness." He stopped a strange girl in his church one day. "Is it you who have written to me, my child?" "Yes, M. l'abbé." "Very well. You must not worry. You will enter the convent all right. You will hear from the reverend mother in a few days." And it was so: nor had he communicated with the abbess concerned. Mlle Henry, a shopkeeper at Chalon-sur-Saône, came to ask M. Vianney to pray for the cure of her sick aunt. He told her to go back home at once, for "while you are here you are being imposed on!" She returned accordingly and found her assistant making free with the stock; and the aunt recovered. The numerous miracles of bodily healing reported of the Curé of Ars were mostly attributed by him to the intercession of St Philomena, and his first demand of those that sought them was fervour of faith: something of the faith by which he himself was enabled miraculously to provide money and goods when one or other of his charities was in straits. But the schoolmaster of Ars, echoing the well-known words about St Bernard, saw where was the greatest miracle of all: "The most difficult, extraordinary and amazing work that the Curé did was his own life." And every day after the noon *Angelus*, when he left the church to go to the presbytery to eat the food brought in from *La Providence*, there was a manifestation of recognition, love, and respect for his goodness. It sometimes took him over twenty minutes to cross that dozen yards. The sick in soul and body knelt to ask his blessing and his prayers: they seized his hands, they tore pieces from his cassock. It was one of his hardest mortifications: "What misguided devotion!" he exclaimed at it. It is not surprising that as time went on M. Vianney longed more and more for solitude and quiet. But there is more to it than that: every one of his forty-one years at Ars was spent there against his own will; all the time he had to fight his personal predilection for the life of a Carthusian or Cistercian. He left the village three times, "ran away" in fact, and in 1843, after a grave illness, it needed the diplomacy of the Bishop and of M. des Garets to get him to return.

In 1848, under rather delicate circumstances which have not

failed to arouse comment and speculation, the Sisters of St Joseph from Bourg took over the direction and administration of *La Providence*, which was to be carried on just as M. Vianney had planned it. However, only the school survived; the orphanage being reduced to only a few children when they took over, the sisters allowed it to lapse. In the following year more religious were introduced into the village, namely, teaching Brothers of the Holy Family from Belley, to whom the *curé* entrusted the boys' school which he had established and run under lay masters for many years. Their superior, Brother Athanasius, conducted the school until 1890, and was one of the chief witnesses to the last ten years of the *curé's* life. In 1852 Mgr. Chalandon, the new Bishop of Belley, made M. Vianney an honorary canon of the chapter; he was invested almost by force and never again put on his *mozzetta*, which indeed he sold for fifty francs which he required for some charitable purpose. Three years later well-meaning but insensitive officials obtained for him further recognition in the form of a civil decoration: he was made a knight of the Imperial Order of the Legion of Honour. But with this he positively refused to be invested, and no persuasion could induce him to have the imperial cross pinned to his cassock, even for a moment. " What if, when death comes, I were to appear with these toys and God were to say to me: ' Begone! You have had your reward?' " " I can't think why the Emperor has sent it to me," he added, " unless it is because I was once a deserter ! " In 1853, just when without his knowledge arrangements had been made to exchange his rather unsatisfactory curate for a more promising one, M. Vianney made his last attempt at flight from Ars. It is a moving story, of the old and worn-out priest cajoled back to his presbytery on behalf of the numerous poor sinners who were unable to do without him. " He imagined he was doing the will of God by going away," said Catherine Lassagne in innocent surprise. And it may well have been the will of God that His servant should now have some few years of repose and peace, to practise that contemplation which had already borne fruit in some of the highest experiences of ecstasy and vision. It is not impossible that the Bishop of Belley should be mistaken in not allowing him to resign his cure. But such a possibility was not one which M. Vianney would entertain; he devoted himself to his ministry more assiduously than ever. In the year 1858–59 over one thousand pilgrims visited Ars; the *curé* was now a very old man of seventy-three, and the strain was too much. On July 18 he knew the end was at hand, and on the 29th he lay down on his bed for the last time: " It is my poor end. You must send for M. le curé of Jassans," he said. Even now he sent for several souls to kneel by his death-bed and finish their confessions. As the news spread people flocked into Ars from all sides : twenty priests accompanied the Abbé Beau when he brought the last sacraments from the church ; " It is sad to receive holy Communion for the last time," murmured the dying priest. On August 3 the Bishop of Belley arrived in haste, and at two o'clock in the morning of the 4th, amid a storm of thunder and lightning, the earthly life of the Curé of Ars came to a gentle end.

The cause of St John-Mary-Baptist Vianney was introduced at Rome in 1874. He was beatified by Pope Pius in 1905 and canonized by Pius XI in 1925. The same Pope made him principal patron-saint of the parochial clergy throughout the world in 1929.

The most satisfactory source of information concerning this great saint is duly emphasized in that recent biography written by the Abbé François Trochu, which has been " couronné " by the Académie Française and is likely for a long time to hold the field. The Abbé Trochu's Life of the Curé d'Ars, as its title-page proclaims, has been founded upon a careful study of the evidence submitted in the process of beatification and canonisation. Moreover it clears up a number of points left obscure by such earlier biographers as the Abbé Monnin, and M. Joseph Vianney, and both in its Bibliographical Introduction and in the footnotes it provides full details concerning the sources which have been utilized. There is an English translation by Dom E. Graf. A still more recent volume in Italian of over 800 pages, *Ars e il suo curato S. Giovanni Maria Vianney*, by Angelo Maria Zecca (1929), is not so much a biography of the saint as an agreeable record of the impressions of a pilgrim visiting Ars. Among slighter sketches that of Henri Ghéon, translated by F. J. Sheed, *The Secret of the Curé d'Ars*, deserves special commendation.

ST ROMANUS, Mart.

A.D. 258

According to the *Liber Pontificalis* Romanus was a doorkeeper of the Roman Church who, with three other clerics, Severus a priest, Claudius a subdeacon, and Crescentius a reader, suffered martyrdom at the same time as St Laurence the Deacon. The legendary *acta* of St Laurence, adopted in the Roman Martyrology, make of him a soldier in Rome at the time of the martyrdom of Laurence. Seeing the joy and constancy with which that holy martyr suffered persecution, he was moved to embrace the Faith, and was instructed and baptised by him in prison. Confessing aloud what he had done, he was arraigned, condemned, and beheaded, the day before the execution of St Laurence. Thus he arrived at his crown before his guide and master. The body of St Romanus, the doorkeeper, was first buried on the road to Tivoli in the cemetery of Cyriaca, and his grave is mentioned as being there in the itineraries of the seventh century.

The example of the martyrs and other primitive saints by the grace of God had not less force in converting infidels than the most obvious miracles. St Justin observed to the heathen that many of them by living among Christians and seeing their virtue if they did not embrace the Faith at least were led to a change of manners, became meek and kind from being overbearing, violent, and passionate; and by seeing the patience, constancy, and contempt of the world of Christians had learned themselves some degree of those virtues. Thus are we also bound to glorify God by our lives, and Christ commands that our good works shine before men. Clement of Alexandria says that it was the usual saying of the apostle St Matthias that "The Christian sins if his neighbour sins." Such ought to be the care of every one to instruct and edify his neighbour by word and conduct. But woe to us on whose hearts no good examples or instructions, even of saints, make any impression! And there is a still more dreadful woe to those of us who by our lukewarmness and scandalous lives are a stumbling-block to others and draw the reproaches of infidels on our holy religion and its divine founder.

Mgr. Duchesne's note in his edition of the *Liber Pontificalis*, vol. i, p. 156, supplies all the information which is available. Romanus is mentioned in the itineraries of the seventh century, as De Rossi, *Roma Sotteraanea*, vol. i, pp. 168 and 179, has pointed out. His resting-place was on the Via Tiburtina. See also Quentin-Delehaye, *Acta Sanctorum*, Nov., vol. ii, part 2, p. 428.

SS. NATHY, Priest, and PHELIM, Bp.

Sixth Century

Though not associated with one another so far as is known, these two saints are celebrated throughout Ireland by a common feast on this day. St Phelim (Fedhlimidh) was the son of Dediva, a lady who was married four times, and had several saints among her children, including Dermot, Abbot of Inis Clothram, brother-german to Phelim. We have no particulars or even legends of St Phelim, but he is traditionally venerated as the first bishop of Kilmore; he was probably a regionary bishop in the Breffney country. Another PHELIM, named on the 18th or 28th of this month, was son of Crimhthainn and king of Munster in the ninth century; according to the exploits of his life he must have been included in the Martyrology of Donegal either in error or as a penitent.

St Nathy Cruimthir, that is "the Priest," was a native of the Luighne district in Sligo and is mentioned in the *acta* of St Attracta, who was probably his contemporary. He is said to have been put at Achonry by St Finian of Clonard, though the name by which he was known makes it unlikely that he was a bishop. At his monastic school he formed St Fechin, who founded the monastery of Fore in West Meath, and St Kenan, who became a monk of St Martin's at Tours.

No biography either in Latin or Irish seems to be available in either case. Nathy is commemorated under this day in the Felire of Oengus. See O'Hanlon, *Lives of Irish Saints*, vol. viii.

ST OSWALD, KING OF NORTHUMBRIA, MART.
A.D 642

After the death of Ida, founder of the kingdom of Northumbria, the northern part called Bernicia was preserved by his children, but Deira, that is, the southern part, was occupied by Ælla, and after his death was recovered by Ethelfrid, grandson of Ida, who ruled the whole kingdom till he was slain in battle by Redwald, King of the East Angles, in 617. His sons Eanfrid, Oswald, and Oswy took refuge among the Scots, where they were instructed in the Christian faith and received baptism at Iona. In the meantime St Edwin, the son of Ælla, reigned seventeen years over both kingdoms, but in 633 was killed fighting against the united forces of Penda the Mercian and Cadwalla, King of the Britons or Welsh, a Christian by profession but a stranger to his religion. Thereupon the three sons of Ethelfrid returned from Scotland and Eanfrid, the eldest, obtained Bernicia, while Osric, cousin-german to Edwin, was chosen king of Deira. Both these princes apostatized from the Faith which they had embraced, and were both slain the same year by Cadwalla: Osric in battle, and the other by treachery. Oswald, being the son of Ethelfrid and nephew of Edwin, whose sister Acca was his mother, now prepared to gain possession of both parts of Northumbria; he had received Christianity with his whole heart and, far from forsaking Christ as his unhappy brothers had done to court the favour of his subjects, he wished to bring them to the spiritual kingdom of divine grace and to labour with them to secure a crown of eternal glory. While Cadwalla ravaged the Northumbrian provinces, laying everything waste with fire and sword at the head of an army which he boasted nothing could resist, Oswald assembled what troops he was able, and marched confidently, though with a small force, against his enemy. In 635 battle was joined some seven miles north of Hexham. The evening before the engagement, the King caused a great wooden cross to be made, and he held it up himself with both his hands whilst the hole dug in the earth to plant it in was filled up round the foot. When it was fixed, St Oswald cried out to his army (in which only a handful of individuals were Christians), " Let us now kneel down, and together pray to the almighty and only true God that He will mercifully defend us from our fierce enemy ; for He knows that we fight in a just war in defence of our lives and country." All the soldiers did as he commanded, and that same night Oswald had a vision wherein St Columba of Iona appeared to stretch his cloak over his sleeping troops and to promise them victory on the morrow. And so it fell out. God blessed Oswald's faith and the superior forces of Cadwalla were routed and himself killed in the battle. It was a happy omen, says St Bede, that the place where this cross was set up was called in English *Hevenfelth*, that is, " Heaven's field " (though doubtless in fact it was given that name later), because there was erected the first heavenly trophy of faith : before that time no church or altar was known to have been raised in the kingdom of the Bernicians. This cross of St Oswald was afterwards very famous. In St Bede's time many cut little chips of it which were steeped in water, and drunk by sick persons, or sprinkled upon them, and many recovered their health. After the death of King Oswald, the monks of Hexham used to come to the place on the day before the anniversary of his death, there to sing the night-office and to celebrate Mass the next morning. A church was built on the spot some time before Bede wrote. He mentions that one of the monks of Hexham, named Bothelm, then living, having broken his arm by falling on ice, and having suffered a long time from the hurt, was perfectly cured in one night by applying a little moss which was taken off from the cross.

St Oswald, after giving thanks to God, immediately set himself to restore good order throughout his dominions, and to plant in them the faith of Christ. Naturally enough he looked not to Canterbury but to Scotland, where he had received the Faith himself, for help in this task, and asked for a bishop and assistants by whose preaching the people whom he governed might be grounded in the Christian religion and receive Baptism. St Aidan, a native of Ireland and a monk of Iona, was chosen for the arduous undertaking, and he by his mildness repaired the mischief done by another monk, sent before him, whose harshness had alienated many from the gospel which he professed to preach. "It is my opinion, brother," St Aidan had said to him, "that you were more severe to your simple hearers than you ought to have been and did not first, according to the apostolic rule, give them the milk of the more easy doctrine till, being thus by degrees nourished with the word of God, they should be capable of greater perfection and be able to put into practice His more sublime precepts." The King bestowed on Aidan the isle of Lindisfarne for his episcopal see, and was so edified with his learning and zeal that, before the bishop could sufficiently speak the English language, he would himself be his interpreter and explain his sermons and instructions to the people. "From that time many of the Scots [Irish] came daily into Britain and preached the word with great devotion to those provinces of the English over which King Oswald reigned. . . . Churches were built in a number of places; the people gladly gathered to hear the gospel; money and land were given by the King to build monasteries; and the English, high and low, were instructed by their Scottish teachers in the rules and observance of regular discipline, for most of them that came to preach were monks" (Bede).

Oswald, whilst he was governing his temporal kingdom, was intent to labour and pray also for an eternal crown. He often continued in prayer from Matins at midnight (for which he rose with the monks) till daylight; and by reason of his praying and giving thanks to our Lord at all times, it is said that whenever he was sitting he would have his hands on his knees turned upwards, toward Heaven. St Bede says that he reigned over Britons, Picts, Scots, and English. The kingdom of Northumberland then extended as far as the Firth of Forth, and Mercia also paid him a kind of submission; so great was his power that all the other kings of England recognized in him some sort of nominal overlordship (*bretwalda*), so that St Adamnan, in the "life" of St Columba, styles him "Emperor of all Britain." St Bede gives the following example of the humility and charity of this great king amidst his prosperity. One Easter Day, whilst he was sitting down to dinner, an officer whose business it was to take care of the poor came in and told him there was a multitude of poor people at his gate, asking alms. The King sent them a large silver dish full of meat from his own table, and ordered the dish to be broken into small pieces and distributed among them. Upon this, St Aidan, who happened to be at table, taking him by the right hand, said, "May this hand never perish." After St Oswald's death his right arm was cut off and remained incorrupt at least till the time of Simeon of Durham (d. *c.* 1135), when it was kept at the minster of Peterborough. St Oswald married Cyneburga, daughter of Cynegils, the first Christian king of Wessex; he stood sponsor for him at his baptism and lent his authority to St Birinus in his mission among the West Saxons. Oswald had one child, a son, Ethelwald, who became king of Deira and was little credit to his father; but he endowed the monastery which St Cedd founded at Lastingham, in Yorkshire.

When St Oswald had reigned six years war broke out with the pagan Penda of Mercia, who was overlord of the Christian East Angles whom Oswald wished to bring under his sway. Penda again allied himself with the Welsh and the struggle lasted for two years, until a decisive battle was fought at Maserfield, a place which has not been certainly identified. St Oswald met him with an inferior force, and was killed in the battle. When he saw himself surrounded with his enemies, he offered his last prayer for the souls of his soldiers, and it became a proverb : " O God, be merciful to their souls, as said Oswald when he fell." He was slain in the thirty-eighth year of his age, on August 5, 642. His relics were eventually distributed to various places and St Bede chronicles some of the many miracles of which they were the occasion ; nor is it to be wondered at that the sick should be healed by him when dead, for while he lived he never ceased to provide for the poor and infirm, and to bestow alms on them and aid them. St Oswald was formerly remembered as one of the great national heroes of England, and his veneration extended to Scotland, Ireland, southern Germany, and Switzerland, where he is patron of Zug. His memory is now somewhat dim, but his feast is observed in several English dioceses on 9th August; he is named in the Roman Martyrology on the 5th.

We know little of St Oswald beyond what has been recorded in Bede's *Ecclesiastical History*, Bk. iii, but C. Plummer gives (vol. ii, p. 161) a list of subsequent Lives of the holy king. That by Drogo (11th cent.) is printed in the *Acta Sanctorum*, August, vol. ii ; that by Reginald of Durham may be found in Arnold's edition of Simeon of Durham (Rolls Series). It is remarkable, as Plummer again points out in detail (pp. 159–160), how widespread was the *cultus* of St Oswald in Central Europe. Plummer's notes upon Bede's text are also valuable, as well as those in the edition of Mayor and Lumby (1881).

BD. JOHN OF SALERNO, CONF.

A.D 1242

John Guarna was born at Salerno about the year 1190, of a family allied to the Norman royal house of Naples and the Sicilies. While studying at Bologna he met St Dominic ; they were mutually attracted one to the other, and John received the habit of the new order. In 1219 thirteen friars were sent to preach in Etruria and of these, though he was easily the youngest, John of Salerno was made superior. A house was given them at Ripoli, near Florence, from whence they went out to the whole neighbourhood, but particularly to Florence itself, where John every day preached in the streets and sought the sheep that were lost. This arrangement was soon found to be too inconvenient and wasteful of time, and the community moved to San Pancrazio, adjoining the walls of the city. Here Bd. John had a trying experience with a young woman of undisciplined desires who had given herself up to a passion for him. She pretended she was ill, went to bed, and sent for Brother John to hear her confession; the friar went at once, only to discover his "penitent" taking brazen advantage of their being alone. He rebuked the girl severely and tried to bring her to reason but she took no notice, so he could only go away and leave her. But he did not forget her, and his prayers eventually brought the girl to repentance towards God and humble apology to himself. This incident is said to have been made public in the following way. A possessed woman was being exorcized by a priest when the evil spirit, speaking by her mouth, exclaimed, " Only he who was unburned in the midst of the fire can drive me out !" He was adjured to explain who and what he meant, and he named the prior of the Dominicans and told the story; Bd. John was sent for and the woman was freed. He had the gift of reading minds and consciences, and would sometimes abash or enlighten a penitent or one of his subjects by his knowledge of them.

In August 1221 he was summoned to the death-bed of St Dominic at Bologna, and on his return found his community turned out of the church in which they had been wont to meet to say the Divine Office; he soon established them at Santa Maria Novella, whose famous present church was begun fifty years later, and the old convent at Ripoli he peopled with nuns. Florence was greatly troubled at this time by the Patarines, a Manichæan sect which had penetrated into Italy from Bosnia through Dalmatia; some years before they had murdered the governor of Orvieto, St Peter Parenti, who had been sent to deal with them. In consideration of the tactful ability with which he had undertaken the reform of the monks of St Anthimus at Chiusi, Pope Gregory IX commissioned Bd. John to deal with these heretics in Florence, whose tenets and life were similar to those of the Albigensians who had first exercised St Dominic. They were indignant at his campaign but he refused to be intimidated by their threats or ruffled by their insults, and succeeded in bringing large numbers back to the Church and to a Christian life. While he lay dying Bd. John exhorted his brethren to unswerving fidelity to God and their rule, and reminded them that a religious is bound to aim at repentance in all his actions and that no one of them requires so much care, devotion and purity as the reception of holy communion. His *cultus* was approved by Pope Pius VI in 1783.

A Life of this Beato, by John Caroli, O.P., of Florence, has been printed in the *Acta Sanctorum*, September, vol. iii, but with *lacunæ*, which, in the *Analecta Bollandiana*, vol. vii (1888), pp. 85–94, have been made good from a recovered copy of the text. Père Mortier speaks of Blessed John in his *Histoire des Maîtres Généraux O.P.*, vol. i, pp. 106 *seq.* See also Procter, *Lives of Dominican Saints*, pp. 226–228. A fuller bibliography is supplied in Taurisano, p. 11.

BD. JOHN OF ALVERNIA, Conf.

A.D. 1322

Is sometimes called " of Fermo " in the Marches, where he was born in 1259, but usually " of Alvernia " because he lived for many years and died on the mountain of La Verna. When seven years old he was already notable for his piety, spending much time in thinking about our Lord's passion and practising child-like mortifications; he was only ten when he was received among the canons regular at St Peter's in his native town, presumably to be educated. In 1272 desire for a life of greater perfection caused him to join the Friars Minor, with whom he made his novitiate under the direction of Brother James of Fallerone, and after his profession he was sent by the minister general, St Bonaventure, or his successor, to La Verna, where St Francis had received the *stigmata*. Here he lived in a cell formed in a cave in the mountain-side, sleeping only a few hours when absolutely necessary, and then on the bare ground with a stone for pillow. In this solitude of penance and contemplation he spent some years, and frequent ecstasies and visions of our Lord and of the saints are recorded of him; one All Souls' day while saying Mass he saw numberless souls released from Purgatory and ascending to Heaven, and for a space of three months he was conscious of the habitual presence of his guardian angel, who conversed with him. After a time his austerities became excessive and St Francis himself in vision ordered him to moderate them lest he unfit himself for the active service of his neighbour to which he was soon to be called. This took the form of preaching and pastoral work, first in the towns and villages around La Verna and then throughout central and northern Italy. He had the gifts of infused knowledge and of reading souls, and his exhortations brought back many who were sinners to Christ and excited the admiration of good and learned men. He never wrote out his sermons, and when it was pointed out to him that this had its disadvantages he replied, " When I go into the pulpit I just remind myself that it is not I, a poor sinner, who is to preach, but God Himself who will teach divine truth through my mouth. Do you suppose, dear brethren, that God can ever fail in His words ? " Bd. John was a close friend of the poet Bd. Giacopone da Todi and gave him the last sacraments as he lay dying on Christmas day, 1306 ; and John himself is alleged to be the author of the proper preface sung by the Friars Minor in the Mass of St Francis. He was at the friary of Cortona, on his way to Assisi, when he felt death approaching ; he therefore hurried to La Verna, and there died on August 10, 1322. To the brothers who were present he said, as his last message, " If you would have a good conscience, wish to know Jesus Christ only, for He is the way. If you would have wisdom, wish to know Jesus Christ only, for He is the truth. If you wish to have glory, wish to know Jesus Christ only, for He is the life."

The *cultus* of Bd. John of Alvernia was approved by Pope Leo XIII in 1880. The Capuchin friars minor keep his feast on August 13, and join with it that of BD. VINCENT OF AQUILA, a Franciscan lay-brother who died at San Giuliano in 1504 ; " a man of great humility, of prayer, temperance, and patience, adorned with the spirit of prophecy."

There is more than one sketch of the life of Blessed John de Fermo printed in the *Acta Sanctorum,* August, vol. ii, and there is another early account which has been edited in the *Analecta Franciscana,* vol. iii (1879), pp. 439–447. See also Léon, *Auréole Séraphique* (Eng. Trans.), vol. ii, pp. 553 *seq.*, and more especially L. Oliger, *Il beato Giovanni della Verna,* 1913.

BD. JOHN OF RIETI, CONF.

c. A.D. 1350

Was born about the beginning of the fourteenth century at Castel Porziano in Umbria, a member of the Bufalari family and brother to St Lucy of Amelia. Little is known of his life, except that it was uneventful, but none the less significant in that he grew daily in grace and virtue. He early determined to leave the world and joined the order of Hermits of St Augustine (Austin friars) at Rieti, whose rule he observed with great exactness. He was ever at the service of his neighbour, especially the sick and strangers, and delighted to wait on guests who came to the monastery; he spent long hours in contemplation and especially valued the opportunities provided by serving Mass in the friary church for loving converse with God. He had the gift of tears, not only for his own faults but for those of others; when walking in the garden he would say, " How can one not weep ? For we see all around us trees and grass and flowers and plants germinating, growing, producing their fruit, and dying back again into the earth in accordance with the laws of their Creator : while men, to whom God has given a reasoning intelligence and the promise of a transcendent reward, continually oppose His will." A simple reflection whose force, if rightly understood, is not lessened by the consideration that the vegetable creation could not do otherwise if it would. The exact date of the death of Bd. John is not known, but his holy life and the miracles taking place at his tomb were the cause of a *cultus* which persisted and was formally confirmed by Pope Gregory XVI in 1832.

See Torelli, *Secoli Agotiniani*, vol. ii, and P. Seeböck, *Die Herrlichkeit der Katholischen Kirche* (1900), pp. 299–300.

AUGUST 10

ST LAURENCE, Mart.

A.D. 258

THERE are few martyrs in the Church whose names are so famous as that of St Laurence, in whose praises the most illustrious among the Latin Fathers have written, and whose triumph, to use the words of St Maximus, the whole Church joins in a body to honour with universal joy and devotion. The ancient Fathers make no mention of his birth or education (the Spaniards call him their countryman), nor are any particulars known of him except that he was one among the seven deacons who served the Roman Church; this was a charge of great trust, to which was annexed the care of the goods of the Church, and the distribution of its alms among the poor. The Emperor Valerian in 257 published his edicts against the Church, and that by cutting off the shepherds he might disperse the flocks, he commanded all bishops, priests, and deacons to be put to death without delay. The holy Pope St Sixtus, the second of that name, was apprehended the year following and put to death, and on the fourth day after the faithful Laurence followed him to martyrdom. That is all that is known for certain of the life and death of St Laurence, but Christian piety has adopted and consecrated as its own the details supplied by St Ambrose, the poet Prudentius, and others, which they probably had on oral tradition and the historical value of which is slight.

According to these, as Pope St Sixtus was led to execution, his deacon Laurence followed him weeping; and, sorrowing because he was not to die with him, said to him, "Father, where are you going without your son? Should the priest go to sacrifice without the deacon?" The Pope answered, "I do not leave you, my son. You shall follow me in three days." Laurence was full of joy, hearing that he should be so soon called to God; he set out immediately to seek all the poor, widows, and orphans, and gave among them all the money which he had in his hands; he even sold the sacred vessels to increase the sum, employing it all in the like manner. The church at Rome had then, besides the necessary provision of its ministers, to maintain many widows and orphans, and fifteen hundred poor people, of whose names the bishop or his chief deacon kept the list; and it often sent large alms into distant countries. When then the prefect of Rome was informed of these charities, imagining that the Christians had hid considerable treasures, he wanted to secure them: for he was no less a worshipper of gold and silver than of Jupiter and Mars. With this view he sent for St Laurence, and said to him, " You Christians often complain that we treat you with cruelty, but no tortures are here thought of; I only inquire mildly after what concerns you. I am informed that your priests offer in gold, that the sacred blood is received in silver cups, and that in your nocturnal sacrifices you have wax tapers fixed in golden candlesticks. Bring out these hidden treasures; the Emperor has need of them for the maintenance of his forces. I am told that according to your doctrine you must render to Cæsar the things that belong to him. I do not think that your God causes money to be coined; He brought none into the world with Him; He only brought words. Give us therefore the money, and be rich in words." St Laurence replied, without showing any concern, " The Church is indeed rich; nor hath the Emperor any treasure equal to what it possesses. I will show you a valuable part; but allow me a little time to set everything in order, and to make an inventory." The prefect did not understand of what treasure Laurence spoke, but, imagining the hidden wealth already in his hands, was satisfied with this answer and granted him three days. During this interval Laurence went all over the city, seeking out the poor who were supported by the Church. On the third day he gathered together a great number of them, and placed them in rows, the decrepit, the blind, the lame, the maimed, the lepers, orphans, widows, and maidens; then he went to the prefect and invited him to come and see the treasure of the Church. The prefect, astonished to see such an assembly of misery and misfortune, turned to the deacon with threatening looks, asked him what all this meant, and where the treasures were which he had promised to show him. St Laurence answered, " What are you displeased at? These *are* the treasure of the Church." The prefect's anger was not allayed but redoubled, and in a fury of rage he shouted, " You mock me! The axes and the fasces, the ensigns of the Roman power, are not to be insulted! I know that you desire to die: that is your madness and vanity: but you shall not die immediately, as you imagine. You shall die by inches!" Then he had a great gridiron made ready, and glowing coals put under it, that the martyr might be slowly burnt. Laurence was stripped and bound upon this iron bed over the slow fire, which roasted his flesh by little and little. His face appeared to the Christians to be surrounded with a beautiful light, and his suffering body to give off a sweet smell; but the unbelievers neither saw this light nor perceived this smell. The martyr felt not the torments of the persecutor, says St Augustine, so passionate was his desire of possessing Christ: and St Ambrose observes that whilst his body burned in the material flames, the fire of divine love was far more active within his breast and made him regardless of the pain: having the law of God before his eyes, his agony was as a refreshment and a comfort. Having suffered a long time, he turned to the judge and said to him, with a cheerful smile, " Let my body be turned; one side is broiled enough." When the executioner had turned him, he said, " It is cooked enough, you may eat." Then, having prayed for the conversion of the city of Rome that the faith of Christ might spread thence throughout the world, St Laurence gave up the ghost.

Prudentius ascribes to his prayer the entire conversion of Rome, and says God began to grant his request at the very time he made it; for several senators who were present at his death were so moved by his heroic fortitude and piety that they became Christians upon the spot. These noblemen took up the martyr's body on their shoulders and gave it an honourable burial on the Via Tiburtina. His death, says Prudentius, was the death of idolatry in Rome, which from that time began to decline; and now (c. 403) the senate itself venerates the tombs of the apostles and martyrs. He describes with what devotion and fervour the Romans frequented the church of St Laurence and commended themselves to his patronage; and the happy issue of their prayers proves how great his power is with God. St Augustine assures us that God wrought in Rome many miracles through the intercession of St Laurence, and St Gregory of Tours, Fortunatus, and others, relate several in other places. St Laurence has been one of the most venerated martyrs of the Roman Church since the fourth century, and he is named in the canon of the Mass. He was certainly buried in the cemetery of Cyriaca *in agro Verano* on the Via Tiburtina, where Constantine built the first chapel on the site of what is now the church of St Laurence-outside-the-Walls, the fifth patriarchal basilica of the city.

In St Laurence we have a demonstration of the power of the grace of Jesus Christ, which is able to sweeten whatever is bitter and harsh to flesh and blood. If we had the resolution and fervour of the saints in the practice of devotion we should find all seeming difficulties, which discourage our lukewarmness, to be mere shadows and phantoms. A lively faith, like that of the martyrs, would make us disdain with them the honours and pleasures of the world, and measure and judge the goods and evils of this life not by nature but by the light and principles of faith only ; and did we sincerely love God, as they did, we should accept His holy will with joy in all things, have no other desire, and find no happiness but in it. If we are dejected or impatient under troubles, murmur and complain, or call ourselves unhappy in them, it is evident that too much self-love is in our hearts, and that we seek our own inclinations more than the will of God. Suffering is the true test of our love, by which we may judge whether we do what is agreeable to ourselves for love of God or merely because we like doing it. If we find self-love in our sufferings, all the rest of our lives is to be suspected of the same disorder.

Much confusion and inconsistency prevail in what purport to be the "Acts" of St Laurence, though in fact this document is only an item in a series of similar narratives. See the *Bibliotheca Hagiographica Latina*, n. 6884, as compared with nn. 7801 and 4753. The poem of Prudentius, however, which Ruinart prints among his "Acta Sincera," affords a relatively clear statement, followed in the main by Butler above. Is this merely a poetical fiction, or does it represent some genuine tradition handed down either orally or in documents which have perished ? St Ambrose (see, *e.g.*, his *De Officiis*, i, 41) undoubtedly shared the belief that the martyr was roasted to death, and so did other early Fathers. P. Franchi de' Cavalieri (*Römische Quartalschrift*, xiv, 1900, pp. 159–176 ; and *Note agiografiche*, v, pp. 65–82) and Père Delehaye (*Analecta Bollandiana*, xix, 1900, pp. 452–453 ; as also in the *Acta Sanctorum*, Nov., vol. ii, part 2, 1932, pp. 431–432) reject altogether the gridiron tradition ; but it still finds defenders. See, for example, Dom H. Leclercq in the *Dictionnaire d'Archéologie*, etc., article "Gril" (vol. vi, cc. 1827–1831) and article "Laurent" (vol. viii, cc. 1917–1947). The great devotion inspired by the memory of St Laurence in Rome is strikingly illustrated in the newly recovered Life of St Melania the Younger (see Rampolla's edition, pp. 5–6), as also by the fact of the numerous dedications of churches and oratories. See J. P. Kirsch, *Die römischen Titelkirchen in Altertum*, pp. 80–84, and Huelsen, *Le Chiese di Roma nel medio evo*, pp. 280–297. *Cf.* also Duchesne "Le Sanctuaire de S. Laurent," in *Mélanges d'Archéologie*, etc., xxxix (1921), pp. 3–24.

BD. AMADEUS OF PORTUGAL, Conf.

A.D. 1482

The name by which Bd. Amadeus was known in Portugal was João Mendez da Silva. He was born in 1420, the son of Roderigo, Count of Portalegre, and so was the elder brother of Bd. Beatrice da Silva, foundress of the Conceptionist nuns. At the age of twenty-two he became an Hieronymite at the monastery of Our Lady of Guadalupe in Spain ; here he spent ten years, learning the principles of the religious life and exercising himself in virtue. At one time, fired with the desire of martyrdom, he went to Granada to preach to the Moors; he was seized as a spy, beaten, and sent back to his own country. He then decided to become a Friar Minor and went to their house at Ubeda, whence he was sent to Italy with letters of recommendation to the minister general who, however, refused to accept him. After other rebuffs he was received at Assisi as a lay-brother in 1453. He became sacristan there and at Perugia, but when he had been transferred to Milan his reputation for sanctity caused him to be pestered with visitors. He therefore got permission to retire, first to Marignano and then to Oreno, where he rebuilt a ruined convent for his followers. After giving himself for a while to solitary contemplation, he determined to establish a new house of his order in which the observance of the rule should be more primitive and severe. He was ordained in 1459, and with the approval and help of the Archbishop of Milan founded such friaries at Marignano, dedicated in honour of our Lady of Peace, and at Oreno, from whence, in the face of much difficulty and opposition, other similar houses were set up in Italy. The new Franciscan minister general, Friar Francis della Rovere, extended his encouragement and protection to Bd. Amadeus, and when he became pope, as Sixtus IV in 1471, called him to Rome to be his confessor and established the reform at the church of San Pietro in Montorio. Bd. Amadeus wrote a book on revelations and prophecies, and earned an ever-increasing reputation for holiness which, after his death at Milan in 1482, developed into the popular *cultus* which has existed ever since. The Reform of Marignano, or Amadeists, was carried on by George de Val-Canonique, John the German, and others, and at its height had twenty-eight friaries in Italy and one near Cartagena, given by Pope Innocent VIII, in Spain. But it came to an end in 1568, when Pope St Pius V united all their houses to the other Observant Franciscans.

A full account of Amadeus as well as of his sister Beatrice (known in Portuguese as Dona Brites da Silva) will be found in Frei Jeronymo de Belem, *Chronica Serafica da Santa Provincia dos Algarves* (Lisboa, 1753), vol. ii, pp. 727–748. It would seem, however, that there has been no confirmation of the *cultus* of the former and that his feast is not kept liturgically by any branch of the Franciscan Order.

AUGUST 11

SS. TIBURTIUS, Mart., and CHROMATIUS, Conf.

c. A.D. 288

AGRESTIUS CHROMATIUS was prefect of Rome, and had condemned several martyrs in the reign of Carinus. In the first years of Diocletian, St Tranquillinus was brought before him, and he assured him that, having been afflicted with the gout, he had recovered perfect health on being baptised. Chromatius was troubled with the same disorder, and being convinced by this miracle of the truth of the gospel, he sent for Polycarp, the priest who had baptised Tranquillinus, and receiving the sacrament of Baptism was freed from his infirmity: by which miracle God was pleased to give him a sensible emblem of the spiritual health which that holy cleansing conferred on his soul. From that time he harboured many Christians in his house to shelter them from the persecution, and resigned his dignity, in which he was succeeded by one Fabian. Chromatius's son Tiburtius was ordained subdeacon, and was soon after betrayed by an apostate, Torquatus, to the persecutors. He was brought up before the said Fabian, and walked unharmed over burning embers by the power of his faith. But the miracle was set down to magic and he was beheaded on the Via Labicana, three miles from Rome, where a church was afterwards built. These particulars are found in the *acta* of St Sebastian, and therefore no reliance can be placed on them, but this martyr Tiburtius certainly existed.

We have no reliable evidence of the existence of any Chromatius, who is not even mentioned in the Roman Martyrology, but Tiburtius is famous from an epitaph by Pope Damasus which ends with the line:

Care Deo ut foveas Damasum precor alme Tiburti.

See the texts quoted by Delehaye in the *Acta Sanctorum*, Nov., vol. ii, part 2, p. 434; and *cf.* the article of J. P. Kirsch " Die Martyrer der Katakombe ' ad duas Lauros ' " in *Ehrengabe deutscher Wissenschaft dargeboten von Katholischen Gelehrten* (1920), pp. 577–601.

ST PHILOMENA OR PHILUMENA, VIRG. AND MART.
DATE UNKNOWN

On May 24, 1802, in the catacomb of St Priscilla on the Via Salaria Nova an inscribed *loculus* was found, and on the following day it was carefully examined and opened. The *loculus* was closed with three tiles, on which was the following inscription in red paint:

LUMENA PAXTE CUM FI

together with certain symbols, namely, two anchors, two arrows, a javelin, a palm, and a flower (or torch). One theory about this inscription was that it had originally run:

[Fi]lumena pax tecum fi[at],
"Philumena, peace be with thee. So be it";

that the *loculus* had had to be closed in a hurry, and that the mason's tools had obliterated the first two and last two letters. But it is now generally accepted that the tiles were put in a wrong order, again either through hurry or by one who could not read, and that the inscription should read:

Pax tecum Filumena,
"Peace be with thee, Philumena,"

which is obtained by putting the first of the three tiles at the end. Within the *loculus* was found the skeleton of a female of from thirteen to fifteen years old, the principal bones entire except the skull, which was much broken. Embedded in cement was a small glass phial or vase, with vestiges of what was taken to be blood. This was one of the so-called "blood-ampullæ" which, before the researches of V. de Buck, Kraus, and Rossi, when found in conjunction with the palm symbol was accepted as proof of the grave of a martyr. Accordingly, in accordance with the knowledge of the time and the current regulations of the Congregation of Sacred Rites, the remains were taken to be those of a virgin-martyr named Philomena, they were reverently gathered up, and deposited in the *custodia generale* of sacred relics.

No more attention was paid to them until the summer of 1805, when Pope Pius VII gave them into the care of the Reverend Don Francis di Lucia, and on June 8 they were translated to Mugnano del Cardinale in the diocese of Nola and enshrined under one of the altars of the parish-church. Miracles and favours, spiritual and temporal, consequent on invocation of St Philomena and in the presence of her relics, were immediately reported, and with the consequent increase of devotion marvels multiplied. Her fame spread throughout Italy and was increased by the credence popularly, but not officially, given to certain private revelations claimed by Sister Mary-Louisa-of-Jesus, a canoness of Naples*; on the strength of these Don Francis di Lucia wrote a " life " of the unknown St Philomena, including a completely fictitious account of her martyrdom. The church of Mugnano became a great pilgrimage shrine, she became known in France, and from thence devotion to her spread throughout the world. The holy alliance, so to say, between St Philomena and St John-Baptist Vianney is well known ; she was his " dear little saint," his " agent in Heaven," she would do anything he asked : " And why not ? For Almighty God Himself obeys me every day upon the altar." Nor was he the only one among the heroes of religion in nineteenth-century France to be distinguished for devotion to St Philomena : St Madeleine-Sophie Barat, Bd. Peter-Julian Eymard, Bd. Peter-Louis Chanel, the Venerable Countess de Bonnault d'Houet were among them. But it is likely enough that if the Curé of Ars had not sounded her praises for the space of thirty years, she would not have enjoyed the immense popularity that became hers. On the other hand, the most influential single event in the diffusion of the *cultus*, and the one which did much to move the Roman authorities to action, was the miraculous cure of the Venerable Pauline Mary Jaricot, foundress of the Association for the Propagation of the Faith. During 1834 her life was despaired of, but she determined to make the journey from Lyons to Mugnano, lying at full length in a chaise, to ask the intercession of St Philomena at her shrine. While passing through Rome she stayed at a convent where she was twice visited by Pope Gregory XVI, who betrayed his idea of her condition by asking her to pray for him as soon as she got to Heaven. Mlle Jaricot, almost at the point of death, arrived at Mugnano on August 8, 1835 ; two days later, when receiving holy Communion in St Philomena's church on the saint's feast, she was completely cured of her disease. On her way home she stopped again at Rome, " to show herself to the priest," and Gregory promised at once to examine the cause of this wonder-working Philomena. On January 30, 1837, he signed a decree authorizing her public *cultus*, with permission for the clergy

* The value of these alleged revelations may be somewhat gauged by the fact that the nun said the saint told her that her name was derived from Latin and signified " daughter of light " (*Filia luminis*). It is, in fact, a quite well-known name from the Greek φιλουμένη, " beloved."

of the diocese of Nola to celebrate on August 11 in her honour the Mass *Loquebar* and Office from the common of a virgin-martyr, with a proper fourth lesson at Matins; this feast soon was extended to other dioceses, including Rome itself. In 1855 Pope Pius IX approved a proper Mass and Office for the feast; but her name has not been inserted in the Roman Martyrology. The lessons of her office remark that " it is to be regretted that her life, her acts, and the kind of martyrdom that she suffered have remained hidden," but definitely state that she was a virgin and a martyr; these same lessons do not anywhere say in so many words that the bones found in the sepulchre " wherein the body of St Philomena had been laid " were those of that person; nevertheless, it cannot be denied that the implication of the lessons is that they were.

The Congregation of Sacred Rites accepted the evidence of the symbols on the inscription and of the phial within the *loculus* as proofs positive of martyrdom; it must now be recognized in the light of more accurate knowledge that this cannot safely be done. The miracles and spiritual helps granted by God to the faithful who have called on St Philomena cannot, however, be reasonably called in question as proofs of sanctity—but the sanctity of whom? Professor Marucchi has cast very grave doubt indeed on the identity of the bones in the sepulchre with those of the Philomena commemorated on its outside; he makes out an exceedingly strong case for the tiles not having been disarranged accidentally, but that they were originally used to close the grave of one Philomena between the middle and end of the second century, and later used again, in the wrong order, to close another, of a maiden unknown. The real body of the Philomena of the inscription, likely enough a martyr, but not certainly, was probably translated with many others to one of the churches of the city by Pope St Paul I or Pope St Pascal I (eighth to ninth centuries); the relics of the second burial in Philomena's grave are, of course, at Mugnano, very imposingly enshrined.

Some clients of St Philomena, especially those who have received kindness at her hands, view with suspicion and even resentment the results of the efforts of learned men (men not less religious than themselves) to establish the truth about their patron. They fear that the effect of those researches is to " do away with St Philomena," to nullify the testimony of all who are under practical, spiritual or temporal obligation to her, from the sainted Curé of Ars to her most obscure client. This is not so, nor is it possible: but we must not, in the name of piety, deceive ourselves with knowledge we have not got. The miracles and benefactions wrought by God when we ask for the intercession of a certain saint, whom we call on by the name of Philomena, are indubitably known to us : nothing can shake them, or our gratitude to her. But we do not know certainly whether she was in fact named Philomena in her earthly life, whether she was a martyr, whether her relics now rest at Mugnano or in some place unknown. And these questions are of only relative importance : the spiritual influence of her whom we call St Philomena is what really matters ; we may accommodate to this subject (and to others like it) the words of our Lord : " Is not the life more than the meat and the body more than the raiment ? "

This is one of the cases in which we seem to have on the one side a number of critical scholars agreeing in a practically unanimous verdict, and on the other a devout credulity which is mainly impressed by reputed miracles and revelations. Prof. Marucchi's conclusions have not undergone any change since he published in *Miscellanea di Storia Ecclesiastica*, ii (1904), pp. 365–386, his " Osservazioni archeologiche sulla Iscrizione di S. Filomena," and supplemented this with further arguments in the *Nuovo Bullettino di arch. crist.*, vol. xii (1906), pp. 253–300. On the other hand Padre G. Bonavenia, S.J., has replied to Marucchi in two essays—*Controversia sul celeberrimo Epitaffio di S. Filomena*, 1906, and *La Questione puramente archeologica*, etc., 1907. Further the Abbé Trochu, the author of the excellent Life of the Curé d'Ars, has also published a monograph, *La " petite Sainte " du Curé d'Ars*, 1924, defending the historicity of the martyr. A great deal has been written upon the question of St Philomena, and a very full bibliography may be found in the *Dictionnaire d'Archéolgie*, vol. v, cc. 1604–1606.

ST ALEXANDER THE CHARCOAL-BURNER,
Bp. of Comana, and Mart.

A.D. 250

The Christian community of Comana in Pontus having grown to be sufficiently large to require a bishop, St Gregory the Wonderworker, Bishop of Caesarea, went thither to preside at the election. He rejected all the candidates, put forward by the clergy and people, especially one who was favoured because of his high birth and wealth, reminding them that the Apostles were poor and common men. Whereat a wag exclaimed, " Very well then. Why not appoint Alexander the charcoal-burner ? " St Gregory, knowing that the Holy Ghost was as likely to make Himself heard by means of this sarcastic suggestion as any other way, was moved to send for the said Alexander, who presented himself all dirty and blackened from his trade. Gregory looked at him and saw through the grime and the rags ; he took him aside and questioned him, and soon discovered that Alexander was a man of good birth and education, who had given away his goods and taken up this trade the more literally to follow Christ; the Roman Martyrology says that he was "a most learned philosopher," though there is no reason to think that anything more is meant by this than that he was a man of wisdom. St Gregory accordingly put Alexander forward, he having signified his willingness, as his own choice for the vacant see, it was ratified by the people, and the new bishop was consecrated. St Gregory of Nyssa, who relates this happening, speaks highly of St Alexander as a bishop and teacher. He eventually gave his life for the Faith, being martyred by fire in the persecution under Decius. St Alexander was naturally revered as a patron of charcoal-burners.

See the *Acta Sanctorum*, August, vol. ii.

ST SUSANNA, Virg. and Mart.
A.D. 295

The Church on this day celebrates St Tiburtius, spoken of above, and joins with him this maiden martyr. Susanna was nobly born in Rome, and is said to have been a daughter of St Gabinius and niece of Pope St Caius. Having made a vow of virginity, she refused to marry Galerius Maximian, the Emperor's son; therefore she was impeached as a Christian, and suffered a cruel martyrdom, being beheaded in her father's house. No genuine acts of her life are now extant: but she is commemorated in many ancient martyrologies, and a famous church has borne her name ever since the fifth century, when it was one of the *tituli* or parish-churches of Rome. It is built on the site of the adjoining houses of Gabinius and Caius, near to the place of burial of St Tiburtius.

Sufferings were to the martyrs a crowning mercy, an extraordinary grace, and the source of the greatest glory. All afflictions which God sends are in like manner mercies and blessings; they are precious talents, to be improved by us to the increasing of our love for God and the exercise of self-denial, patience, humility, and penance. They are also most useful and necessary to bring us to the knowledge of ourselves and our Creator, which we are too apt to forget without them. Wherefore whatever crosses or calamities befall us, we must be prepared to bear them with a patient resignation to the divine will; we ought to learn from the martyrs to comfort ourselves and to rejoice in them. It is cowardly and foolish if, by neglecting to take advantage of sickness, losses, and other afflictions, we make precious mercies our heaviest curse. By honouring the martyrs we show ourselves the path we must tread.

The story of St Susanna as it is related in her fictitious "Acts" has already been touched upon in the February volume of this series, pp. 262-264. The germs of historic truth which have been incorporated in the story are of curious interest. The primitive "Hieronymianum" would seem to have contained a notice in this form—" In Rome at 'the Two Houses' beside the baths of Diocletian, the birthday of Saint Susanna." These brief data are quite reliable, but they have probably provided the nucleus from which the story of Gabinius and Pope St Caius in their two houses was evolved. See Delehaye's commentary in the *Acta Sanctorum*, Nov., vol. ii, part 2, p. 435. Besides Mgr. Duchesne's article in the *Mélanges d'Archéologie*, xxxvi (1916), pp. 27-42, consult also P. Franchi de' Cavalieri, *Note Agiografiche*, vol. vii, pp. 184-202. The "Title of St Susanna" does not seem to have been known under that name much before the end of the sixth century. *Cf.* Lanzoni, *I Titoli presbiterali di Roma*, pp. 34-40.

ST ATTRACTA OR ARAGHT, VIRG.
FIFTH CENTURY (?)

As with so many Irish saints, there is some uncertainty about the chronology of St Attracta; her alleged association with St Patrick would put her in the fifth century, but others mentioned as her contemporaries lived in the sixth. According to her legend she was the daughter of a noble house, and when her father Talan refused to allow her to dedicate herself to God, she fled into Greagraighe (Coolavin), where she is said to have received the nun's veil from St Patrick, and to have miraculously provided him with a paten when he came to say Mass and found he had not got one. Some writers say her veil was produced in the same way. She then established herself on Lough Gara, and founded a hospice for travellers in a place where seven roads meet, now called after her Killaraght. This hospice continued its good work until 1539. Later, she went into Roscommon, where she wished to have a cell close to St Conal (said to have been her half-brother) at Drum, near Boyle. This was forbidden by him and St Dachonna, and St Attracta expressed her indignation with a freedom which strikes us as Irish rather than holy: she hoped that the time would come when their respective churches would be reduced to insignificance, and their offerings to nothing, by the rising of another church near by, "and many other things that were disagreeable," some of which are "not set down in her *acta*." It is fanciful to see a fulfilment of this in the foundation centuries later of the Cistercian abbey of Boyle, but the churches of Drumconnell and Eas Dachonna (Assylin) were soon after overshadowed by the rise of the episcopal churches of Achonry and Elphin. When a raiding-party of the men of Luighne (Lugna) were fleeing from the King of Connacht, St Attracta enabled them to escape by dividing the waters of Lough Gara; two natural weirs on the lake are still connected with her name. Another miracle attributed to her is the harnessing of forest deer with her own hair, to drag timber for the construction of a fort by the King of Connacht, when he had unjustly summoned her to take part in the work: doubtless he remembered the affair of the men of Lugna. This saint has been commemorated on various dates, but her feast is now celebrated throughout Ireland on August 11; she is patron of the diocese of Achonry. The cross of St Attracta, venerated at Killaraght in the fourteenth century, was for long in the hereditary keeping of the O'Mochains (Mochain was the name of her servant who fled from home with her); its whereabouts is now unknown.

There is a Latin Life, unfortunately mutilated, printed by Colgan, as well as in the *Acta Sanctorum* under February 9, and in the form " Tarakata." Although St Attracta is mentioned as in personal relation with St Patrick both in Tirechan's Collections and in the Tripartite Life, there seems to be no reference to her in the *Félire* of Œngus.

ST EQUITIUS, ABBOT AND CONF.

A.D. 540

He flourished in the Abruzzi at the time when St Benedict was establishing his rule at Monte Cassino, and in his youth suffered greatly from temptations of the flesh. He sought solitude in the province of Valeria, where by prayer and discipline he brought his body into subjection and attained the virtues of the spirit. When he had learned to govern himself he undertook the direction of others and founded first a monastery at Pescara (Amiternum) and then other houses, both of men and women. St Gregory the Great describes Equitius from accounts he had received from Albinus, Bishop of Rieti, and others who knew him personally: " Zeal for the salvation of souls so burned in his heart that, in spite of his responsibility for so many monasteries, he travelled about diligently, visiting churches, towns, villages, and particularly men's houses, to stir up the hearts of those that heard him to a love of heavenly joys. His clothes were so mean and shabby that those who did not know who he was would not deign to salute him, even if he greeted them first. Wherever he went he rode on the most forlorn beast he could find, with a halter for bridle and a sheep's skin for saddle. He carried his books of divinity in leather bags, hung on either side of his horse, and to what place soever he came he opened there the spring of sacred Scripture and refreshed the souls of his hearers with the heavenly water of his words. His grace in preaching was so great that the fame thereof reached Rome itself." Like many of the early abbots St Equitius was not in holy orders, and a patrician called Felix challenged him for presuming to preach when he was neither ordained nor licensed thereto by the Bishop of Rome. " I myself have seriously considered the matter on which you speak," replied Equitius, " but on a certain night a young man stood by me in a vision and touched my tongue with such an instrument as is used in letting blood, and said to me : ' Behold ! I have put my word into your mouth. Go your way and preach.' And since that day I can talk only of God, whether I would or no." This did not satisfy some of the Roman clergy, who complained to the Pope that " this countrified fellow has taken on himself authority to preach and, ignorant as he is, usurps the office of our apostolic ruler," and asked that he be sent for to be dealt with. A cleric called Julian was therefore sent to his monastery to fetch Equitius, and he found the abbot in hob-nailed boots, mowing grass, who, when he received the Pope's message, prepared to set out at once. Julian was tired with his journey and wanted to stay there the night, and St Equitius agreed, but, " I am very sorry," he said, " for if we go not to-day, to-morrow we shall not." And so it fell out, for the next morning a messenger arrived from the Pope to tell Julian that he had had a vision from God about Equitius and the holy man was not to be disturbed. St Equitius died on March 7 about the year 540, and on this day his body was translated to the church of St Laurence at Aquila ; some of his relics are now in St Martin's, at Benevento.

The Bollandists have dealt with St Equitius on March 7, but there is also a similar collection of fragmentary data in Mabillon, *Acta Sanctorum, O.S.B.*, vol. i, pp. 655–658.

ST BLAAN OR BLANE, BP. AND CONF.

c. A.D. 590 (?)

There is considerable uncertainty about the chronology of this Scots bishop, who was born in Bute, the son of Ertha, a sister of St Cathan. He spent seven years in Ireland under the instruction of St Comgall and St Canice (Kenny), and presumably became a monk there. He then returned to the isle of Bute (" in a boat without oars "), and put himself under the discipline of his uncle Cathan, who gave him holy orders, and he devoted his life to apostolic work in Scotland. He eventually became a bishop and is said to have gone on pilgrimage to Rome, returning on foot through England. A number of miracles are attributed to him, as that he raised a youth to life who had died in his sins and rekindled the church lights, which had gone out during the night office, by striking fire from his finger-nails. He died and was buried at Kingarth in Bute, and on the site of his monastery the pre-Reformation cathedral of Dunblane was built; his bell is still preserved there. Devotion to St Blaan early became popular, and his feast is still observed in the dioceses of Saint Andrews, Dunkeld (which includes the former see of Dunblane), and Argyll.

There is an account of the Saint in the *Acta Sanctorum*, Aug., vol. ii, which is taken mainly from the lessons of the Aberdeen Breviary; but see rather Forbes, *Kalendars of Scottish Saints*, pp. 280–281. St Blane is mentioned in the *Félire* of Œngus, and this as well as the Aberdeen Martyrology enters his name under August 10.

ST GAUGERICUS OR GERY, Bp. OF CAMBRAI AND ARRAS, CONF.

c. A.D. 625

He was a native of Yvois, in the diocese of Trier, a small town in the duchy of Luxemburg. He was brought up at home in the study of sacred learning and in the practice of self-denial, prayer, and almsdeeds. During an episcopal visitation St Magnericus, the successor of St Nicetas in the bishopric of Trier, coming to Yvois, was much delighted with the sanctity and talents of St Géry, and ordained him deacon (but not till he knew the whole psalter by heart, says his biographer); from that moment the saint redoubled his fervour in the exercise of good works, and applied himself with zeal to the functions of his sacred ministry, especially to the instruction of the faithful.

The reputation of his virtue and learning raised him to the episcopal chair of Cambrai and Arras, which sees were united for a period of six hundred years, until 1093. King Childebert II confirmed the election and Géry was consecrated by the Archbishop of Reims. The saint devoted his episcopate to the rooting out of the paganism which was by no means dead in his diocese. At Cambrai he founded a monastery, called by him after St Médard, and to him is attributed the foundation of the city of Brussels, for he is said to have built a chapel on an island in the Senne (now Place Saint-Géry) around which a village grew up. In 613 he was sent by King Clotaire II to distribute alms at the shrine of St Martin at Tours, and in the following year assisted at the Council of Paris. Among other miracles recounted of him, it is related that at Yvois a leper was healed by being baptised by him: which aptly represented the interior cleansing of the soul from sin. St Géry was called to rest after occupying his see for thirty-nine years, about the year 625, and was buried in the church which he had built in honour of St Médard. This being demolished by the Emperor Charles V for the building of the citadel, the canons were removed and took with them the relics of the saint, to the old church of St Vedast, which from that time has borne the name of St Géry.

The oldest life of St Géry has only been printed in relatively modern times, i.e., in the *Analecta Bollandiana* vol. vii, (1888), pp. 388–398. Since then it has been re-edited by Bruno Krusch in the *Monumenta Germanica Scriptores rerum Meroving*, vol. iii, pp. 652–658. It seems to have been written about fifty or sixty years after the death of the saint and in very barbarous Latin. Cf., the *Neuer Archiv*, vol. xvi (1891), pp. 227 *Seq.*; van der Essen, *Saints Mérovingiens*; and Duchesne, *Fastes Épiscopaux*.

BD. PETER FABER, Conf.

A.D. 1546

Peter Faber (le Fèvre) was the senior of the first companions of St Ignatius Loyola and held the highest place in his master's estimation after St Francis Xavier; and he was the first among the Jesuits to come to grips with the Protestant Reformation. He was a Savoyard by birth, born in 1506 of a family of substantial farmers, and while still a shepherd-boy of ten years old showed aptitude for both study and preaching. To his great joy he was sent to school, first with a priest at Thônes and then to a local college. The master of this last, Peter Villiardi, made a life-long impression on his pupil, who revered him as an uncanonized saint. In 1525 Peter Faber went to Paris and was entered at the college of Sainte-Barbe. Here he shared the lodging of a Navarrese student, one Francis Xavier, and was appointed to supervise the studies of a backward undergraduate from Salamanca, Ignatius Loyola. The three became firm friends, and Peter put himself under the spiritual direction of the man he was coaching in philosophy. In 1530 he received his mastership in arts on the same day as Xavier, but for a time he could not make up his mind what profession he should pursue: medicine, law, teaching, by turns attracted him, and he as yet heard no clear call to "leave the world." At last, after making the "spiritual exercises," he decided to throw in his lot with Ignatius; he completed his theological studies, was ordained priest in 1534, and on August 15 of the same year said the Mass at Montmartre when the seven first Jesuits took their vows. Bd. Peter was in charge of the little company that met St Ignatius at Venice, early in 1537, only to find that their way to the Holy Land, where they planned to be missionaries, was barred by the Turkish war. At the end of the year he went with Ignatius and Lainez to Rome, where they were appointed missionary preachers by the Holy See, and for a time he was professor of sacred Scripture at the University. He was then sent by Pope Paul III with Father Lainez and the Cardinal of Sant' Angelo to Piacenza and Parma, where he preached with much profit.

At this time the Emperor Charles V was trying to compose the religious troubles of Germany by convoking a series of conferences, called "diets," of the Catholic and Protestant leaders, and Bd. Peter was appointed by the Pope to go with the imperial envoy, Ortiz, to that of Worms, in 1540; from this abortive meeting he went on to assist at the equally useless diet of Ratisbon in the following year. But Bd. Peter saw clearly what both the Emperor and high ecclesiastics could not or would not see, that what Germany needed was not discussions with heretics but a reformation in the life and discipline of Catholics, both clergy and lay-people. He was appalled by the state of the country in general and by the lethargy and ill-living of Catholics in particular, and he devoted himself with great success to preaching and direction in Speyer and Ratisbon and Mainz; at the last-named place Peter Canisius, then a layman, made the "spiritual exercises" under his direction and was received into the Society of Jesus. Among those whom Bd. Peter turned from a diplomatic and vacillating to an earnest and religious fulfilment of their office was Cardinal Albert of Brandenburg, who became a true defender of the Faith and an upholder of the Jesuits. After having practically eradicated heresy in Cologne, whose archbishop, Herman von Wied, was himself a Protestant, and helping to found the first Jesuit residence there, he was called from Germany first to Portugal and then to Spain. While travelling through France he was imprisoned for seven days, and during that time made a vow to accept no stipends for celebrating Mass or preaching whenever he could refuse them without injustice to others. In Spain, as elsewhere, he gave retreats to lay-people as well as to the clergy, using the Spiritual Exercises of St Ignatius with the happiest results of confirming the zealous, reviving fervour in the weak, and converting the indifferent and the fallen; he made a Latin version of the Exercises for the use of the Carthusians of Cologne. Among those in Spain whose life was permanently influenced by Peter Faber was Francis Borgia, then Duke of Gandia, and he was chosen as the spiritual adviser of his prince, the Duke of Savoy. He returned to Germany in 1542, and the Catholicity of the Rhineland to-day is to a considerable degree due to his labours then, till he was summoned from the University of Louvain by Philip II who wanted him again in Portugal and Spain.

In 1540 the King of Ethiopia had sent a request to the King of Portugal that he would ask the Holy See to send an ecclesiastic to rule the Abyssinian Church in place of the nominee of the Monophysite Patriarch of Alexandria, and King John III suggested to St Ignatius that Bd. Peter would be suitable for the office. However it was not until nine years after Peter's death that a Portuguese Jesuit, Father Nuñez Barreto, was nominated to that exotic charge, for Pope Paul III wished to have Father Peter as his theologian at the Council of Trent. He was not anxious to go, but, "on a Sunday which fell on October 22, 1542, I determined to fall in with the wish of the Archbishop of Mainz, who wanted me to go with him to the Council of Trent, which was to begin on the first day of November. Before I took that determination I had various feelings in my mind and some sadness, from which our Lord delivered me by virtue of holy and unquestioning obedience, which knows better than to consider either one's own insufficiency or the difficulty of the things which are commanded." In 1546 the Pope's summons to the same assembly confirmed his resolution of obedience, and he set out at once though he was sick and the summer heat was overpowering. The effort was too much. Though only forty years old, Bd. Peter was exhausted by his laborious journeys and the strain of his work, and soon after his arrival in Rome he died of fever in the arms of St Ignatius, on August 1.

Bd. Peter Faber left behind in his *Memoriale* a detailed account of his spiritual life during a long period, describing the action of God in his soul, especially at Mass and Divine Office, almost from day to day. The following is a characteristic entry: "One day I went to the palace to hear the sermon in the prince's chapel and the porter, not knowing me, would not let me in. So I had to stop outside, and it came into my mind how many times I had given entrance into my soul to vain thoughts and evil imaginings, while refusing it to Jesus who was knocking at the door. I reflected, too, how He is everywhere badly received by the world, and I prayed for myself and for the porter that the Lord would not make us wait long in Purgatory before admitting us to Heaven. Many other good thoughts came to me at that time, and so I felt very kindly towards that porter who had been for me the occasion of so much devotion." The mind that turned to such gentle reflection was naturally opposed to any sort of coercion when dealing with Protestants, and he had little faith in diets and formal conferences. When it was required of him he could and would meet such opponents as Bucer and Melancthon face to face, and confute them in argument, and such victories were not without good effect. But he attached far more importance to winning men to a change of heart, to amend their lives, and so lead them back to Christ and His Church. " The wish came to me that I might work and suffer in every way, not only generally but particularly, even for one single soul : in imitation of Christ who gave His life, who suffered and died, for each one in particular." There was a grace and sweetness about Bd. Peter that Father Simon Rodriguez met in no other man ; " I am at a loss for words to express the way in which, by his lovable and pleasing manner, he earned everyone's good-will and affection and won all who met him to the love of God. When he spoke of divine things it was as though he had the keys of men's hearts on his tongue, so powerfully did he move and attract them ; and the love he inspired was equalled by the reverence they had for the sweet gravity and firm virtue which informed all he said." The *cultus* of Bd. Peter Faber was confirmed and ratified by Pope Pius IX in 1872.

Ever since the publication by the Spanish Jesuits of the *Monumenta Historica Societatis Jesu*, an immense amount of material has become accessible regarding the activities of St Ignatius' first companions. A special volume of nearly 1000 pages, under the title *Fabri Monumenta*, contains a critically revised text of Blessed Peter's letters, of his *Memoriale*, and of the documents of the process of beatification, including a " processus informativus " begun informally in 1596 but ratified in 1607 by the ordinary, the Bishop of Geneva, who was then no other than St Francis of Sales. Modern Lives are numerous, including that by Father Bocro, translated into English for the Quarterly Series, a French biography by Fr. A. Maurel, one in German by R. Cornely, and one in Spanish by F. Maruri. Most of Blessed Peter's extant letters, written to St Ignatius and other Jesuits, are in Spanish and he signs himself " Pedro Fabro," but in a French letter he signs " Pierre Favre," and " Favre " seems to have been the name of many collateral descendants of his who gave evidence in the process.

AUGUST 12

ST CLARE, Virg. and Abbess,
Foundress of the Poor Clares
A.D. 1253

"THE Lady Clare, shining in name, more shining in life, most shining in conversation, was a native of Assisi, of noble birth and by grace nobler, a maiden most pure in heart, young in years but hoary in determination, most steadfast in purpose, but withal wise and meek and a marvellous lover of Christ," was born about the year 1193. Her mother was Bd. Ortolana di Fiumi and her father is commonly said to have been Favorino Scifi, Count of Sasso-Rosso, but to what families, and whether noble or simple, her parents really belonged is not certainly known. Clare had a younger sister, Agnes, and perhaps another, Beatrice, but of her childhood, adolescence and home-life there are no certain facts. When she was eighteen St Francis came to preach the Lenten sermons at the church of San Giorgio in Assisi; his words fired her, she sought him out secretly, and asked him to help her that she too might live "after the manner of the holy Gospel." Francis spoke to her of contempt for the world and love of God, and strengthened her nascent desire to leave all things for Christ. On Palm Sunday in the year 1211 Clare, in holiday dress, attended at the cathedral of Assisi for the blessing of palms; when all the rest went up to the altar-rails to receive their branch of olive a sudden shyness kept her in her place, which the bishop seeing, he went from the altar down to her and gave her the branch. She attended the procession; but the evening following she ran away from home and went a mile out of the town to the Portiuncula, where St Francis lived with his little community. He and his brethren met her at the door of the chapel of our Lady with lighted tapers in their hands, and before the altar of the Blessed Virgin she put off her fine clothes, and St Francis cut off her hair, and gave her his penitential habit, which was a tunic of sackcloth tied about her with a cord. The holy father not having yet any nunnery of his own, placed her for the present in the Benedictine convent of St Paul, where she was affectionately received. It would seem that the relatives of St Clare (her father was probably dead) had proposed a particular marriage that did not recommend itself to her, but that she did not entirely renounce the idea of matrimony in general until the burning words of Francis persuaded her to commit her maidenhood finally to God. Then followed what Mr. Chesterton has discriminatingly called this "regular romantic elopement," in which the bridegroom was Christ and St Francis the "knight-errant who gave it a happy ending."

No sooner was her action made public but her friends and relations came in a body to draw her out of her retreat. Clare resisted and held to the altar so fast as to pull its cloths half off when they endeavoured to drag her away ; and, uncovering her head to show her hair cut, she said that Christ had called her to His service and that she would have no other husband, and that the more they should continue to persecute her, the more God would strengthen her to resist and overcome them. And God triumphed in her. St Francis soon after removed her to another nunnery, that of Sant' Angelo di Panzo. There her sister Agnes joined her, which drew on them both a fresh persecution. Agnes's constancy proved at last victorious, and St Francis gave her also the habit, though she was only fourteen years of age. (It may be noted that in the bull of canonization Pope Alexander IV makes no mention of any violence being used in the attempt to dissuade Clare and her sister from their new life.) Eventually St Francis placed them in a poor house contiguous to the church of San Damiano, on the outskirts of the city of Assisi, and appointed Clare the superior. She was later joined by her mother and others, to the number of sixteen, among whom three were of the illustrious family of the Ubaldini in Florence, who held for truer greatness the sackcloth and poverty of St Clare than the estates and riches which they possessed, seeing they left them all to become humble disciples of so admirable a mistress. St Clare saw founded within a few years monasteries at Perugia, Arezzo, Padua, Rome, Venice, Mantua, Bologna, Spoleto, Milan, Siena, Pisa, and in many towns in France and Germany. Bd. Agnes, daughter to the King of Bohemia, founded a nunnery of the order in Prague, in which she took the habit, and was called by Clare, " my half self."

St Clare and her community practised austerities which till then had scarcely been known among women. They wore neither stockings, shoes, sandals, not any other covering on their feet ; they lay on the ground, observed a perpetual abstinence from meat, and never spoke but when they were obliged to it by necessity and charity. The foundress recommended this holy silence as the means to avoid innumerable sins of the tongue, and to preserve the mind always recollected in God and free from the dissipation of the world which, without this guard, penetrates even the walls of cloisters. Not content with the fasts and other general mortifications of the Rule, she always wore next her skin a rough shift of hair or of bristles cut short; she fasted on vigils and all Lent on bread and water; and on some days she ate nothing at all. All her austerities were on the same scale and after a time it became necessary for Francis and the Bishop of Assisi to oblige her to lie upon a mattress and never pass one day without taking at least some bread for nourishment. Discretion came with experience, and years later she wrote to Bd. Agnes of Bohemia: " Since our bodies are not of brass and our strength is not the strength of stone but rather are we weak and subject to corporal infirmities, I implore you vehemently in the Lord to refrain from that exceeding rigour of abstinence which I know you practise, so that living and hoping in the Lord you may offer Him a reasonable service and a sacrifice seasoned with the salt of prudence." St Francis wished that his order should never possess any rents or other property even in common, subsisting on daily contributions, and St Clare possessed this spirit in such perfection that before she left her home she gave the whole of her goods to the poor without reserving one single farthing for the monastery. Pope Gregory IX desired to mitigate this part of her rule, and offered to settle a yearly revenue on the Poor Ladies of San Damiano; but she in the most pressing manner persuaded him by many reasons, in which her love of evangelical poverty made her eloquent, to leave her order in its first rigorous establishment. When the Pope offered to dispense from the vow of strict poverty St Clare replied, " I need to be absolved from my sins, but I do not wish to be absolved from the obligation of following Jesus Christ." Gregory accordingly granted in 1228 the *Privilegium paupertatis*, that they might not be constrained by anyone to accept possessions: " He who feeds the birds of the air and gives raiment and nourishment to the lilies of the field will not leave you in want of clothing or of food until He come Himself to minister to you for eternity." The convents of Perugia and Florence also received this privilege, but others thought it more prudent to accept a mitigation.* After the death of Gregory IX (who as Cardinal Ugolino had drawn up the first written rule for the Poor Ladies of San Damiano), Innocent IV in

* Thus began the two observances which have ever since been perpetuated among the Poor Clares. The mitigated houses are called " Urbanist " from the modification of the rule given to them in 1263 by Pope Urban IV.

1247 published another recension of the rule which in some respects brought it nearer to Franciscan than to Benedictine observance, but which *permitted* the holding of property in common ; he wrote to the Cardinal-bishop of Ostia that he did not wish to force this rule on any community unwilling to accept it. St Clare was unwilling, and she, as the living depository of the spirit and tradition of St Francis himself, set to work to draw up a rule which should truly express them, and which unequivocally provides that the sisters shall possess no property, either as individuals or as a community. It was not until two days before she died that this rule was approved for the convent of San Damiano by Pope Innocent.

From the time when she was appointed abbess, much against her will, by St Francis in 1215, St Clare governed the convent for forty years. But it was her wish always to be the servant of servants, beneath all, washing and kissing the feet of the lay-sisters when they returned from begging, serving at table, attending the sick. When she prayed for the sick she sent them to other sisters, that their recovery might not be imputed to her prayers or merits. She had as it were wings to fly wherever St Francis directed her, and was always ready to do anything or to put her shoulders under any burden that was enjoined her : " Dispose of me as you please ; I am yours by having given my will to God. It is no longer my own." Whilst her sisters took their rest she watched long in prayer, and was the first that rose, rung the bell in the choir, and lighted the candles. She came from prayer with her face so shining (like that of Moses coming down from conversing with God) that it dazzled the eyes of those that beheld her ; and she spoke with such a spirit and fervour as to enkindle those who did but hear her voice. She had a wonderful devotion towards the Blessed Sacrament, and even when sick in bed (she ailed grievously for the last twenty-seven years of her life) she made fine linen corporals and cloths for the service of the altar, which she distributed among the churches of Assisi. The powerful force and efficacy of her prayer is well illustrated by a story told by Thomas of Celano, which may well be true. In 1244 the Emperor Frederick II cruelly ravaged the valley of Spoleto, because it was the patrimony of the Holy See. He had in his army many Saracens, and these infidels came once in a great body to plunder Assisi, and as San Damiano stood without the walls they first assaulted it. Whilst they were scaling the walls, St Clare, though very sick, caused herself to be carried to the gate of the monastery and the Blessed Sacrament to be placed there in a pyx in the very sight of the enemies, and, prostrating herself before It, prayed with many tears, saying, " Does it please Thee, O my God, to deliver into the hands of these beasts the defenceless children whom I have nourished with Thy love? I beseech Thee, good Lord, protect these whom I am now not able to protect." And she heard a voice like the voice of a little child saying, " I will have them always in my care." Then Clare prayed for the city of Assisi, and again the voice came, reassuring her, and she turned to the trembling nuns and said, " Have no fear, little daughters; trust in Jesus." Terror at the same time seized the assailants and they fled with such precipitation that several were hurt without being wounded by any enemy. Shortly after, Vitale di Aversa, a general of the same Emperor and a cruel and proud man, laid siege to Assisi for many days. St Clare said to her nuns that they, who received corporal necessaries from that city, owed to it all assistance in their power in its necessity. She therefore bid them cover their heads with ashes, and in this suppliant fashion to beg of Christ the deliverance of the town. They continued this with many tears a whole day and night till " God in His mercy so made issue with temptation that the besiegers melted away and their proud captain with them, for all he had sworn an oath to take the city."

Another popular story, namely, of St Clare and one of her nuns leaving the cloister of San Damiano and going to the Portiuncula to sup with St Francis, and of the marvellous light which radiated from the room, is less deserving of credence. The event, in itself exceedingly unlikely, is mentioned by no contemporary or by any writer for at least one hundred and fifty years; and Thomas of Celano, who often heard St Francis warning his followers to avoid any injudicious association with the Poor Ladies, states categorically that St Clare never left the walls of San Damiano. Unhappily even during her life, and for long after her death at intervals, there was disagreement between the Poor Clares and the Friars Minor as to the relations of the two orders: the observant Clares maintaining that the friars were under obligation to serve them in things both spiritual and temporal. In this connection Thomas of Celano has a story which, if it is the source of much trouble to historians, at least is illuminating on the subject of the stalwart and inflexible character of Clare. When Pope Gregory IX in 1230 forbade the friars to visit the convents of nuns without his special licence, she feared that this would mean a loss of the spiritual help to be obtained from the friars and a severing of the ties St Francis had wished should subsist between them. She thereupon dismissed every one of them attached to the convent, saying, " Now that he has deprived us of our spiritual almoners, let him also take them that serve our material needs ": if she couldn't have the one, she wouldn't have the other. At which the Pope referred the matter to the minister general of the Friars Minor.

St Clare bore years of sickness with sublime patience, and at last in 1253 the long-drawn-out agony began. Twice during its course she was visited by Pope Innocent IV, who gave her absolution, saying, " Would to God *I* had so little need of it," and she exclaimed to her nuns, " Praise the Lord, beloved daughters, for on this most blessed day both Jesus Christ and His Vicar have deigned to visit me." For the last seventeen days she was able to eat nothing, " and during that weary time of labour the faith and devotion of the people increased more and more. Every day prelates and cardinals came to call on her, for all men were firmly convinced that this dying woman was truly a great saint." Her sister St Agnes was there, and three of the companions of St Francis, Leo, Angelo, and Juniper, who read aloud to her the passion of our Lord according to St John as they had done at his death-bed twenty-seven years before. And when Brother Reginald exhorted her to patience, she replied, " Dear brother, ever since by means of His servant Francis I have known the grace of our Lord Jesus Christ, I have never in my whole life found any pain or sickness that could afflict me." Seeing all her spiritual children weep, she comforted them and tenderly exhorted them to be constant lovers and faithful observers of holy poverty, and gave them her blessing, calling herself the little plant of her holy father Francis. And to herself she was heard to say, " Go forth without fear, Christian soul, for you have a good guide for your journey. Go forth without fear, for He that created you has sanctified you, has always protected you, and loves you as a mother." " Thus was the passing of Blessed Clare. It was on the morrow of Blessed Laurence that she received her laurel crown, for on that day the temple of her body was dissolved, her most holy soul went forth and, exulting in its freedom, soared on the wings of gladness to the place which God had prepared for it." It was the forty-second year after her religious profession, and the sixtieth of her age. She was buried on the day following, on which the Church keeps her festival. Pope Innocent IV came again from Perugia and assisted in person with the Sacred College at her funeral. Alexander IV canonized her at Anagni in 1255. Her body was first buried in the church of San Giorgio at Assisi till the year 1260, when her relics were translated to a new church which bears her name. In 1850 the skeleton was discovered deep down beneath the high altar, and twenty-two years later was transferred to a new shrine in the crypt.

The example of this young girl, who renounced all the softness, superfluity, and vanity of her station and persevered in a life of so much severity, is a reproach to our sloth and sensuality. Such extraordinary rigours are not required of us ; but constant practice of self-denial is indispensably enjoined us by the rule of the gospel, which we all have solemnly professed. Our backwardness in fulfilling this duty is owing to our lukewarmness, which creates in everything imaginary difficulties and magnifies shadows. St Clare, notwithstanding her austerities, the opposition she had suffered, and the pains of a sharp and tedious disease, was surprised when she lay on her death-bed to hear anyone speak of her patience, saying that from the time she had first given her heart to God she had never met with anything to suffer or to exercise her patience. Such was the effect of her burning charity. Let none seek to enter her order, or any other, without a fervour which inspires a cheerful eagerness to comply in the most perfect manner with all its rules and exercises and without seriously striving to obtain, and daily improve in their souls, her spirit of poverty, humility, obedience, silence, mortification, recollection, prayer, and divine love. In these consist their sanctification ; in these alone they will find all present and future blessings and happiness.

A vast literature has grown up around the story of St Clare, but the sources themselves, apart from the Saint's connection with general Franciscan history, are not overwhelmingly abundant. First comes the Life commonly attributed to Thomas of Celano which must have been written before 1261, that is, at latest, within eight years of her death. The short metrical Life adds nothing of any value, but there are occasional references in the so-called *Speculum Perfectionis* (see the second edition published by the British Society of Franciscan Studies, Manchester, 1928), in the *Actus B. Francisci*, (which supplies so much of the material of the *Fioretti*,) and in other early documents. Besides these we have a few letters written by St Clare, we have the Rule which bears her name, and her " Testament," with a certain number of papal bulls. An early Life of the Saint in English was translated from a compilation by Francis Hendricq, and printed at Douai in 1635 under the title of " The History of the Angelicall Virgin, glorious S. Clare " and dedicated to the Queen's Most Excellent Majesty (*i.e.* Queen Henrietta Maria). But there have been many admirable books in English since then. It must suffice to mention " The Life of S. Clare ascribed to Thomas of Celano," translated by Fr. Paschal Robinson, which also contains a translation of the Rule of St Clare, Philadelphia, 1910. E. Gilliat Smith, *St Clare of Assisi*, London, 1914 ; C. Balfour, *The Life and Legend of the Lady St Clare*, London, 1910. From a more erudite point of view the *Archivum Franciscanum Historicum*, vols. vi, vii, xii, and xiii, contains several valuable articles, particularly that on the canonisation of the Saint in vol. xiii (1920), pp. 403-507.

ST EUPLIUS, Mart.

A.D. 304

On August 12, 304, during the persecution of Diocletian, at Catania in Sicily, Euplius, a deacon, was brought to the governor's hall and, while waiting outside the curtain, cried out, " I am a Christian, and shall rejoice to die for the name of Jesus Christ." The governor, Calvisian, heard him and ordered that he who had made that noise should be brought in. Euplius went in with the book of the gospels in his hand. One of Calvisian's friends, named Maximus, said to the deacon, " You ought not to keep such writings, contrary to the edicts of the emperors." Calvisian asked, " Where did you get those writings ? Did you bring them from your own house ? " Euplius replied that he had no house, but that he was seized with the book about him. The judge bid him read something in it. The martyr opened it, and read : " Blessed are they that suffer persecution for justice' sake, for theirs is the kingdom of Heaven." And in another place, " If any man will come after Me, let him deny himself and take up his cross, and follow Me." The judge asked what that meant. The martyr answered, " It is the law of my Lord, which has been delivered to me." Calvisian said, " By whom ? " Euplius answered, " By Jesus Christ, the Son of the living God." Calvisian then ordered, " Since his confession is evident, let him be examined on the rack." This was immediately done, and while they were torturing him Calvisian asked him whether he persisted in his Christianity. Euplius, making the sign of the cross on his forehead with the hand that he had at liberty, said, " What I said before I say again : that I am a Christian and read the holy Scriptures," and added that he durst not deliver up the sacred writings, by which he would offend God ; that death was preferable and thereby he would gain eternal life. Calvisian ordered him to be more cruelly tormented, and the martyr cried out, " I thank Thee, O Lord Jesus Christ, that I suffer for Thy sake : save me, I beseech Thee." Calvisian said, " Lay aside this folly ; adore our gods, and you shall be set at liberty." Euplius answered, " I adore Jesus Christ and I detest the false gods. Do what you please ; torture me anew ; for I am a Christian and I have long desired to suffer for Christ." After the executioners had tormented him a long time, Calvisian told them to stop, and addressing Euplius said, " Wretched man, worship Mars, and Apollo, and Æsculapius." Euplius replied, " I adore the Father, the Son, and the Holy Ghost. I worship the Holy Trinity, and there is no other god." Calvisian said, " Sacrifice, if you would be set free." The martyr answered, " I sacrifice myself now to Jesus Christ, my God. All your efforts to move me are wasted. I am a Christian." Whilst the executioners were exerting their utmost Euplius prayed thus, " I thank Thee, my God. Jesus Christ, help me! It is for Thy name's sake that I suffer." This he repeated several times. When his strength failed him, his lips were seen still to move, continuing the same or the like prayer with his lips when he could no longer do it with his voice. At length Calvisian went behind the curtain and dictated his sentence, which a secretary wrote. Afterward he came out with a tablet in his hand, and read it : " I command that Euplius, a Christian, be put to death by the sword, for defying the emperor's edicts, blaspheming the gods, and not repenting. Take him away." The executioners hung the book of the gospels, which the martyr had with him when he was seized, about his neck, and the public crier proclaimed before him, " This is Euplius the Christian, an enemy to the gods and the emperors." But Euplius was full of joy, and repeated as he went, " Thanks be to Jesus Christ, my God. Confirm, O Lord, what Thou hast wrought in me." When he was come to the place of execution, he once more returned thanks, and bared his neck to the executioner, who cut off his head. The Christians carried off his body, embalmed it with spices, and buried it.

The Acts of Euplus or Euplius make a favourable impression. They exist both in Latin and Greek. The former will be found in the *Acta Sanctorum*, Aug., vol. ii, and in Ruinart; the latter in Cotelerius, *Ecclesiæ Græcæ Monumenta*, vol. i, pp. 192-200. But a much improved edition of both, with other new texts, will be found in *Studi e Testi*, vol. xlix (1928), where P. Franchi de' Cavalieri in the seventh series of his *Note agiografiche* has discussed the whole question. St Euplus is duly entered in the " Hieronymianum," and the notice is discussed in the *Acta Sanctorum*, Nov., vol. ii, part 2, p. 436. The Acts of Euplus are also to be found in Krüger-Knopf, *Ausgewählte Martyrerakten* (1929), a revised and enlarged edition of Knopf's previous collection.

ST MUREDACH or MURTAGH, Bp. and Conf.
Sixth Century (?)

Was of the royal family of Laoghaire, King of Ireland, and is reputed to have been the first bishop in Killala, by the appointment of St Patrick. It seems probable, however, that he lived at a later date, for in the " life " of St Corbmac it is stated that the harbour of Killala was blessed by Patrick, Brigid, Colmcille, Kenny, and Muredach, which, as Canon O'Hanlon says, doesn't sound as if

Patrick and Muredach were contemporaries; moreover, he is stated to have met St Colmcille at Ballysodare, near Sligo, after Colmcille's conference with the Irish king at Drumkeith in 575. St Muredach's feast is kept throughout Ireland. On the same day was venerated another St Muredach, who was a monk at the monastery of Iniskeen in Lough Erne, in the seventh century.

> There seems to be no Life of this Saint either in Latin or Irish; but there is a curiously obscure reference to him on this day in the *Félire* of Œrigus. See also O'Hanlon, *Lives of the Irish Saints*, vol. viii, pp. 177 *seq.*

ST PORCARIUS AND HIS COMPANIONS, MM.

c. A.D. 732

At the beginning of the fifth century the great abbey of Lérins was founded on an island off the coast of Provence now known after the founder as Saint-Honorat, opposite Cannes. By the eighth century the community numbered over five hundred monks, novices, *alumni*, and familiars, and about the year 732 the head of this great body, Abbot Porcarius, the second of that name, was warned that they were threatened by a descent of infidel barbarians from the sea. The mediaeval account of the martyrdom calls these marauders Saracens, that is, probably Moors from Spain or North Africa, but they may have been Norsemen or Danes. Porcarius at once sent off to a place of safety all for whom there was room on ship-board, namely, the *alumni* or boys being educated in the monastery, and thirty-six of the younger religious, and gathered together the remainder of his community and prepared them for death, exhorting them to suffer bravely for the faith of Christ. The pirates landed, broke into the abbey, and slaughtered every one of its inmates with the exception of four, whom they carried off as slaves. St Porcarius and his monks have always been regarded as martyrs: they are mentioned in the Roman Martyrology and their feast is kept in the diocese of Fréjus.

> The texts printed in the *Acta Sanctorum*, August, vol. ii, give all the information which seems obtainable; they are, however, of very late date. See further B. Munke, *Die Vita S. Honorati* (1911) in *Beihefte zur Zeitschrift für romanische Philologie*, No. 32, pp. 23 *seq.*

AUGUST 13

ST HIPPOLYTUS, Mart.

A.D. 258

THE Roman Martyrology to-day mentions that Hippolytus the martyr who is mentioned in the *acta* of St Laurence. According to that very unreliable document Hippolytus was an officer in charge of Laurence when he was in prison for the Faith, and was by him converted and baptized. He assisted at the burial of the martyr, and for so doing was summoned before the Emperor, who rebuked him for disgracing the imperial uniform and commission by " conduct unbecoming an officer and a gentleman," and ordered him to be scourged and otherwise tortured. At the same time St Concordia, the nurse of Hippolytus, and nineteen others were beaten to death with leaded whips. St Hippolytus himself was sentenced to be torn apart by horses—a suspicious circumstance in the narrative when we remember the fate of Hippolytus, the son of Theseus who, flying from the anger of his father, met a monster the sight of which affrighted his horses, so that he fell from his chariot and, being entangled in the harness, was dragged along and torn to pieces. No sooner was the order given in respect of the converted soldier but the people set themselves to work in assisting the executioners. Out of the country, where untamed horses were kept, they took a pair of the most furious and unruly they could meet with, and tied a long rope between them to which they fastened the martyr's feet. Then they provoked the horses to run away by loud cries, whipping and pricking them. The last words which the martyr was heard to say as they started were, " Lord, they tear my body ; receive Thou my soul." The horses dragged him away furiously into the woods, through brooks and over ditches, briers, and rocks ; they beat down the hedges, and broke through everything that came in their way. The ground, the thorns, trees, and stones were sprinkled with his blood, which the faithful that followed at a distance weeping, dipped up from every place with kerchiefs, and they gathered together all the mangled parts of his flesh and limbs which lay scattered about.

This story would appear to be a romance, and the martyr Hippolytus commemorated by the Church on this day is probably a

Roman priest who lived during the early part of the third century. He was a man of great learning and the most important theological writer in the early days of the Roman Church. He is said to have been a disciple of St Irenæus and of Clement of Alexandria; St Jerome called him a " most holy and eloquent man "; St John Chrysostom praises him as a " source of light, a faithful witness, a most virtuous teacher, and a man full of sweetness and charity "; Theodoret ranks him with St Irenæus as a " spiritual fountain of the Church." St Hippolytus censured Pope St Zephyrinus for being, in his opinion, not quick enough to detect and denounce heresy, and on the election of his successor, St Callistus I, he severed communion with the Roman Church and permitted himself to be set up as an anti-pope. With Pope St Pontian he was banished to Sardinia during the persecution of Maximinus in 235, and was reconciled to the Church. He died a martyr by his sufferings on that unhealthy island, and his body was afterwards translated to the cemetery of St Cyriaca on the Via Tiburtina. Prudentius who, led astray by the inscription of Pope St Damasus over his grave, confuses this Hippolytus with a priest of that name who was led away by the Novatian schism but went to martyrdom repudiating his errors, testifies that as often as he had prayed at the tomb of St Hippolytus for the remedy of his infirmities, whether of body or mind, he had always found relief; but professes that he was indebted to Christ for all favours received, because He gave to his martyr Hippolytus the power to obtain for him the divine succour. He adds that the chapel which contained the relics shone within with silver, and on the outside with bright marble like glass, the whole being ornamented with gold. He says that from the rising to the setting of the sun, not only the inhabitants of Rome but many from remote countries resorted to this place to worship God; and that especially on the martyr's festival, on the Ides (13th) of August, both senators and people came thither to implore the divine mercy, and kiss the shrine which contained the relics. " In the morning they rush to greet him; all the youth worship; they come, they go, till the setting of the sun. They press kisses on the shining metal of the inscription; they pour out spices; they bedew his tomb with tears. And when . . . his feast-day returns, what throngs are forced thither by their earnest zeal . . . the wide fields can scarce contain the joy of the people." It is further evidence of the great veneration which St Hippolytus formerly enjoyed that he is named in the canon of the Ambrosian Mass of Milan.*

* In the county of Hertford, two miles south-east from Hitchin, is the village of Ippollitts or Saint Ippolitts (formerly Hippolits, Eppalets or

In the year 1551 was dug up in the cemetery of St Hippolytus on the road to Tivoli, under the Vigna Gori (Caetani), a third-century statue of marble, representing the saint sitting in a chair, on the sides of which are inscribed his two Greek cycles, for eight years each ; on the right side is the cycle of the several fourteen days of the moons, and on the left that for the Sundays. On the side of this cycle is engraved a catalogue of St Hippolytus's works. This statue is now in the Lateran museum. The writings of St Hippolytus show how careful the primitive Christians were to have the divine judgement constantly before their eyes, a trait which St John Climacus describes as the character of the true servant of God. By this means they maintained themselves always in fear and penitence ; solicitous and watchful in all their actions. By this they were encouraged to despise a false and transitory world and to suffer with joy torments and every barbarous kind of death rather than consent to sin. Especially in time of temptation this consideration was their shield and defence, according to the rule which St Basil, that great master of a spiritual life, lays down : " If ever you are tempted to sin, call to mind the terrible judgement-seat of God, at which all men must appear."

It is only within the last half-century or so that the true importance of St Hippolytus in the early history of the Roman Church has come to be recognised. Butler had not the data before him, for he wrote a hundred years before the discovery of the *Philosophoumena*, and even the excellent account of Hippolytus in Mgr. Duchesne's *Histoire ancienne de l'Église* (vol. i, pp. 292–323) has to be supplemented by Dom R. H. Connolly's important discovery that the so-called " Egyptian Church Order " dates from Hippolytus and forms the foundation document of the far-famed *Apostolic Constitutions*. (See the Cambridge *Texts and Studies*, vol. viii, No. 4, 1916.) For the personality and writings of the historical presbyter Hippolytus the reader may be referred to Lightfoot, *Apostolic Fathers*, vol. ii, pp. 316–477, and to Amann's excellent article in the *Dictionnaire de Théologie*, vol. vi, cc. 2487–2511. A. d'Alès, *La Théologie de S. Hippolyte* (1906) is also a book of great value. Whether Hippolytus the writer was identical with the Hippolytus venerated at Portus cannot be certainly determined. The fantastic story of the martyrdom by wild horses seems to be a pure invention ; but as Prudentius testifies, there was already a fresco of the incident painted over the tomb. Hippolytus was buried in a

---

Pallets), which takes its name from the parish-church of St Hippolytus. Formerly it had a shrine of the saint to which sick horses were brought, " out of the North Street, through the North Gate, and the North Door of the church, which was boarded on purpose to bring up the horses to the altar." Having regard to the story of the martyrdom and the significance of the name (" horse-leader "), it is natural that the saint should be looked on as a patron of horses and their riders.

cemetery on the Via Tiburtina, opposite to that of St Laurence, and a story had to be fabricated for him in order to complete the Laurentian cycle. See especially Delehaye in the *Acta Sanctorum*, November, vol. ii, part 2, pp. 439–440 ; and H. Leclercq in *Dictionnaire d'Archéologie*, vol. vi, cc. 2409–2483.

ST CASSIAN, Mart.
A.D. 304 (?)

In a single feast with St Hippolytus the Church joins St Cassian, though there was no connection between the two martyrs. He was a Christian schoolmaster, and taught children to read and write at Imola, a city twenty-seven miles from Ravenna in Italy. A violent persecution being raised against the Church, probably that of Diocletian, he was taken up, and interrogated by the governor of the province. As he constantly refused to sacrifice to the gods, the barbarous judge, learning of what profession he was, commanded that his own scholars should stab him to death with their iron pens.* He was exposed naked in the midst of two hundred boys, " by whom," says the Roman Martyrology, " he had made himself disliked by teaching them ! " Some threw their tablets, pens, and knives at his face and head, and often broke them upon his body ; others cut his flesh, or stabbed him with their knives ; and others pierced him with their pens, some only tearing the skin and some penetrating more deeply, or making it their barbarous sport to cut letters out of his skin. Covered with blood and wounded in every part of his body, he cheerfully bade the little fiends not to be afraid and to strike him with greater force ; not meaning to encourage them in their sin, but to express the willingness he had to die for Christ. He was buried by the Christians at Imola, where afterward his relics were honoured with a rich shrine. Prudentius tells us that in his journey to Rome he visited this martyr's tomb, and before it implored the divine mercy for the pardon of his sins with many tears. He mentions a picture of this saint's martyrdom over the altar, representing his cruel death in the manner he has recorded it in verse. Through an error this St Cassian is venerated at Brixen in Tirol as first bishop and apostle of Seben, a see that no longer exists.

* At that time it was the custom in schools to write upon wax laid on a board of box wood, in which the letters were formed with an iron *stylus* or pen, sharp at one end but blunt and smooth at the other, to erase what was to be effaced or corrected.

On this same day the Roman Martyrology mentions another St Cassian, Bishop of Todi, said to have been martyred under Diocletian ; there is confusion between him and the above. And on the previous day is commemorated a St Cassian who was bishop of Benevento in the fourth century.

The " Passio " of the martyr, printed in Mombritius, seems merely to be a prose resetting of Prudentius' poem in *Peristephanon IX*. The stylus-prodding by schoolboys is probably a reminiscence of an incident in Apuleius (see P. Franchi de' Cavalieri, *Hagiographica*, p. 124) and bears a more than suspicious resemblance to the torture of St Mark of Arethusa (see vol. iii of this series, p. 433). But of the historical existence of the martyr of Imola there can be no reasonable doubt. See Lanzoni, *Le Leggende di S. Cassiano d'Imola in Romagna*, 1913 ; *Didaskaleion* (1925), pp. 1–44 ; and Delehaye in *Acta Sanctorum*, November, vol. ii, part 2, pp. 440–441.

ST SIMPLICIAN, Bp. of Milan, Conf.

A.D. 400

When a priest of the Roman Church of advanced age and corresponding experience, this Simplician was sent by Pope St Damasus to Milan in 375 as adviser to St Ambrose, then newly elected to that see. He was distinguished not only by that responsible trust but also by the friendship of St Augustine, in whose life he played an important part. To him Augustine gave an account of the round of his wanderings and errors, and mentioned his reading certain books of the Platonists, which had been translated into Latin by Victorinus, who had been professor of rhetoric in Rome and died a Christian. Simplician commended his choice of these books, and related to him how he himself had been instrumental in the conversion of Victorinus, that very learned old man, who taught most of the senators of Rome and had the honour of a statue set up in the Forum. A fear of offending his friends, from whom he apprehended great storms of malice would fall upon him, made him defer his baptism for some time ; but being encouraged by Simplician he overcame that temptation and, trampling the world under his feet, was instructed and baptised by him. When Julian the Apostate forbade Christians to teach the sciences, Victorinus quitted his school. Augustine was strongly touched by so generous an example, but he envied the happiness of Victorinus more than he admired his courage; for he was still held captive under the slavery of his passions. But the influence of St Simplician and the example of Victorinus led Augustine perceptibly nearer to his own conversion in 386. In several places in his writings St Ambrose praises the learning, the prudent judgement, and glowing faith of Simplician, and when he was dying, overhearing someone suggest the priest as his successor, he cried out emphatically, " Simplician is old, but he is a good man." Simplician in fact succeeded to the see of Milan, but survived to govern it for only three years. Being troubled by certain difficulties found in St Paul's epistle to the Hebrews he referred them to St Augustine; his work *Quæstiones diversæ ad Simplicianum* was written in reply. One of the devotional practices of St Simplician (and of St Ambrose and St Augustine) was the wearing of a black leather belt on account of a vision said to have been experienced by St Monica in which our Lady told her to wear such an one in her honour. This belt was adopted as part of the habit of the Augustinian friars. St Simplician is named on August 16 in the Roman Martyrology, but the friars just mentioned and other congregations keep his feast on the 13th; neither date is that of his death, which took place in May.

There is no early Life of Simplician, but some later accounts with references to SS. Ambrose and Augustine and a quotation from Enuodius will be found in the *Acta Sanctorum*, August, vol. iii.

ST RADEGUNDE, Matron and Queen

A.D. 587

" The figure of St Radegunde," writes M. Godefroid Kurth in his Life of St Clotilde, " is undeniably the most authentic and the best known of her century. All the light which history throws on that period converges on her personality, since her life has been traced by two biographers who lived on intimate terms with her, without counting Gregory of Tours, who was in the ranks of her respectful admirers." She was born in 518 at Erfurt, the daughter of Berthaire, a pagan king of part of Thuringia in Germany, who was assassinated by his brother, Hermenfrid. In 531 Theoderic, King of Austrasia, and his half-brother, Clothaire I, King of Neustria, fell upon Hermenfrid, vanquished him, and carried home a great booty. Among the prisoners, Radegunde, then about twelve years old, fell to the lot of King Clothaire, who is said to have had her instructed in the Christian religion and baptised, but it is more probable that she was already a Christian when she was seized from her father. Until her eighteenth year she lived at Athies, near Péronne, distinguished for her personal beauty, her goodness, and her devotion to religion;

and then she was called to Vitry to become the wife of the King. Clothaire I was the youngest son of Clovis, the first Christian king of the Franks, but he was a man of shocking character, " sensual and a brute," the Abbé Aigrain justly calls him. His matrimonial alliances have never been properly disentangled ; he was married at least five times and it is even possible that his union with Radegunde was polygamous. She bore her lot with fortitude and, though now become a queen, she continued no less an enemy to dissipation and vanity than she was before, and divided her time chiefly between the church and care of the poor, the sick, and captives. She also founded a hospital for lepers, whom she waited on herself, and was one day seen kissing their diseased bodies. A friend remonstrated, saying that after that no one would dare kiss her. " If you don't want to kiss me, I really do not mind at all," retorted Radegunde. Clothaire allowed her full liberty in her devotions ; but after his affection began to be alienated from her he reproached her for her pious exercises, saying he had married a nun rather than a queen, who converted his court into a monastery. His complaints were unjust ; for she made it the first point of her devotion never to be wanting in any duty of her state and to show the King all possible complaisance. She accepted his infidelities and taunts on her childlessness with patience and courtesy, but after six years of marriage Clothaire committed a crime which Radegunde could not overlook : he murdered her brother, who had been captured with herself at the battle of the Unstrut and of whom she was very fond.

Radegunde asked her husband's leave to retire from the court, which was granted. Whether she had already made up her mind not to return but concealed this from Clothaire, as some authorities state, is not certain ; he had given her ample grounds for separation. But, once gone, she fled to Noyon and asked the bishop, St Médard, to give her the religious veil. He hesitated, for she was in a somewhat equivocal position and the King was notoriously violent and unscrupulous. But when she appeared before him in church, dressed in a nun's habit, and charged him, " If you will not consecrate me you fear man more than God, and He will ask you an account of my soul," Médard gave in and consecrated her a deaconess. After a pilgrimage to the tomb of St Martin at Tours St Radegunde first withdrew to Saix, an estate which the King had given her in Poitou, living a penitential life there for six months ; she employed almost her whole revenue in alms, and served the poor with her own hands. She went after to Poitiers, and there built a monastery of nuns, of which she arranged for a friend, named Agnes, to be made the first abbess, and paid her an implicit obedience, not reserving to herself the disposal of the least thing. King Clothaire about this time went as far as Tours with his son Sigebert, upon a religious pretence but intending to go to Poitiers and carry her again to court. She was alarmed, and wrote to St Germanus of Paris, beseeching his help. The bishop went to the King and, throwing himself at his feet before the tomb of St Martin, implored him to leave his innocent wife alone. Germanus's interference was so effectual that Clothaire sent him to Poitiers to beg Radegunde's forgiveness for him and her prayers that he might find God's pardon also. His better frame of mind was only passing ; among other subsequent enormities he burned alive in a cottage his own son and grandchildren. He is said to have died penitent, but it is not surprising to read that during his last illness he showed great alarm and disturbance of mind at the remembrance of his crimes ; but he left St Radegunde in peace and was even a benefactor of her monastery. This abbey, at first called St Mary's, but afterwards Holy Cross, was one of the first double monasteries, for men and women, in the West, and on this account was also one of the first to insist on a strict and permanent enclosure. The rule chosen was that of St Cæsarius of Arles, in accordance with which the nuns had to spend two hours every day in study, and Radegunde herself knew Latin and some Greek ; under her influence Holy Cross became a meeting-place for scholars and, traditional accompaniment of learning, a centre for the maintenance of peace. Whenever rumours of war were heard, St Radegunde sent letters to the combatants, urging them in the name of Christ to desist ; but she used violence unsparingly to her own body. St Cæsaria the Younger, abbess of St John's at Arles, sent to Poitiers with a copy of the Cæsarian rule a letter of advice for the nuns. In it she says that persons who desire sincerely to serve God must apply themselves earnestly to prayer, asking continually of God that He will be pleased to make known to them His holy will, and directs them to follow it in all things ; that they must diligently hear, read, and meditate on the word of God, which is infinitely more precious than that of men, and a mine which can never be exhausted ; that they must never cease praising God, and giving Him thanks for His mercies ; that they must give alms to the utmost of their ability, and must practise austerities according to the rule of obedience and discretion. She prescribes that every nun shall learn the psalter by heart, and be able to read ; and she gives the strictest caution to be watchful against particular friendships or familiarities in communities.

St Radegunde wrote to a council of bishops that was assembled at Tours in 567, asking them to confirm the foundation and rule of her monastery, which they did. She had already enriched the church she had built with the relics of a great number of saints, but was very desirous to procure a particle of the true cross of our Redeemer, and sent clerks to Constantinople, to the Emperor Justin, for that purpose. The Emperor sent her a piece of that sacred wood, adorned with gold and precious stones, a book of the Gospels beautified in the same manner, and the relics of several saints. They were carried to Poitiers, and deposited in the church of the monastery in the most solemn manner, with a great procession, wax tapers, incense, and singing of psalms; this ceremony was carried out, at the command of King Sigebert, by St Euphronius, Archbishop of Tours, the Bishop of Poitiers having for some reason refused to have anything to do with it. It was for that occasion that St Venantius Fortunatus composed the hymn, *Vexilla regis prodeunt*, which was solemnly sung for the first time on this 19th November, 569. Venantius was at that time a priest of Poitiers, and a close friend of St Radegunde, whose "life" he wrote; he corresponded freely with her and the Abbess Agnes, writing letters to them in Latin verse about their austerities and their health, acknowledging gifts of food and sending in return flowers.

Much of Radegunde's last years was spent in complete seclusion, and she died peacefully on August 13, 587. "When we heard of her death," writes St Gregory of Tours, "we went to the monastery which she had founded at Poitiers. We found her lying in her coffin, her face shining with a brightness surpassing the beauty of lilies and roses. Around her stood nuns to the number of about two hundred, who, inspired by the words of the saint, led a perfect life within their cloister. In the world many of them had belonged to senatorial families, and some of them were even of royal blood." The nun Baudonivia, who had been brought up by St Radegunde and was present at her funeral, relates that during it a blind man recovered his sight, and other miracles were attributed to her both before and after death. On one occasion she cured a sick nun, miraculously or not, by giving her a hot bath—for two hours. Following St Cæsarius, she always insisted on the excellent practice of bathing, and when at Saix used to bath sick people twice a week. This Baudonivia wrote a biography of their holy foundress, at the order of her abbess, not, as she says, "to repeat those things which the apostolic bishop Fortunatus wrote in his life of the blessed one, but to record those which he in his prolixity passed over." "Human eloquence," he had written, "has in its astonishment but little power to show in what piety, self-denial, charity, sweetness, humility, uprightness, faith and fervour Radegunde lived," but his own eloquence had done its best. St Radegunde is named in the Roman Martyrology and her feast is observed in many places; she is one of the three contitulars of the Cambridge college commonly known as Jesus College.

As stated above, we owe our knowledge of St Radegunde to the Lives by Venantius Fortunatus, and the nun Baudonivia, together with certain passing references in Gregory of Tours. The two former sources have been edited, after Mabillon and the Bollandists, by Bruno Krusch in the *Monumenta Germaniæ, Scriptores rerum Meroving.*, vol. ii, pp. 364–395. There are modern Lives by Leroux (1877) and Briand (1899), but that by the Abbé R. Aigrain in the series "Les Saints" is mentioned with high commendation in the *Analecta Bollandiana*, vol. xxxix (1921), pp. 192–194. For English readers attention may be called to F. Brittain, *St Radegund, Patroness of Jesus College, Cambridge* (1925), and to a re-edition (1926) of an English poem (probably by Henry Bradshaw), *the Lyfe of Seynt Radegunde*, published originally by R. Pynson about 1510.

ST MAXIMUS HOMOLOGETES, ABBOT OF CHRYSOPOLIS, MART.

A.D. 662

Maximus is called the Confessor because he gave his life for the Faith, or "the Theologian," for he was one of the foremost divines of the seventh century, a pillar of orthodoxy against the Monothelite heresy, and a zealous supporter of the teaching authority of the Holy See. He was born about the year 580 and belonged to a noble family of Constantinople; when he grew up he was placed at the imperial court and became the principal secretary of the Emperor Heraclius. But after a time he resigned this post (it is likely that he was made uncomfortable by the Emperor's support of what he recognized as heretical opinions) and became a monk at Chrysopolis (now known as Scutari); there he was soon elected abbot of the monastery and wrote some of his mystical treatises. He went into Palestine and Africa to consult St Sophronius, Patriarch of Jerusalem, who had been a hermit and whom Maximus calls his master, father, and teacher, and when the patriarch died, a refugee from the Arabs, at Alexandria in 638 he took his place as the champion of orthodoxy against the Monothelism (the attribution of only one, a divine, will to our Lord) of the Emperor Heraclius and his successor Constans II. He defended the memory of Pope Honorius from the charge of having held that heresy, and in a letter about Pyrrhus, who had been exiled from the see of Constantinople, he says, "If the Roman see recognizes Pyrrhus to be a heretic as well as a reprobate, it is obviously certain that everyone who anathematizes those who have condemned Pyrrhus, anathematizes the see of Rome, that is, the Catholic Church. . . . Let him hasten before all else to satisfy the Roman see, for if it is satisfied all will agree in calling him pious and orthodox . . . [that] Apostolic See which has received universal and supreme dominion, authority, and power of binding and loosing over all the holy churches of God throughout the world, from the incarnate Son of God Himself and also by all holy councils. . . ." In 645 Gregory, the governor of the African province and a friend of Maximus, arranged a public disputation between the saint and Pyrrhus, as the result of which Pyrrhus went to Rome to abjure his Monothelite heresy before Pope Theodore I. Three years later the Emperor Constans II issued a decree in favour of Monothelism, called the *Typos*, and St Maximus went to Rome to assist at the Council of the Lateran summoned by Pope St Martin I, at which this document was condemned. In 653 the Pope was dragged from Rome by the imperial exarch, banished to the Chersonese, and there bullied and starved to death, the last martyred pope. St Maximus remained in Rome until, having argued against the *Typos* before an imperial legate, he too was seized, being now an old man of seventy-five, and carried off to Constantinople. He was put on trial on a charge of conspiring against the Empire; he said that he supported Rome in the matter of the *Typos*, and when it was objected that he thereby condemned the Church of Constantinople he replied, " I condemn no one ; but I would rather lose my life than depart from the least point of the Faith." He was sentenced to banishment at Bizya, in Thrace, where he suffered greatly from cold, hunger, and neglect. After some months a commission was sent to interview him, headed by Theodosius, Bishop of Caesarea in Bithynia. Maximus so eloquently demonstrated to them the two natures in Christ and the depravity of keeping silence on the true faith that Theodosius was convinced, gave the confessor money and some clothes (which were stolen by the Bishop of Bizya), and promised that he would submit to the Holy See. St Maximus was then removed to a monastery at Rhegium, and there arrived the Bishop of Caesarea and another deputation, offering him honours from the Emperor if he would accept the *Typos*. Maximus reminded Theodosius of his promise, which he had ratified " on the holy Gospels, on the cross, and on the image of the Mother of God," to which the bishop could only reply, " What could I do ? The Emperor took another view." Maximus remained firm ; he was struck and spat upon, his money and few other possessions were taken away from him, and the next day he was taken to Salembria and thence to Perberis, where his two friends and supporters, Anastasius the Abbot and Anastasius the Apocrisiarius, were already in captivity.

Here they remained in great hardship and distress for six years, and then were brought back to Constantinople to appear before a tribunal of Monothelites. All three were condemned, and with them the memory of St Martin I and St Sophronius, and they were sentenced to be scourged, to be deprived of their tongues and their right hands, thus mutilated to be pilloried in each of the twelve quarters of the city, and to be imprisoned for life. Tongueless, they could no longer preach the true faith, handless, they could no longer write it ; but they could still confess it by suffering with patience and dying with fortitude. St Maximus survived only a few weeks, after a terrible journey to Schemari, in Colchis on the Black Sea ; one Anastasius died even sooner, but the other lived on until 666. This great confessor of the Faith and supporter of the Holy See suffered thus in his eighty-second year ; he left many writings, including allegorical commentaries on the Scriptures and the works of Denis the Areopagite, a dialogue on the spiritual life between two monks, and a number of letters, and is accounted the father of Byzantine mysticism.

The history of St Maximus is mainly derived from a Greek biography originally edited by Combefis, and now accessible in Migne, *P.G.*, vol. xc, cc. 68–109, followed by letters or tractates of his, and other documents concerning him. But of late years better texts have become available which correct prevailing misconceptions in many details. See especially R. Devreesse in the *Analecta Bollandiana*, vol. xlvi (1928), pp. 5–49. *Cf.* also Mgr. Duchesne, *L'Église au VIème Siècle*, pp. 431–460.

ST WIGBERT, Abbot of Fritzlar, Conf.
c. A.D. 746

There were at least seven missionaries with St Boniface who were named Wigbert, and it is sometimes difficult to distinguish one from another. This one, the most important of them, was an Englishman who, despising the world in his youth, embraced a monastic state. There is a letter extant addressed to the monks of Glastonbury and attributed to this Wigbert, but he does not seem to have belonged to that monastery. About the year 734 St Boniface invited him to join in the labours of the conversion of the Germans, and made him abbot of Fritzlar, a monastery three miles from Cassel. A few years later he was transferred to Ohrdruf, in Thuringia, and he successfully formed and organized both these foundations, himself setting an impeccable example of monastic observance; when called out by duty he spoke to no one on the road, and made haste back to his monastery. His biographer speaks much of St Wigbert's virtues and accomplishments, but tells us little of the events of his life. Towards its end St Boniface gave him permission to return to Fritzlar, where he could live more quietly to prepare himself for death. His last sickness could not make him mitigate the severity of his penances and fasts, and he died about the year 746, famous for miracles. His body was translated to the monastery of Hersfeld by St Lullus, in 780. This saint must not be confused with the St Wigbert, a disciple of St Egbert, who tried to evangelise the Frisians at the end of the seventh century.

The Life, written about 100 years after Wigbert's death by Servatus Lupus, in which the miraculous element is very prominent, after being printed by Mabillon and the Bollandists, was re-edited in Pertz, *Monumenta Germaniae, Scriptores*, vol. xv, pp. 37–43. See also H. Timerding, *Die christliche Frühzeit Deutschlands*, Zweite Gruppe, 1929; and *cf.* Stanton's *Menology*, pp. 391–392.

ST NERSES GLAIËTSI, Katholikos of the Armenians, Conf.

A.D. 1173

Nerses, called the Gracious or Felicitous because of the beauty of his writings, was born at Hromglah in Cilicia, his mother being of the family of St Gregory the Illuminator and his father the Prince Priat. He was educated first by his uncle, the Katholikos Gregory II Vekaiaser, who had favoured the reunion of his heretical church with Rome, and then by a great Armenian doctor, Stephen Manug. Nerses was ordained by his elder brother, the Katholikos Gregory III Pahlawuni, and accompanied him to the Catholic Synod of Antioch in 1139, at which the Latin Patriarch of Jerusalem was deposed for his cruelty and schismatical tendencies. This Gregory, whom both Catholic and dissident Armenians venerate as a saint, was also present at Catholic synods at Jerusalem in 1136 and 1143, and two years after the last sent to Bd. Eugene III legates who on his behalf submitted to the Holy See. When in 1166 Nerses succeeded his brother as katholikos (the fourth of his name), he maintained this union, which, however, was not formally confirmed until the coronation of King Leo II at Tarsus in 1199. Nerses moreover worked for the reconciliation of the Orthodox Greeks, and manifested a militant faith in the primacy of the Roman Pontiff; writing to the Emperor

Manuel Comnenos he refers to the Pope as "the First of all the Archbishops and successor of the apostle Peter." He is the most famous writer of the twelfth-century Armenian renaissance, both in prose and verse; he wrote a book of prayers for every hour of the day and poems on religious and historical subjects, but his greatest works are his liturgical hymns, which are sung every day in the Armenian Divine Office. In one of them the Roman Church is thus apostrophized: "Thou, O Rome the illustrious and venerable, mother of all cities! Thou, the see of the great Peter, prince of the Apostles! Thou, inviolate Church, immovably built on the rock of Kephas, art invincible by the gates of Hell and art the seal of the guardian of the gates of Heaven!" St Nerses died on August 13, 1173, but his feast is kept on the 3rd, and he is named in the great intercession of the Armenian Liturgy both by Catholics and dissidents.

A full account of St Nerses and of his attitude to Monophysite teaching will be found in Tournebize, *Histoire politique et religieuse de l'Arménie* (1901), especially pp. 239–253. References to Armenian authorities are there supplied. See also Balzy, *Historia doctrinæ christianæ inter Armenos*, pp. 33 *seq.*, and Nilles, *Kalendarium Utriusque Ecclesiæ*, vol. ii, p. 598.

BD. GERTRUDE OF ALTENBERG, Virg.

A.D. 1297

A few weeks after the death in September 1227 of her husband Louis at Otranto, on his way to the crusade in the Holy Land, St Elizabeth of Hungary gave birth in her castle on the Wartberg to their third daughter, who was christened Gertrude. Before his departure on the previous St John's day Bd. Louis had agreed with his wife that their coming child should be dedicated to the service of God as a thank-offering for their years of happiness together: if a boy, with the monks of Romersdorf, if a girl with the Premonstratensian canonesses at Altenberg, near Wetzlar. Friar Conrad of Marburg, under whose direction the Landgravine had put herself and who ruled her rigorously, insisted that this should be done when the child was still short of two years old, and to Altenberg the baby Gertrude was taken. When she grew up she elected to ratify the wish of her parents, by then both dead; she was received into the community, and by the age of twenty-two was abbess. Following in the footsteps of her mother, she expended the inheritance she received from her uncle, the Margrave of Meissen, on building a new church for her monastery and an almshouse for the poor; the conduct of the last she made her own personal business and, at a time when abbesses, especially royal abbesses, tended to be very great ladies indeed, was in her works and mortifications indistinguishable from the other nuns. During the seventh crusade Bd. Gertrude, in memory of her father's chivalry, " took the cross," on behalf of herself and her community : not indeed with the obligation of going to the Holy Land, but binding themselves to support it unweariyingly by their prayers and penances. She also obtained permission for the celebration of the feast of Corpus Christi in her monastery ; this was in 1270 and she was in consequence one of the first to introduce it into Germany. When Dietrich the Dominican was writing his *vita* of St Elizabeth of Hungary in 1289 he noted that her daughter the Abbess Gertrude was still living, and she lived on for another eight years, dying in the fiftieth year of her abbacy. Her feast was granted to Altenberg by Pope Clement VI half a century afterwards, and is now kept by the Premonstratensians and in the diocese of Trier.

See the *Acta Sanctorum*, August, vol. iii, and *cf.* the *Stimmen aus Maria Laach* (1893), ii, pp. 415 *seq.* Most Lives of St Elizabeth of Hungary contain some notice of Blessed Gertrude.

BD. FRANCIS OF PESARO, Conf.
vulgo Bd. Cecco
A.D. 1350

Cecco was born in Pesaro and, his parents having died and left him well off, he determined while still a young man to devote his wealth to the needy and himself to God. Accordingly in the year 1300 he joined the third order of St Francis, and retired to a hermitage which he had built on the slope of Monte San Bartolo, by Pesaro. Here he soon had a number of disciples, to whom he carefully taught the principles of the solitary life, detachment from the world, subjection of the body to the spirit by mortification, and union with our Lord, without which all else is useless. To help support his followers he begged from place to place, and so became known and loved far and wide for his goodness and benevolence. Bd. Francis, who was more usually known to his friends as Cecco, lived thus for some fifty years, and a number of remarkable occurrences were associated with his name. Having been with his disciples to Assisi to gain the Portiuncula indulgence on the feast of the dedication of St Mary of the Angels, he was detained in Perugia and sent his companions on before him ; to their astonishment he was there waiting for them when they arrived at the hermitage. However, this does not necessarily mean anything more than that he had a good knowledge of short-cuts across the country; such simple incidents as this in the lives of the saints have been too easily magnified into miracles by enthusiastic biographers. Bd. Francis was not at all "stand-offish" and would sometimes accept invitations to dine with people in the world; but on these occasions he took great care not to give way to any excessive pleasure in unaccustomed good food, and dealt mercilessly with any sign of gluttony in himself: nor was he slow in rebuking this failing in others. Once when he was ill he lost his appetite altogether, and his followers killed a cockerel, intending to cook it carefully in the hope of thereby coaxing him to eat. But Francis missed the bird's crowing and enquired after it, and when he was told that it had been killed, he rebuked them. "You ought," he said, "to have been too grateful to it for its crowing at midnight and dawn to have taken its life away, even though it was out of your kind compassion to myself. Its voice in the morning was a reproach to my laziness and stirred me to be up and about in the Lord's service." His biographer goes on to say that he prayed over the cockerel, which was not only dead but plucked, and its life was restored, together with its plumage! Bd. Francis helped Bd. Michelina Metelli to found the Confraternity of Mercy at Pesaro and build a hospice for tramps and pilgrims at Almetero. He also founded another hermitage, dedicated in honour of our Lady, on Monte Granaio, and here he was called to his reward; his body was laid in the cathedral of Pesaro and his ancient *cultus* confirmed by Pope Pius IX.

There is a short medieval biography printed in the *Acta Sanctorum*, August, vol. i. See also Mazara, *Leggendario Francescano* (1679), vol. ii, pp. 199–202, and Léon, *Auréole Séraphique* (Eng. trans.), vol. ii, pp. 547 *seq*.

BD. WILLIAM FREEMAN, Mart.

A.D. 1595

William Freeman (*alias* Mason) was born in the East Riding of Yorkshire about 1558. He was educated at Magdalen College, Oxford, where he took his B.A. degree in 1581, and then lived for a time in London. He had been brought up a Catholic, but took to outward conformity with the new religion until 1586. In that year he was present at the martyrdom of Bd. Edward Stransham at Tyburn, and he was so deeply impressed that he at once went over to Rheims and was ordained in the following year. He was sent to England in 1589 and worked for six years on the borders of Worcestershire and Warwickshire, where he was in touch with several of the friends of Shakespeare. He was then engaged by a Mrs. Heath of Stratford-on-Avon to be tutor to her son, but in January 1595 a special commission was sent to search her house at the instance of Whitgift, Archbishop of Canterbury, and Mr. Freeman was arrested. He managed to conceal the fact that he was a priest, but he was betrayed by a fellow-prisoner, and at the end of seven months' imprisonment was convicted and sentenced as a seminary priest. He was accordingly hanged, drawn, and quartered at Warwick, on August 13, 1595. Certain criminals were put to death before him and in his presence, in the hope that the terrifying sight would make him apostatize; but he protested that if he had many lives he would most willingly lay them down for the sake of Him who had been pleased to die upon a cross for his redemption, and devoutly recited Psalm xli, " As the hart panteth after the fountains of water."

See Challoner, *Lives of Missionary Priests* (Ed. Pollen), pp. 227–228, and *Publications of the Catholic Record Society*, vol. v, pp. 345–360.

AUGUST 14

ST EUSEBIUS, Conf.

Middle of the Fourth Century

THIS Eusebius was a priest of a patrician family at Rome; his *acta* are extant, but are entirely or in great part spurious. These relate that, Pope Liberius having signed the semi-Arian formula of Sirmium as the price of his permission from the Emperor Constantius for his return to Rome (in itself a matter by no means certain), St Eusebius publicly preached against both the Pope and the Emperor, and celebrated the Holy Mysteries in his own house after he had been forbidden the churches. He was therefore imprisoned in a tiny room of the same house, where he died after seven months. Whatever his true history, he was buried in the cemetery of St Callistus on the Appian Way by his friends Gregory and Orosius, with the inscription over his tomb: " To Eusebius, the Man of God." The church of Sant' Eusebio on the Esquiline is built over the house wherein he is said to have died; in later martyrologies he is sometimes called a martyr.

Every Christian, however lowly his estate in this world, should remember that an eternal kingdom, compared to which all the sceptres of the earth are nought, is offered him by God, and that it is in his power, through the divine grace, to obtain it; for Heaven is justly called in the holy Scriptures a kingdom, and all its glorious inhabitants are kings, God communicating to every one of them a full partnership in that honour, in an entire possession of overflowing joy, of all honour, power, and liberty of doing and commanding, according to their own will, which is in all things subject and conformable to the divine. Our faith must be weak if we do not, with the saints, labour unceasingly to make sure our election; if we do not find joy in the suffering and disgrace here by which we purchase eternal glory; and if we do not scorn from our hearts this little point of the earth, with all its empty enjoyments and false promises, using its goods only as steps to conduct us to God's kingdom, which is framed by His almighty hand to display His infinite power, love, and goodness towards His faithful servants to all eternity.

This is one of the cases in which we have clear evidence of the historical existence of a person who was afterwards the object of a certain *cultus*, though the story subsequently told is quite untrustworthy. Eusebius beyond doubt founded what we may call a parish church in Rome which was known as the " titulus Eusebii." As founder an annual commemorative Mass was offered for him, which in course of time was regarded as a Mass celebrated in his honour, and in 595 we find that the parish was always referred to as the " titulus sancti Eusebii." See Delehaye, *Sanctus* (1927), p. 149; and also Mgr. Wilpert in *Römische Quartalschrift*, vol. xxii, pp. 80–82; J. P. Kirsch, *Die römischen Titelkirchen*, pp. 58–61; with the whole discussion in *Acta Sanctorum*, Nov., vol. ii, part 2, pp. 443–444.

ST EUSEBIUS, Mart.
End of the Third Century

In the reign of Diocletian and Maximian, before they had published any new edicts against the Christians, Eusebius, a holy priest, suffered death for the faith, probably in Palestine. An information was lodged with Maxentius, governor of the province, against Eusebius, because he had distinguished himself by his zeal in preaching Christ, and he was brought before him. Maxentius, whom the people stirred up against the servant of Christ, said to him, " Sacrifice to the gods freely, or you shall be made to do it against your will." The martyr replied, " There is a greater law which says : Thou shalt worship the Lord thy God, and Him alone shalt thou serve." Maxentius urged, " Choose! Either sacrifice or suffer torture." Eusebius answered, " It is not consistent with reason for a person to worship stones." " These Christians are a hardened race," said Maxentius, " it seems to them more desirable to die than to live." " Because it is impious to despise the light for the sake of darkness," replied Eusebius, and the governor turned on him, saying angrily, " You grow more obstinate under kindness and entreaties. I therefore lay them aside. Unless you sacrifice, you shall be burnt alive." " As to that, I am in no trouble. The more cruel the torments are, the greater will be the crown." At this Maxentius had him racked, and Eusebius only repeated, " Lord Jesus, preserve me. Whether we live or die we are yours." The governor ordered that he should be taken off the rack, and said to him, " Do you know the decree of the senate which commands all to sacrifice to the gods ? " Eusebius answered, " The command of God comes before that of man." Maxentius thereupon commanded that he should be led to the fire as if he were to be burnt alive.

Eusebius walked out with a composure which struck the bystanders with amazement, and the prefect called after him, " You go to an unnecessary death ; your obstinacy astonishes me. Change your mind." The martyr said, " If the Emperor commands me to worship dumb metal in contempt of the true God, let me appear before him." This he said, knowing the Emperor Maximian was in the neighbourhood, and because he was impeached upon old laws, the present emperors not having yet made any new ones against the Christians. Maxentius therefore said to his guards, " Keep him till to-morrow " : and forthwith went to the Emperor, to whom he said, " I have found a seditious man who is disobedient to the laws, and even denies to my face that the gods have any power, and refuses to sacrifice or to adore your name." The Emperor said he would like to see him, but one present, who had seen him at the prefect's tribunal, said, " If you see him, you will be moved by his speech." " Is he such a man that he can change even me ? " asked Maximian, and Maxentius replied, " He will change not only you, but the minds of all the people. If you once see him you will feel yourself strangely moved in his favour." The Emperor, however, ordered that he should be brought in, and when he saw Eusebius he fixed his eyes steadfastly on him as if he beheld in him something divine, and at length spoke thus, " Old man, why are you brought before me ? Speak, and be not afraid." Seeing him still silent, he repeated, " Speak freely ; answer my questions. I desire your safety." Eusebius answered, " If I hope to be saved by man, I can no longer expect salvation from God. If you excel in dignity and power we are, nevertheless, all mortal alike. Neither will I be afraid to repeat before you what I have already declared. I am a Christian, and cannot worship wood and stone ; but I most readily obey the true God whom I know, and whose goodness I have experienced." The Emperor said to the president, " What harm is it if this man worships the God of whom he speaks, as above all others ? " " Be not deceived, O Emperor," answered Maxentius, " he does not call what you imagine God, but some Jesus or other, whom our people and fathers never knew." Then the Emperor said, " Go you forth, and judge him according to justice and the laws. I will not be judge in this business." This Maximian was a rough and savage man, yet the undaunted and modest goodness of this stranger struck him with awe. He wished to save Eusebius but, like Pilate, would not give himself any trouble or risk incurring the criticism of those whom on other occasions he despised. So cowardly are worldly and wicked men in the practice of virtue, who in vice are unbridled and daring.

Maxentius ascended his tribunal, and for the last time commanded Eusebius to sacrifice to the gods. He answered, " I will never sacrifice to those which can neither see nor hear." Maxentius again threatened him with fire and torture, saying, "He whom you fear is not able to deliver you from them," to which Eusebius replied, "Neither fire nor the sword will work any change in me. Tear my body to pieces, do what you will with it. My soul is God's and cannot be hurt by your torments. I persevere in the holy law to which I have belonged from my cradle." Then he was condemned to be beheaded, and he said aloud, "I thank Thy goodness and praise Thy power, O Lord Jesus Christ, that by calling me to the trial of my fidelity Thou hast treated me as one of Thine own," and he heard as it were a voice from Heaven saying to him, "If you had not been found worthy to suffer, you could not be admitted into the court of Christ and to the seats of the just." Being come to the place of execution, he knelt down, and his head was struck off.

On the 12th August is commemorated another ST EUSEBIUS, Bishop of Milan, who opposed the Monophysites, repaired the ravages of the Huns, and died about the year 462.

A strange obscurity rests upon this martyr. There seem to be no indications of *cultus*, but Butler has translated the alleged Acts (printed in the *Acta Sanctorum*, August, vol. iii) almost entire.

ST MARCELLUS, BP. OF APAMÆA, MART.
A.D. 389

Among the undertakings of the Emperor Theodosius the Great was the attempt completely to Christianize the Roman Empire, and in 380 he and the co-emperor, Gratian, issued a decree that all their subjects were to profess the faith of the Bishops of Rome and Alexandria. Eight years later he sent an officer into Egypt, Palestine, Syria, and Asia Minor, whose duty it was to enforce an edict that all pagan temples were to be destroyed; this violent policy, doubtless made necessary by conditions obtaining in those times, was carried out very roughly and not unnaturally aroused the anger and resentment of the pagans. When the imperial prefect arrived at Apamæa in Syria he set his soldiers to work to pull down the temple of Zeus there, but it was a large building and well built and the soldiers, being inexpert at systematic demolition, made little progress. The bishop of the place was one Marcellus, who had been governor of Cyprus until in 381 the people and clergy of Apamæa had chosen him for their ecclesiastical head; he told the prefect to take off his men to their next job and in his absence means would be sought efficiently to destroy the temple. The very next day a navvy came to the bishop and said that, if he would pay him double wages, he could do the work himself. St Marcellus agreed, and the man proceeded to demolish the temple by the simple device of undermining some of the supporting columns, holding up the foundations with timber, and then burning it away, in much the same way as a tall chimney-stalk is brought down to-day. Marcellus proceeded to have other temples dealt with in this manner, until he went to that of Aulona, near Apamæa; this building was stoutly defended by those who worshipped in it, and the bishop had " to take up a position some way from the scene of conflict, out of the reach of the arrows, for he suffered from gout and so was not able either to fight or to run away." But while he was watching from this point of vantage, some of the pagans stole a march on him, seized him, and put him to death by setting fire to his clothes. The sons of St Marcellus (he had been married) afterwards wanted to take vengeance on his murderers, but the council of the province forbade them, saying they should rather rejoice that God had accounted their father worthy to die in His cause. St Marcellus is named as a martyr in the Roman Martyrology; the historian Theodoret, who tells the story of the destruction of the temple of Zeus, says that he used to bless water with the sign of the cross, one of the earliest references to holy water. He must not be confused with another St Marcellus, born at Apamæa and abbot in Constantinople, whose feast is observed on 29th December.

The account in the *Acta Sanctorum*, August, vol. iii, seems to have gathered up all that is known concerning this Marcellus. Theodoret, *Eccles. Hist.*, Bk. v, ch. 21, is the main authority.

ST FACHANAN, Bp. and Conf.
End of the Sixth Century

This saint's feast is observed liturgically throughout all Ireland and he is patron of the diocese of Ross, where he was probably the first bishop. He came of the royal family of Corca Laighde and was born at Tulachteann about the year 540. He was one of the pupils of St Ita of Killeedy, and founded the monastery of Molana on an island in the Blackwater, near Youghal. But his great achievement was the establishment of the great monastic school of Ross, at what is now Rosscarbery, in county Cork, one of the most famous schools of Ireland, which flourished for three hundred years and survived in some form until the coming of the Normans. Among its professors was St Brendan, who had been a fellow-pupil of Fachanan under St Ita. Fachanan suffered for a time from blindness, from which he recovered at the intercession of Ita's sister, who was about to give birth to St Mochoemoc. St Fachanan was revered as a "wise and upright man," with a great gift for preaching ; St Cuimin of Connor said of him that he was "generous and steadfast, fond of preaching to the people and saying nothing that was base or displeasing to God." The St Fachanan honoured on this day as the patron of Kilfenora diocese may be a different person from him of Ross.

St Fachanan or Fachtna is another Irish saint of whom no early biography survives. He is mentioned, however, on this day in the *Félire* of Œrigus and is described as "son of Mongach, the son of the wright, a fair captive." There is also a passing reference to him and to his school in the Latin life of St Mochæmog. See O'Hanlon, *Lives of the Irish Saints*, vol. viii, pp. 191 *seq.*

ST ATHANASIA, Matron
A.D. 860

She was born on the island of Ægina, in the gulf of that name, and was brought up religiously by her father Nicetas. She married an officer in the army, but only sixteen days after their union he was killed while fighting against the Arabs who had made a descent on the Grecian coast. Athanasia was now anxious to become a nun, especially as she had had a dream or vision in which the passingness of all earthly things had been strongly impressed on her. But she was persuaded by her parents to marry again. Her second husband was a devoted and religious man, and shared in and encouraged his wife's good works. She gave alms liberally and helped the sick, strangers, prisoners, and all who stood in need ; after the Liturgy on Sundays and holy-days she would gather her neighbours round her and read and explain to them a passage from the holy Scriptures. After a time her husband decided he wanted to become a monk, which with Athanasia's consent he did, and she turned her house into a convent, of which she was made abbess. These nuns followed a life of excessive austerity, till at the end of four years they came under the direction of a holy abbot called Matthias ; he found that they had by mortifications reduced themselves to such weakness that they could hardly walk. He therefore insisted to St Athanasia that she should modify the austerities of her subjects, and also arranged for the community to move from their noisy house in a town to one more quiet and suited for monastic life at Timia. Here so many came to them that their buildings had to be enlarged, and the fame of St Athanasia caused her to be called away to the court of Constantinople as adviser to the Empress Theodora. She had to live there for seven years, being accommodated in a cell similar to that which she occupied in her own monastery. She had not been allowed to return to Timia long when she was taken ill ; for twelve days she tried to carry on as usual, but at last she had to send her nuns to sing their Office in church without her, and when they returned their abbess was dying and survived only long enough to give them her blessing. St Athanasia is sometimes called "Anastasia."

The evidence for this history is unsatisfactory, for though the author of the Life which the Bollandists have translated from the Greek (*Acta Sanctorum*, August, vol. iii) claims to be virtually a contemporary, such pretensions are not of themselves convincing. No great *cultus* seems to have existed, but an account of Athanasia is given in some texts of the Synaxaries on April 4. Martinon, *Annus Ecclesiasticus Graeco-Slavicus*, pp. 107-108, speaks of her on April 12. One point of interest in the Greek life is the stress laid upon the commemoration on the fortieth day after burial, which amongst the Greeks corresponded to the "Month's Mind" in Western lands.

BD. EBERHARD, ABBOT OF EINSIEDELN, CONF.

A.D. 958

Was of the ducal family of Suabia and became provost of the chapter of the cathedral of Strasburg. In the year 934 he gave up this dignity and went to the hermitage of Einsiedeln in Switzerland, to join his friend Bd. Benno, who had been one of his canons at Strasburg and then bishop of Metz. Benno already had a few followers there and the coming of Eberhard, who enjoyed a wide reputation for spiritual wisdom and holiness, considerably increased their numbers. He therefore devoted his fortune to building a monastery to shelter them and a church wherein they might worship, and after the death of Bd. Benno he was recognized as first abbot of the monastery of our Lady of the Hermits. He obtained from the Emperor Otto I confirmation of possession of the abbey lands and recognition of its right to free election of its abbots and exemption from civil and episcopal jurisdiction. In 942 there was a great famine in Alsace, Burgundy, and Upper Germany, and Bd. Eberhard and his monks gave a large supply of corn for the relief of the suffering people. The consecration of the abbey-church of Einsiedeln by our Lord himself, assisted by the four Evangelists, St Peter, and St Gregory the Great, is fabled to have taken place in 948, ten years before the death of Bd. Eberhard. He was buried near Bd. Benno, in the church he had built, and his feast is kept at Einsiedeln Abbey.

See O. Ringholz, *Geschichte desf. Stifts Einsiedeln* (1904), vol. i, pp. 33-43 ; R. Henggeler, *Reliquien der Stiftskirche Einsiedeln* (1927), pp. 7 seq.

BD. ANTONY PRIMALDI AND HIS COMPANIONS, MM.

A.D. 1480

In the year 1480 the Turks under Mohammed II captured and pillaged the city of Otranto in southern Italy, putting to the sword over ten thousand of its inhabitants and defenders, including the archbishop, Stephen Pendinelli, who was sawn apart. Some of these victims are regarded as martyrs, having died for the Faith, principal among them being Bd. Antony Primaldi and the eight hundred who suffered with him. He was an old man, an artizan, and well known in the city as a good workman and a good Christian. When the Turks rounded up those males who had escaped the first massacre, sacking their houses and carrying off their wives, Antony and the others were led out into a valley near the town, and offered the restoration of their liberty, their wives, and their goods if they would apostatize and become Moslems. Bd. Antony, as spokesman for the rest, replied that they confessed there was only one God, and that the Lord Jesus Christ was His divine Son, and that on no account would they abandon that faith. The Turkish general threatened them with fearful torments and some began to waver, seeing which Bd. Antony loudly appealed to them: " We have fought for our city and for our lives. Now we must fight for our souls and for Jesus Christ ; He died for us ; we must die for Him." The waverers rallied to him, and it was ordered that all be beheaded. Bd. Antony was the first to die, and it is said that his headless body remained upright on its feet, as it were to encourage the others, until all the rest were slain. The place where this massacre took place is to this day called the Valley of the Martyrs, and there their bodies lay unburied during the twelve months that the Turks occupied the country. When Otranto was retaken by Alfonso, Duke of Calabria, the apostolic nuncio, Bd. Angelo Carletti, ordered their relics to be transported into the cathedral, and the *cultus* of these martyrs thus begun confirmed was by Pope Clement XIV in 1771.

There is a long account of these martyrs in the *Acta Sanctorum*, August, vol. iii, under the heading " Martyres Hydruntini," at the end of which the evidence of certain witnesses is printed in full. Unfortunately these depositions were not taken until A.D.1539, fifty-nine years after the event ! See also the *Dictionnaire d'Histoire et de Gèographie ecclésiastiques*, vol. iii, cc. 805–806, which gives further references. There seems to be some doubt whether the proper name of the most prominent martyr was Primaldi or Grimaldi.

AUGUST 15

THE BLESSED VIRGIN MARY
On the Feast of her Assumption into Heaven
First Century a.d.

ON this festival the Church commemorates the happy falling asleep of the Virgin Mary, and her translation into the kingdom of her Son, in which she received from Him a crown of immortal glory and a throne above all the other saints and heavenly spirits. After Christ, triumphant conqueror of death and Hell, ascended into Heaven, His blessed Mother remained at Jerusalem, persevering in prayer with the disciples till, with them, she had received the Holy Ghost. St John the Evangelist, to whom Christ recommended her on His cross, took her under his protection. The prelates assembled in the general council which was held at Ephesus in 431 mention as the highest prerogative of that city that it had sheltered St John the Evangelist and the Mother of God. Some conjecture that she died at Ephesus; but others think rather at Jerusalem, where in later ages mention is made of her sepulchre, cut in a rock at Gethsemani. Nothing is known of the day, year, or manner of her death, but all authorities agree that she lived to a very advanced age, improving daily in perfect charity and all other virtues. She paid the common debt of nature, none among the children of Adam being exempt from that law. But the death of the saints is rather to be called a sleep than death; much more that of the queen of saints, who had been exempt from all sin.

Mary was a Jewish maiden of the house of David and the tribe of Judah, whose parents are commonly referred to as St Joachim and St Anne. At her conception, that is, when God infused a soul into her embryonic body, she was preserved by Him from all taint of original sin (the Immaculate Conception, 8th Decr.); her birth, which the Church celebrates on September 8, may have taken place at Sepphoris or Nazareth, but a general tradition favours Jerusalem, at a spot adjoining the Pool of Bethesda, close to a gate still called by Mohammedans (but not, curiously enough, by Christians), *Bab Sitti Maryam*, the Gate of the Lady Mary. She is believed to have been a child of promise to her long childless parents, and on 21st November the Church keeps a feast of her presentation in the Temple, though upon what occasion is not certain. According to apocryphal writings she remained within the Temple precincts in order to be brought up with other Jewish children, and at the age of fourteen was betrothed to a carpenter, Joseph, her husband being indicated to the High Priest by a miracle. While still only betrothed she was visited by the archangel Gabriel (the Annunciation, March 25) and the Second Person of the Blessed Trinity became incarnate by the power of the Holy Ghost in her womb. This was at Nazareth, and she now journeyed into Judæa to see her cousin St Elizabeth, who also was with child, St John the Baptist (the Visitation, July 2). The marriage with St Joseph was duly ratified, and in due course, going up with him to Jerusalem for the enrolment ordered by Cæsar Augustus, Mary gave birth in a rock-hewn stable at Bethlehem to Jesus Christ, the God-Man (Christmas Day, December 25). Forty days later, in accordance with the Jewish law, she presented herself and her Child in the Temple for her ritual purification (February 2), an observance abrogated by the law of Christ which sees nought but honour in sanctified child-bearing. Warned by an angel, St Joseph fled with his wife and the holy Child into Egypt, to avoid the jealous rage of King Herod; it is not known how long they lived there, but when Herod was dead they returned to their old home at Nazareth. For the thirty years before the public ministry of Jesus began Mary lived the outward life of any other Jewish woman of the common people. There are some who, concentrating their hearts and minds on our Lady in her glorified state as Queen of Heaven, or as participating in the chief mysteries of the life of her Son, lose all memory of her day by day life as a woman in this world. The sonorous and beautiful titles given to her in the Litany of Loreto; representations of her in art, from the graceful delicate ladies of Botticelli to the prosperous *bourgeoises* of Raphael; the efforts of writers and preachers who feel that ordinary language is inadequate to describe her perfections; these and many other influences help to glorify the Mother of God—but somewhat tend to make us forget the wife of Joseph the carpenter. The Lily of Israel, the Daughter of the princes of Judah, the Mother of all Living, was also a peasant-woman, a Jewish peasant-woman, the wife of a working-man. Her hands were scored with labour, her bare feet dusty, not with the perfumed powder of romance but with the hard stinging grit of Nazareth, of the tracks which led to the well, to the olive-gardens, to the synagogue, to the cliff whence they would have cast Him. And then, after those thirty years, those feet were still tired and dusty, but now with following her divine Son from afar in His public life, from the rejoicings of the wedding-feast at Cana to His dereliction and her desolation on Mount Calvary, when the sword spoken of by Simeon at the purification pierced her heart. The dying Jesus confided her to the care of St John, " and from that hour the disciple took her to his own." Many have supposed that the first appearance of the risen Christ was to His mother; we do not know. It would have been appropriate, but the suggestion of St John's Gospel that the risen Saviour of sinners was first seen by the penitent Mary Magdalen is not less appropriate. On the day of Pentecost the Holy Ghost descended on our Lady when He came upon the Apostles and other disciples gathered together in the upper room at Jerusalem: that is the last reference to her in the sacred Scriptures. The rest of her earthly life was probably passed at Jerusalem, with short sojourns at Ephesus and other places in company with St John and during the times of Jewish persecution.

Mary is the mother of Jesus, Jesus is God, therefore she is the Mother of God; the denial of this was condemned by the third general council at Ephesus in 431. Both before and after her miraculous child-bearing she was a virgin and so remained all her days, according to the unanimous and perpetual tradition and teaching of the Church. That she remained for her whole life absolutely sinless is affirmed by the Council of Trent. As the "second Eve" Mary is the spiritual mother of all living, and veneration is due to her with an honour above that accorded to all other saints; but to give divine worship to her would be idolatry, for Mary is a creature, like the rest of human-kind, and all her dignity comes from God. It is a traditional belief in the Church, not indeed an article of faith but, according to Pope Benedict XIV, a probable opinion the denial of which would be impious and blasphemous, that the body of the Blessed Virgin was preserved from corruption and soon after taken into Heaven and re-united to her soul, by an unique anticipation of the general resurrection. This doctrine can be traced back to the fourth and perhaps to the second century. This preservation from corruption and assumption to glory was a privilege which seems justly due to that sacred body which was never defiled by any sin, which was ever the most holy and pure temple of God, preserved from all contagion of Adam and the common curse of mankind: that body from which the eternal Word received His own flesh, by whose hands He was nourished and clothed on earth, and whom He vouchsafed to obey and honour as His mother. So great was the respect and veneration of the Fathers towards this most exalted of all creatures that St Epiphanius dared not affirm that she ever died, because he had never found any mention of her death and because she might have been preserved immortal, and translated to glory without dying. Much more must we receive with deference a tradition so ancient and so well recommended as is this of the corporal assumption of the Virgin Mary.* This festival is in old martyrologies referred to as the Birthday, Death, Falling Asleep, Passing-over, of St Mary. Did it commemorate only the assumption of her soul, and not of her body as well, its object would still be the same. For, as we honour the departure of other saints out of this world, so we have great reason to rejoice and praise God on this day when the Mother of Christ entered into the possession of those joys which He had prepared for her. The assumption of the Virgin Mary is the greatest of all the festivals which the Church celebrates in her honour, and is the titular feast of all churches dedicated in her honour without any special invocation. It is the consummation of all the other great mysteries by which her life was made wonderful; it is the birthday of her true greatness and glory, and the crowning of all the virtues of her whole life, which we admire singly in her other festivals. It is for all these gifts conferred on her that we on this day praise and thank Him who is the author of them, but especially for that glory with which He has crowned her.

Whilst we contemplate the glory to which Mary is raised on this day, we ought for our own good to consider how she arrived at this honour and happiness, that we may walk in her steps. That she should be the mother of her Creator was the most wonderful miracle and the highest dignity; yet it was not properly this that God crowned in her. So near a relation to God had to be adorned with the greatest graces, and Mary's fidelity to them was the measure of her glory. It was her virtue that God considered in the recompense He bestowed upon her: He regarded her charity, her humility, her purity, her patience, her meekness, her paying to God the most perfect homage of worship, love, praise and thanksgiving. Charity, or the love of God, is the queen and the most excellent of all virtues; it is also their *form* or soul: because no other virtue can be meritorious of eternal life unless it proceed from the motive of holy charity. In this consists the perfection of all true sanctity. Mary surpassed all others in sanctity in proportion as she excelled them in charity. This virtue she exercised and improved continually in her soul by

* There is no unequivocal reference to her bodily assumption in the Mass of the feast, but there is in the lessons of the second nocturne of Matins from a sermon of St John Damascene.

the ardour with which she served Christ, both in person and in His members, the poor; by obedience to the divine law in all things; by resignation and sacrifice of herself to God's will; by patience and meekness and prayer. But if charity was the perfection of her sanctity, its groundwork was humility: this was the source of her charity and of all her other virtues by drawing from Heaven those graces into her soul. And it raised her to the highest throne among the blessed, for the assumption of Mary in glory was only the triumph of her humility. Hereof we have the most authentic assurance: "Because He hath regarded the humility of His handmaid: for behold from henceforth all generations shall call me blessed." She was exalted above all other creatures because she was of all the most humble. Therefore did charity and every other virtue strike so deep roots in her heart, and raise their head like a palm-tree in Cades and like a cedar on Libanus; spreading their shade like a cypress on mount Sion, and diffusing their sweet smell as a rose-plant in Jericho, like cinnamon and balm and myrrh. Therefore she ascends so high because in her own estimation of herself she was so low.

The prayers of the Virgin Mary whilst she lived on earth were certainly of great efficacy: more than those of Abraham, Job, or Elias. Now, raised to a state of bliss, she cannot have lost the power to intercede with God for us; on the contrary, it must be much greater, for she is now seated near the throne of mercy. If the angels who are before the throne of God offer our prayers to Him, and themselves pray for us, and if the saints in glory employ their mediation in our favour, shall not the most holy Mother of God do the same? That she is most ready so to do no one can doubt, seeing that among all creatures there never was any charity equal to hers, who bore Charity itself in her womb. She received from Him that zeal for the glory of God and that tenderness and compassion for the souls of poor sinners which surpasses that of angels and men. Now she beholds the divine Essence and is made all love by being transformed in glory and united to Him who is love itself; now she sees all that can kindle her charity, in our miseries, in God's goodness, and in the glory which will redound to Him from our salvation. Can she then forget us? No, certainly. Her compassion for us must be much increased. And if Esther could prevail with Assuerus in favour of her nation; if the woman of Thecua could move David to show mercy to Absalom; if Judith could save her people by her prayers; if the saints both on earth and in Heaven can avert the divine wrath and work wonders, what shall we not be able to obtain through the mediation of Mary? As St Bonaventure repeats from St Bernard: "You have secure access to God where you have the Mother addressing the Son, and the Son the Father on your behalf. She shows to her Son in your favour the breasts which gave Him suck, and He shows to the Father His wounds and open side." The constant doctrine and tradition of the Church throughout all ages recommends to us the practice of invoking this holy Virgin; it would be superfluous and tedious to load these pages with the quotations of those writers who in every age vouch for this article of the Catholic faith, and witness to the homage which the Church, taught by the Holy Ghost, has never failed to pay to the glorious Mother of God. It is confirmed from the watchful care with which the Church has condemned all errors that have been broached contrary to it, whether, on the one hand, of such as those who affirmed that she had not remained a virgin, and that after the birth of Christ she had children by St Joseph, or, on the other, of those who offered up cakes to her, honouring her with sacrifices as a kind of divinity and thus changing piety and devotion into superstition and idolatry.

To discuss in brief space the introduction and development of our Lady's Assumption feast would not be easy. For fuller details the writer of this note must be content to refer to an article of his which appeared in *The Month* for August 1917 (pp. 121–134). Three points seem clear. First that the building of churches in veneration of Mary, the Theotokos, inevitably brought in its train the celebration of some sort of dedication feast. That such churches dedicated to our Lady existed both in Ephesus and at Rome in the first half of the fifth century is certain, and Baumstark (*Römische Quartalschrift*, 1897, p. 55) thinks it probable that " a commemoration of the ever-virgin Mary, Mother of God " was known at Antioch as early as A.D. 370. Secondly in such a commemoration, or annual feast of the Blessed Virgin, no stress was at first laid upon the manner of our Lady's departure from this world. In her case, as in the case of the martyrs and other saints, it was simply the heavenly " birthday " (*natalis*) which was originally honoured, and the festival was spoken of indifferently either as the " birthday," or the " falling-asleep " (*dormitio*), the " passing away " (*transitus*), the " deposition," or the " Assumption." Thirdly, according to an apocryphal but ancient belief, the Blessed Virgin actually died on the anniversary of her Son's birth, *i.e.* on Christmas day. As this day was consecrated to the veneration of the Son, any distinctive commemoration of the Mother had to be postponed. In some parts of the world this separate feast was assigned to the winter season. Thus we know from St Gregory of Tours (*c.* 580) that a great feast in Mary's honour was then kept in Gaul in the middle of January. But it is equally certain that in Syria (see Mrs. Smith Lewis in *Studia Sinaitica*, vol. xi, p. 59) there was a summer feast on the fifth day of the month Ab, roughly August. This, with some fluctuations, was also adopted in the West, and in England St Aldhelm (*c.* 690) speaks plainly of our Lady's " birthday " being kept in the middle of August. See also Cabrol in the *Dictionnaire d'Archéologie*, etc., vol. i, cc. 2995–3001; Jugie in *Échos d'Orient*, vols. xxv, xxvi, and xxix; and Delehaye in *Acta Sanctorum*, November, vol. ii, part 2, pp. 444–445.

ST TARSICIUS, Mart.
Third–Fourth Century

"At Rome, on the Appian Way, the passion of St Tarsicius the acolyte, whom the heathen met bearing the sacrament of the Body of Christ and asked him what it was that he carried. He judged it a shameful thing to cast pearls before swine, and so was attacked by them for a long time with sticks and stones, until he gave up the ghost. When they turned over his body the sacrilegious assailants could find no trace of Christ's sacrament either in his hands or among his clothing. The Christians took up the body of the martyr and buried it with honour in the cemetery of Callistus." Thus the Roman Martyrology sums up the later form of the story of St Tarsicius, " the boy martyr of the holy Eucharist," which is derived from the fourth-century poem of Pope St Damasus, wherein it is stated that one Tarsicius, like another St Stephen stoned by the Jews, suffered a violent death at the hands of a mob rather than give up " the divine Body* to raging dogs."

This bare fact is certainly true, but we do not know that Tarsicius was a boy or an acolyte. It may be, especially having regard to the reference of St Damasus to the deacon St Stephen, that he was a deacon, for it was the deacon's special office to administer holy Communion in certain circumstances and to carry the Blessed Sacrament from one place to another when necessary, *e.g.* that part of the consecrated Host, called *Fermentum*, which the Pope sent from his Mass to the presbyters of the principal Roman churches, symbolizing the unity of the holy Sacrifice in place and the union subsisting between the bishop and his flock. But then, as now, in times of dire persecution, anybody, cleric or lay, young or old, male or female, may be entrusted with the sacred Host in case of necessity, and the tradition about St Tarsicius since the sixth century is that he was a young acolyte commissioned to take communion to certain Christian prisoners, victims of the persecution of Valerian. He was

---

* *Tarcisium sanctum Christi sacramenta gerentem,*
Cum male sana manus peteret vulgare profanis ;
Ipse animam potius voluit dimittere cæsus
Prodere quam canibus rabidis cœlestia membra.

Cardinal Wiseman, who uses the story in *Fabiola*, says of " [Christi] cœlestia membra" that the words, " applied to the Blessed Eucharist, supply one of those casual, but most striking, arguments that result from identity of habitual thought in antiquity, more than from the use of studied or conventional phrases." An example, in fact, of " unity of indirect reference."

buried in the cemetery of St Callistus, but his grave has never been positively identified; probably his body eventually rested with those of Pope St Zephyrinus and others in the basilica of St Sixtus and St Cæcilia; but his relics are claimed by San Silvestro in Capite. The great increase of devotion to the Blessed Sacrament in recent years has brought about a corresponding extension of the *cultus* of St Tarsicius.

See Wilpert, *Die Papstgräber und die Cäciliengruft* (1909), pp. 92–98. Tarsicius was certainly not the deacon of Pope Zephyrinus, as has been suggested. *Cf.* also Marucchi in *Nuovo Bullettino di arch. christ.*, vol. xvi (1910), pp. 205–225.

ST ARNULFUS, or ARNOUL, Bp. of Soissons, Conf.
A.D. 1087

Was born about 1040 at Tydenhem, of the noble family of Pamèle, and in his youth distinguished himself in the armies of Robert and Henry I, Kings of France. He was called to a more noble warfare, resolving to employ for God the labour which till then he had consecrated to the service of the world. He became a monk in the great monastery of St Médard at Soissons; and after he had for some time made trial of his strength in the cenobitic life, he, with his abbot's leave, shut himself up in a narrow cell and in the closest solitude, almost without any intercourse with men, and devoted himself to assiduous prayer and the most austere penance. He led this manner of life until he was called to be abbot of the monastery. It was in 1082 that a council, held at Meaux by a legate of Pope Gregory VII, at the request of the clergy and people of Soissons resolved to place him in that episcopal see. To the deputies of the council who came to inform him Arnoul said, "Leave a sinner to offer to God some fruits of penance; and do not compel such a fool as myself to take up a charge which requires so much wisdom." He was, however, obliged to shoulder the burden. He set himself with great zeal to fulfil every part of his ministry; but finding himself not able to correct certain grievous abuses among the people, and fearing the account he should have to give for others no less than for himself, and having, moreover, been driven from his see by a usurper, Ursio, he obtained leave to resign his dignity. He afterward founded a monastery at Aldenburg (Oudenbourg) in Flanders, where he died in 1087. At a council at Beauvais in 1120 the then Bishop of Soissons showed a "life" of St Arnoul to the assembly and demanded that his body should be enshrined in the church. "If the body of my predecessor were in my diocese," he said, " it would have been brought in out of the churchyard long ago." The translation was accordingly made into the abbey-church of Aldenburg in the following year.

On the 22nd of this month is named another ST ARNULF, a hermit who lived at Eynesbury, near the Huntingdonshire Saint Neots, and died there towards the end of the ninth century. The date is arbitrarily chosen because it coincides with the commemoration of another French St Arnoul, a bishop ; but the English Arnoul may be an imaginary incarnation of St Arnoul of Metz, of whom there were relics at Eynesbury.

The Life by Hariulfus has been printed by the Bollandists and Mabillon, but has been more critically edited in Pertz, *Monumenta Germaniæ, Scriptores*, vol. xv, part 2, pp. 872–904. See also H. Claeys, *Het Leven van Sint Arnold*, 1895.

AUGUST 16

St Joachim, Father of the Blessed Virgin Mary

"IN the records of the twelve tribes of Israel was Joachim, a man exceedingly rich; and he brought double offerings, saying, 'There shall be of my superabundance for all the people, and these shall be the offering for my forgiveness to the Lord for a propitiation for me.' For the great day of the Lord was at hand, and the sons of Israel were bringing their offerings. And there stood over against him Rubim, saying, 'It is not meet for thee first to bring thine offerings, because thou hast not raised up seed in Israel.' And Joachim was exceedingly grieved, and went away to the registers of the twelve tribes of the people, saying, 'I shall see the registers of the twelve tribes of Israel, as to whether I alone have not raised up seed in Israel.' And he searched and found that all the righteous had raised up seed in Israel. And he remembered the patriarch Abraham, that in the last day God gave him a son, Isaac. And Joachim was exceedingly grieved and did not come into the presence of his wife; but he retired to the desert and there pitched his tent, and fasted forty days and forty nights, saying within himself 'I will not go down either for food or for drink until the Lord my God shall look upon me; prayer shall be my food and my drink.'" And Anne his wife also prayed and lamented, and an angel of the Lord appeared to her and told her that she would conceive and that her child should be spoken of in all the world. And an angel likewise appeared to Joachim, and he came down to the Temple rejoicing and offered ten lambs to God, with twelve calves for the priests and elders, and a hundred goats for the people; and his offering was accepted, and he knew that God had forgiven his sins and that he, the childless man, should beget a child.

This account of the father of our Lady is taken from the *Protevangelium of James*, a work to which the Church denies the authenticity of holy Scripture but which with other similar apocryphal works is the only source of information we have about the parents of Mary; even their traditional names, Joachim and Anne, must ultimately be traced to them. Of St Joachim, as of St Anne, we know absolutely nothing with certainty; but we are at liberty to retain as pious beliefs anything in an uncanonical book that does not conflict with the teaching of the Church, and it is a widely held tradition that our Lady was a child of promise as related in the so-called Gospel of James.

The feast of both Parents of the all-holy Mother of God has been observed in the East, on 9th September, from early times, but in the West not till very much later. That of St Joachim is not heard of before the fifteenth century; it was assigned to 20th March by Pope Julius II, but some fifty years later suppressed by St Pius V; it was restored by Paul V in 1621 for the Sunday after the Assumption, and Leo XIII made the feast a double of the second class in rank. Its present date was only fixed in 1913. The Roman Martyrology notes 20th March as St Joachim's birthday in Judæa. The Benedictines, as well as some Eastern Catholics, celebrate Joachim and Anne together, on 26th July.

Whether or no St Joachim was "a man exceedingly rich" in temporal goods, he must have been one wealthy in humility to be deemed by God worthy to be the father of the immaculate Mother of Jesus, and free of all pride in the worldly position and goods which had been bestowed upon him. We, too, if we consider the benefits of God, must humble ourselves, and bow down our heads. And if we consider our sins we must likewise humble ourselves and bow down our heads. A man must know that whatever is of his own growth is opposite to his own good; and he must give to others what is theirs, and never appropriate to himself what belongs to another: that is, he must ascribe to God all his good and all advantages which he enjoys and acknowledge that all his evil is of his own growth. Blessed is he who accounts himself as mean and base before men as he is before God. Blessed is he who walks faithfully in obedience to another. He who desires to enjoy inward peace must look on every man as his superior and as better and greater before God. Blessed is he who knows how to keep and conceal the favours of God. Humility knows not how to speak, and patience dares not speak, for fear of losing the crown of suffering by complaints, with a firm conviction that a person is always treated above his deserts. Humility dispels all evil, is an enemy to all sin, and makes a man nothing in his own eyes. By humility a man finds grace before God, and peace with men. God bestows the treasures of His grace on the humble, not on the proud. A man ought always to fear pride, lest it cast him down headlong; for he is of himself poor and sinful, rich only by the divine gifts: these then he must love, and despise himself.

The "Protevangelium of James," which appears under various names and in sundry divergent forms, may be conveniently consulted in the English translation of B. H. Cowper, *Apocryphal Gospels*, edition of 1874, but the text here in question is called by him " the Gospel of Pseudo-Matthew." See also E. Amann, *Le Protévangile de Jacques et ses remaniements* (1910); and the original Greek, with translation, in Ch. Michel, *Évangiles Apocryphes*, vol. i (1911), in the Collection Hemmer et Lejay, " Textes et Documents."

ST ARSACIUS, HERMIT

A.D. 358

Was a Persian by birth and a soldier by profession, and was also employed as superintendent of the imperial menagerie. He became a Christian and suffered for the faith under the Emperor Licinius, but was not put to death. He then lived as a solitary in a small tower at Nicomedia where, among other marvels, he had prevision of a terrible calamity that was about to overtake the city. He went at once to the clergy and told them to offer public prayer for the averting of disaster and to urge the people to penitence, but no notice was taken of him and he returned to his tower to pray alone for the city. There was a terrible earthquake, in which the tower of Arsacius was one of the few buildings to escape destruction; when people ran to it to seek safety he was found on his knees—but dead. Though St Arsacius is named in the Roman Martyrology on this day, the earthquake at Nicomedia took place on 24th August, in the year 358. His story is told by the historian Sozomen in his *Ecclesiastical History*, who says he got his information from people who had got it from others who knew Arsacius personally, and that many miracles were done at his intercession.

An account of St Arsacius, or Ursacius, is furnished in the *Acta Sanctorum*, August, vol. iii, based upon Sozomen, *Hist. Eccles.*, Bk. iv, ch. 16. It is curious that no *cultus* of Arsacius seems to be traceable in the Eastern Churches. On the other hand through the *Historia Tripartita* of Cassiodorus he found his way into the Western martyrologies; moreover copious, but very unreliable, accounts are furnished of the translation of his relics.

ST ARMEL, Abbot and Conf.

c. A.D. 570

Armel, whose name takes various forms (*e.g.* Ermel, Erme, Arzel, Arkel, Arthmael, even Ermyn), is the eponymous saint of Ploermel and of other places in France. He was born in the cantref of Penychen in Glamorgan, the son of Hywel ap Emyr Llydaw and cousin of SS. Cadfan, Samson, and others, towards the end of the fifth century. His youth was spent under the abbot Carentmael, and he was remarkable for piety and aptness in studies. It is related of him, as of other saints, that one day he entered a church just as the deacon was singing the words : " And whosoever doth not carry his cross and come after Me cannot be my disciple " ; and he heard this as a call from God direct to himself to give up all for His sake. He therefore followed the example of so many other Britons of his age and went over into Armorica, perhaps with St Paul Aurelian in 510, together with his master and other companions. They landed in Finistère, but while living an evangelical life together at Plouarzel they were disturbed by the activities of the usurper Conmor, who had killed Jonas, the true chieftain of those parts. They therefore went to Paris to seek the protection of King Childebert, who kept Armel by him for a time. After the son of Jonas had, with the help of St Samson, defeated and slain Conmor in 555, St Armel was granted some land near Rennes whereon to establish his community anew (Saint-Armel-des-Boscheaux). He founded another monastery at Ploermel in Morbihan and there died in peace. His feast is observed in the diocese of Rennes, and was noted in the Sarum calendar of 1498.

See Baring Gould and Fisher, *Lives of the British Saints*, vol. i, pp. 170 *seq.*, and Stanton, *Menology*, pp. 395–396.

BD. LAURENCE LORICATUS, Hermit

A.D. 1243

Was born at Fanello, near Siponto in Apulia, and while still a young man had the misfortune accidentally to kill another. In expiation he made a pilgrimage of penance to Compostella, and on his return in 1209 went to Subiaco, where he joined the community but was soon given permission to be a solitary. He lived in a mountain cave nearby for thirty-three years, and practised terrific mortifications of the body: the name *Loricatus*, "the cuirassier," was given to him because of the coat of mail studded with sharp points which he wore next his skin. His *cultus* was approved in 1778 and his relics are preserved in the *Sacro Speco* of St Benedict at Subiaco.

An account of him is given in the *Acta Sanctorum*, August, vol. iii, which possesses interest from the fact that it embodies documents compiled in 1244 during an investigation undertaken at the instance of Pope Innocent IV.

ST ROCH, Conf.
Fourteenth Century

We find this servant of God venerated in France and Italy during the fifteenth century, not very long after his death, but we have no authentic history of his life. No doubt he was born at Montpellier and nursed the sick during a plague in Italy (perhaps that of 1348), but that is all that can be affirmed about him. His two "lives" are simply collections of popular legends about the saint, which may have a basis in fact but cannot now be checked. According to the older, written by a Venetian, Francis Diedo, in 1478, Roch was son of the governor of Montpellier, and upon being left an orphan at the age of twenty he gave away his patrimony to the poor and went on a pilgrimage to Rome. Finding Italy plague-stricken he visited numerous centres of population, Acquapendente, Cesena, Rome, Modena, Mantua, Parma, where he not only devoted himself to care of the sick but cured large numbers simply by making the sign of the cross on them. At Piacenza he was infected himself, and not wishing to be a burden on any hospital he dragged himself out into the woods to die. Here he was miraculously fed by a dog, whose master soon found Roch and looked after him; when he was convalescent he returned to Piacenza and miraculously cured many more folk, as well as their sick cattle. At length he got back to Montpellier where, it being war-time, he was taken for a spy and imprisoned, and so he remained five years, till he died. When they came to examine his body it was recognized who he really was, the son of their former governor, by a cross-shaped birth-mark on his breast. He was therefore given a public funeral, and he performed as many miracles when dead as he had done when alive. The popularity and rapid extension of the *cultus* of St Roch, a veneration by no means extinct to-day, was remarkable, and he soon became the saint *par excellence* to be invoked against pestilence. During the Council of

Constance (1414–18) he was said by his intercession to have stopped a local epidemic, and the Council approved his cult. St Roch is named in the Roman Martyrology, and his feast is kept in many places, on 16th August; there is no evidence that he was a Franciscan tertiary, but the Franciscans venerate him as such and observe his feast on 17th August.

Nothing more seems now to be known about the life of St Roch than what was already published by the Bollandists 200 years ago in the *Acta Sanctorum*, August, vol. iii. But the saint is vastly popular, as anyone may learn who consults the long list of books and articles noted in the *Bio-bibliographie* of Chevalier. There is a volume by Chavanne, *St Roch, histoire complète* (1876); but perhaps the best modern book of general interest is that of G. Ceroni, *San Rocco nella vita, nel culto, nell'arte* (1927). On St Roch in art see, beside the *Ikonographie* of Künstle, vol. ii, A. Fliche, *Saint Roch*, in the series "L'Art et les Saints" (1929). It is curious that St Roch seems even to have left traces of *cultus* here in England. The present St Roche's Hill in Sussex was St Rokeshill in 1579. A short English account of the Saint may be found in Léon, *Auréole Séraphique* (Eng. Trans.), vol. iii, pp. 11–21.

AUGUST 17

ST HYACINTH, Conf.

A.D. 1257

ST HYACINTH, whom church historians call the Apostle of the North, was of the ancient house of the counts of Odrowaz, which afterwards gave St Stanislaus Kostka to the Church. His grandfather, a great general against the Tartars, left two sons. Ivo, the younger, was chancellor of Poland and bishop of Cracow. Eustace, the elder, was count of Konski, the first child of whose marriage was Hyacinth, born in 1185, at the castle of Lanka in Silesia. His parents encouraged his natural disposition for virtue, and he kept an unspotted innocence through youth during his studies at Cracow, Prague, and Bologna, in which last university he took the degrees of doctor of laws and divinity. Returning to the Bishop of Cracow, St Vincent Kadlubek, he was given a canonry at Sandomir, and employed as his assistant and counsellor. Hyacinth showed prudence, capacity, and zeal in his exterior occupations, but never suffered them to be an impediment to his spirit of prayer and recollection. He was assiduous in assisting at the Divine Office, and in visiting and serving the sick in the hospitals; most of his ecclesiastical revenue he bestowed in alms. When St Vincent gave up his office to become a Cistercian, Ivo of Konski succeeded him in the see of Cracow and soon after made a visit to Rome on the occasion of his translation to Gnesen. He took with him his two nephews, Hyacinth and Bd. Ceslaus, who was probably Hyacinth's brother. St Dominic was then at Rome, and Ivo and the Bishop of Prague, charmed with his personality and impressed by his discourses and sermons, begged some of his preachers for their dioceses, which lay open to the influence of the Tartars, the Finns, and other pagans. St Dominic had sent away so many that he was not able to supply them, but four of the attendants of Ivo desired to join his new order, namely, Hyacinth and Ceslaus, a German gentleman, Herman, and Henry, a Czech. They received the habit at the hands of St Dominic, in his convent of St Sabina, and at once began by disengagement from things of this world, mortification of the senses, denial of their own will, and a keen desire to glorify God in all their actions and sufferings, to lay a solid foundation for the work which they were to do. They made their solemn vows by dispensation after a short novitiate, and then set out for Poland in April 1220. They entered Upper Carinthia where they stayed six months, and St Hyacinth gave the habit to several priests and others, founded a friary at Friesach, and left Herman to govern it. The Archbishop of Salzburg received them with all possible respect and the apostolic men passed through Styria, Austria, Moravia, and Silesia, preaching everywhere the word of God, Henry remaining behind to work in the last two provinces.

In Poland they were received with joy and honour. At Cracow the first sermons of St Hyacinth were attended with much success, and in a short time the infamous life of the capital was greatly improved, as the spirit of prayer and charity and the use of the sacraments were revived. Reconciliations of enemies and restitutions for injustices, which had been despaired of, were effected, and some of the nobility set the people an example of edifying docility. The power of the words of this apostle and the example of his life were supported by an extraordinary spirit of prayer and also by miracles, though he strove to conceal them. Hyacinth founded a convent of his order, called of the Holy Trinity, in Cracow : another at Sandomir, and a third at Plock, on the Vistula. He was a very notable wonder-worker and his bull of canonization mentions a miracle in Moravia attested by over four hundred witnesses. He came with three companions to the banks of the Vistula, going to preach at Wisgrade, but the flood was so high that none of the boats dare venture over. Hyacinth, having made the sign of the cross, walked upon the waters of that deep and rapid river as if it had been firm land, in the sight of a multitude of people waiting for him on the opposite bank. A like incident is related later in his life when preaching to the Russians, and again when he fled from Kiev before the Tartars and walked over the Dnieper bearing the Blessed Sacrament and a statue of our Lady.

Having preached in the principal cities of Poland, he undertook to carry the gospel into the wild and semi-pagan countries of the North. He could not allow himself any rest whilst he saw souls perishing in ignorance of God ; and the length, difficulties, and dangers of the journeys were not able to discourage his heroic soul, which could think nothing difficult which was undertaken for so great an end. He preached and built convents of his institute in Prussia, Pomerania, and other countries lying near the Baltic, and then went on into Denmark, Sweden, and Norway, in all which countries there still remained many idolaters. To conserve and carry on his labours he everywhere founded monasteries of Preaching Friars, and left disciples to people and extend them. After the above missions he went into the Ukraine and Ruthenia, where he tried to induce the prince to abjure the Greek schism. He there built the convents of Lwów (Lemberg) and of Halicz, and from thence penetrated as far as the Black Sea. Returning towards the north, he entered Muscovy, or Russia proper, where there were heathens, Jews and Mohammedans in large numbers, as well as the native schismatics; the few Catholics remaining there had not so much as one church to assemble in. He found the Grand Duke Vladimir IV deaf to his appeals, but obtained of him permission to preach to the Catholics and to establish a friary at Kiev, then the capital of both Russias. The ensuing conversions gave uneasiness to the Grand Duke, who began to persecute the Catholics; at the same time the Tartars, after an obstinate siege, took Kiev by assault, sacked it, and set it on fire, the Dominicans being driven out.

St Hyacinth then returned to Cracow, and enjoyed some rest in his house of the Holy Trinity, still continuing to preach and instruct both in the city and the country round. About 1239 he made a visitation of his communities among the Danes, Swedes, Prussians, and others, and penetrated among the Cuman Tartars. To preach on the Danube to these fierce idolaters had been the unfulfilled desire of St Dominic himself, and some Dominican preachers had entered this province in the year 1228. St Hyacinth baptized a number of them, including one of their princes, and then, returning into Poland again, entered Little Russia, and there converted many from the schism. The inhabitants of Podolia, Volhynia, and Lithuania were visited again and encouraged by his sermons to penance and to a change of life; the convent he founded at Vilna became the mother-house of a large province of his order. After having arrived once more at Cracow, in the year 1257, he soon realized that his long and amazingly strenuous life was nearly at an end. A last great miracle is recorded of him. Primaslava, a noble lady, having sent her son to invite the saint to come and preach to her vassals, the young nobleman was drowned on his return in crossing a river. The sorrowing mother caused the body to be laid at the feet of St Hyacinth who, after a fervent prayer, took him by the hand and restored him to her alive and sound. On the following feast of St Dominic he was taken ill, and on the vigil of the Assumption he talked for the last time to his brethren, recommending to them especially meekness and humility of heart and to have great care always to preserve mutual love and charity, and to esteem poverty as men that have renounced all things of the earth. " For this," said he, " is the testament, the sealed deed, by which we claim eternal life." The next morning he assisted at Matins and Mass, received the Viaticum and Extreme Unction at the steps of the altar, and died in a few hours, being seventy-two years old. St Hyacinth was canonized by Pope Clement VIII in 1594.

All Christians are not called to the apostolic work of the ministry, but every one is bound to preach to his neighbour by the modesty of his manners, by a spirit of patience, charity, and religion, by fidelity in all duties, by enthusiasm in the divine service, by temperance and mortification. Passion and ill humour, if not suppressed, easily scandalize and injure those who observe them. Nothing is more contagious than self-love. He who is fretful, hard to please, full of himself, or a slave to sensuality easily infects even those who see and condemn it in him : but no sermon is more powerful than the example of a man of prayer and of a Christian spirit.

What commonly passes current as the Life of St Hyacinth partakes more of the nature of a saga than of a sober historical record. This is pointed out both by Knöpfler in the *Kirchenlexikon* and by the modern Bollandists (*e.g.* in *Analecta Bollandiana*, vol. xlv, 1927, pp. 202–203). The earliest and practically the only source of information down to quite recent times was the account of St Hyacinth's (or, as the Poles called him, St Iaccho's) life and miracles, written by Father Stanislaus of Cracow a hundred years after the saint's death. It is printed in the *Monumenta Poloniæ Historica*, vol. iv, pp. 841–894. Later biographers only embroidered this account with further extravagances, and consequently even such Lives as that by the Comtesse de Flavigny, *S. Hyacinthe et ses compagnons* (1899), must be read with great caution, and the account of Alban Butler, in part reproduced above, is certainly not an exception. The most valuable contribution which has so far been made to the perplexed history of St Hyacinth is that of B. Altaner, *Die Dominikanermissionen des 13 Jahrhunderts* (1924). For the traditional account see Mortier, *Histoire des Maîtres Généraux O.P.*, vol. i, pp. 215–218 and 377–388 ; Procter, *Lives of Dominican Saints*, pp. 229–232 ; and for a fuller bibliography Taurisano, p. 16.

ST MAMAS, Mart.

c. A.D. 275

St Basil and St Gregory Nazianzen inform us that St Mamas was a shepherd at Cæsarea in Cappadocia who, seeking from his childhood the kingdom of God with his whole heart, distinguished himself by his fervour in the divine service. Being apprehended by the persecutors, he suffered cruel torments with joy and attained the crown of martyrdom. According to Eastern tradition he suffered under Aurelian by stoning, while yet a boy; but the Roman Martyrology says that he underwent "a prolonged persecution from youth to old age." The late Greek *acta* say that he was born in prison, the child of SS. Theodotus and Rufina, but other writers make him a Roman senator; we can be sure of little but his existence, occupation, and the place of his martyrdom. His feast is still observed in many churches in the East and a few in the West.

The vogue enjoyed by St Mamas as an object of popular devotion was undoubtedly very great. One has to read the panegyric of St Basil and the allusions of St Gregory Nazianzen to appreciate the depth of feeling involved. See Delehaye, *Origines du Culte des Martyrs*, p. 133, and *Passions des Martyrs et les Genres littéraires*, pp. 198-200.

SS. LIBERATUS AND HIS COMPANIONS, MM.

A.D. 483

Huneric, the Arian Vandal king in Africa, in the seventh year of his reign, published fresh edicts against the Catholics and ordered their monasteries to be everywhere demolished. Seven monks who lived in a monastery near Capsa, in the province of Byzacene, were at that time summoned to Carthage. Their names were Liberatus the abbot, Boniface deacon, Servus and Rusticus subdeacons, Rogatus, Septimus, and Maximus, monks. They were first tempted with great promises to conform to Arianism, but they answered with one accord, "We confess one Lord, one faith, and one baptism. As to our bodies, do with them what you please, and keep those riches which you promise us, and which will surely perish." As they remained constant in the belief of the Trinity and of one baptism, they were put in irons and thrown into a dungeon. The faithful having bribed the guards, visited them day and night to be taught by them, and mutually to encourage one another to suffer for the faith of Christ. The King being informed of this, he commanded them to be more closely confined, and after a time condemned them to be put into an old ship and burnt at sea. The martyrs walked cheerfully to the shore, ignoring the insults of the Arians as they passed along. Particular endeavours were used by the persecutors to gain Maximus, who was very young, indeed, a boy, who was being educated by the monks. But God, who makes the tongues of children to praise His name, gave him strength to withstand all their efforts, and he boldly told them that they would never be able to separate him from his abbot and brethren, with whom he had begun to learn the labours of a penitential life for the sake of everlasting glory. An old vessel was filled with sticks, the seven martyrs were put on board, and it was set adrift; fire was put to it several times, but it would not kindle, and all their attempts to get the ship burning failed. Huneric therefore ordered that they should be brought back to land, and there the martyrs' brains were brutally dashed out with oars. Their bodies were thrown into the sea, whence they were recovered and buried at a monastery near the church of St Celerinus. The feast of St Liberatus and his companions is kept by the Augustinians of the Assumption on August 19.

All our information comes from a "Passio," formerly, but as it would seem wrongly, ascribed to Victor of Vita. The "Passio" with comments is printed in the *Acta Sanctorum*, August, vol. iii.

ST CLARE OF MONTEFALCO, Virg.
A.D. 1308

There has been much discussion between the Franciscans and the Augustinians as to whether this holy nun belonged to one order or the other; the solution of the difficulty which appears to satisfy both parties is that the community of pious young women, under the direction of her sister Joan, to which Clare belonged from six years of age, consisted of secular tertiaries of St Francis: but that when they wished to adopt a regular conventual life the Bishop of Spoleto gave them the Augustinian rule. Their convent, of the Holy Cross, was erected in 1290 and, her sister dying, St Clare much against her will was elected abbess. Her life was already notable for its austerities and they were now increased: for a breach of silence she stood barefoot in snow while she said the Our Father a hundred times. Her words and example kept alive in her community a great desire of perfection, and the union of her heart with God gave them a model of recollection. A number of miracles were attributed to her, frequent ecstasies, and supernatural gifts, which she utilized for the good of those outside her convent as well as those within; she confuted heretics and reconciled enemies. St Clare had a very great devotion to the passion of our Lord. She once said to a sister, "If you seek the cross of Christ, take my heart; there you will find the suffering Lord." These words were taken literally, and when her heart was examined after death in 1308 an image of the crucifix was said to have been found imprinted on it. St Clare of Montefalco was canonized in 1881.

The Bollandists having been refused access to the original sources preserved at Montefalco, had to be content with reprinting (*Acta Sanctorum*, August, vol. iii) the Life of St Clare by Masconio (1601), which is of no great value. But in presenting the case for the canonisation of the saint, the more reliable documents came in the last century to be better known and are now generably accessible in print. The most important is the Life, said to have been compiled in 1309 by Berengarius, Vicar-General of Spoleto. It may be read in Faloci Pulignani, *Vita di santa Chiara da Montefalco* (1885). Apart from her faithful observance and the austerity of her penance, she is alleged to have been honoured by three divine favours of exceptional interest. First the marvellous incorruption of her remains. See on this Mr. John Addington Symonds in the *Cornhill Magazine*, October 1881, p. 446, who describes what he himself had seen at Montefalco: " Only her hands and the exquisitely beautiful pale outline of her face (forehead, nose, mouth, and chin, modelled in purest outline, as though the injury of death had never touched her) were visible. Her closed eyes seemed to sleep." Secondly the cross and other instruments of the Passion formed solidly within her heart in some fibrous tissue. She spoke of this during life, and after death when her heart was opened, it was found to be as she had said. The evidence for this strange phenomenon is certainly not contemptible. Thirdly the alleged liquefaction and ebullition of her blood. Upon this last, in particular, consult Ian Grant, *The Testimony of Blood* (1929), pp. 79–122. As to modern literature see also Tardi, *Vita della b. Chiara da Montefalco* (Eng. trans., New York, 1884); T. de Töth, *Vita* (1908); Merlin, *Ste Claire de' la Croix de Montefalco* (1930); and Faloci Pulignani, *Miscellanea Francescana*, vol. xiv (1913), pp. 129–152.

AUGUST 18

ST AGAPITUS, Mart.

A.D. 274

AGAPITUS was a Christian boy, only fifteen years old, who was brought before the governor Antiochus at Præneste (Palestrina), and upon refusing to abjure his faith was scourged, imprisoned, and beheaded, under the Emperor Aurelian. In his *acta* these simple facts have been embroidered in the usual way: after being beaten he was confined in a foul cell without food or drink for four days; burning coals were poured over his head and he was hung up by his feet over a smoking fire; boiling water was poured upon him, and the bones of his jaw broken. The cruel and disappointed Antiochus had a seizure and died before his victim. Agapitus was beheaded only because the beasts in the arena refused to touch him: a sight that so impressed the tribune Anastasius that he was converted on the spot. Exactly similar details, unconvincing in themselves, can be found in the *acta* of many other martyrs and were inserted to fill out a story and edify the hearers; but in fact they add nothing to the lesson of the simple heroism of young St Agapitus and the other martyrs of whom they are told.

The early *cultus* of St Agapitus is well attested, not only by the mention of him under this day in the sacramentaries, but by traces of the ruins of his basilica a mile out of Palestrina and of an epitaph bearing his name. We may note also the dedication to him of several other churches in the eighth and ninth centuries. See the *Acta Sanctorum*, November, vol. ii, part 2, pp. 448–449; add also A. Kellner, " Der hl. Agapitus von Præneste," in *Studien und Mitteilungen*, 1930, pp. 404–432; and a number of notices by O. Marucchi duly indicated in the Bollandist volume just quoted.

SS. FLORUS AND LAURUS, MM.

SECOND CENTURY

According to a Greek tradition Florus and Laurus were brothers, stone-masons, who were employed upon the building of a pagan temple in Illyria. After it was finished those responsible for putting up the temple, Proculus and Maximus, were converted to Christianity, and their two masons with them, whereupon they broke down the images of the heathen gods and delivered the building over to Christian worship; they were seized by the governor and all four buried alive in a dry cistern or drowned in a deep well. The story is chiefly interesting because an ingenious attempt has been made to show that we have here a survival of the worship of the Dioscuri, that SS. Florus and Laurus are Castor and Pollux disguised as Christians and that from the earliest times there was a monthly festival in honour of the twins. The theory is based on the coincidence on the 18th and 19th of most months from April to December of the commemorations of martyred brothers with consonant names (*e.g.*, Mark and Marcellinus, Gervase and Protase) and of martyrs whose names resemble or are associated with Castor and Pollux (*e.g.*, Dioscorus, Polyeuctes, Castor). Florus and Laurus are particularly important to the argument because on their day occurs the feast of St Helen, and Helen was the name of the sister of Castor and Pollux. There is nothing in this speculation, as Père Delehaye has no difficulty in showing. He points out that some of the dates of these martyrs as given by the theorists do not agree with the dates in the martyrologies; that the 18th of the month in the Julian calendar does not correspond with the 18th in Greek, Syrian, or Asiatic calendars; and that St Helen occurs on August 18 in the Roman Martyrology quite fortuitously. For the day of her celebration traditional in the East is May 21 and was formerly February 8 in many churches of the West; the concurrence of the three saints on August 18 in the Roman Martyrology is no older than the sixteenth century, before which SS. Florus and Laurus did not appear in it at all.

These are obscure saints whose very existence is doubtful. See, regarding Castor and Pollux, Delehaye, *The Legends of the Saints* (Eng. trans.), pp. 182–184, and sundry other references in the *Analecta Bollandiana*, *e.g.* vol. xxiii, pp. 427–432. *Cf.* also *The Month*, August 1906, pp. 202–207; where it is pointed out that there is no real assonance between Florus and Laurus, as Dr. Rendel Harris pretends, except for an Englishman who adheres to his native pronunciation of Latin; and secondly that a much stronger case than any Dr. Harris presents could be made out to prove that SS. Ced and Chad were Dioscuri; yet nobody dreams of disputing the account which Bede gives of these two bishops of his own time.

ST HELEN, Empress
A.D. 330

St Helen was born, so far as can be ascertained, at Drepanum in Bithynia about the year 250, the daughter of an inn-keeper. Somewhere about 270 the Roman general Constantius Chlorus met her there and, in spite of her humble birth, married her; but when in 292 he was made Cæsar by Diocletian he was persuaded to divorce her and marry Theodora, the stepdaughter of the Emperor Maximian. Eight years earlier she had given birth at Naissus (Nish in Serbia) to Constantine the Great, who always had a deep regard and affection for his mother, and afterwards conferred on her the title of "Venerabilis et Piissima Augusta," changing the name of her birth-place to Helenopolis. "We are assured," says Alban Butler, "by the unanimous tradition of our English historians that this holy empress was a native of our island." This is so, but the oft-repeated statement of mediæval chroniclers that Constantius married Helen, daughter of Coel* of Caercolvin (Colchester), is without historical foundation. Supported by misunderstood passages in certain panegyrics of Constantine, the legend arose from confusion with another Constantine and Helen, namely the Helen, daughter of Eudaf of Ewyas, who married Magnus Clemens Maximus, who was emperor in Britain, Gaul, and Spain from 383 to 388 (the Macsen Wledig of Welsh romance); they had several sons, one of whom was called Constantine (Cystennin). This lady received the epithet *Lluyddawg* (" of the hosts "), later transferred to the other Helen, and already in the tenth century there is a statement that Constantine was the " son of Constrantius [sic] and Helen Luicdauc, who went out of Britain to seek the Cross so far as Jerusalem, and brought it thence to Constantinople." It has been suggested that the churches dedicated in honour of St Helen in Wales, Cornwall, and Devon refer to Helen Lluyddawg, as the name of the ancient Welsh road, Sarn Elen, certainly does. There is in another part of the dominions of Maximus an independent and equally erroneous tradition of St Helen: namely, that she was born at Trier and gave her own palace to be turned into a cathedral, to which she gave the " Holy Coat." The nucleus of the present building is a basilica built by Valentinian I, over thirty-six years after her death, and there is no reason to suppose that she was ever in the city.

Constantius Chlorus lived for fourteen years after the repudiation of St Helen, and when he died in 306 their son Constantine was

---
* *i.e.* " old King Cole."

proclaimed Cæsar by his troops at York, and eighteen months later Emperor. He entered Rome after the battle of the Milvian Bridge on October 28, 312, and by the Edict of Milan early in the following year Christianity was tolerated throughout the Empire. It appears from Eusebius that St Helen was converted only at this time, when she was about sixty-three years old (Constantine himself was a catechumen until his death-bed): "She became such a devout servant of God under [her son's] influence that one might believe her to have been a disciple of the Saviour of mankind from her very childhood." Though she was so advanced in years before she knew Christ, her fervour and zeal were such as to make her retrieve the time lost in ignorance; and God prolonged her life many years to edify by her example the Church which her son laboured to exalt by his authority. Rufinus calls her faith and holy zeal incomparable, and she kindled the same fire in the hearts of the Romans; she assisted in the churches amidst the people in modest and plain attire, and to attend at the divine offices was her greatest delight. She made use of the treasures of the Empire in liberal alms, and was the mother of the indigent and distressed. She built numerous churches, and enriched them with precious vessels and ornaments, and when after his victory over Licinius in 324 Constantine became master of the East, the noble lady went to Palestine to venerate the places made sacred by the bodily presence of our Lord.

After Golgotha and the holy Sepulchre had been laid bare by the removal of the terrace and temple of Venus with which the Emperor Hadrian had over-built them, Constantine wrote to Macarius, Bishop of Jerusalem, ordering a church to be built, "worthy of the most marvellous place in the world." St Helen, then fourscore years of age, took the charge on herself to see this work executed, desiring at the same time to discover the sacred cross on which our Redeemer died. Eusebius, in his "Life" of Constantine, mentions no other motive for her journey but her desire of adorning the buildings in the holy places and of relieving the poor in those parts, out of devotion to the mysteries of our divine Redeemer's sufferings; but other early writers attribute it to visions, to admonitions in her sleep, to divine warnings, and St Paulinus says that one of its definite objects was to find the cross. Constantine in his letter to Macarius commissions him to make search for it on Mount Calvary. The finding of three crosses in a rock-cistern just to the east of Calvary and the difficulty in deciding which was the cross of Christ, has been related herein under May 3, on which date the Church celebrates this discovery, and under

St. Macarius, Vol. III, page 167. But it must be noted here that neither the pilgrim Ætheria, who visited Jerusalem *circa* 395, St Cyril of Jerusalem, writing in 351, nor Eusebius, all of whom mention the finding of the cross, directly connect its discovery with the name of St Helen. The first known ascription of it to her is in a sermon of St Ambrose, preached in 395, who remarks that St Helen, when she had discovered the holy cross, " adored not the wood, but the King, Him who hung on the wood. She burned with an earnest desire of touching the guarantee of immortality." Several other writers about the same time mention her as playing a principal part in the recovery of the cross, but it is noteworthy that St Jerome, who lived at Bethlehem, was not among them. A large part of the precious relic was given in charge of the Bishop of Jerusalem and kept in the basilica built to the east of the *Anastasis* and over the cistern where it was found ; it was contained in a silver-gilt reliquary and exposed for veneration every Good Friday. Another part was sent to Rome, where the *Liber Pontificalis* says that " Constantine built a basilica in the Sessorian palace, to which he gave a portion of the wood of the holy cross of our Lord Jesus Christ, enshrined in gold and jewels, and called the church by the name of Jerusalem, which it retains to this day," *i.e.*, Santa Croce in Gerusalemme ; the Sessorian palace was the residence of St Helen.

Whether or no she actually took an active part in the finding of the cross, it is beyond dispute that her last days were spent in Palestine and, says Eusebius, " In the sight of all she continually resorted to church, appearing humbly dressed among the praying women ; and she adorned the sacred buildings with rich ornaments and decorations, not passing by the chapels of the meanest towns." She was kind, and charitable to all, but especially to religious persons ; to these she showed such respect as to serve them at table as if she had been a servant, set the dishes before them, pour them out drink, hold them water to wash their hands, " though empress of the world and mistress of the empire she looked upon herself as servant of the handmaids of Christ." Whilst she travelled over the East with royal pomp and magnificence she heaped all kinds of favours both on cities and private persons, particularly on soldiers, the poor, and those who were condemned to the mines : distributing money and garments, and freeing many from oppression, chains, and banishment. The latest coins which, by order of her son, bore her name, Flavia Julia Helena, were minted in 330, which presumably was the year of her death. This took place apparently in the East, perhaps at her birth-place. Her body was taken with much pomp to Rome. St Helen is named in the Roman Martyrology on August 18, on which day her feast is kept in the dioceses of Liverpool, Salford, and Brentwood; it is observed universally in the East, but on May 21, with that rather equivocal person, her son Constantine: the Byzantines refer to them as "the holy, illustrious and great emperors, crowned by God and equal with the Apostles."

This holy Empress paid all possible honour to bishops and pastors of the Church. He who truly loves and honours God and religion has a great esteem for whatever belongs to it and consequently respects its ministers; the first Christian princes were well aware that it is impossible to inspire the people with a just value and reverence for religion and its immediate object without such reasonable respect. It was upon this principle that immunities were granted to the Church. On the other hand, notorious scandals in pastors are execrable sacrileges. Circumspection is necessary that we be not drawn aside or imposed upon by any because, like Alcimus, they are of the seed of Aaron; but a propensity to censure rashly and detract from those persons who are invested with a sacred character is inconsistent with a religious mind and leads to revolt. True pastors indeed, in the spirit of the Apostles, far from resenting, or so much as thinking of, any slights that may be put upon them, or desiring, much less seeking, any kind of respect for themselves personally, are satisfied with contempt, which in their hearts they sincerely acknowledge to be only their due. Humility is the ornament and badge of the sacred order which they hold in the Church of Christ.

> The principal source is the Life of Constantine by Eusebius, the relevant passages of which are quoted in the *Acta Sanctorum*, August, vol. iii. But see also M. Guidi, *Un Bios di Constantino* (1908). Among more popular accounts of St Helen may be mentioned R. Couzard, *Ste Hélène d'après l'histoire et la tradition* (1911), and A. M. Rouillon, O.P., *Sainte Hélène* (1908) in the series " Les Saints." In both these books too much stress seems to be laid upon the very questionable translation of the relics of the saint to the monastery of Hautvillers in France. St Helen, as Père Delehaye shows (*Acta Sanctorum*, Nov., vol. ii, part 2, p. 450), after Duchesne, was buried, not in Constantinople, but in Rome on the Via Lavicana. In the series " L'Art et les Saints " an interesting little brochure has been written concerning St Helen by Jules Maurice (1929).

ST ALIPIUS, Bp. of Tagaste, Conf.
c. A.D. 430

He was of a good family, and born about the year 354 at Tagaste in Africa, of which town St Augustine, only a few years older than himself, was also a native. He studied grammar at Tagaste and rhetoric at Carthage, both under St Augustine, till a disagreement happened between his master and his father. Alipius still retained a great affection and respect for Augustine, and was reciprocally much beloved by him. At Carthage Alipius was engrossed by the circus, to which the inhabitants of that city were extravagantly addicted. Augustine was much afflicted that so hopeful a young man would be, or rather was already, lost in what was an exceedingly dangerous interest, but he had no opportunity to warn him as Alipius by that time was not allowed by his father to be any longer one of his scholars. Alipius happened, however, one day to go into his school, and hear some part of the lecture, as he did sometimes by stealth. Augustine, in expounding the subject which he had in hand, borrowed a similitude from the shows of the circus, with a smart rebuke for those who were involved in their excesses. This he did without any thought of Alipius. But he imagined it had been spoken purely for him and, being a well-disposed youth, was angry with himself for his weakness, and determined to overcome it. Thus God, who sits at the helm and guides the course of all things which He has created, rescued from this danger one whom He was to adopt one day among His children, and raise to the dignity of a bishop and a dispenser of His sacraments. After this, Alipius persuaded his father that he might again attend Augustine's lectures. For a time, attracted by its plausibility and the virtue of some of its adherents, he shared his master's addiction to Manichæism.

Whilst he was a student at Carthage Alipius found a hatchet in the street, which a thief, who had attempted to cut off and steal some lead railings and was closely pursued, had dropped to save himself. Alipius innocently took up the hatchet and, being found with it, was carried before the judge, where he was treated as the true thief. As the officers were leading him to prison he was met by an architect who had care of the public buildings and knew Alipius, whom he had often seen at the house of a certain senator. This man, surprised to see him in such hands, inquired how such a misfortune had befallen him; and having heard his case, he asked some of the crowd to go along with him and he would try to prove the innocence of the prisoner. He went to the house of a man whom he suspected of being the true culprit, and met a child at the door who innocently told the whole matter. For on being shown the hatchet, and asked whose it was, the child answered, " It is ours." Whereupon Alipius was released and " he that was to be a dispenser of God's word and a judge of many causes in His Church departed, more experienced and more wise." This accident, according to the remark of St Augustine, was an act of divine providence, that he might learn from it to be careful of the reputation of others and to guard against rash judgement; for, generally, common report is no ground for condemning a man.

Alipius, pursuing a career in the world according to the wishes of his parents, went to Rome to study the law. He had already moved some distance on the road towards conversion, but soon had a serious set-back. Some of his friends meeting him one day led him, much against his will, to some barbarous sports. He resisted all the way, and said to them, " If you haul my body thither, can you force me to turn my mind or my eyes upon these shows? I shall be absent therefore, though present in body." Yet they did not desist, but carried him with them. When they had taken their seats, and the spectacle began, Alipius shut his eyes, that his soul might not take any delight in such scenes; and would to God, says St Augustine, he had shut his ears too. For hearing a great shout of the people, he was overcome by curiosity and opened his eyes, meaning only to see what the matter was, and then shut them again. But, showing us how much our safety depends upon our shunning the occasions of evil and shutting out all dangerous objects from our soul, by this curiosity he fell. One of the combatants was wounded; and Alipius no sooner saw the blood of the wounded gladiator than, instead of turning away his eyes, he fixed them on the savage sight, sucked in all the fury, and was made drunk with the insensate cruelty of those criminal and barbarous combats. He was not now the man he came, but one of the multitude with which he mingled. He looked on gloatingly, he shouted, he took fire, he carried away with him a madness which compelled him to return again and to draw others with him. He relapsed into his former passion for the diversions of the circus, some of them innocent, some barbarous, and some gross. From these misfortunes he learned to fear his own weakness, and trust in God alone, after he had been rescued by the strong and merciful hand of his Creator. But this was long afterwards.

In the meantime Alipius followed his studies, lived chaste, behaved with integrity and honour, and was made assessor of justice in the court of the treasurer of Italy. In this charge he gave clear proofs of justice and disinterestedness, and opposed an unjust usurpation by a powerful senator whose favour was courted by many, and whose enmity was dreaded by all. When a bribe was promised, Alipius scornfully rejected it; and when he was approached with threats, he despised them. The judge himself was restrained by the integrity of his assessor; for if he had passed an unjust decree, Alipius would have left the bench. When St Augustine came to Rome he stuck close to him, went with him to Milan in 384, and shared his conversion. Their names were inscribed together among the *competentes* at the beginning of the Lent of 387. Alipius followed with exactness and fervour the exercises of catechumens before Baptism, and received that sacrament with St Augustine from St Ambrose on Easter Eve. Some time after they returned to Rome and, having spent a year there in retirement, went back to Africa. They lived together at Tagaste, in a small community of devout persons, in the fervent practice of penance, fasting, and prayer. Worldly habits just discarded stood in need of such a retreat, and habits of all virtues were to be formed and strengthened. Such a solitude was also a necessary preparation for the apostolic life, which these holy men afterwards undertook. They lived thus three years at Tagaste when, St Augustine being made priest of Hippo, they all removed thither and continued the same manner of life in a monastery which had been built there. Alipius made a pilgrimage of devotion to Palestine, where he met and conversed with St Jerome. Upon his return into Africa he was consecrated bishop of Tagaste, about the year 393. He was St Augustine's chief assistant in all his public work, and wrote against the Donatists and the Pelagians. He assisted at many councils, and preached and laboured with indefatigable zeal in the cause of God and His Church. St Augustine in a letter which he wrote to him in 429 calls him old, and he seems not to have long survived that year. His name occurs in the Roman Martyrology on August 15, but the Augustinian canons regular and others keep his feast on the 18th.

A sufficient account of St Alipius, pieced together mainly from the writings of St Augustine will be found in the *Acta Sanctorum*, August, vol. iii.

LITTLE ST HUGH OF LINCOLN, Mart.

A.D. 1255

The charge against the Jews of a general practice of ritual murder, a charge which arose from the story of Little St William of Norwich in the twelfth century, has been amply refuted by both Jewish and Christian writers; nor has any particular sporadic example of it ever been proved. This does not do away with the possibility of accidental or deliberate killing of Christian children by Jews out of hatred for their religion (or even more of hatred for those that professed it), even to the extent of crucifixion and mockery of the passion of Christ; but this again has never been proved against them in any specific example, nor is there now evidence to show that the famous cases of William of Norwich and Hugh of Lincoln were exceptions to this.

The story is that Hugh was a child of nine years old, the son of a widow. On the occasion of some Jewish gathering at Lincoln one Koppin enticed him into his house on July 31, 1255, where he was kept until the following August 27, a Friday. On that day Koppin and his fellow Jews tortured and scourged him, crowned him with thorns and finally crucified him in derision. They tried to dispose of the body by burial, but the earth refused to cover it, and it was thrown down a well. Hugh's school-fellows directed suspicion towards the Jew's house and Koppin was arrested, together with ninety-two other Jews of the city. Koppin is alleged to have confessed the crime, to have denounced his accomplices, and to have stated (certainly falsely) that it was Jewish custom to crucify a Christian boy once a year. By an order of King Henry III and his parliament assembled at Reading Koppin was dragged to death at the heels of a young horse and eighteen others were hanged at Lincoln; the remainder were imprisoned in London, but set free on payment of large fines. Their release was attributed to the kind offices of the Franciscans, who interceded for them; but Matthew Paris asserts that they were bribed to do this by the wealth of Jewry. Immediately Hugh's body was recovered from the well a blind woman was restored to sight on touching it and invoking the martyr; other miracles followed, and the chapter of Lincoln solemnly translated the relics from their parish church to a shrine next to the tomb of Grosseteste. It is impossible to tell now whether the Jews were innocent or guilty of the crime attributed to them; the universal mediæval conviction that St Hugh suffered *in odium fidei* is still recognized in the diocese of Nottingham, where his feast is kept on August 18. The account of Little St Hugh in Chaucer's *Prioresse's Tale* is well known, and both he and St William of Norwich were favourite ballad subjects ; a pathetic song about William, with a sweet simple tune, was sung in country parts within living memory.

The account given above is that of Matthew Paris. The Burton Annalist attributes the intervention in favour of the Jews to the Dominicans, not to the Franciscans, and Mr. C. Trice Martin in his Preface to the *Registrum Epistolarum J. Peckham* (Rolls Series), vol. ii, pp. lxxxviii and xcvi, seems to agree with him. See also the French account described by T. D. Hardy in his *Catalogue of British History*, vol. iii, p. 144 ; where, as in some other sources, the name of the principal culprit is given as Jopin, not Koppin. *Cf.* further what has been said regarding these cases of supposed ritual murder in vol. iii of this series, pp. 388–390.

BD. ANGELO AUGUSTINE MAZZINGHI, CONF.

A.D. 1438

Was born at Florence in 1377 of a family rivalling in distinction those of the Corsini and Pazzi. Having entered the Carmelite order, he became lector in theology, and was successively appointed prior of the Carmels of Le Selve, Frascati, and Florence, and then provincial of Tuscany. In these offices he showed himself a model of virtue ; his religious devotion to the Blessed Sacrament and to our Lady, his observance, mortifications, and humility, touched all hearts, and warmed the zeal of every monastery with which he came into contact. He had great success as a preacher, which certain old pictures indicate by representing him with garlands of flowers coming from his mouth and entwining among his hearers. At the end of his term as provincial he went back to Le Selve and devoted the rest of his life to the reform of his order, which had been begun by Friar James Alberti in 1413 and had taken root at Le Selve, Gerona, and Mantua. The last-named Carmel gave its name to this movement, which four years after Bd. Angelo's death became a quasi-independent congregation with its own vicar general ; among its principles on which Bd. Angelo insisted was the abolition of the use of all private property and that no friar might accept or retain a post which involved his living outside his monastery. He died at the *Carmine* of Florence on August 16, 1438, after predicting the day of his death. The ancient *cultus* of

Bd. Angelo, supported by many miracles, was confirmed by Pope Clement XIII in 1761.

A sketch of the life of Blessed Angelo Agostini was printed at Saragossa at the time of his beatification: R. A. Faci, *Noticia breve de la vida de S. Angelo Augustini* (1761). See also Villiers, *Bibliotheca Carmelitana*, vol. i, pp. 104–105, and *Dictionnaire d'Histoire et de Géographie ecclésiastiques*, vol. iii, c. 40.

BD. BEATRICE DA SILVA, Virg., Foundress of the Conceptionists

A.D. 1490

This Beatrice, known in Portugal as Brites, was born in 1424 of the family of Portalegre, a branch of the Portuguese royal house, and was a sister of Bd. Amadeus, initiator of the Franciscan "reform of Marignano." She was brought up in the household of the Princess Isabel and at the age of about twenty accompanied her to Spain when she married John II of Castile. The beauty and attractiveness of Beatrice excited the jealousy of the Queen, or, as some say, she listened too readily to the ill-natured gossip of jealous ladies of the court, and Beatrice was imprisoned for three days without food. When she was released she had had enough of court life and, a vision of our Lady having shown her the will of God, she was given leave to retire to the Dominican convent at Toledo. Here she was honoured with the friendship of the famous daughter of her former mistress, Isabel the Catholic, a woman of learning and piety who always honoured those qualities in others; she aided Beatrice in her project for a new order of women and in 1484, four years after Isabel was recognized as queen of Castile, the Congregation of the Immaculate Conception of the Blessed Virgin Mary was founded at Toledo. The Queen gave the castle of Galliana to be the house of the first community, who followed an adaptation of the Cistercian rule, wore a white habit with a blue mantle, after the form in which our Lady had appeared to the foundress, and had a special devotion to the Immaculate Conception. This institute was approved by Pope Innocent VIII in 1489, but ten days before its solemn inauguration Bd. Beatrice died, on September 1, 1490. Soon after the new order came under the influence of the Franciscan Cardinal Ximenez de Cisneros, Archbishop of Toledo, and when its approval was confirmed by Pope Julius II in 1506 it was with a modification of the rule of the Poor Clares; it still exists in Spain, Belgium, Italy, and before the persecution of 1926–29 in Mexico.

The strong *cultus* of Blessed Beatrice da Silva in Spain and elsewhere was solemnly confirmed by Pope Pius XI in 1926.

The decree confirming the cult of Blessed Beatrix da Silva is printed in the *Acta Apostolicae Sedis*, vol. xviii (1926), pp. 496–499, and contains a short sketch of her history. See also Jeronymo de Belem, *Chronica Serafica da santa Provincia dos Algarves*, vol. ii, pp. 736–748. Upon the Conceptionist Order, of which the famous mystic Maria Coronel d'Agreda was a member, see Heimbucher, *Die Orden und Kongregationen der Kath. Kirche*, vol. ii, pp. 488 seq.

BD. AIMO TAPARELLI, Conf.

A.D. 1495

Belonged to the family of the Counts of Lagnasco and was born at Savigliano in Piedmont in 1395. He was an attractive and quick-witted youth, who joined the Dominicans and studied at the University of Turin, where he afterwards taught. He preached with much effect throughout Piedmont, both for the reconciliation of heretics, the reformation of ill-livers, and the edification of good Christians. As prior in his native town and then as vicar provincial he promoted regular discipline and was most particular that the Divine Office and conventual Mass should be carried out fittingly. He attracted the attention of Bd. Amadeus, who became Duke of Savoy in 1455, and was appointed to preach at his court, and he continued to counsel and encourage that holy but unfortunate prince in the troubles which followed his abdication. Bd. Aimo's favourite text was, " To serve God is to reign " ; he wrote those words on the wall of his cell, and in a more simple form above the door of the friars' church at Savigliano : " Salvation consists in serving God ; everything else is delusion." His own long life was simply a commentary on that text : all his time he was serving God either directly or by service of his neighbour for God's sake ; and when the world was too much with him he would retreat for a time of uninterrupted divine contemplation to a mountain near Saluzzo. And the world and the Devil were often very much with him, for northern Italy was overrun by heretics and it was the Dominicans' business to deal with them. In 1466 the commissary of the Inquisition, Bd. Bartholomew, a fellow-townsman of Bd. Aimo, was done to death by heretics at Cerverio ; he was the third of the four inquisitors produced by Savigliano, and the third to be martyred. Aimo was appointed to take his place and shortly after was made inquisitor general for Upper Lombardy and Liguria ; the post was as dangerous as it was difficult and laborious, but Aimo, already over seventy, took it up without a word and carried out its duties till the end of his life, nearly thirty years. On August 13, 1495, when reciting the office of the day he came to the words, "The saints shall rejoice in glory," and it seemed to him that a choir of angels made the response, "They shall be joyful in their beds," and at once he had a premonition that his death was at hand. And so it was. Two days later, the feast of the Assumption, when he had said his office and received the last sacraments, he clasped a crucifix to his breast and quietly died. He was a hundred years old. The people immediately flocked to venerate his body, and the *cultus* that then began was confirmed by Pope Pius IX in 1856.

The case presented for the confirmation of the *cultus* of Blessed Aimo seems to have been largely based upon a manuscript chronicle compiled by Father Peronino Sereno at the beginning of the sixteenth century. A full account is given in the *Analecta Juris Pontificii*, ii (1856), cc. 2337–2346. See also Arnaud, *Vita del b. Aimone* (1802), and Procter, *Lives of Dominican Saints*, pp. 45–47.

AUGUST 19

ST JOHN EUDES, Conf., Founder of the Congregation of Jesus and Mary

A.D. 1680

IN the second half of the sixteenth century there lived at Ri, in Normandy, a certain Isaac Eudes. He was what we should call a yeoman farmer, who had been at first intended for the priesthood, but when an epidemic carried off his brothers in 1587 he took over the family land, responsibility for which had thus devolved on him. Eleven years later, when he was about thirty-two years old, he married Martha Corbin and when after two years they had no children the couple made a pilgrimage to a neighbouring shrine of our Lady, and nine months later a boy was born to them; subsequently they had three daughters and two more sons, one of whom was François Eudes de Mézeray, well known in France as an historian. The first-born was baptized John, and he led an exemplary childhood; it is recorded of him that, when he was nine, a play-mate hit him in the face and he literally fulfilled the gospel precept and turned his other cheek to be slapped also. But such actions are by no means confined to children who will grow up to be saints, and too much significance must not be attached to them. When he was fourteen he was sent by his parents to the Jesuit college at Caen. They wished him to marry and carry on his father's estate, but John had taken a private vow of celibacy and when he had finished his arts and philosophy courses in 1621 he received minor orders and returned to Caen to study theology, with the idea of enrolling himself among the parochial clergy. But by the advice of his confessor he decided to offer himself to the Congregation of the Oratory of France, which had been founded in 1611 by M. (afterwards Cardinal) Peter de Bérulle, and after with difficulty obtaining the consent of his parents he was accepted by the superior general at Paris early in 1623. As he had been an exemplary child and youth, so was he an exemplary cleric, and he made so great an impression upon Bérulle that he permitted him to preach while yet in minor orders. After a year of trial at Paris John Eudes was sent to Aubervilliers to be under the instruction of M. de Condren, a priest who, in the words of St Jane Frances de Chantal, was "fit to instruct angels." The aim of the Oratory is the perfection of sacerdotal life, and John Eudes was happy in having his first steps along that path directed by two such men as Condren and Bérulle, men who took as their model in direction " our Lord training His priests ; the Word incarnate, not living at a distance just to be an example, but living within the priest so as to communicate His own life to him, to make one with Himself the priest whom He intended to make a fellow priest, a fellow victim, a fellow guide and shepherd." On December 20, *O Clavis*, 1625, John Eudes became himself a priest, and at midnight of Christmas offered the Holy Sacrifice for the first time.

Two years later a virulent epidemic of plague broke out in Normandy and St John volunteered to go and work among the sufferers of his own countryside. He was given permission and Bérulle sent him to the Bishop of Séez, with a letter of introduction in which he said, "The order of charity demands that his gifts should be used in the service of the province wherein he received life, grace, and holy orders, and that his own diocese should be the first to have the fruits that are to be expected from his ability, goodness, wisdom, energy, and life." For a time St John could find no priest who would share his labour and danger, but at length the Abbé Lament came forward, and together they spent two months ministering spiritually and medically to the sick, dying, and endangered. He was then sent to the Oratory of Caen, where he remained quietly till a visitation of plague to that city in 1631 called him out again ; during that time, in order to avoid the danger of infecting his brethren, he lived in a large barrel in the middle of a field, receiving his food daily from a nearby convent. In spite of this precaution the Oratorian fathers began to sicken, and the care of them was added to his responsibility ; thanks largely to his devoted work only two of them died. For the following ten years St John was chiefly engaged in giving missions and incidentally gaining much experience for the work which he was afterwards to undertake. It was a time in which were inaugurated popular missions as we now understand them and, amid many able and some preeminent mission-preachers, St John Eudes was the most distinguished ; and from the pulpit he went to the confessional for, as he said, "the preacher beats the bushes but the confessors catch the birds!" So competent a judge as Mgr. le Camus, Bishop of Belley, a friend of St Francis de Sales, said of him, "I have heard all the best preachers in Italy and France but I have never heard anyone who touches the heart so deeply as does this good father." He preached in his life-time one hundred and ten missions.

Among the matters that troubled St John during the course of his mission was the difficult position of women and girls who were reclaimed by God's grace from a disorderly life. For a time he tried to deal with the problem by finding for these penitents temporary homes with religious people, where there would be less temptation for them to revert to a life of sin, but this arrangement was soon seen to be inadequate. A certain woman of humble origin, Madeleine Lamy, who had taken charge of several of these girls, strongly realized the unsatisfactoriness of the position and wanted St John to make some more permanent provision. "Where are you off to now?" she demanded of him one day, "To some church, I suppose, where you'll gaze at the images and think yourself pious. And all the time what is really wanted of you is a decent home for these poor creatures who are being lost for want of attention and guidance." These words and the laughter of his companions made a deep impression on St John, and in 1641 a house was rented as a refuge for penitent women until honest work could be found for them, and it was put in charge of a lady named Margaret Morin, who was soon joined by Mlle de Saint André and others. Unfortunately Mlle Morin was a headstrong and difficult character; her harshness drove Mlle de Saint André from the house, she insisted on trying to introduce the Ursuline rule in opposition to Père Eudes, who favoured that of the Visitation nuns, and eventually she threw up her work and left the refuge with several others, leaving the whole thing on the hands of Mlle de Taillefer and St John's niece, Marie Herson, who was a mere child. He now saw that it was necessary for the work to be in the hands of a religious congregation and offered it to the Visitandines of Caen, who accepted it in 1644 and made Mère Frances Patin the superior. She continued to administer it successfully for some years and received a number of novices, but it progressed only slowly and in the face of considerable difficulties. In 1643 Père Eudes, after several years of prayer, consideration, and consultation with his superiors and high ecclesiastics, severed his connection with the Oratorians. He had learnt in the course of his missions that the clergy needed reform even more than their flocks, and became convinced that the first necessity was to establish seminaries, and that until this was done the Congregation of the Oratory could not hope to have its full effect. His views were shared by Père de Condren, who had become superior general, but his successor Père Bourgoing would not countenance the plan of a seminary in connection with the Oratory of Caen. Père Eudes then formed the project of a new congregation of secular priests whose object should be the formation of a zealous and virtuous parochial clergy by the conduct of seminaries, and with the approval of Cardinal de Richelieu such a congregation was founded at Caen on the feast of the Annunciation, 1643. It was called the Congregation of Jesus and Mary and was modelled on that of the Oratory, consisting of secular priests who were not bound by vows; the first members were St John Eudes and five others, and they were consecrated to " the Most Holy Trinity as the first principle and last end of priestly dignity and holiness." The badge by which they were to be distinguished was the hearts of Jesus and Mary regarded as mystically one, and he prescribed devotions in its honour to both of his congregations, to the heart of flesh united to the Divinity and symbolizing the eternal love of Jesus. The new venture met with immediate criticism and opposition, particularly from the Jansenists and from the French Oratorians, who were both influenced by the first-named and jealous of the Eudist fathers; when in 1646 Père Eudes sent Père Mannoury to Rome to try and get papal approval for his foundation the opposition was so strong that he was unsuccessful. The same thing happened in the following year, but in 1648 the Congregation of Propaganda gave it indirect approbation by recognizing the establishment at Caen as a Tridentine seminary.

In 1650, therefore, the Bishop of Coutances invited St John to set up a seminary in that city and in the following year he was invited by M. Olier, who regarded him as " the marvel of his age," to give a ten weeks' mission at the parish-church of St Sulpice in Paris. During the course of it news was brought that the sisters at the Refuge in Caen, having separated from the Visitandines, were recognized by the Bishop of Bayeux as a separate congregation, under the name of the Sisters of Our Lady of Charity of the Refuge; aspirants were to be selected with great care and the penitents were to be forbidden to talk about their past life either to one another or to the nuns. In the following year Mère Patin, having discharged her time of office at the Visitation convent and her health being marvellously improved, returned to the Refuge, which she successfully directed till the end of her life. St John founded a seminary at Lisieux in 1653 and another at Rouen in 1659, and in 1661 he accompanied the Bishop of Evreux to Rome, where he made personal representations for the formal approbation of his work; but even saints do not do everything properly and herein Père Eudes failed, in part through his own disregard for prudence and tact. But a year after his return, in 1666, the Refuge sisters by a bull of Pope Alexander VII were erected as a recognized institute, with enclosure and solemn vows, with a fourth added, to labour for the reclamation of unchaste women and to care for penitents from among them. This work begun by Père Eudes and the devoted Madeleine Lamy had then been going on for thirty years, during twenty of which it had been directed by Mère Patin; having seen it thoroughly established and recognized, she went to her rest two years later. St John continued to give long and successful missions and founded two more seminaries, at Evreux in 1666 and at Rennes in 1670.

In the latter year he published a book entitled *The Devotion to the Adorable Heart of Jesus;* he had already given a feast of the Holy Heart of Mary to his congregation, which in 1648 had been celebrated at Autun and afterwards in other French dioceses, but in this book was included a proper Mass and Office of the Sacred Heart of Jesus. On August 31, 1670, this feast was first observed in the seminary chapel at Rennes, with the bishop's consent; on October 20 it was celebrated at Coutances, and five other dioceses took it up. He wrote to his congregation on the subject: " Although we have not hitherto observed a special feast of the adorable Heart of Jesus we have never meant to separate two things which God has so closely joined together as the most majestic Heart of His Son and the heart of His blessed Mother. On the contrary, our intention has always been to look upon and honour these two Hearts as one in unity and spirit, in sentiment and in affection, as is clear in the salutation with which every day we greet the divine Heart of Jesus and Mary and in the prayer and several parts of the Office and Mass which we celebrate on the feast of the sacred heart of the Blessed Virgin." It will be seen therefore that, while St John Eudes can hardly be called the first apostle of devotion to the Sacred Heart as we know it to-day, nevertheless he was " the institutor of the liturgical *cultus* of the sacred Heart of Jesus and the holy heart of Mary," as Pope Leo XIII called him in 1903 : " He was the first to think— and that not without a divine inspiration—of rendering to them liturgical worship," says his decree of beatification. In 1674, the year before St Margaret Mary's " great revelation," Pope Clement X issued six briefs of indulgences for the confraternities of the Heart of Jesus and Mary erected in Eudist seminaries.

In 1671 this Pope had celebrated the jubilee of his priesthood, and on that occasion Père Eudes was invited to preach before King Louis XIV at Versailles. He preached there an ordinary mission sermon and, as his biographer records, with more fruit than was gained by more accomplished orators ; Bossuet himself was impressed by the power which so great holiness gave to his discourses.

Among his personal friends were St Vincent de Paul and the holy Carmelite, Margaret-of-the-Blessed-Sacrament, the second daughter of *la belle Acarie* (Bd. Mary-of-the-Incarnation). He also knew the famous demoniac, the unfortunate Marie des Vallées, whom he exorcised and whose conversation he wrote down. During the last years of his life he spent much time on his great treatise *The Admirable Heart of the Most Holy Mother of God*, at which he had been working for many years and which he finished less than a month before his death. His last mission had been at Saint-Lô in 1675, where in wintry weather he had preached in the open *place* nearly every day for nine weeks; from this ordeal the old man never properly recovered and his days of active work were practically ended. St John Eudes died on August 19, 1680, was beatified in 1909, and canonized in 1925, when his feast was added to the general calendar of the Western Church. Of his foundations, the Congregation of Jesus and Mary (" Eudists ") prospered after his death but was almost extinguished by the Revolution; it was reconstituted in 1826 and took a new lease of life in 1851, but it never recovered its seminaries in France and is now chiefly engaged in mission work and secondary education in various parts of the world. But the Sisters of Our Lady of Charity of the Refuge have gone on from strength to strength, and in 1835 there was formed from it, by the vigorous efforts of the Ven. Mary-of-St-Euphrasia Pelletier, the separate institute of the Sisters of Our Lady of Charity of the Good Shepherd, well known in Great Britain as the " Good Shepherd nuns," who add to the work of the original institute the conduct of reformatories, inebriates' homes, *etc*.

The most famous saying of St John Eudes is that to celebrate the Holy Sacrifice of the Mass properly three eternities would be required: the first to prepare for it, the second to celebrate it, and the third to give thanks for it; and in a book which he wrote during the early years of his ministry, *The Life and Reign of Jesus in Christian Souls*, he sums up in a sentence the principle of his own life and of his own works: " Our wish, our object, our chief preoccupation must be to form Jesus in ourselves, to make His spirit, His devotion, His affections, His desires, and His disposition live and reign there. All our religious exercises should be directed to this end. It is the work which God has given us to do unceasingly."

The later biographers of St John Eudes have done well to draw largely upon his correspondence, much of which still remains unpublished. The first formal Life was written by one of his congregation, Père Hérambourg, who had not personally known him, but who in joining the institute two years after the founder's death had had abundant opportunities of conversing with those who had lived with him in the most intimate personal relation. No full bibliography can be attempted here. The most exhaustive study so far published is the Life by Père Boulay in four stout volumes (1905); but the Eudist Father, Émile Georges, in his *Saint Jean Eudes, missionaire apostolique* (1925), has sketched on a less ample canvas a very thorough portrait of the saint and of his manifold activities. Excellent also is the still more handy volume of Henri Joly in the series " Les Saints." It must suffice to add a reference to Henri Bremond's chapters on Eudes in his *Histoire littéraire du Sentiment religieux en France*, etc., vol. iii, pp. 583-671; and to Émile Dermenghem, *La Vie Admirable et les Révélations de Marie des Vallées* (1926). There is a good article also under the heading " Eudes " in the *Dictionnaire de Théologie Catholique*, vol. v, with an adequate bibliography.

ST ANDREW THE TRIBUNE, Mart.

c. A.D. 303

The authentic *acta* of this famous martyr have not survived, and the legend which we have has been amplified and embroidered, probably during the tenth century. So far as the story can be plausibly reconstructed Andrew was a captain under Antiochus in the army of Maximian Galerius sent by Diocletian against the Persians. During an engagement with the enemy Andrew called on the name of Christ (of whom he had heard as a mighty protector) and told his men to do the same; when their arms were successful they attributed the victory to these prayers, and Andrew and some others resolved to become Christians. For this they were denounced to Antiochus, who was not certain what steps he ought to take with regard to this breach of discipline among his troops, and wrote to Galerius to enquire. The general was unwilling to risk spoiling the *morale* of the army by executing brave soldiers at a moment of victory and so ordered Antiochus to discharge the offenders from the service, but to punish them later on when a more suitable opportunity should arise. Andrew therefore with the other converts made his way to Peter, Bishop of Cæsarea in Cappadocia, by whom they were baptized. Seleucus, the military governor of Cilicia, heard of what had happened and sent a detachment to arrest the neophytes, who fled for refuge into the Taurus mountains. Here they were tracked, surrounded, and put to death. St Andrew is the object of a great devotion in the East, where he is one having the title of " the Great Martyr." The number of his companions is not known, but is given by a Syrian menology as 2995, which figure has been copied (with variations) by some Western martyrologies.

There is no early evidence for the cult of this St Andrew, though the fictitious story of the martyrdom was popular at a later date. The Greek text is given in the *Acta Sanctorum*, August, vol. iii. There is an Andrew in the " Hieronymianum " on July 22, but there is nothing to connect him with this date or with the story told in the alleged " Acts."

SS. TIMOTHY, AGAPIUS, AND THECLA, MM.

A.D. 304

Whilst Diocletian held the reins of government and signalized his rage and cruelty against the Christians, in the second year of the general persecution, orders were received by Urban, the governor of Palestine, to proceed against the Christians in his province. St Timothy, Bishop of Gaza, for having boldly confessed his faith was inhumanly scourged, his sides were torn with iron combs, and he was at length burnt to death at a slow fire at Gaza on May 1, 304, giving by his patience a certain proof that his charity was perfect. SS. Agapius and Thecla were condemned by the same judge to be led to Caesarea, and there exposed to wild beasts. Thecla was despatched by the beasts in the amphitheatre ; but Agapius was kept back for the time being, and detained two years longer in prison, till Maximian Caesar gave orders that this confessor should be one of the victims to grace a festival, unless he would abjure the Christian faith. His sufferings had no way abated his constancy, and the delay of his crown had increased his desire speedily to join his companions in glory. In the amphitheatre he was brought out in the presence of the Emperor himself and in company with a common felon, a slave who had murdered his master. This man, not being at once killed by the beasts, was pardoned and set free ; clemency was likewise offered to the innocent Agapius if he would sacrifice to the gods. He was therefore left to be mauled by a bear, but as the animal did not kill him outright he was taken back to prison, and on the next day drowned in the sea. In the martyrdom of St Agapius we see examples both of our Lord's saying that His followers should confess His name before the kings of the earth and of the repetition of the choice of a Barabbas to be released before a just man unjustly condemned.

Eusebius' *De Mart. Palestinæ* is a trustworthy authority for the martyrdom of this group. The *cultus* of Timothy is well attested ; see Delehaye, *Les Origines du Culte des Martyrs*, pp. 75, 218, 221. A basilica was built at Gaza in which St Timothy's remains were venerated.

ST SIXTUS OR XYSTUS III, POPE

A.D. 440

Sixtus was one of the principal clergy of the Roman Church before his pontificate, and of sufficient importance to be triumphantly claimed by the Pelagians as one of themselves, which caused him to raise his voice against the heresy. He corresponded with St Augustine about it, and a letter written by Augustine to him in 418 and circulated by the monk Florus, was the cause of the dispute in the African monastery of Hadrumentum in 424 in which some of the monks violently opposed the teaching of the Bishop of Hippo. When St Sixtus III succeeded Pope St Celestine I in 432 St Prosper of Aquitaine wrote that, " We trust in the protection of the Lord, and that what He has done for us in Innocent, Zosimus, Boniface, and Celestine He will do also in Sixtus ; and as they guarded the flock against declared and openly professed wolves, so he may drive off the hidden ones," referring to the teachers of Semipelagianism. He was not disappointed, but St Sixtus was of a peace-loving nature and conciliatory in his policy, so that some of the hot-heads of orthodoxy were dissatisfied and did not scruple to accuse the Pope of Pelagian and Nestorian leanings. He confirmed the decrees of the Council of Ephesus, held under his predecessor, and admonished Nestorius to retract his errors, but that heresiarch had eventually to be banished to a monastery in the Libyan desert. A legacy of the controversy was the antagonism between St Cyril, Patriarch of Alexandria, and John, Patriarch of Antioch, who had supported Nestorius ; St Sixtus joined his efforts to those of the Emperor, Theodosius II, and of St Simeon Stylites, to heal this breach, which was eventually accomplished. It is often stated that Sixtus III was accused by the consul Bassus of an infamous crime, but that Bassus was convicted of calumny and pardoned by the Pope ; it is now known that the story is apocryphal, resting on the testimony of a forged document.

St Sixtus III notably upheld the dignity of the Roman Church both abroad, where he maintained his jurisdiction over the bishops of Illyricum against Proclus, Archbishop of Constantinople, and at home. In the city he built the basilica of St Laurence *in Lucina*, for the service of the cemetery where SS. Peter and Paul and, later, St Sebastian, had lain ; set up a tablet bearing the names of the popes who lay there in the papal crypt of St Callistus ; and restored the Liberian basilica, now called St Mary Major, which he dedicated in honour of our Lady as a memorial of the Council of Ephesus which had vindicated her right to be called the Mother of God. In it he set up this noble inscription: "O Virgin Mary, I, Sixtus, have dedicated a new temple to thee, an offering worthy of the womb that brought to us salvation. Thou, a maiden knowing not man, didst bear and bring forth our Salvation. Behold! These martyrs, witnesses to Him who was the fruit of thy womb, bear to thee their crowns of victory, and beneath their feet lie the instruments of their passion—sword, flame, wild beast, water, and cruel poison: one crown alike awaits these divers deaths." Over the arch of the apse can still be read the words in mosaic: "Sixtus the bishop for the people of God." This Pope consecrated a number of churches, and the dedications of two of them are feasts universal in the Western Church, St Peter-in-Chains (August 1) and St Mary Major (August 5). He was till 1922 commemorated on March 28, but now on August 19, the more likely date of his death.

The *Liber Pontificalis*, with Duchesne's notes, vol. i, pp. 232–237, is the most important source. See also Grisar, *Geschichte Roms und der Päpste*, §§ 224–226, and with regard to the forgeries mentioned above § 468. Some further references are given above in the bibliographical notes to St Peter in Chains and Our Lady of the Snow, pp. 3 and 62.

ST MOCHTA, BP. AND CONF.

EARLY SIXTH CENTURY

Mochta (Mochteus) is mentioned in the lives of St Patrick and there is a late Latin "life" of himself which is "crammed with fables"; he is regarded as the first bishop in Louth, but it is not certain that he was ever consecrated: sometimes he is called bishop, sometimes archpriest, sometimes priest, or even simply a "holy man." He was a Briton by birth and while still a child was brought over to Ireland by his Christian parents. With them travelled a heathen bard, one Hoa, who when a grievous storm sprang up during the voyage wanted to throw young Mochta overboard as a propitiatory sacrifice; but the tempest was miraculously calmed and later on Mochta converted Hoa. Mochta became a disciple of St Patrick and was sent to Rome where, according to the *acta*, he was made bishop by Pope St Leo I, and he presented to the Pope a tablet on which he had learned writing under the tuition of an angel. When he had collected twelve suitable young men as missionaries he returned to Ireland; one of these, Edan, got left behind *en route*, so he put to sea on the bough of a tree—and got there first. St Mochta settled first at Omeath and then at Louth, where he was soon surrounded by a large community of followers; for these he wrote a rule of life, and the sixty senior monks were dispensed from manual labour. It is recorded that he never uttered a false word nor a foolish one, and that he never ate a morsel of fat—not from finicalness but by way of curbing his appetite for such food. Among the fables told of St Mochta is that he lived for three hundred years: this was in accordance with a sentence pronounced on him by St Patrick because, when reading the Bible, Mochta had questioned the accuracy of the ages attributed to the antediluvian patriarchs. If the evidence which we have may be trusted he probably lived to be one hundred, and was the last of St Patrick's personal disciples.

The best text of the Latin Life referred to above is that edited by Père de Smedt from the Codex Salmanticensis, pp. 903-914; but the Life is also printed after Colgan in the *Acta Sanctorum*, August, vol. iii. Mochta's death is assigned in the *Annals of Ulster* to A.D. 535, but see further J. Ryan, *Irish Monasticism*, pp. 126-127.

ST BERTULF, Abbot of Bobbio, Conf.

A.D. 640

Among the many relatives of St Arnoul of Metz who were venerated as saints Bertulf was one of the chief; he had been brought up a pagan, but the example and teaching of Arnoul brought him to the Church of Christ, and in 620 (at what age is not known) he became a monk at Luxeuil. Bertulf remained there for several years, learning the principles of the religious life and the discipline of St Columban from his successor St Eustace. Then he attracted the attention of St Attala, who had succeeded Columban as abbot of Bobbio; he was given permission to migrate to that monastery, and in 627 became its abbot on the death of Attala. St Bertulf was worthy of his predecessors in holiness, learning, and apostolic zeal. Within the monastery he rigorously maintained the austere rule of St Columban; outside it he vigorously opposed Arianism, which was rife in northern Italy. The year following St Bertulf's election the Bishop of Tortona, taking advantage of a new abbot, claimed jurisdiction over the monastery. Bertulf appealed to Arioald, the Lombard king, who was a convert from Arianism (previous to his conversion he had had a monk of Bobbio murdered because he refused ceremonial courtesy to the heretical prince), but he would not take responsibility for a decision and referred the matter to a council. It was then carried to Rome and Arioald paid the expenses of the abbot to go there to state his case; he took with him the monk Jonas of Susa, his secretary, who afterwards wrote the life of St Bertulf, as well as of St Columban, St Attala, St Eustace, and others. Pope Honorius I, knowing the great reputation of the monastery and the exactness of its observance, declared it to be exempt from episcopal control and immediately subject to the Holy See; this was the first exemption of its kind and began a new era in the relationship of the " regular " clergy to the bishops. Jonas relates that on the way home Bertulf was stricken down with a fever, from which he seemed likely to die; but on the vigil of SS. Peter and Paul he fell into a deep sleep, during which he had a vision of St Peter, and upon waking up was completely recovered. Jonas also records a number of miracles of the saint, of which he claims to have been a witness.

There is a short Latin Life by Jonas I, abbot of Bobbio, which was printed both by Mabillon and the Bollandists, and finally has been edited by B. Krusch in the *Monumenta Germaniæ, Scriptories rerum Meroving.*, vol. iv, pp. 280 seq. There is also an encomium in verse by Hodoard. *Cf.* Cipolla and Buzzi, *Codice diplomatico del Monastero di Bobbio* (1918), **vol. i.**

ST SEBALD, CONF.

EIGHTH CENTURY (?)

St Sebald, patron of Nuremberg in Bavaria, seems to have come to that city from somewhere south of the Danube, perhaps as a follower of St Willibald. He lived as a hermit in the Reichswald, preaching the gospel of Jesus Christ among his neighbours, and already in 1072 was recognized as the patron of Nuremberg. His "life" is of uncertain date, and full of anachronisms and inconsistencies. According to it he was a solitary near Vicenza for some time and was in Rome both during the pontificate of St Gregory II and when SS. Willibald and Winebald were there; when St Gregory III sent Willibald into Germany he accompanied him. One of the reliefs on the base of his shrine at Nuremberg, the best-known work of Peter Vischer, on which he was working from 1505 to 1519, represents the miracle of the icicles, attributed to St Sebald: one snowy night he took shelter in a peasant's cottage, but found it almost as cold within as without, for the fire was low and small. Sebald suggested that more fuel might be put on, but the man answered that he was too poor to keep up a decent fire, so Sebald

turned to the housewife and asked her to bring in a bundle of the
long icicles hanging from the eaves; this she did, Sebald threw
them on the fire, and they blazed up merrily. Other miracles of
his are recorded on the shrine, namely, giving sight to a blind man,
filling a jug with wine from nowhere, and causing a mocker to be
swallowed up by the earth.

By a recent decree of the Congregation of Sacred Rites (Jan. 26, 1927)
the name of St Sebald has been inserted in the Roman Martyrology. The
unsatisfactory Life mentioned above is printed in the *Acta Sanctorum*,
August, vol. iii. See also the *Kirchenlexikon*, vol. xi, cc. 24–26; and
Stamminger, *Franconia Sancta*, pp. 534 *seq.*

ST LOUIS OF ANJOU, Bp. of Toulouse, Conf.

A.D. 1297

This saint was born at Brignoles in Provence in 1274, second
son to Charles II surnamed the Lame, King of Naples and Sicily,
and Mary, daughter of Stephen V, King of Hungary; he was therefore a grand-nephew of St Louis of France and connected with the
family of St Elizabeth of Hungary.

In 1284, two years after the general revolt of the two Sicilies,
Louis's father, Charles, then Prince of Salerno, was taken prisoner
in a sea-fight by the King of Aragon. His father, Charles I, died
within a few months, and he was saluted by his friends as King of
Sicily, but he remained four years prisoner and was only released
on hard conditions: being, moreover, obliged to send into Aragon
as hostages fifty gentlemen and three of his sons, of whom Louis
was one. He remained seven years at Barcelona in captivity, under
which he was always cheerful and encouraged his companions, reminding them that adversity is a help to those who make profession
of serving God. We learn by it patience, humility, and resignation
to the divine will, and by it are better disposed for the exercise of
virtue. Prosperity blinds the soul, drugs it, so as to make her forget
both God and herself; it emboldens and strengthens the passions,
and flatters pride and the inordinate love of ourselves. Not content
with what he suffered from his captivity, he practised voluntary
austerities, fasted several days every week, rejected dangerous amusements, and avoided the company of women except in public. He
recited the Church's office, and went every day to confession before
he heard Mass, that he might assist at that tremendous sacrifice with
greater purity of soul; and, as the whole city of Barcelona was his

prison, he often attended the sick in the hospitals. He was educated by the Friars Minor and came under the influence of the great Spiritual, Peter John Olivi, so that when he was attacked by a severe illness at the castle of Sciurana he made a vow to join that order if he should recover. He got leave for two Franciscan friars, who were appointed to attend him, to live with him in his own apartments; he rose to pray with them in the night, and under them he applied himself diligently to the studies of philosophy and theology. At his release he seemed to have no other joy than in the power of fulfilling his engagement to become a religious. Already before that took place Pope St Celestine V had given faculties to Friar Francis of Apt to confer minor orders on Louis and appointed him administrator of the archdiocese of Lyons, though neither of these things seems to have been done.

St Louis was set at liberty in 1295, by a treaty concluded between the King of Naples, his father, and James II, King of Aragon, one condition of which was the marriage of his sister Blanche with James. Both courts had at the same time the project of a double marriage, and that the Princess of Majorca, sister to King James, should be married to Louis, on whom his father promised to settle the kingdom of Naples (which he had in part recovered), his eldest brother, Charles Martel, having been already crowned King of Hungary; but the saint's resolution of dedicating himself to God was inflexible, and he resigned his right to the crown of Naples, which his father conferred on his next brother, Robert. Thus it was his ambition to follow Jesus Christ poor and humble, rather than to be raised to honour in the world, which has no other recompenses to bestow on those who serve it but temporal goods. "Jesus Christ," said he, "is my kingdom. If I possess Him alone, I shall have all things: if I have not Him, I lose all." The opposition of his family obliged the superiors of the Friars Minor to refuse for some time to admit him into their body, wherefore he took holy orders at Naples, where he befriended a poor scholar of Cahors, James d'Euse, who afterwards became Pope John XXII and canonized his benefactor. Pope Boniface VIII gave him a dispensation to receive priestly orders in the twenty-third year of his age, and afterwards for the episcopate, together with his nomination to the bishopric of Toulouse, and a severe injunction in virtue of holy obedience to accept it. He first went to Rome to fulfil his vow, and made his religious profession among the Friars Minor, in their convent of *Ara Cœli*, on Christmas Eve, 1296, and received the episcopal consecration in the beginning of the February following.

He travelled to his bishopric as a poor religious, but was received at Toulouse with the veneration due to a saint and the magnificence that became a prince. His modesty and devotion inspired love in all that beheld him. It was his first care to provide for the relief of the poor and his first visits were made to the hospitals. Having taken an account of his revenues, he reserved to his own use a very small part, allotting the rest entirely to the poor, of whom he entertained twenty-five every day at his own table, serving them himself. He extended his charities over all his father's kingdom, and made the visitation of his whole diocese, leaving everywhere memories of his charity and sanctity. He banished the use of gold and silver plate and jewelled vessels from his episcopal dwelling, substituting therefor pewter and wooden bowls, and wore an old darned habit, as befitting a Franciscan and as an example to his clergy, who gave too much thought to their dress. As a bishop he abated nothing of his austerities, said Mass every day, and preached frequently. He was very severe in the examination of the abilities and piety of those whom he admitted among his clergy. But he soon found the episcopal office too much for him, and asked leave to resign it. He answered to some that opposed his inclination, " Let the world call me mad ; provided I may be discharged from a burden which is too heavy for my shoulders, I am satisfied. Is it not better for me to try to throw it off than to sink under it ? " The Holy See so far refused to grant his request as to make him as well administrator of the newly erected diocese of Pamiers, but God pleased to grant him what he desired by calling him to Himself. Returning from a visit to his sister in Catalonia he fell sick at the castle of Brignoles. Finding his end draw near, he said to those about him, " After a dangerous voyage I am arrived within sight of the port which I have long desired. I shall now enjoy my God whom the world would rob me of ; and I shall be freed from the heavy charge which I am not able to bear." He received the Viaticum on his knees, and died on August 19, 1297, being only twenty-three years and a half old. He was buried in the convent of Franciscan friars at Marseilles, as he had ordered. Pope John XXII canonized him at Avignon in 1317, and addressed a brief thereupon to his mother, who was still living ; a rhythmical office for his feast was written by his younger brother, Robert of Naples, but is no longer in use, though the feast is observed by the Franciscans and at Toulouse, Valencia, and elsewhere.

Attention has recently been directed to this saint by the publication at Manchester by Miss Margaret R. Toynbee, in connection with the British Society of Franciscan Studies, of a volume on *St Louis of Toulouse and the Process of Canonisation in the Fourteenth Century* (1929). We possess in fact a record of the depositions of witnesses in the process of canonisation, and this important source, long ago utilised by the Bollandists (*Acta Sanctorum*, August, vol. iii), is now being critically edited by the Franciscans of Quaracchi. Another principal source, the Life written by St Louis's confessor, John de Orta, has been printed in the *Analecta Bollandiana*, vol. ix (1890), pp. 278-353 (*cf*. also vol. xlvi, pp. 344-354). It is interesting to note that Richard Middleton (de Media Villa), an English Franciscan who was also a famous theologian, was one of St Louis' tutors; also that St Aloysius Gonzaga's extreme, and as some may well think exaggerated, modesty in avoiding all relations with the opposite sex, not even excepting his own mother, was apparently imitated from the conduct of his patron, St Louis of Anjou. See *The Month* for August 1924, pp. 158-160. An ample bibliography may be found in U. Chevalier, *Bibliographie*; and for St Louis in art see the *Archivum Franciscanum Historicum*, vol. ii (1909), pp. 378 *seq*.

BD. EMILY BICCHIERI, Virg.

A.D. 1314

Emily Bicchieri was born at Vercelli in 1238, and having lost her mother at an early age put herself under the special protection of the all-holy Mother of God. She combined a healthy aversion from worldliness with an efficient care for her widowed father's household, and he, good man, seeing only the one, planned for her a respectable marriage by which his daughter, himself, and the husband-to-be would all benefit. But when she was sixteen Emily upset all this by telling him she wanted to be a nun; at first Peter Bicchieri would not hear of such a thing, but he was a Christian and reasonable man and at length gave in to his daughter's importunities. He went further, and built and endowed a convent at Vercelli, dedicated in honour of St Margaret, of which Sister Emily became prioress at the age of twenty. These nuns were under the direction of the Friars Preachers and followed the rule of St Augustine according to the constitutions of the Sisters of Penance; according to one of several theories of the origins of Third Orders, this was the first convent of Dominican regular tertiaries. Having been elected prioress against her will, Bd. Emily governed with tact and ability, and was careful to tell no one to do what she would not do herself—except that she would never interview the fashionable ladies of Vercelli in the parlour if she could possibly help it. In directing her sisters she laid particular stress on " knowing what you were after " and on the purity of that intention : otherwise, she would say, one is like a person going to market who does not know with whom to deal or what price to pay ; and God's glory must be the last end of all their actions and the motive of their religious obedience. Those were the days, albeit the Ages of Faith, when frequent Communion was not customary, and Bd. Emily was remarkable in the practice and privilege of receiving the Blessed Sacrament three times a week and on all great feast-days. It is related of her, as of several other saints, that having once been prevented from communicating by duties in the infirmary, she afterwards received holy Communion at the hands of an angel. She was distinguished by a notable spirit of gratitude both to God and man, and by her love for liturgical prayer. She is reputed to have had the gift of miracles and to have stopped by her prayers and the sign of the cross a disastrous fire in the convent (though that is almost a commonplace of hagiology, and must often be put down to "common form"); to have had frequent visions of our Lord and His Mother; and to have participated in the sufferings of the Passion, especially those caused by the crown of thorns, to which at all times she had a great devotion. Bd. Emily died on her birthday, May 3, at the age of seventy-six. Her *cultus* was approved by Pope Clement XIV in 1769.

See the *Acta Sanctorum*, May, vol. vii, in the Appendix; Ganay, *Les Bienheureuses Dominicaines*, pp. 121 seq.; Mortier, *Maîtres Généraux O.P.*, vol. ii, p. 9; and P. B. Berro, *La beata Emilia* (1914). A fuller bibliography will be found in Taurisano, *Catalogus Hagiographicus O.P.*, p. 17.

AUGUST 20

ST BERNARD, Abbot of Clairvaux, Doctor of the Church

A.D. 1153

ST BERNARD was the third son of Tescelin Sorrel, a Burgundian noble, and Aleth, who was daughter of Bernard, lord of Montbard. He was born in 1090 at Fontaines, a castle near Dijon and a lordship belonging to his father. His parents were persons of virtuous life and his mother, not content to offer him to God as soon as he was born, as she did all her seven children, consecrated him to His service in the Church, as Anne did Samuel, and from that day considered him as not belonging to her but to God; and she took a special care of his education, in hopes that he would one day be worthy to stand at the altar. Indeed she brought up all her children with the greatest care and never trusted them to nurses. Their names were Bd. Guy, Bd. Gerard, St Bernard, Bd. Humbeline, Andrew, Bartholomew, and Bd. Nivard. They were all well educated and learned Latin and verse-making before the sons were applied to military exercise and feats of arms; but Bernard was sent to Chatillon on the Seine, to pursue a complete course of studies in a college of secular canons. He even then loved to be alone, largely at first because of shyness; his progress in learning was far greater than could be expected from one of his age; and he was soon alert to listen to what God by His holy inspirations spoke to his heart. One Christmas-eve, while waiting with his mother to set out for Matins, he fell asleep and seemed to see the infant Jesus newly born in the stable at Bethlehem; from that day he ever had a most tender devotion towards that great mystery of love and mercy, and in speaking of it always seemed to surpass himself in the sweetness of his words. He began the study of theology and of the Holy Scriptures at Chatillon, and was nineteen years old when he returned finally to his home, having been thirteen years at the school. In that same year his mother died. Her charities and attendance in the hospitals, her devotion and all her other virtues, had gained her the reputation of a saint. Bernard was greatly attached to Aleth and her loss was a heavy blow; he was in danger of becoming morbidly despondent till he was rallied out of his brooding and inertia by his lively sister Humbeline.

Bernard was now his own master, and made his appearance in the world with all the advantages and talents which can make it attractive to a young man, or which could make him loved by it. His personal attractiveness and wit, his affability and sweetness of temper, endeared him to everybody; but in these very advantages lay his chief danger, and for a time there was serious risk of his becoming lukewarm and indifferent. His keen sensibility and personal beauty laid him open to strong temptations against chastity; once an impudent woman forced herself on him; but he drove her from his room by waking the house with a cry of "Thieves!" By these and other temptations of the world Bernard was made to think of forsaking it and the pursuit of letters, which greatly attracted him, and of going to Cîteaux, where only a few years before SS. Robert, Alberic and Stephen Harding had established the first monastery of that strict interpretation of the Benedictine rule, called after it "Cistercian." He wavered for some time in his mind, and one day going to see his brothers, who were then with the Duke of Burgundy at the siege of the castle of Grancey, in great anxiety he went into a church by the road and prayed that God would direct him to discover and follow His holy will. He arose steadily fixed in the resolution of following the severe Cistercian life. His friends endeavoured to dissuade him from it; but Gaudry, lord of Touillon, his uncle, who had gained great reputation by his valour in the wars, although a man with a wife and family, came to the same resolution. Bartholomew and Andrew, two younger brothers of Bernard, also declared that they would come too. Guy, the eldest brother, was also appealed to. He had obligations which seemed to fix him in the world, for he, too, was married, and had two daughters; but his wife Elizabeth eventually consented and herself became a nun at Jully. Gerard, the second brother, was not to be so easily won, being a soldier of reputation and full of his profession, but he was soon after wounded in his side by a lance and taken prisoner, and during his convalescence God called him, and he, too, went to join his brothers. Hugh of Mâcon (who afterward founded the monastery of Pontigny, and died Bishop of Auxerre), an intimate friend of St Bernard, wept bitterly at the thought of separation, but by two interviews was induced to become his companion. Nor were these the only ones who, with apparently no previous thought of the religious life, suddenly decided to leave the world for the austere life of Cîteaux. Bernard induced in all thirty-one men to follow him—he who himself had been uncertain of his call only a few weeks before. It is a happening unparalleled in Christian history. Bernard's eloquent appeals were irresistible; mothers hid their sons, wives their husbands, lest they came under the sway of that compelling voice and look. They all assembled in a house at Chatillon, preparing to consecrate themselves to God, and on the day appointed for their meeting Bernard and his brothers went to Fontaines to take farewell of their father and beg his blessing. They left Nivard, the youngest brother, to be a comfort to him in his old age. Going out they saw him at play with other children, and Guy said to him, " Adieu, my little Nivard ! You will have all our estates and lands to yourself." The boy answered, " What ! you then take Heaven, and leave me only the earth. The division is too unequal." They went away; but soon after Nivard followed them, so that of the whole family there only remained in the world the old father and his daughter, Bd. Humbeline.

After they had stayed six months at Chatillon to settle their affairs they all departed for Cîteaux, which had been founded fifteen years and was at that time governed by St Stephen. The company arrived there about Easter in 1112 and begged to be admitted to join the monks. St Stephen, who had not had a novice for several years, received them with open arms. St Bernard was then twenty-two years old. He entered this house with the desire to die to the remembrance of men, to live hidden, and be forgotten, that he might be occupied only with God. To guard against sloth he repeated often to himself the saying of the great St Arsenius, " What have you come here for ? " and practised what he afterwards used to say to postulants who presented themselves to his monastery at Clairvaux : " If you desire to live in this house, you must leave your body ; only spirits can enter here "; that is, persons who live according to the Spirit. So rigidly did he guard his eyes that it is said that after a year's novitiate he did not know whether the top of his cell was vaulted or covered with a ceiling, nor whether the church had more than one window.

After his novitiate he made his profession into the hands of St Stephen with all his companions except one, and continued his exemplary cloistered life. Not being able to reap corn so as to keep up with the rest, his superior ordered him other work ; but he begged of God that he might be enabled to use a hook properly, and soon equalled the best hands. At his work his soul was continually occupied in God, and he used afterwards to say that he never had any other master in his studies of the Holy Scriptures but the oaks and beeches of the forest : for that spiritual learning of which he became so great a doctor was a gift of the Holy Ghost, obtained by purity of heart, meditation, and prayer. The peace of his soul shone through his countenance, in which the charm of heavenly grace captivated and surprised those that beheld at first only a face that was emaciated, pale, and wan. He suffered all his life from stomach troubles, without ever speaking of them or using any indulgence, unless compelled by those who took notice of them. He used to say, "Our fathers built their monasteries in damp, unwholesome places so that the monks might have the uncertainty of life more clearly before their eyes." But these monasteries built in uncultivated deserts or swampy lands were by the monks' industry drained of their morasses and converted into gardens and meadows. St Bernard was a great lover of poverty in his habit, cell, and all other things, but called dirtiness a mark of laziness or of affectation. He seemed to have lost all taste for food, and often took one for another when offered him by mistake, so that he once drank oil instead of water.

The number of monks being grown too great at Cîteaux, St Stephen founded in 1113 the monastery of La Ferté, in Burgundy, and in 1114 that of Pontigny in Champagne. Hugh, Count of Troyes, offered ground on his estates, whereon to found a third monastery; and the abbot, seeing the great progress which Bernard had made and his extraordinary abilities, gave him a cross, appointed him abbot, and ordered him to go with twelve monks, among whom were his brothers, to found a new house in the diocese of Langres in Champagne. They walked in procession, singing psalms, with their new abbot at their head, and settled in a place called the Valley of Wormwood, surrounded by a forest, which had often been a retreat for robbers. These thirteen monks grubbed up a sufficient area and, with the assistance of the bishop and the people of the country, built themselves a house. This young colony had much to suffer and was often relieved in some need in a sudden and unexpected manner; and these effects of providence St Bernard made use of to excite confidence in God. These fervent monks, animated by the example of their abbot, lived through a period of extreme and grinding hardship. The land was poor and their bread was usually made of coarse barley; and boiled beech leaves were sometimes served up instead of vegetables. Bernard at first was so severe in his discipline, coming down upon the smallest distractions and least transgressions of his brethren, whether in confession or in chapter, that although his monks behaved with the utmost humility and obedience they began to be discouraged, which made the abbot sensible of his fault. He condemned himself for it to a long silence. At length, being admonished by a vision, he resumed his preaching with extraordinary fruit, and provided that meals should be more regular, though the food was still of the coarsest, as William of St Thierry relates. The reputation of the house, and of the sanctity of the abbot, in a short time became so great that the number of monks in it amounted to one hundred and thirty ; the name of the valley had now been changed to Clairvaux, because it was situated right in the eye of the sun.

St Bernard was attacked by a serious illness so that his life was almost despaired of about the end of the year 1118. His great admirer, the learned and good Bishop of Châlons, William of Champeaux, went to the chapter of the order then held at Cîteaux and obtained authority to govern him as his immediate superior for one year. With this commission he hastened to Clairvaux, and lodged the abbot in a little house outside the enclosure, with orders that he should not observe even the rule of the monastery and that he should be entirely freed from all care of the affairs of his community. Here the saint lived under the direction of a physician from whose hands he received treatment which was calculated to kill him even quicker than his disease, but he carried it out without complaint and after a year returned in better health to his monastery. His aged father Tescelin and the young Nivard had followed him there in 1117, and received the habit at his hands. The four first daughters of Cîteaux, namely La Ferté, Pontigny, Clairvaux, and Morimond, became each a mother-house to many others, and Clairvaux had the most numerous offspring. St Bernard founded, among many others, in 1117 the abbey of Trois Fontaines, in the diocese of Châlons, that of Fontenay, in the diocese of Autun, Rievaulx and Fountains in England, and that of Foigny, in the diocese of Laon. The last was in 1121 and in the same year he wrought his first miracle, restoring, while he sang Mass, his power of speech to a certain lord, his relation, called Josbert de la Ferté, that he might confess his sins before he died, three days after, having made restitution for numerous acts of injustice. When the saint had confidently promised this restoration of Josbert, his uncle Gaudry and his brother reproved him for his imprudence, but Bernard repeated the assurance in stronger terms ; the saints have a supernatural instinct when for the divine honour they undertake to work a miracle. The author of St Bernard's life adds an account of other sick persons cured instantaneously by the saint's making the sign of the cross upon them, attested by eye-witnesses of weight and unexceptionable veracity. We are also told that the church of Foigny was infested with flies till, by the saint's saying he " excommunicated " them, they all died. The malediction of the flies of Foigny became famous as a proverb in France.

In consideration of his ill-health the general chapter dispensed Bernard from work in the fields and ordered him to undertake extra preaching instead. This led to his writing, at the request of the Abbot of Fontenay, his treatise on the Degrees of Humility and Pride, which was the first of his published works (1121). It includes a study of character which, says the Abbé Vacandard, "the most expert psychologist would not disavow." In 1122 he had to take a journey to Paris where, at the request of the bishop and archdeacon, he preached to the students who were candidates for holy orders; some of whom were so moved by his discourse that they accompanied him back to Clairvaux, and persevered there. Several German gentlemen who called to see the monastery were so strongly affected by all they saw that they agreed to return, hung up their swords, and took the habit. Their conversion was the more wonderful as till that day they had been interested chiefly in war, tilts and tournaments. Humility made Bernard sincerely regard himself as unworthy and incapable of moving others; but charity opened his mouth, and he poured forth his thoughts with such eloquence, that, aided by God's grace, it brought about these and similar conversions. He received into his monastery monks who came from other orders that were less austere, but declared that he was most willing to give leave to any of his own who should desire to pass to any other religious institute from the motive of seeking their greater perfection. Peter the Venerable, Archabbot of Cluny, having addressed an expostulation to Clairvaux, charging the Cistercians with hypocrisy and with vilifying the Cluniacs, St Bernard replied in an *apologia*, in which he refutes the charge of slander and makes serious adverse criticism of Cluniac life. Charity was admirably maintained on either side, and in the event Peter and Suger, Abbot of Saint Denis, inaugurated a reform. During the year 1125, in which during a famine he had often exhausted the provisions of his monastery to feed the poor, Bernard was once again brought to the very gates of death. It happened in this illness that he once appeared to those about him as if he were actually dying, and he fell into a trance, in which he seemed to himself to see the Devil accusing him before the throne of God. To the charge he made only this answer, "I confess myself unworthy of the glory of Heaven, and that I can never obtain it by my own merits. But my Lord Jesus possesses it upon a double title: that of inheritance, by being the only-begotten Son of His eternal Father; and that of purchase, He having bought it with His precious blood. This second title He has conferred on me, and by it I claim the reward of Heaven." The Devil was confounded and disappeared. Then Bernard saw himself waiting on the sea-coast to board a vessel, but it stood out to sea and left him. Finally our Lady appeared and laid her hands on him, and when he awoke his sickness had left him. St Bernard's works sufficiently declare his devotion to the blessed Virgin. In one of his missions into Germany, being in the great church at Spires, it is said he spontaneously sang during a procession, "O clemens, O pia, O dulcis Maria," which words the Church added to the anthem *Salve Regina* (the word "virgo" before "Maria" is a later addition still). The custom was introduced from this incident of singing that anthem every day with great solemnity in the cathedral of Spires. Notwithstanding St Bernard's love of retirement, obedience and the Church's needs frequently drew him from his cell. Like several other great saints who have had in a supreme degree the gift of contemplation and wished only to live alone with God in the retirement of a monastery, he had for years on end to be about his Father's business in active and public, even political, affairs. In 1137 he wrote that his life was "over-run in all quarters with anxieties, suspicions, cares, and there is scarcely an hour that is left free from the crowd of discordant applicants, from the trouble and care of business. I have no power to stop their coming and cannot refuse to see them, and *they do not leave me even the time to pray.*" So great was the reputation of his learning and sanctity that princes desired to have their differences determined by him and bishops regarded his decisions with the greatest respect, referring to him the most important affairs of their churches. The popes looked upon his advice as the greatest support of the Holy See, and all people had a profound respect and veneration for his person and his opinion. It may be said of him that in his solitude he governed all the churches of the West. The first occasion which called for his help outside was a dissension between the Archbishop and citizens of Reims, whom the saint reconciled, confirming his words by the miraculous cure of a boy that was deaf, blind, and dumb. He opposed the election of unworthy persons to the episcopacy or other ecclesiastical dignities, which raised him many enemies, who spared him neither slanders nor abuse. Their common complaint was that a monk ought to confine himself to his cloister. To this he answered that a monk was a soldier of Christ as much as other Christians, and ought to defend the truth and the honour of God's sanctuary. By his example Henry, Archbishop of Sens, and Stephen, Bishop of Paris, renounced the court and their secular manner of living; and Suger, Abbot of Saint Denis, who was minister to King Louis the Fat and for some time regent of the kingdom, and who lived in great state accordingly, laid aside his worldly habits, resigned all his posts, and shut himself up in Saint Denis, where he banished the court out of his abbey and re-established regular discipline. He often reminded ecclesiastics of their strict obligation of giving whatever they enjoyed of church revenues, above a necessary maintenance, to the poor. Thus he wrote to the Dean of Languedoc: " You may imagine that what belongs to the Church belongs to you, while you officiate there. But you are mistaken : for though it be reasonable that one who serves the altar should live by the altar, yet it must not be to promote either his luxury or his pride. Whatever goes beyond bare nourishment and simple plain clothing is sacrilege and theft." Bernard had, much against his will, to assist at the synods of Troyes, Arras, Châlons, and others, in the course of which he encouraged and co-operated in the founding of the Knights Templar and concurred in the deposition of the Bishop of Verdun and the Abbot of Saint Sepulchre. The severity of these disciplinary measures was imputed entirely to St Bernard and drew upon him a rebuke from the Chancellor of the Roman Church; in reply he amply justified the part he had taken, protested his unwillingness to be present at the councils, and asked that he should not be summoned again.

After the death of Honorius II in 1130, Innocent II was chosen pope on the same day by the greater number of cardinals. But, at the same time, a faction attempted to invest with that supreme dignity Cardinal Peter de Leone, who took the name of Anacletus. He had formerly been a monk of Cluny, was an ambitious worldly man, and so powerful that he got the strongholds of Rome into his hands. Innocent II was obliged to fly to Pisa. A council of French bishops was held at Etampes, twenty-five miles from Paris, to which St Bernard was invited. He strenuously maintained the justice of Innocent's cause, he was recognized by the council, and soon after came into France, where he was splendidly received by King Louis the Fat. St Bernard waited on him, and accompanied him to Chartres, where he met Henry I, King of England, who was at first inclined to favour the antipope, but was persuaded by St Bernard to acknowledge Innocent. The saint followed the Pope into Germany, and was present at the conference which he had with the Emperor Lothaire, who recognized the lawful pope on the condition of receiving the right of giving the investitures of bishoprics. St Bernard's remonstrances overwhelmed Lothaire and made him withdraw the condition, which Innocent had refused. His Holiness held a council at Reims in 1131, and went from Auxerre to visit Clairvaux, where he was received in procession, as in other places, but without any splendour : the monks were clad in coarse habits and before them was carried a homely wooden crucifix. The bread which was served at table was made of coarse flour that had never been sifted; the other food was vegetables and herbs, with one small fish for the Pope, of which a chronicler says the other guests had to be satisfied with admiring it from a distance. Nor was there any wine. Innocent insisted on keeping Bernard by his side and in the year following he attended the Pope into Italy, and reconciled to him Genoa and some other cities. He arrived with him at Rome, whence he not long after was sent into Germany as papal legate to make peace between the Emperor Lothaire II and the two nephews of Henry V, his predecessor. He marked every stage of his journey by supporting the cause of the true pope and by the conversion of sinners, among others, of Alois, Duchess of Lorraine, sister to the Emperor, who had for a long time dishonoured her rank and religion by her scandalous behaviour; having pacified the troubles of Germany he returned into Italy, being obliged by the Pope to assist at the council of Pisa in 1135, in which the schismatics were excommunicated. Afterwards he went to Milan to reconcile that city to the Holy See. He wrought there many miracles, and wherever he came was received as a man sent from Heaven. He induced the Milanese to renounce the schism and reconciled them with the Emperor, and the grateful citizens established at Chiaravalle the first Cistercian house in Italy. In November he was allowed to return to Clairvaux, and among the postulants he took with him was a canon of Pisa, Peter Bernard, who was to become Pope Eugenius III; for the present he was put to stoke the fire in the monastery calefactory.

In the previous year St Bernard had been called into Aquitaine where William, the powerful duke of that province, persecuted those that adhered to the true pope, and had on that account expelled the Bishops of Poitiers and Limoges. Gerard, Bishop of Angoulême, an abettor of the schism, encouraged him in these excesses. This William was a prince of immense wealth, gigantic stature and strength of body, and extraordinary abilities in worldly affairs, but was in his youth impious, haughty, and impatient of the least control. He seemed not to be able to live out of war, and was openly living with his brother's wife. St Bernard was not afraid of this formidable person, the Duke listened to his arguments for a week, and was finally won over. But directly Bernard was gone the Bishop of Angoulême undid his work. The saint, who had learned never to despair of the most obstinate sinner, redoubled his prayers and endeavours, till he had the comfort to see William begin to come again to the obedience of the rightful pope, but could not prevail upon him to restore the two bishops whom he had unjustly deprived of their sees. At length he had recourse to more powerful arms. He went to say Mass, the duke and other schismatics staying at the door, as being excommunicated persons. After the giving of the kiss of peace before communion, the abbot put the Host upon the paten and, carrying It out, his eyes sparkling and his countenance all on fire, spoke to the Duke no longer as a suppliant but with a voice of authority : " Hitherto I have entreated you and prayed you, and you have despised me. Several servants of God have joined their entreaties with mine, and you have never regarded them. Now, therefore, the Son of the Virgin, the Lord and Head of that Church which you persecute, comes in person to see if you will repent. He is your judge, at whose name every knee bends, in Heaven, Earth, and Hell. Into His hands your obstinate soul will one day fall. Will you despise Him ? Will you scorn Him as you have done His servants ? Will you ? " The Duke, not being able to hear any more, fell down in fear. St Bernard lifted him up, and bade him salute the Bishop of Poitiers, who was present. The Duke was not able to speak, but went to the bishop, and kissed him, and afterwards led him by the hand to his cathedral-church, expressing by that action that he renounced the schism and restored the bishop to his see. After this, the saint returned to the altar and finished the sacrifice. A particular impulse of the Holy Ghost, the great authority of the saint, and the dignity with which he was enabled to perform so extraordinary an action, make it an object of admiration, though not of imitation. As for Duke William, it made so deep an impression upon his mind that his conversion was complete. He founded a Cistercian monastery and undertook a penitential pilgrimage to Compostella, on which he died. Thus by the efforts of St Bernard was the schism extinguished in many places, but it was still protected by Roger, King of Sicily and Duke of Calabria. The Pope called the saint to Viterbo in 1137, and thence sent him to this prince. Bernard, in a public conference at Salerno, convicted Anacletus's partisans of schism, and brought over many persons of distinction to the union of the Church, including Cardinal Peter of Pisa ; but Roger remained inflexible. The death of the antipope in 1138 opened the way to the peace of the Church for, though the schismatics chose Gregory Conti, the activities of Bernard in Rome so damaged his cause that he surrendered his pretensions to Innocent II. Hereupon Bernard asked the Pope for permission to return to his monastery, which he was at last permitted to do.

In 1139 St Bernard was elected to the archiepiscopal see of

Reims; it was not the first time he had been called to the episcopacy—it was in fact the fifth—but he resolutely refused the dignity and his refusal was again respected; he was present at the tenth general council, Lateran ii. All this time he had continued diligently to preach to his monks, notably those discourses on the Canticle of Canticles, and he now for the first time made the acquaintance of St Malachy (Maelmhaedhoc o'Morgair), who had recently retired from the see of Armagh; the ensuing friendship between the two lasted until Malachy's death in Bernard's arms nine years later. In 1140 he wrote his famous letter to the metropolitan chapter of Lyons protesting against their introduction of the feast of the Conception of our Lady, which was not known in the West until comparatively late. Bernard wrote in the belief that the canons wished to celebrate, not the infusion by God of the soul into the human embryo, but her " active conception," *i.e.*, the generative act of her parents. From other passages in his writings it may be gathered that St Bernard believed in the Immaculate (passive) Conception of our Lady, a doctrine which in those days was not yet defined by the Church to be of faith. Later in the same year he preached for the first time in a public pulpit, primarily to the students of Paris. They are the two most powerful and trenchant of his discourses preserved to us, in which he says much of " things hellish and horrible "; they effected some good and a number of conversions among the students, who were at first superior to their fervent " evangelicalism."

If St Bernard was the most eloquent and influential man of his age, the next was the brilliant and unhappy Peter Abelard, who was, moreover, of far wider learning. The two were bound to come into collision, for they represented two currents of thought which, not necessarily opposed, were not yet properly fused: on the one hand, the weight of traditional authority and " faith not as an opinion but a certitude "; on the other, the new rationalism and exaltation of human reason. In 1121 Abelard's orthodoxy had come under suspicion and after a synod at Soissons he had had to burn a book he had written containing certain opinions on the mystery of the Holy Trinity, but about 1136, after a brief career as abbot of St Gildas de Rhuys, he returned to teach enthusiastic audiences in Paris. In 1139 William of St Thierry, a Cistercian of Signy, denounced some of Abelard's teachings and writings, and informed Geoffrey, Bishop of Chartres, who was legate of the Holy See, and St Bernard, saying they were the only persons who could crush the mischief. St Bernard had three private conferences with Abelard, at which he promised to abandon his dangerous doctrines, but he did not keep his promise, and Bernard attacked him publicly and before the authorities. Thereupon Abelard challenged him to substantiate his charges before an assembly of bishops which would meet at Sens at the Pentecost of 1140. Bernard was unwilling to appear, telling the bishops it was their business, so that Abelard triumphed, and his friends said Bernard was afraid to encounter him face to face. The saint therefore was obliged to be present. But Abelard, who dreaded the eloquence of the abbot above all things, only presented himself at the council to hear the charges drawn up by St Bernard out of his own book read against him; he declined to give any answer, though he had liberty given him to do it, had very favourable judges, and was in a place where he had no reason to fear anything. Instead, he appealed to the Pope, and then withdrew from the synod with his party. The bishops condemned seventeen propositions extracted out of his works, and wrote to Pope Innocent II, who confirmed their sentence. Stopping at Cluny on his way to Rome, Abelard heard of this confirmation and he was persuaded by the abbot, Peter the Venerable, to recall whatever he had written which gave offence, and to meet St Bernard. He did so, and was reconciled to him. With the Pope's leave he resolved to spend the remainder of his life at Cluny, being now really sorry for his pride and aberrations. St Bernard himself has since been grievously criticized for his unrelenting pursuit of Abelard: but he had detected in him vanity and arrogance masquerading as science, and rationalism masquerading as the use of reason, and his ability and learning made him the more dangerous. St Bernard wrote to the Pope: "Peter Abelard is trying to make void the merit of Christian faith, when he deems himself able by human reason to comprehend God entirely . . . the man is great in his own eyes."

Probably about the beginning of the year 1142 the first Cistercian foundation was made in Ireland, from Clairvaux, where St Malachy had put some young Irishmen with St Bernard to be trained. The abbey was called Mellifont, in county Louth, and within ten years of its foundation six daughter-houses had been planted out. At the same time Bernard was busied in the affair of the disputed succession to the see of York, set out in the account of St William of York (June 8), in the course of which Pope Innocent II died. His third successor, within eighteen months, was the Cistercian abbot of Tre Fontane, that Peter Bernard of Pisa to whom reference has been made, who is known to history as Bd. Eugenius III. St Bernard wrote a charming letter of encouragement to his former subject, addressed: "To his most dearly loved father and master,

Eugenius, by the grace of God Sovereign Pontiff, Bernard, styled Abbot of Clairvaux, presents his humble service." But Bernard was also rather frightened, for Eugenius was shy and retiring, not accustomed to public life, and he wrote also to the College of Cardinals, a letter beginning: "May God forgive you what you have done! You have put back among the living a man who was dead and buried. You have again surrounded with cares and crowds one who had fled from cares and crowds. You have made the last first, and behold! the last state of that man is more perilous than the first." Later he wrote for Pope Eugenius's guidance the longest and most important of his treatises, *de Consideratione*, impressing upon him the various duties of his office, and strongly recommending to him always to reserve time for self-examination and daily contemplation, applying himself to this still more than to business. He proves to him that "consideration" serves to form and to employ in the heart all virtues. He reminds the Pope that he is in danger of falling, by the multiplicity of affairs, into a forgetfulness of God and hardness of heart: the thought of which made the saint tremble for him, and tell him that his heart was already hardened and made insensible if he did not continually tremble for himself; for if the Pope falls, the whole Church of God is involved. The work has been most highly esteemed by popes and theologians ever since. Bernard also relentlessly pursued Arnold of Brescia, "a man who neither eats nor drinks because, like the Devil, he thirsts only after the blood of souls. His conversation has nothing but sweetness, and his doctrine nothing but poison. He has the head of a dove, but the tail of a scorpion," whose heretical teaching and stirring up of the Roman populace caused the Pope for a time to flee from his city. In the meantime the Albigensian heresy and its social and moral implications had been making alarming progress in the south of France. St Bernard had already been called on to deal with a similar sect in Cologne and in 1145 the papal legate, Cardinal Alberic, asked him to go to Languedoc. Bernard was ill and weak and hardly able to make the journey, but he obeyed, preaching at Bergerac, Périgueux, Sarlat, and Cahors on the way. Geoffrey, who was for some time the saint's secretary, accompanied him, and relates many miracles to which he was an eye-witness. He tells us that at Sarlat, in Périgord, Bernard, blessing with the sign of the cross some loaves of bread which were brought, said, "By this shall you know the truth of our doctrine, and the falsehood of that which is taught by the heretics, if such as are sick among you recover their health by eating of these loaves." The Bishop of Chartres, who stood near the saint, being fearful of the result, said, "That is, if they eat with a right faith, they shall be cured." But the abbot replied, "I say not so; but assuredly they that taste shall be cured, that you may know by this that we are sent by authority derived from God, and preach His truth." And a number of sick persons were cured by eating that bread. When the saint lodged at St Saturnin's, a house of regular canons at Toulouse, one of the canons lay at the point of death, so weak that he could not rise from his bed; but by a visit and prayer of the saint he was restored to perfect health. "That instant," says Geoffrey, "he rose from his bed, and following after, overtook us and kissed the blessed man's feet with an eager devotion which can only be imagined by those who saw it." The bishop of the place, the legate, and the people went to the church, the man who had been sick leading the way, and gave thanks to God for His blessing. Bernard preached against the heresy throughout Languedoc; its supporters were stubborn and violent, especially at Toulouse and Albi, but in a very short time he had restored the country to Catholic orthodoxy and returned to Clairvaux. But he left too soon, the restoration was more apparent than real, and twenty-five years later Albigensianism had a stronger hold than ever. Then came St Dominic.

On Christmas-day, 1144, the Seljuk Turks had captured Edessa, centre of one of the four principalities of the Latin kingdom of Jerusalem, and immediate appeals for help were at once sent to Europe, for the whole position was in danger. King Louis the Young announced his intention of leading an expedition to the East, and the Pope commissioned St Bernard to preach the holy war. He began at Vézelay on Palm Sunday 1146, when Queen Eleanor and many nobles were the first to take the cross, and were followed by such large numbers of people, moved by the monk's burning words, that the supply of cloth badges was exhausted and he had to tear strips off his habit to make others. When he had roused France, he wrote letters to the rulers and peoples of England, Italy, Sicily, Spain, Poland, Denmark, Moravia, Bohemia, and Bavaria, and then went in person into Germany. First he had to deal with a half-crazy monk, called Rudolf, who in his name was inciting the people to massacre the Jews, and then made a triumphant journey through the Rhineland, confirming his appeals by an amazing succession of miracles, vouched for by his companions. The Emperor Conrad III received him with honour, took the cross from him at Spires, and set out on the crusade with an army in the May of 1147, followed by Louis of France. This, the second, crusade was a miserable failure; Conrad's forces were cut to pieces in Asia Minor and Louis did not get beyond laying siege to

Damascus. Its ill success is chiefly ascribed to the treachery of the Greek Emperor, Manuel Comnenus, but was also in no small measure due to the crusaders themselves, of whom a great part were led by no other motive than the prospect of plunder, were lawless, and committed every kind of disorder in their march. To those who were led by motives of sincere penance and religion, these afflictions were trials for the exercise of their virtue, but the ascetical exercise was dearly bought. This unfortunate expedition raised a great storm against St Bernard, because he had seemed to promise success. His answer was that he confided in the divine mercy for a blessing on an enterprise undertaken for the honour of the divine name; but that the sins of the army were the cause of its misfortunes; further, who could judge the extent of its success or failure, and " how is it that the rashness of mortals dares reprove what they cannot understand ? "

In 1151 Gunnar, King of Sardinia, made a visit to Clairvaux, and was so edified with what he saw practised there that he returned the year following, and made his religious profession in that house, and the like was done by Prince Peter, brother to King Alfonso of Portugal, and by Prince Henry, third son of King Louis VI. In 1147 Pope Eugenius visited Clairvaux, and afterwards assisted at the general chapter of the order held at Cîteaux, at which the whole Benedictine congregation of Savigny, consisting of thirty or more monasteries, passed into that of Cîteaux and, out of respect for St Bernard, became a filiation of Clairvaux. After the return of the crusaders Bernard, in concert with Abbot Suger, who had opposed the former venture, energetically started to organize another, and in 1150 Bernard himself was elected to lead the Christian army to victory; he wrote to the Pope, reproaching him for his lack of enthusiasm, and preparations went on apace. But at the beginning of the next year Suger died, and France being again on the brink of civil war the project was never put into execution. Bernard urged the Emperor to proceed against Arnold of Brescia, who still held Rome against the Pope, but Conrad died suddenly in 1152 and Bd. Eugenius in 1153, and in the beginning of that year St Bernard too entered on his last illness. He had long dwelt in Heaven in desire, though this desire he by humility ascribed to weakness, not to charity. " The saints," said he, " were moved to pray for death out of a desire of seeing Christ; but I am forced hence by scandals and evil. I confess myself overcome by the violence of the storm for want of courage." For a time he mended a little in the spring, and was called on for the last time to leave Clairvaux to succour his neighbour. The inhabitants of Metz having been attacked and defeated with great slaughter by the Duke of Lorraine, they were vehemently bent on revenge. To prevent the shedding of more blood the Archbishop of Trier went to Clairvaux, and earnestly implored Bernard to journey to Metz in order to reconcile the parties that were at variance. At this call of charity he forgot his corporal infirmity and immediately made his way into Lorraine, where he prevailed on both sides to lay aside their arms and accept a treaty which he drew up. When he was back at Clairvaux his illness returned with more grievous symptoms; his stomach was scarcely able to bear the least nourishment even taken in liquids, his arms and legs swelled as if he had dropsy, and he was hardly able to sleep for a few minutes at a time. When he received the last sacraments and his spiritual children assembled about him in tears, he comforted and encouraged them, saying that the unprofitable servant ought not to occupy a place uselessly, and that the barren tree ought to be rooted up. His love for them inclined him to remain with them till they should be gathered with him to God; but his desire to enjoy Christ made him long for death. "I am straitened between two," he cried, "and what to choose I know not. I leave it to the Lord; let Him decide." And God took him to Himself, on August 20, 1153; he was sixty-three years old, had been abbot for thirty-eight, and sixty-eight monasteries had been founded directly from Clairvaux. He was canonized by Pope Alexander III in 1174, and in 1830 formally declared a Doctor of the Church: *Doctor mellifluus*, the Honey-sweet Doctor, as he is now universally called.

St Bernard "carried the twelfth century on his shoulders, and he did not carry it without suffering"; he was during his life the oracle of the Church, the light of prelates, and the reformer of discipline; since his death he continues to comfort and instruct by his writings. The great French lay scholar of the seventeenth century, Henry Valois, did not hesitate to say they are the most useful for piety among all the works of the Fathers of the Church, though he is the youngest of them in time, and Sixtus of Siena, the converted Jew, said, "His discourse is everywhere sweet and ardent: it so delights and warms that from his tongue honey and milk seem to flow in his words, and a fire of burning love to break forth from his breast." To Erasmus he was "cheerful, pleasant, and vehement in moving the passions," and in another place, "He is Christianly learned, holily eloquent, and devoutly cheerful and pleasing." From Pope Innocent II to Cardinal Manning, from Luther to Frederic Harrison, Catholics and Protestants of eminence have recognized the sanctity of St Bernard and the greatness of his writings, in which he is equally gentle and vigorous; his style is sublime, lively, and pleasant; his charity appears even in his reproaches and shows that he reproves to correct, never to insult. This gives such a force to his strongest invective that it gains the heart and instils both awe and love: the sinner whom he admonishes can only be angry with himself, not with the reprimand or its author. He had so meditated on the Holy Scriptures that in almost every sentence he borrows something from their language, and diffuses the marrow of the sacred text with which his own heart was filled. He was well read in the writings of the early Fathers of the Church, especially SS. Ambrose and Augustine, and often takes his thoughts from their writings and by a new turn makes them his own. Though he lived after St Anselm, the first of the scholastics, and though his contemporaries are ranked in that class, yet he treats theological subjects after the manner of the ancients. On this account, and for the great excellence of his writings, he is reckoned among the Fathers. And though he is the last among them in time, he is one of the greatest to those who desire to study and to improve their hearts in sincere religion. A perfect spirit of humility, devotion, and divine charity reigns throughout his writings and strongly affects his readers, for it is the language of his own heart, always glowing with love and penitence.

Almost all the principal materials for the Life of St Bernard have been printed in the *Latin Patrology* of Migne, vol. 185. The most important source, known as the *Vita prima*—the best text is that of Waitz in Pertz, *Monumenta Germaniæ, Scriptores*, vol. xxvi—is made up of five sections by different authors, his contemporaries, *i.e.* William of St Thierry, Arnold of Bouneval, and Geoffrey of Auxerre, supplemented by a collection of the miracles. There are also other accounts of his life by Alan of Auxerre, John the Hermit, etc., and a good deal of more or less legendary matter in later compilations, notably the *Exordium Magnum* of Conrad of Eberbach, and the *Liber Miraculorum* of Herbert. All these sources as well as the saint's correspondence have been very carefully discussed by G. Hüffer in his *Vorstudien* (1886) and in the first chapter of F. Vacandard's *Vie de Saint Bernard*, which last book still remains after nearly forty years the most authoritative biography of the great founder of Clairvaux. More popular Lives such as those by G. Goyau (1927), F. Höver (1927), and A. Luddy, *Life and Teaching of St Bernard* (Dublin, 1927), are numerous, but the accuracy of the rather bulky work last named cannot always be relied upon. Father Luddy, for example, adopts with Butler the legend that the last line of the *Salve Regina* was due to a spontaneous outburst of St Bernard at Spires; but there are manuscripts in existence containing this line which are of older date than St Bernard's visit to Spires. Many non-Catholic biographies or histories, notably those of J. Cotter Morison, R. S. Storrs, and G. G. Coulton (*Five Centuries of Religion*, vol. i), also pay tribute to St Bernard's greatness.

ST AMADOUR, Hermit
Date Unknown

St Amadour is honoured in Quercy and the Limousin as founder of the shrine of our Lady now known throughout Christendom as Rocamadour, and as the first hermit of Gaul. There is in fact nothing whatsoever known about him, neither of the events of his life nor the age in which he lived. His extant *acta* were written in the twelfth century at the earliest, and before then there is no documentary reference to him; even the discovery at Rocamadour in 1166 of an incorrupt body, said to be his, is not mentioned in a collection of local miracles of 1172. The pilgrimage to Rocamadour certainly existed before the twelfth century, and one hypothesis is that St Amadour was an early solitary in the valley of Alzon and gave his name to the spot.

According to the *acta*, which are sheer fiction, Amadour was a servant of the Holy Family and afterwards married St Veronica. Driven from Palestine by persecution, they landed in Gaul and, under the direction of St Martial (who lived not in the first but in the third century), evangelized the neighbourhood of Bordeaux and Cahors. Amadour was sent to Rome to report Martial's progress to St Peter, where he was present at the martyrdom of the Apostles; on his return he continued his preaching, founded monasteries, and, after the death of Veronica, retired to his lonely cell in Quercy where he built the chapel of our Lady which became the great sanctuary. In the fifteenth century a fresh turn was given to this legend when St Amadour was gratuitously identified with the Zachæus of St Luke xix; but none of the fictitious events of Amadour's life find a place in any legend of Zachæus. The finding of the incorrupt body " of St Amadour " is still remembered in the popular saying, " With skin and bones like Amadour."

The curious and manifestly incredible legend of St Amadour, owing to the popularity of the shrine and pilgrimage of Roc-Amadour, has attracted much attention in France. The subject has been critically and soberly dealt with by E. Rupin, first in his monograph *Roc-Amadour; étude historique et archéologique* (1904); and then in his *Légende de Saint Amadour* (1909). In this last he replied convincingly to the booklet *Notre-Dame de Roc-Amadour* (1908) written by an uncritical assailant, J. T. Layral. *Cf.* also the article of E. Albe, " La Vie et les Miracles de S. Amator " in the *Analecta Bollandiana*, vol. xxviii (1909), pp. 57–90. In this the fictitious character of the whole tradition is here made apparent by another line of argument.

ST OSWIN, King of Deira, Mart.
A.D. 651

When his father Osric, King of Deira, was killed by the British Cadwalla in 634, the young Oswin was taken into Wessex for safety, where he was baptized and educated; but after the death of the holy and great prince St Oswald in 642 he returned to the north and took possession of his kingdom. He governed it for seven years with virtue, prudence, and prosperity, beloved by all, and enjoyed every spiritual and temporal advantage. He was tall, good-looking, liberal and affable to all, especially to the poor, sober at table, modest and most devout. For an instance of his humility St Bede relates that he had bestowed on the bishop St Aidan a horse on which, though he usually made his journeys on foot, he might sometimes ride and cross rivers. Soon after, the bishop met a poor man who asked an alms, and not having anything else, he gave him this horse with all his rich harness. Next time he waited on the King, before he sat down to table the King asked him why he had given so fine a horse, which he intended for his own use, to a beggar, pointing out that he had horses of less value or other presents which would have supplied his wants. The Bishop answered, " Is then, O king, a colt or a mare of more value in your eyes than a son of God ? " When they entered the hall the bishop took his seat, but the King being just come in from hunting stood by the fire with his servants, warming himself. Here, calling to mind the bishop's words, he suddenly put off his sword and going in haste cast himself at Aidan's feet, begging his pardon for having found fault with his charity, and promising never again to complain whatever of his goods he should give to the poor. The bishop raised him up in confusion, and assured him he was well satisfied, on condition Oswin was cheerful and sat down. The King hereupon expressed great joy at table, but Aidan appeared sorrowful, and said to his attendants in the Scottish language, which the King and his courtiers did not understand, that he was assured so humble and so good a king would not live long, because the nation was not worthy of such a ruler.

His prediction was soon verified. Oswin incurred the jealousy of his cousin Oswy, King of Bernicia, the two fell out, and Oswy declared a state of open warfare. Oswin, seeing his own weakness and being desirous to spare human blood (or, as St Bede says, from simple prudence, but doubtless for both considerations), dismissed his forces at a place called Wilfaresdon, ten miles north-westward from Catterick. Attended with one faithful soldier, he retired to a town called Gilling, near Richmond in Yorkshire, which estate he had lately bestowed on Earl Hunwald. He hoped under his protection to lie concealed here, or at least that Oswy would content himself with possessing his kingdom and would suffer him to live; but Oswy feared that so long as a prince so much beloved was alive, his usurpation could not be secured to him. He therefore ordered one Ethelwin, with a body of soldiers, to march in search of him and to kill him. Hunwald treacherously betrayed his guest. When Oswin saw the castle surrounded with soldiers he courageously prepared himself for death, only entreating Ethelwin to content himself with his life and spare that of his faithful servant. But both were slain together, and buried at Gilling. Queen Eanfleda, daughter to St Edwin and wife of Oswy, with her husband's leave founded a monastery at Gilling, in which prayers might be ever offered up for both kings. It was afterward destroyed by the Danes, before whose incursions the body of St Oswin, whose shrine was made illustrious by many miracles, was translated to Tynemouth. Here it was lost sight of during the Danish troubles, but in 1065 a monk of Tynemouth discovered it in consequence of a vision, and it was accordingly enshrined again in the year 1100.

We know little of St Oswin beyond what is told us in Bede's *Ecclesiastical History*, Bk. iii, ch. 14. There is, however, a twelfth-century Life with two homilies and some liturgical matter. This has been used by Plummer in his notes to Bede. See also Stanton's *Menology*, pp. 401–403.

ST PHILIBERT, Abbot of Jumièges, Conf.
A.D. 684

He was born about 608 at Eauze in Gascony. His father, Philibaud, having received holy orders, was made bishop of Vic-Jour, and the young Philibert was educated under the eyes of his father, who sent him to the court of Clotaire II, where the example and instructions of St Ouen made so deep an impression on him that at the age of twenty years he took the habit in the abbey of Rebaix, in the diocese of Meaux, founded by St Ouen. Here he was appointed successor to St Aile in the government of this house, but left it on finding some of the monks refractory, and his own inability through inexperience to deal with them. After having visited the most celebrated houses which professed the rule of St Columban, he retired into Neustria, where Clovis II gave him ground in the forest of Jumièges. Here he founded a monastery, not far from that of

Fontenelle, of which St Wandrille was superior. He inured his subjects to hard labour, obliging them to remove the rocks and drain the morasses which covered the country; and the community of Jumièges increased in a short time to a large number of monks. He also built a monastery for women at Pavilly, on a piece of ground given him by Amalbert, lord of that district, whose daughter Aurea took the veil there, and appointed St Austreberta its first abbess. St Philibert having some business at the court of Thierry III in 674, boldly reproached Ebroin, mayor of the palace, for his many acts of injustice. This brought on him the vengeance of that minister, who persecuted him so violently that he was imprisoned for a time at Rouen and obliged to quit Jumièges. The saint then retired to Poitiers, and afterward to the little island of Her, on the coast of Poitou, where he founded a monastery, called Hermoutier, then Nermoutier or Noirmoutier. He likewise founded the priory of Quinçay, near Poitiers, the government of which he gave to St Achard, whom he afterwards made abbot of Jumièges. These he peopled with monks from his first foundation. Two years before his death he had a further responsibility put upon him, when Ansoald, Bishop of Poitiers, founded a monastery at Luçon, which he put under the supervision of St Philibert as a cell of Hermoutier. He died and was buried at the last-named house in 684.

There is an early Life of St Philibert which has been printed both by Mabillon and in the *Acta Sanctorum*, August, vol. iv. But the best text and the most valuable contribution to the subject is that of R. Poupardin, *Monuments de l'histoire des Abbayes de Saint-Philibert* (Paris, 1905), which contains a discussion of the authorship and recensions of the Life, as well as the record of the miracles of St Philibert, and much supplementary matter.

AUGUST 21

ST JANE-FRANCES DE CHANTAL, Widow and Abbess
A.D. 1641

THE father of St Jane de Chantal was Bénigne Frémyot, president of the parliament of Burgundy, famous for his loyalty to Henry IV in opposing the League and for his piety and modesty. By his wife, Margaret de Berbisy, he had three children; Margaret, who was afterwards married to John de Neufchèzes, Baron des Francs in Poitou, Jane, who was born at Dijon on January 23, 1572, and Andrew, who died archbishop of Bourges. M. Frémyot was left a widower whilst his children were yet in their infancy; but he took such care of their education that nothing was wanting for forming them in the practice of every religious duty and preparing them for life; they were the more carefully instructed in Christian doctrine because the Calvinists were very active in Burgundy at that time. Jane, who at her Confirmation was called Frances, profited above the rest and was tenderly beloved by her father, who gave her in marriage when she was twenty years of age to Christopher de Rabutin, Baron de Chantal, then twenty-seven years old, an officer of distinction in the French army and an accomplished but penitent duellist; on his mother's side he was descended from Bd. Humbeline, whose feast is kept on this same day. The marriage was solemnized at Dijon, and a few days after she went with her husband to his seat at Bourbilly. She found an estate and household which since the death of her husband's mother had not been much accustomed to regularity, and the Baronne made it her first care to establish order and good management. The Baron de Chantal was a nobleman of honour and virtue, and, after three children had died soon after birth, they were blessed with a boy and three girls who throve. Nothing, therefore, which the world could afford was wanting to complete their happiness. And they strove to be worthy of God's blessings. When someone commented on the Baronne's modest clothes when her husband was away, she replied, " The eyes which I want to please are a hundred leagues from here "; and the remark of St Francis of Sales was as true in the early days as when he made it, " In Madame de Chantal I have found the valiant woman whom Solomon had difficulty in finding in Jerusalem."

But the happiness of Bourbilly lasted only nine years. One day in the year 1601 M. de Chantal, in company with a friend who had come to see him, went out shooting; the circumstances are not known, but accidentally M. d' Aulézy shot him in the thigh. He survived nine days, during which he suffered great pain from the efforts of an unskilful surgeon and received the sacraments with edifying resignation; he caused his pardon of M. d'Aulézy to be recorded in the registers of the parish church, strictly forbidding anyone to prosecute or trouble him. Madame de Chantal's life, thoughts, and actions were bound up in her beloved husband, and when she was left a widow at twenty-eight years of age her grief is not to be expressed; yet she bore it with such constancy and resignation that she sometimes said she was surprised to see herself receive so great a shock with such equanimity. Offering herself to suffer whatever crosses God should be pleased to lay upon her, she made an entire sacrifice of herself to Him by a vow of perpetual chastity, in accordance with a resolution made some time before with her husband that the survivor of them should do so. For four months she was sunk in grief and dejection, until she was roused by a letter of rebuke from her father, who reminded her of her obligations towards her children, and now she found some comfort and joy at the thought that she was at liberty to give herself more perfectly to the divine service. To testify her perfect forgiveness of him who had been the cause of her husband's death, she did him every good office in her power, and stood godmother to one of his children. She doubled her alms, distributed her rich clothes among the poor, determining not to wear any but what were made of linen; she discharged most of her servants; and divided her time between the instruction and care of her children, her prayers, and her work. She declared that had it not been for her four little children she would have fled to the Holy Land and there ended her days: and it was her earnest and continual prayer that God would free her from whatever could hinder her from loving and serving Him, and that He would show her a truly holy guide, by whom she might be instructed in what manner she might best accomplish His will. One day, when she was speaking to our Lord on this matter she saw suddenly a man of the same stature and features as St Francis of Sales, in a black cassock with a rochet and biretta, just as he was the first time she saw him afterwards at Dijon. Another time, being in a little wood, she seemed to be trying to get into a church that was near, but in vain. Here it was given her to understand that divine love must consume all the rust of self-love in her, and that she should meet with a great many troubles, both from within and without.

During the year of her mourning her father sent for her to his house at Dijon, where she lived with her children for a time until, in order to safeguard their property and try to do something for her father-in-law, she had to go with them to Monthelon, near Autun, to live with the old Baron de Chantal, who was then seventy-five years of age. She gave up her beautiful and deeply loved Bourbilly for an unprepossessing *château*, occupied by a vain, fierce, and extravagant old man and ruled by an insolent housekeeper of bad reputation. Jane never let fall a word of complaint, and, though she was never allowed to take her rightful place in the house, her compliance in everything was cheerful and agreeable; she gave much of her time to prayer. It happened in the year 1604 that St Francis of Sales came to preach the Lent at Dijon, and she went to stay with her father there that she might have the opportunity of hearing the sermons of so celebrated a preacher. The first time she saw him she at once recognized him as the person she had seen in vision and knew him to be the spiritual director she had long begged of God to send her; the bishop too knew her in the same way. St Francis dined frequently at her father's house, and, by hearing his conversation she gained a great confidence in him. It was her wish to put her difficulties before him, but she was hindered by a scruple on account of a vow she had made by the advice of an indiscreet religious, her director, not to address herself to any other than to himself for spiritual advice. She, however, took care to profit by the presence of the Bishop of Geneva, and he in his turn was greatly impressed by and attracted to her. One day, seeing her dressed better than usual, he said, " Madame, do you wish to marry again ? " " No, indeed, my lord ! " she replied. " Very well," he said with a smile, " but then you should pull down your flag." She took the hint, and St Francis, who knew that nothing is little that is done with a desire to please God, was delighted with her ready obedience.

The perplexities about her indiscreet vow being removed, she made several confessions to him, and a general one of her whole life, and received great light and comfort by the wholesome counsels of St Francis. By his advice she regulated her devotions and other exercises so as to conform herself to what she owed to the world whilst she lived in the houses of her father and father-in-law. In this she was so successful that the significant remark was made, " Madame prays always, and yet is never troublesome to anybody." She got up at five o'clock, without a fire and without the attendance of a maid, made an hour's meditation, and then woke and dressed her children, and went with her family to Mass. After dinner she read the Bible for half an hour; at evening catechized her children and some others of the village; read again, and said the rosary before supper; said evening prayers with her children; and retired at nine o'clock. She mortified her taste in what she ate, yet without showing it, and wore very plain clothes; she visited the poor that were sick in the neighbourhood and watched whole nights by the bedside of those that were dying. The sweetness and mildness of her temper showed how she had already co-operated with the grace of God; she was by nature strong, firm, and forceful, but there was a certain hardness and rigidity in her character which was only removed by long years of prayer, suffering, and patient guidance. And this was the work, under God, of St Francis of Sales, whom she visited at Annecy and who corresponded freely with her. He strictly limited her bodily mortifications, reminding her that St Charles Borromeo, " a man with a true spirit of liberty acting from charity," did not disdain to drink toasts with his hearty neighbours, and that St Ignatius Loyola ate meat on a Friday on the bare word of his doctor, " when a narrow man would have argued about it for at least three days." And he never allowed her to forget that she was still a woman in the world, an old man's daughter, and, above all, a mother; he spoke much to her about her children's upbringing and softened her tendency to over-strictness in their regard, so that they profited almost as much from his friendship as their mother did.

For some time various considerations, including the presence of Carmelite nuns at Dijon, inclined Madame de Chantal to enter a cloister. When she had talked to St Francis about this he took some time to recommend the matter to God, and at length proposed to her several religious orders. Her only answer was that she desired to embrace whatever state he judged best. He then unfolded his project of forming a new establishment, a congregation of the Visitation of the Virgin Mary. St Jane welcomed the proposal with joy; but the grief of her aged father, the requirements of her children, and the situation of the affairs of her family, raised great obstacles and gave her much suffering, for no one who lies under any obligations of justice to others can, without first discharging them, lawfully take up any way of life incompatible with them. To the objection that the obligation which Madame de Chantal owed to her children could not be complied with unless she remained with them in the world, St Francis replied that they were no longer infants and that in a cloister she would be able to watch over them with no less vigilance, and perhaps even with greater advantage to them, than by continuing always with them, especially as the two eldest were about to go "into the world"; and these and other objections were eventually overcome, though even Madame's brother, the Archbishop of Bourges, had supported them.

Before she left the world St Jane-Frances married her eldest daughter to St Francis's brother, the young Baron de Thorens. Her two younger daughters she determined to take with her: one died in a short time; the other she afterwards married to M. de Toulonjon. Her son, Celse-Bénigne, was fifteen years old, and him she left under the care of her father and of tutors. Taking leave of her father-in-law, the old Baron de Chantal, at Monthelon, she fell on her knees, begged his pardon if she had ever displeased him in anything, asked his blessing, and recommended her son to him. The old man, remorseful for his unkindness to her, was inconsolable and, embracing her, wished her all happiness. The inhabitants of Monthelon, especially the poor, who thought that in her they lost their all, crowded round and broke into tears and lamentations. She bade them all farewell and asked their prayers. At Dijon she had again to bid adieu to all her friends, and as she came to leave the room Celse-Bénigne, who had tried in vain to shake her resolution at the last moment, threw himself to the ground across the doorway in a paroxysm of grief. Here was a last inducement to choose the easier way, and stay; she chose the harder—and stepped over his body. In the porch her aged father was waiting. She fell on her knees with streaming eyes and asked him to bless her. He laid his hands on her head and said, " I cannot blame you for what you do. You go with my consent, and I offer you to God, a daughter dear to me as ever Isaac was to Abraham. Go where God calls you. I shall be happy, knowing you are in His house. Pray for me. Come! We must not weep more, lest our friends may think our determination is weakening." She again said good-bye, staying her tears with the thought that her action having been judged, after the most mature deliberation and advice, to be the call of Heaven, it was her duty to follow it, and a happiness to make to God an entire sacrifice of all that was most dear. St Francis having provided a house, called the Gallery House, on the edge of the lake at Annecy, he inaugurated his convent on Trinity Sunday, 1610. With St Jane-Frances were clothed two other sisters, Mary Favre and Charlotte de Bréchard, and a servant, Anne Coste, and they were soon joined by ten others. So far the institute had no name, and indeed the founder had no certain idea of its scope, except that it was to be a haven for those whose health, age, or other considerations, debarred them from the already established orders, and that he wished the sisters to be unenclosed and so more free to undertake work for souls and bodies.

It encountered much opposition, from the usual failure of the narrow and unimaginative to understand anything new, and the Cardinal de Marquemont, Archbishop of Lyons, persuaded St Francis to change the plan of the congregation so far as to make it an enclosed religious order, under the Rule of St Augustine, to which St Francis added constitutions "admirable in their wisdom, moderation, and sweetness." But he refused to give up the name, "of the Visitation of Our Lady," which he had chosen for his nuns, and St Jane-Frances urged him to make no concessions to the Archbishop of Lyons at all. St Francis would have the two sister virtues of humility and meekness to be the basis of the rule. "In the practice of virtues," said he to St Jane-Frances and her religious sisters, "let humility be the source of all the rest; let it be without bounds; make it the reigning principle of all your actions. Let an unalterable meekness and sweetness on all occasions become by habit natural to you." He gave them excellent instructions on the great duty of prayer, that heavenly exercise being the chief fruit and end of religious retirement, and he wrote specifically for St Jane and her more experienced sisters his famous treatise *On the Love of God*. One saint so far profited by the direction of the other saint that Mother de Chantal, who was fast progressing on the mystical road, was allowed to make a vow always to do what was the more perfect in the sight of God. And she faithfully and prudently governed her community in the spirit of their founder and director.

The affairs of her children, after the death of her father and the foundation of new convents, obliged her often to leave Annecy. The year after she took the habit, upon the death of her father, she went to Dijon and stayed there some months to settle her affairs, and place her son in a college; after a youth which gave much anxiety to his mother, this young man in 1624 married the pretty, rich, and virtuous Mary de Coulanges. While at Dijon St Jane-Frances was tormented by her relatives to return to the world. "Why do you bury yourself like that under two yards of bombasine? That ridiculous veil should be torn to bits!" exclaimed one excitable lady. St Francis of Sales wrote the last word: "If you had married again, some gentleman from the farthest end of Gascony or Brittany, you would have had to leave your family—and no one would have made a single objection...." After convents had been established at Lyons, Moulins, Grenoble, and Bourges, St Francis from Paris sent for Mother de Chantal to see about a foundation there, which she was able to bring about in 1619 in the face of open hostility and

Aug. 21] ST JANE-FRANCES DE CHANTAL

underhand intriguing ; God strengthened and comforted her under it, and her meekness and patience gained her the admiration of those who had been her bitter adversaries. She governed her convent at Paris for three years, during which St Vincent de Paul directed it at the request of St Francis, and she made the acquaintance of Angélique Arnauld, abbess of Port Royal, who failed to get permission to resign her office and join the Visitation order. In 1622 the death of St Francis was a grievous affliction to her, which her resignation to the divine will made her bear with unshaken constancy ; his body was buried with great honour in the church of her convent at Annecy. In 1627 her son was killed fighting against the English and the Huguenots in the isle of Ré, in his thirty-first year, leaving his wife with a daughter not a year old, who became the celebrated Madame de Sévigné. St Jane received this news with heroic fortitude ; she offered her heart to God, saying, " Destroy, cut, burn, whatever opposes Thy holy will." During the following year a terrible plague ravaged France, Savoy, and Piedmont, causing great suffering to several Visitation convents. When it reached Annecy St Jane-Frances refused the importunities of the Prince and Princess de Carignano to leave the town, put all the resources of her convent at the disposal of the sick, and whipped up the local authorities to greater efforts on behalf of the sufferers. In 1632 came the news of the death of Celse-Bénigné's widow, and then of her much-loved son-in-law, Antony de Toulonjon, and of M. Michael Favre, the confessor of St Francis and a close and devoted friend of the Visitandines. To these bereavements were added interior anguish, darkness, and spiritual dryness which she sometimes experienced to a terrible degree, as appears from several of her letters. Thus does God suffer those souls which are most dear to Him seemingly to lose themselves and wander in mists and darkness, amid disturbance of mind. Yet these are certain and direct paths to happiness, and lead to the source and centre of all light.

During the years 1635–36 St Jane-Frances made a visitation of the convents of the order, which now numbered sixty-five and many of which had never seen their spiritual mother ; in 1638 the Duchess of Savoy called her to Turin, to found there a convent, and in 1641 she went into France on an errand of charity to Madame de Montmorency. It was her last journey. She was invited to Paris by the Queen of France, Anne of Austria, and to her distress was treated there with the greatest distinction and honour. On her return she fell ill on the road, in her convent at Moulins. There it was that, having received the last sacraments and given her last instructions to her nuns, she died on December 13, 1641, being sixty-nine years old. Her body was taken to Annecy and buried near St Francis of Sales; she was beatified in 1751 and canonized by Pope Clement XIII in 1767. St Vincent de Paul said of her: " She was full of faith, and yet all her life long had been tormented by thoughts against it. While apparently enjoying that peace and easiness of mind of souls who have reached a high state of virtue, she suffered such interior trials that she often told me her mind was so filled with all sorts of temptations and abominations that she had to strive not to look within herself, for she could not bear with herself: the sight of her own soul horrified her as if it were an image of Hell. But for all that suffering her face never lost its serenity, nor did she once relax in the fidelity God asked of her. And so I regard her as one of the holiest souls I have ever met on this earth."

Apart from her own writings and correspondence and the letters of St Francis of Sales, by far the most important source for any biography of St Jane-Frances is the volume of *Mémoires* of la Mère de Chaugy. This book rightly forms the first of the eight volumes which make up the collection *Sainte Chantal, sa Vie et ses Œuvres* (Paris, 1874–79). St Francis of Sales' letters have now been completely edited in the imposing series of his works (20 vols.) published by the Visitation nuns at Annecy, and these, of course, are of great importance in the light they shed upon the origins of the order. Moreover, the Mother Foundress has been fortunate in finding an almost ideal biographer in modern times. The *Histoire de Sainte Chantal et des Origines de la Visitation* by Mgr. Bougaud, afterwards Bishop of Laval (Eng. trans., New York, 1895), is generally acknowledged to be a *chef-d'œuvre* in hagiographical literature. Besides this there is an able sketch of " Sainte Chantal " in the series " Les Saints " by Henri Bremond, de l'Académie française; and the same author has devoted many pages to the Saint's spiritual influence and inspiration in his important work *Histoire littéraire du sentiment religieux en France*, etc. (1916 and following years); see especially vol. i, pp. 68–127, and vol. ii, pp. 537–584. An interesting episode in St Chantal's story has been treated by A. Gazier, *Jeanne de Chantal et Angélique Arnauld d'après leur correspondance* (1915). See also a selection of her letters published in English in 1918, a short biography by Emily Bowles in the Quarterly Series, and an Anglican Life by E. K. Sanders (S.P.C.K., 1918).

ST ANASTASIUS CORNICULARIUS, Mart.

A.D. 274

This is the converted tribune mentioned in the notice of St Agapitus on August 18; he is an invention of hagiographers, but his name nevertheless occurs, with a statement of his conversion and of his martyrdom at Salona, in the Roman Martyrology of this day. Though they are unconnected, efforts have been made to identify him with St Anastasius the Fuller, a native of Aquileia, martyred at Salona on August 26, 304, who is named in the Roman Martyrology by an error on September 7.

That there has been confusion is certain, and it is likely that the Acts (in *Acta Sanctorum*, September, vol. iii) are altogether fictitious, but we have good evidence that there was a real martyr Anastasius who was probably a fuller and was honoured at Salona. His proper day, as the " Hieronymianum " shows, is August 26. All that we can say is that this one saint has had two different days and two different stories assigned to him. See Delehaye in the *Acta Sanctorum*, November, vol. ii, part 2, pp. 467 and 468, where references are given to several previous articles in the *Analecta Bollandiana*, etc.

SS. LUXORIUS, CISELLUS, AND CAMERINUS, MM.
A.D. 303

According to the late and unreliable *acta* of these martyrs Luxorius was a Roman soldier who, being able to read, had seen a Psalter and was greatly impressed by its contents. When he read in Psalm 85, " There is none among the gods like unto thee, O Lord, and there is none according to thy works. All the nations thou hast made shall come and adore before thee, O Lord, and they shall glorify thy name ; for thou art great and dost wonderful things : thou art God alone," he saw that such a God was none other than the Christians' God. He made the next verse his own, " Conduct me, O Lord, in thy way and I will walk in thy truth," clumsily he made the sign of the cross upon himself, and made his way to a church, and there heard them singing the 118th Psalm : " Give bountifully to thy servant, enliven me, and I shall keep thy words. Open thou my eyes. . . ." He borrowed more of the sacred books, and learned the psalms and the words of the Prophets by heart, and when at least he was permitted to read the Gospels his soul was enlightened by faith and he believed in Jesus Christ, and was baptized.

At that time the persecution of the Emperor Diocletian broke out and Delphius the prefect began to enforce the imperial decrees in Sardinia, where Luxorius was stationed. The soldier was one of the first to be brought before him, and with him two young boys, Cisellus and Camerinus, still wearing the white garments of baptism. Delphius ordered Luxorius to deny Christ, and he refused. So he was tied to a post and scourged, and while this was done he sang psalms, to glorify God, to keep his mind off his own sufferings, and to put heart into his two small companions. And when he could not move them, Delphius had them all three put to death by the sword. This martyrdom took place at Forum Trajanum, but the relics of the martyrs were afterwards translated to Pisa, where on account of his love for the psalms St Luxorius is venerated as patron of the primatial chapter of canons.

It is to be feared that we can be assured of nothing more than the fact of the martyr's existence and early *cultus*. The story of the two boy companions who suffered with him seems to be a mere embellishment. The place of martyrdom, Forum Trajanum, makes one think of Rome, but it is the name of a township in Sardinia now known as Fordingiano. See the *Acta Sanctorum*, November, vol. ii, part 2, pp. 454–5.

SS. BONOSUS AND MAXIMIAN, MM.

A.D. 363

The Emperor Julian the Apostate commanded the cross and name of Jesus Christ, which Constantine had placed on the standard of the army, to be struck off, and had the standards reduced to the form used under the pagan emperors, on which the eagle and the images of false gods were represented. The apostate emperor had made Julian, who was his uncle by the mother's side and an apostate from the Christian faith like himself, *comes* of the East; and he became a more barbarous persecutor of the Christians than his nephew. There were in the Herculean cohort at Antioch two officers of distinguished ability and zealous Christians, named Bonosus and Maximian, who refused to change their standard. Count Julian sternly commanded them to give their troops the new ensign, and to worship the same gods which he and the Emperor worshipped. Bonosus answered, " We cannot worship gods which have been made by the hands of men," and absolutely refused to give up the standard to be altered. The Count ordered him to be tied up, and three hundred lashes to be given him with leathern thongs loaded with lead. Under this Bonosus only smiled, and made no answer when asked if he would obey. The Count then turned to Maximian, who said, " Let your gods first hear and speak to you, and then we will worship them; for you know that we Christians are forbidden to worship deaf and dumb idols." Julian then had them both racked, but when he asked again if they would exchange the representation of the cross on their standard for the images of the gods, they answered, " We cannot obey the Emperor in these matters, because we have before our eyes the invisible immortal God, in whom we trust." Count Julian ordered them back to prison, and left them for some time without food. Then he sent them bread, on which was impressed his personal device; on this was probably engraved the figure of some idol, for they would not eat it. Prince Hurmizd, brother to Sapor, King of Persia (who having left his own country had embraced the Faith and spent the better part of his days in the courts of Constantine and Constantius), paid them a visit in prison, and recommended himself to their prayers. The Count threatened the martyrs in a second and a third interrogation, but they answered they were Christians and were determined to continue such. The Count was for having them tortured again; but the prefect Secundus, himself a pagan, absolutely refused to hear of it (St Gregory Nazianzen, who sat with him on the bench, commends him for his probity and mercy). Julian therefore condemned Bonosus and Maximian and several other Christian prisoners to be beheaded. St Meletius, Bishop of Antioch, and other bishops accompanied them to the place of execution and witnessed their passion.

There is tacked on to the narrative of the trial and death of these martyrs an account of the last days of Count Julian, certainly in its details manifestly false. He is represented as suffering from a disease as revolting as it is impossible; his Christian wife tells him in effect that it serves him right, and urges him to bear the hand of the Lord gladly; and he dies miserably, but calling on the name of the one God. Alban Butler takes the opportunity for a dissertation on the death of a sinner, which is here omitted together with the occasion of it.

> Although the text of this Latin "Passio" is printed by Ruinart amongst his *Acta Sincera*, we lack any satisfactory guarantee of its authenticity. There seems to be no Oriental *cultus*, though the martyrs suffered at Antioch. See, however, P. Allard, *Julien l'Apostat*, vol. iii, p. 153. Dom Leclercq, in his collection *Les Martyrs*, vol. iii, pp. 99–104, has printed a translation of the whole document.

ST SIDONIUS APOLLINARIS, Bp. OF CLERMONT, CONF.

c. A.D. 488

Caius Sollius Apollinaris Sidonius, soldier, poet, statesman, country gentleman, and eventually bishop, was born at Lyons about the year 431, and was of one of the most noble families in Gaul, where his father and grandfather, both named Apollinaris, had been prefects of the prætorium. He was educated in arts and learning under the best masters, and was one of the most celebrated orators and poets of the age in which he lived. From his letters it is clear that he was always religious, humble, extremely affectionate, beneficent, and compassionate, and no lover of " the world," even whilst he lived in it ; on the other hand, he was no rigorous censor, for at a time when Salvianus was writing so fiercely of the corruption of southern Gaul, St Sidonius did not raise his voice in vituperation of the iniquities of his times. For some time he had a command in the imperial army ; and he married Papianilla, by whom he had a son called Apollinaris, and three daughters, Severiana, Roscia, and Alchima. Papianilla was daughter of Avitus, who after having been thrice prefect of the prætorium in Gaul was raised to the imperial throne at Rome in 455 ; Sidonius wrote a panegyric in honour of his father-in-law, who returned the compliment by putting a statue of him among the poets in the Forum of Trajan. Avitus, a weak person if no worse, was made to resign the purple after a reign of ten months, and he died on the road to Auvergne. Majorian, his successor, prosecuted his relations and, coming to Lyons, had Sidonius arrested ; but admiring the way in which he bore his disgrace, and becoming acquainted with his qualifications, he restored his estates to him, and created him count. Sidonius wrote a panegyric of him too. The new emperor was a good soldier and began to curb the barbarians who laid waste the empire, but was slain in 461 by Ricimer the Goth, his own general, who placed the diadem upon the head of Severus. Upon this revolution Sidonius left the court, and retired to Auvergne. Severus was poisoned by Ricimer after a reign of four years, and Anthemius was chosen emperor in 467. Sidonius went again to Rome and, hoping for a revival of the Empire after the death of Thedoric II the Visigoth, wrote another very encouraging panegyric. The feeble emperors of this age were peculiarly susceptible to compliments, and the poet was made prefect of the city. But his hopes of Anthemius came to nothing (he also was eventually murdered and Rome sacked by the soldiers of Ricimer), and he returned to Gaul, to his wife and family and the enjoyment of his estates.

God soon called him from these secular dignities to government in His Church. The bishopric of Arvernum, since called Clermont in Auvergne, falling vacant, the people of that diocese and the bishops of the whole country demanded that he should fill the episcopal office ; they were conscious not only of his high character and abilities, but also of the fact that he was the man best qualified to uphold Gallo-Roman power against the Visigoths.

St Sidonius was then a layman, and his wife was living; he therefore urged the authority of the canons against such an election and opposed it, till fearing at length to resist the will of Heaven he acquiesced, it having been customary on extraordinary occasions to dispense with the canons which forbid laymen to be chosen bishops. He and his wife agreed to a separation, and from that moment he renounced poetry, which till then had been his delight, to apply himself to those studies which were more required by his ministry. He was no stranger to them whilst a layman, and he soon became an authority whom other bishops consulted in their difficulties; he was always reserved and unwilling to decide them and usually referred them to others, alleging that he was not capable of acting the part of a teacher among the brethren whose direction and knowledge he himself stood in need of. St Lupus of Troyes, who had always loved and honoured him, on his being made a bishop wrote a letter of congratulation and advice, in which among other things he told him: " It is no longer by show and a stately household that you are to keep up your rank, but by deep humility of heart. You are placed above others, but must see yourself as below the meanest and last in your flock. Be ready to kiss the feet of those whom formerly you would not have thought worthy to sit at your own. You must make yourself the servant of all." And so St Sidonius did. He kept always a frugal table, fasted every second day and, though of a delicate constitution, seemed to carry his austerities to excess. After he was bishop he looked upon it as a principal duty to provide for the instruction, comfort, and assistance of the poor. In the time of a great famine he maintained at his own charge, with the charitable help of Ecdicius, his wife's brother, more than four thousand Burgundians and other strangers who had been driven from their own country by misery and necessity; and when the scarcity was over he helped to send them to their respective homes. His reputation was so great that, being summoned to Bourges when that see, which was his metropolitan church, was vacant in 472, the prelates assembled with one consent referred the election of a bishop to him, and he nominated one Simplicius. He says that a bishop ought to do by humility what a monk and a penitent are obliged to do by their profession. He gives us an account of Maximus, Archbishop of Toulouse, whom he had before known as a very rich man of the world: he found him in his new spiritual dignity wholly changed; his clothes, mien, and conversation savoured of nothing but modesty and piety; he had short hair and a long beard; his household stuff was plain; he had wooden benches, stuff curtains, a bed without feathers, and a table without a covering; and the food of his household consisted of pulse more than flesh. He testifies that the festivals of saints were kept with great solemnity, and on them the people flocked to the church before day when the monks and clergy sang Matins in two choirs.

Clermont being threatened by Euric, King of the Visigoths, who then controlled the southern provinces of France, the bishop encouraged the people oppose them. He put his brother-in-law Ecdicius in charge of the defence and instituted rogation processions in his diocese to implore the mercy of God. But in 474 Clermont fell, and his previous activities exposed him to the rage of the conquerors after they were masters of the place. He entreated the Arian king to grant concessions in favour of the Catholics, which the barbarian was so far from allowing that he sent the prelate prisoner to Levignac, near Carcassone. Here he was lodged next door to two bad-tempered old women, who made such a noise that he could neither sleep nor read: "Never," complained the poor man, "were two such quarrelsome, restless, and abusive chatterers!" When he was restored to his see he continued to be the protection and support of his people, though grievously troubled by the Goths and by two turbulent and factious priests who interfered in his government. He died in peace about the year 488. St Sidonius Apollinaris was one of the principal writers of the beginning of the second age of Christian literature, or he may be regarded as the last of the Gallo-Roman school. His poetry is inflated and tiresome, but his letters are a valuable witness to the life of Christian gentlemen in southern Gaul during the break-up of the Empire; they were sportsmen, with a taste for literature and the other fine arts, whose Christianity sat rather lightly upon them but was not insincere. The saint shows us himself in his secular days in Auvergne joining in the recreations, physical and intellectual, of his neighbours; looking after his estates and the material and moral well-being of his slaves; and caring for his children: he warns his son against loose talk, forbids *vaudeville* in his house, and declines an invitation to go fishing because his daughter Severiana has a bad feverish cold.

The greater part of our information concerning Sidonius is derived from his letters and other writings. The best text is that edited in the *Monumenta Germaniæ, Auctores Antiquissimi*, vol. viii. There is an excellent short biography by Paul Allard in the series "Les Saints" (1910) and a longer one in two volumes by the Abbé Chaix (1866). An English version of the letters of Sidonius was published by O. M. Dalton in 1915, and an unusually long article has been devoted to him in the *Dictionary of Christian Biography*, vol. iv, pp. 649–661. See also Hauck, *Kirchengeschichte Deutschlands*, vol. i.

BD. HUMBELINE, MATRON AND ABBESS
A.D. 1135 OR 1141

Was born in 1092, the year after her brother St Bernard, with whom she was always on terms of intimate friendship. Like him she was of great physical beauty, and had a lovely voice, was skilled in music, and a good Latinist. When her father and five brothers joined St Stephen Harding at Cîteaux in 1113 she came into a good part of their estates and married herself to a rich nobleman of the house of Lorraine, Guy de Marcy. Some years after the founding of Clairvaux she went to visit Bernard there and in due course arrived, very stylishly dressed and surrounded by an imposing train of attendants. When St Bernard was told that the Lady Humbeline had come, and with what array, he was not at all pleased and refused to see her : he knew his sister and disapproved of her display, and perhaps thought she was " showing off," travelling in that style. She at once guessed what had upset him, or, as tradition says, the brother porter told her, roughly enough, and she sent in a message that if he would come out she would do just as he told her ; and out of enclosure St Bernard accordingly came. Humbeline's life in the world was more notable for dancing than devotion, and it was Bernard's opinion that the balance needed redressing ; he took the opportunity presented, and gently reasoned with her, particularly reminding her of the virtuous and devoted life of their mother, Aleth. This had its effect (even a sister would hesitate about arguing with a St Bernard), and Humbeline went away, considerably chastened. A few years later this interview at Clairvaux had a more unexpected result, when Humbeline got her husband's consent to her becoming a nun. She went to the monastery of the nuns at that Jully near Troyes which is called "les-Nonnais" after them ; here her sister-in-law Elizabeth was abbess, and when she left to found a convent near Dijon, Bd. Humbeline had made such progress in the religious life that she was appointed in her place. She practised severe physical austerities and when her nuns urged her to moderate them she replied, " That is all very well for you, my sisters, who have been serving God in religion all your lives. But I have lived so long in the world and of the world, oblivious of all else, that no penance can be too much for me." In 1132 a colony from Jully founded Tart in the diocese of Langres, the first house of Cistercian nuns ; it is not known what part Bd. Humbeline had in this establishment, but Jully itself always remained Benedictine. In her last illness three of her brothers,

Bernard, Andrew and Nivard, hurried to her bedside, and she died in Bernard's arms on August 21, 1135 (or 1141); but her feast is kept by the Cistercians on February 12. The *cultus* of Bd. Humbeline was approved by Pope Clement XI in 1703, and she is venerated as patroness of the Cistercian nuns of Spain.

There is no early Life of Blessed Humbeline. A short account of her is given in the *Acta Sanctorum*, August, vol. vi, and she stands first in the group of holy women whose history is traced by Henriquez in his *Lilia Cisterciensium* (1633); but almost all Lives of St Bernard devote more or less space to his relations with his only sister.

BD. BERNARD TOLOMEO, Conf., Founder
OF THE OLIVETANS
A.D. 1348

Was born at Siena in 1272 and was baptized Giovanni. He was educated by his uncle, a Dominican friar, who imbued him with a love of learning and a desire for the religious life; but at the wish of his parents he continued his secular studies in the world, specializing in civil law and adding thereto for his own satisfaction theology and canon law. After being a soldier in the service of the King of the Romans, Rudolph of Habsburg, he took up public work in Siena and fulfilled several municipal offices. The story goes that while occupying that of *podestà* he was afflicted with blindness, which befell him as he was about to deliver a lecture on philosophy; it was only temporary, but on his recovery, in 1313, instead of a lecture on philosophy he gave a sermon on contempt of the world, resigned his position and withdrew to a place ten miles from the city and lived there in solitude. This is said to have been done in fulfilment of a vow made to our Lady, to whose intercession he attributed the mending of his sight. He was joined by two other Sienese gentlemen, Ambrose Piccolomini and Patrick Patrici, and the three lived together in the desert land between Siena and the woods of Mont' Amiata, where all was ash-coloured, sterile, and desolate. They built a small chapel and dedicated it in honour of St Scholastica. The reputation of the sanctity of their lives was marred by malicious or mistaken rumours (some thought them mad and there was an attempt to poison Giovanni), which in 1319 caused them to be summoned before Pope John XXII at Avignon to give an account of themselves. Ambrose and Patrick accordingly went, and were able to demonstrate their orthodoxy to the Pope's satisfaction, but he instructed them to put themselves under one or other of the approved monastic rules. Giovanni thereupon consulted Guy of Pietromala, Bishop of Arezzo, who gave them the rule of St Benedict and clothed them in the monastic habit—but white instead of the usual black. It is said that the bishop did this in accordance with a dream in which our Lady had told him to give the Benedictine rule and white habits to some persons who were at that time unknown to him. Giovanni, who was recognized as their leader, took the name of Bernard, their hermitage at Chiusuri was called Monte Oliveto, and the Benedictine congregation of our Lady of Monte Oliveto came into existence. It professed a primitive observance of the rule of St Benedict, to which a number of austerities (including, at first, total abstinence from wine) were added, and its success was instantaneous. Within a few years Bd. Bernard had founded a second monastery at Arezzo, a rich merchant built one at Siena, another was founded at Florence, one at Rome itself, and others elsewhere; their penitential life continued to attract disciples and in 1344 the new congregation was confirmed by Pope Clement VI. Some time afterwards a bad epidemic of plague broke out around Siena, 80,000 died during the summer, and the Olivetan monks gave up themselves entirely to the care of the suffering and the burial of the dead; it seemed as if they were miraculously preserved from contagion, but in August 1348 one of them was struck down: it was their founder himself. He died at Monte Oliveto on the 20th, the feast of his patron, St Bernard of Clairvaux. In 1644 the *cultus* of Bd. Bernard Tolomeo was confirmed, and his name appears in the Roman Martyrology with the title " Blessed "; but he is venerated by the Olivetans, who still exist as a small independent congregation of Benedictines, as " Saint," in accordance with the declaration of the Congregation of Sacred Rites that " he was worthy of veneration among the saints."

The Bollandists in the *Acta Sanctorum*, August, vol. iv, give a long account of Blessed Bernard, though there is no formal biography of early date. The most valuable contribution to the history of the founder of the Olivetani is that of Dom Placido Lugano, *Origine e primordi dell' Ordine di Montoliveto* (1903), who basing his work upon the relatively early chronicles of Antonio de Barga and Alesandro da Sesto has stripped Blessed Tolomeo's life of its legendary accretions, notably of the story which attributes his religious vocation to the miraculous cure of sudden blindness. On the Olivetani as a reformed congregation see Heimbucher, *Orden und Kongregationen der Kath. Kirche*, vol. i, pp. 281–283.

AUGUST 22

SS. TIMOTHY, HIPPOLYTUS, AND SYMPHORIAN, MM.
SECOND TO FOURTH CENTURIES

ON this day the Church commemorates three martyrs totally unconnected with one another. ST TIMOTHY was a priest of Antioch who came to Rome between 311 and 313. He lodged with St Sylvester, afterwards pope, and preached in the city until " he was taken up by the prefect Tarquin and brought low by a long imprisonment. When he refused to sacrifice to idols he was three times scourged, and after passing through most sharp torments was at last beheaded " (Roman Martyrology).

ST HIPPOLYTUS is described both in the lesson at Matins and in the Roman Martyrology as a bishop of Porto, a " man greatly renowned for his learning," who, either at that place or at Ostia, was for his confession of the Faith put to death by drowning ; and was buried in the place of his martyrdom. There is very great uncertainty as to who this martyr was, but it is likely that he is identical with the St Hippolytus, anti-pope and then martyr, who has been mentioned on the thirteenth of this month.

ST SYMPHORIAN was son of Faustus, of a noble Christian family, and suffered at Autun in Gaul soon after the martyrs of Lyons, about the year 180. He is fabled to have been baptized by St Benignus. The city of Autun was one of the most ancient and famous of Gaul, but at that time most superstitious, and particularly addicted to the worship of Cybele, Apollo and Diana. On a certain day of the year, the statue of Cybele was with great pomp carried through the streets in a chariot. Symphorian, because he had not on that occasion adored it, was seized by the mob and carried before Heraclius, governor of the province, who was then at Autun, very busy calling Christians to an account. Heraclius asked him why he refused to adore the image of the mother of the gods. He answered, because he was a Christian and adored the true God ; and that, moreover, if someone would give him a hammer he was prepared to break up their idol. To the judge this reply savoured of rebellion, as well as being impious and sacrilegious, and he inquired of the officers whether he was a citizen of the place. One of them answered,

"He is, and of a noble family." The judge said to Symphorian, "You flatter yourself on account of your birth, or are perhaps unacquainted with the emperor's orders." He then ordered the imperial edict to be read, and said to him, "What say you to this, Symphorian?" The martyr continuing to express his abhorrence of the idol, Heraclius commanded him to be beaten, and sent him to prison. Two days later, he was brought out and presented before the tribunal. Heraclius tried to bribe him, saying, "It would be much better for you to serve the immortal gods and to receive a grant from the treasury with an honourable military office. If you have a mind, the altars shall be adorned with flowers and you may offer to the gods the incense which is due to them." Symphorian despised the offers that were made him, and refused to take any part in the worship of Cybele. At length the judge condemned him to die by the sword for treason towards gods and men, in that he had refused to sacrifice and had spoken of the gods with irreverence. As he was led out of the town to execution, his mother, standing on the walls of the city to see him pass by, cried out to him, " My son, my son Symphorian! remember the living God and be of good courage. Fear not! You go to a death which leads to certain life." His head was struck off and his body buried in a cave, near a fountain, outside the common field. His tomb became famous for miracles, and in the middle of the fifth century St Euphronius, Bishop of Autun, built over it a church in his honour.

It is the reflection of St Augustine that if with the martyrs we seriously considered the rewards that await us, we should account all trouble and pain in this life as nothing; and should be astonished that the divine goodness gives so great a return for so little labour. To obtain eternal rest should require, if it had been possible, eternal labour; to purchase a happiness without bounds, a man should be willing to suffer without bounds. That indeed is impossible; but our trials might have been very long. What are a thousand years, or ten hundred thousand ages, in comparison to eternity? There can be no proportion between what is finite, and that which is infinite. Yet God in His mercy does not ask us to suffer so long. He says, not a million or a thousand years, or even five hundred; but only labour the few years that you live, and in these the dew of my consolations shall not be wanting and I will recompense your patience with a glory that has no end. Though we were to be loaded with miseries, pain, and grief our whole life, the thoughts of Heaven alone ought to make us bear its sharpest trials with cheerfulness and joy.

The conjunction of these three wholly unconnected saints in one common prayer, such as that said in the Roman office and Mass on this day, is a curious liturgical feature. Originally the same prayer was said with the name of Timothy alone, as may be seen in the Gregorian sacramentary; the two other names have been subsequently inserted. Whatever may be thought of the story of St Timothy's martyrdom as recounted in the Acts of St Silvester, his name and his burial on the Ostian Way are entered in the "Depositio Martyrum" of A.D. 354, not to speak of other early testimonies which Father Delehaye has set out in his commentary on the "Hieronymianum." A mention of Timothy on this day in the famous Carthaginian calendar, and a statement in the chronicle known as "the Barbarus of Scaliger" that "Timothy the bishop gloriously suffered martyrdom at Carthage" has raised a doubt whether there may not be two Timothei; just as the question of a second Hippolytus (of Portus) has been much discussed. Symphorian again is a martyr whose existence is established by very early allusions and dedications. On his respectable Acts, printed by Ruinart and elsewhere, see W. Meyer, "Fragmenta Burana" in the *Festschrift* published for the Göttingen Academy in 1901, pp. 161–163. Further references will be found in Delehaye's commentary just mentioned, *Acta Sanctorum*, November, vol. ii, part 2, pp. 456–8.

ST SIGFRID, Abbot of Wearmouth, Conf.

A.D. 689

While St Benedict Biscop was away on his fifth visit to Rome his coadjutor abbot at Wearmouth, St Easterwin, died, and the monks together with St Ceolfrid, coadjutor abbot of Jarrow, elected in his place the deacon Sigfrid. "He was," says St Bede, "a man well skilled in the knowledge of Holy Scripture, of admirable behaviour and perfect continence, but one in whom vigour of mind was somewhat depressed by bodily weakness and whose innocence of heart went along with a distressing and incurable affection of the lungs." Some three years after St Sigfrid's promotion and St Benedict's return to his monasteries both saints were stricken with sickness and had to take to their beds; they knew that death was upon them and wished for a last conference about one another's welfare and that of their monks. Sigfrid therefore was carried on a stretcher to Benedict's cell and laid on his bed, "with their heads on the same pillow," but they were too weak even to embrace one another unaided. After consultation with Sigfrid Benedict sent for Ceolfrid and, with the approval of all, appointed him abbot of both monasteries, that so peace, unity, and concord might be preserved. Two months later St Sigfrid, "having passed through the fire and water of temporal tribulation, was taken to the place of everlasting rest: sending up to the Lord the offerings of praise which his righteous lips had vowed, he entered the mansion of the heavenly Kingdom." He was buried in the abbey-church of St Peter beside his master, St Benedict, and his predecessor, St Easterwin.

All our information comes from Bede's *Historia Abbatum* and the anonymous history which covers the same ground. See the text in C. Plummer and his notes. It is very questionable how far saintship can be claimed in this and many similar cases. There is no trace of any liturgical commemoration, not even so much as an entry in church calendars. *Cf.* Stanton's *Menology*, p. 405.

ST ANDREW, Conf.
End of the Ninth Century

According to his practically worthless *acta* of the fourteenth or fifteenth century this Andrew was a young Irishman who went on a pilgrimage to Rome with his teacher, St Donatus. On their way back they stopped at Fiesole, where the episcopal see was vacant, and Donatus was miraculously designated to fill it; he thereupon ordained Andrew deacon and made him his archdeacon. In this office he served the Church faithfully and holily for some years. He restored the church of St Martin, which had been destroyed by the Magyars, and founded the monastery there. St Andrew had a sister called Brigid to whom he was greatly attached and who also is venerated as a saint; she is said to have followed him to Italy and to have lived as a solitary among the mountains of Tuscany, but according to the legend of Andrew she was miraculously transported from Ireland to her brother's bedside while he lay dying. There is room for confusion about this Brigid, as the preface to the monk Coelan's life of St Brigid of Kildare is attributed to St Donatus of Fiesole. In 1285 the alleged relics of St Andrew were found in the church of San Martino di Mensola at Fiesole, where they are still preserved.

The document which purports to recount the history of St Andrew is printed in the *Acta Sanctorum*, August, vol. iv. It may be noted that Dom Gougaud in his *Gaelic Pioneers of Christianity* makes no mention of Andrew, probably deeming the whole story fictitious.

BB. WILLIAM LACEY and RICHARD KIRKMAN, MM.
a.d. 1582

William Lacey was born at Horton, near Settle, in the West Riding of Yorkshire; he was married to the widow of a man of county family named Creswell, and was a lawyer holding an official position. For long he was reputed to be a Papist at heart and after the visit of Dr. (afterwards Cardinal) William Allen to the north of England in 1565 that suspicion became a certainty. Mr. Lacey was active in the Catholic cause and an open recusant. He almost at once lost his office and for fourteen years was subjected to bitter persecution, in which his wife nobly bore her part; he was repeatedly fined, visited, examined, and once was imprisoned at Kingston-on-Hull, till he eventually fled from his house with his family, and was hunted from place to place. At last Mrs. Lacey broke down under the strain and was taken seriously ill; this did not deter the Archbishop of York from taking steps to have her arrested as a recusant, but the good lady died first. The next year, 1580, Lacey, already a man of considerable age, entered himself as a student at Rheims, continued his studies at Pont-à-Mousson, and finally went to Rome, where he was ordained. In 1581, on the eve of going on the English mission, he wrote from Loreto to a friend in Rome, probably his stepson Joseph (Arthur) Creswell, who was about to become a Jesuit, a letter of leave-taking, full of scriptural quotations and breathing a very tender spirit of humility and happiness. He arrived in England in the early summer but was destined to work only some twelve months for the Catholics of his native Yorkshire. He, together with Bd. William Hart, Mr. Thomas Bell, and other priests, was in the habit of visiting the Catholic prisoners in York castle. Now Mr. Bell had, before his ordination, been imprisoned and tortured for the Faith in that castle, and he conceived the project of now *singing a high Mass* there, as an act of thanksgiving. In those days prisons were not the efficient institutions that they are to-day and a little money, carefully distributed to turnkeys, would go a long way. Early on Sunday, July 22, 1582, that Mass was sung in one of the prisoners' cells, with Mr. Lacey and Mr. Hart assisting as deacon and sub-deacon. Just as it was over, an alarm was given and the authorities began to search the building; Hart and Bell got away, but Lacey was captured. He was examined first by the Lord Mayor and then by Dr. Sandys, Archbishop of York, by whom he was committed to solitary confinement in irons, and after three weeks was brought up for trial. His letter of orders was put in against him, and he openly avowed his priesthood (though it was not at that time high treason for a priest to come into the country); when asked if he acknowledged the Queen as head of the Church, he replied, " In this matter, as well as in all other things, I believe as the Catholic Church of God and all good Christians believe." Whereupon he was convicted and sentenced, at which he said, " God be for ever blessed !

I am now old, and by the course of nature could not expect to live long. This will be no more to me than to pay the common debt a little before the time. I am rejoiced, therefore, at the things which have been said to me : we shall go into the house of the Lord and so shall be with the Lord for ever." Some of the gentry of the county tried to get him pardoned and would probably have succeeded but for the influence of Henry Cheke, secretary to the Council of the North, and on August 22, Bd. William Lacey was hung, drawn, and quartered at the Knavesmire, outside the city of York.

There suffered at the same time and place (they confessed to one another on the way to the scaffold) Bd. Richard Kirkman, also a secular priest and a Yorkshireman. He was born at Addingham, near Skipton, and was ordained at Rheims in 1579. He appears to have been taken into the household of Robert Dymoke, hereditary Champion of England, at Scrivelsby in Lincolnshire, where he was tutor to Dymoke's three younger sons and pastor to the Catholics of the neighbourhood. After eleven months his patron and his wife were indicted for not going to the Protestant service (Dymoke died in prison for the Faith), and Mr. Kirkman had to leave Scrivelsby and seek refuge elsewhere. He worked in Yorkshire and Northumberland until he was arrested near Wakefield merely as a suspected person, but his chalice was found on him and he admitted that he was a priest. The very next day he was brought up at the York assizes, and sentenced to death. When abused by Mr. Justice Wortley as a traitor, he replied, " You might, sir, with the same justice charge the Apostles also with being traitors, for they taught the same doctrine as I now teach and did the same things for which you condemn me." After sentence was pronounced he exclaimed, " It must then be so and I must be honoured with so great a dignity. Good God ! how unworthy I am of it ! But since it is Thy holy will, may it be done on earth as it is in Heaven. Te Deum laudamus, te Dominum confitemur ! " For four days he shared the cell of Bd. William Lacey, but after a private interview with the sheriff and two ministers he was put into a dungeon alone, without light, food, or bed. And here he was left till he was brought out to die.

See Challoner, *Memoirs of Missionary Priests* (Ed. Pollen), pp. 66–70 ; and *Lives of the English Martyrs* (Ed. B. Camm), vol. ii, pp. 564–588, with the authorities there cited.

BD. JOHN WALL, Mart.
A.D. 1679

John Wall (*alias* Francis Johnson, Webb, Dormer) belonged to a good Lancashire family and was born in that county (perhaps at Chingle Hall, near Preston) in 1620. He was sent when young to Douay, entered the Roman College in 1641 and was ordained there in 1645. After a few years on the mission he took the Franciscan habit at St Bonaventure's friary at Douay in 1651, receiving the religious name of Joachim-of-St-Anne, and served there until 1656, filling the offices of vicar and of novice-master, when he returned to England. After he had ministered to the Catholics of Worcestershire for over twenty-two years, his headquarters being at Harvington Hall, he was seized, in December 1678, at Rushock Court, near Bromsgrove, by a sheriff's officer who had come there to look for a defaulting debtor. After five months in prison he was tried before Mr. Justice Atkins as a priest unlawfully come into the realm; of the four witnesses brought against him, three had to be subpœnaed, and he defended himself with great prudence. However, he was sentenced, whereupon he bowed to the judge and said, " Thanks be to God! God save the King! And I beseech God to bless your lordship and all this honourable bench." To which the judge made answer, " You have spoken very well. I do not intend you shall die, at least not for the present, until I know the King's further pleasure." " I was not, I thank God for it," wrote Bd. John, " troubled with any disturbing thoughts either against the judge for his sentence, or the jury that gave in such a verdict, or against any of the witnesses. . . . And I was, I thank God, so present with myself whilst the judge pronounced the sentence that, without any concern for anything in this world, I did actually at the same time offer myself and the world to God." In spite of the good will of Mr. Justice Atkins, the innocent and beloved Franciscan was not to be reprieved, although after being carefully examined in London four several times by Oates, Bedloe, Dugdale, and Prance he was declared by Bedloe in public to be free from any complicity in the Oates " plot." He would not renounce his religion, which was what they really wanted, so after a month he was returned to Worcester for execution. The day before, he was visited in prison by a fellow-Franciscan, Father William Leveson (brother of the venerable martyr, Father Francis Leveson, O.S.F.), who was allowed to spend several hours there and so was able to hear his confession and give him Holy Viaticum. The same friar stood by the scaffold at Redhill the next day and gave him the final absolution when the martyr was hung and quartered, " thirsting after nothing more than the shedding of his blood for the love of his God ; which he performed with a courage and cheerfulness becoming a valiant soldier of Christ, to the great edification of all Catholics and admiration of all Protestants." Bd. John Wall was the only one of the English martyrs to be executed at Worcester ; he was beatified in 1929.

See Challoner, *Memoirs of Missionary Priests* (Ed. Pollen), pp. 550–555 ; B. Camm, *Forgotten Shrines*, pp. 253–280.

BD. JOHN KEMBLE, Mart.
A.D. 1679

Was the son of John Kemble, gentleman, of a family originally of Wiltshire, and Anne, one of the Morgans of Skenfrith and Blackbrooke, and was born in 1599, traditionally at Rhydicar farm in the parish of Saint Weonards, Herefordshire, though some say at Pembridge Castle nearby. They were a Catholic family, and his elder brother was a monk of St Gregory's at Douay. When he was about twelve John was smuggled abroad to the school at Douay, and after six years passed into the seminary, where he was ordained in 1625 and in the same year sent on the mission to work in and around his birthplace. Of these labours nothing at all is known except that they extended over a period of fifty-three years, apparently unbroken save that in the archives of the Old Brotherhood of the Secular Clergy there is an entry in or about the year 1649 which suggests that he was then for a time in London ; it is known from the Westminster archives that in 1643 he was recommended as a suitable person to be made archdeacon of South Wales. During these years he gained that reputation for goodness which persisted among the folk of Monmouthshire almost to our own day and, with the help of the Jesuits at the Cwm in Llanrothal, he formed those mission centres, at the Llwyn, the Graig, Hilston, and elsewhere, which lingered on into the nineteenth century and are now represented only by a desolate burying-ground and a ruined chapel at Coed Anghred on a hill above Skenfrith. During most, if not all, of this time he made his headquarters at Pembridge Castle, the home first of his uncle George, and then of his nephew, Captain Richard Kemble. In 1678 the "Oates' Plot" terror began and in the autumn it reached Herefordshire : the Cwm was sacked and John Kemble's friend David Lewis, S.J., was taken. He was urged to fly, but he would not : " According to the course of nature I have but a few years to live [he was just on eighty] ; it will be an advantage to suffer for my religion, and therefore I will not abscond."

In November Captain Scudamore of Kentchurch, for all his wife and children were Catholics and ministered to by Mr. Kemble, went to Pembridge Castle, arrested the old priest, and dragged him off through the snow to Hereford gaol. There he remained four months, till the March assizes, at which he was condemned to be hung, drawn, and quartered, *pro Sacerd' Seminar.*, " for being a seminary priest," as it is recorded in the Crown Book of the Oxford Circuit. On April 23 an order was signed for him and Bd. David Lewis to be sent to London for examination by the Privy Council ; on the journey he " suffered more than a martyrdom on account of a great indisposition he had, which would not permit him to ride but sideways ; and it was on horseback he was compelled to perform the journey, at least great part of the way." " He was strapped like a pack to his horse going there, but allowed to walk most of the way on his journey back," which he made a few weeks later : as he said at his execution, " Oates and Bedloe not being able to charge me with anything when I was brought up to London (though they were with me) makes it evident that I die only for professing the old Roman Catholic religion, which was the religion that first made this kingdom Christian. . . ." That execution was ordered by Scroggs L.C.J., at the summer assizes, and its date fixed for August 22.

When the under-sheriff, one Digges, arrived at the jail Bd. John asked for time first to finish his prayers and then to smoke a pipe of tobacco and have a drink. The governor and under-sheriff joined him, Digges in his turn delaying in order to finish *his* pipe.* Towards evening he was dragged on a hurdle to Widemarsh Common, where before a huge crowd he denied all knowledge of any plot and made a final profession of faith. He was allowed to hang till he was dead before the remainder of the sentence was carried out, but the hangman's work was so ill done that, old as he was, he lived for half-an-hour after the cart was withdrawn. With the exception of the left hand, now enshrined in the Catholic church at Hereford, Bd. John's remains were buried under a flat stone in Welsh Newton churchyard, where they still lie. The first miracle recorded at the intercession of Bd. John was in favour of the daughter of his denouncer,

* This curious and pleasing incident originated the Herefordshire custom of calling the last pipe of a sitting " the Kemble pipe," a custom only lately fallen into disuse. *Cf.* the footnote on p. 394 of Sir John Hawkins's edition of Izaak Walton's *Compleat Angler* (London, 1808), where Bd. John Kemble is made a Protestant martyr under Queen Mary !

Captain Scudamore, who was cured of an affection of her throat by applying to it the rope with which the martyr was hung ; and Mgr. Matthew Pritchard, O.F.M., Vicar Apostolic for the Western District in 1715, was present when Mrs. Catherine Scudamore was cured of long-standing deafness while praying at his graveside. Protestant witnesses of his execution " acknowledged that they never saw one die so like a gentleman and so like a Christian," and Bd. John Kemble has never been without local veneration ; the annual pilgrimage to his grave is said to have been uninterrupted since his martyrdom. He was beatified by Pope Pius XI in 1929.

There is a pamphlet on Blessed John Kemble by R. Raikes Bromage (1902). But see also Challoner, *Missionary Priests* (Ed. Pollen), pp. 555–7 ; and B. Camm, *Forgotten Shrines*, pp. 333–342.

AUGUST 23

ST PHILIP BENIZI, Conf.

A.D. 1285

THIS principal ornament and propagator of the religious order of the Servites in Italy was of the noble families of Benizi and Frescobaldi in Florence, and a native of that city. He was born on August 15, in the year 1233, which is said by some to be the very feast of the Assumption on which the seven Founders of the Servites had their first vision of our Lady. His parents, Giacomo and Albaverde, had been long married but childless, and Philip was a child of prayer. Through their care, assisted by grace, Philip preserved his soul untainted by vice and the world, and daily advanced in the fear of God. At the age of thirteen, having gone through preliminary studies in his own country, he was sent to Paris to apply himself to the study of medicine, in which charity was his motive; and Galen, though a heathen, was a strong spur to him in raising his heart continually from the contemplation of nature to the worship and praise of its Author. From Paris he removed to Padua, where he pursued the same studies, and took the degree of doctor in medicine and philosophy at the age of nineteen. After his return to Florence he took some time to deliberate with himself what course to steer, earnestly begging God to direct him into the path in which he should most perfectly fulfil His will. For a year he practised his profession, spending his leisure time in the study of sacred Scripture and the Fathers and in prayer for guidance, especially before a certain crucifix in the abbey-church at Fiesole and before a picture of the Annunciation in the Servite chapel at Carfaggio, just outside the walls of Florence.

At this time the Servites, or Order of the Servants of Mary, had been established fourteen years, having been founded by seven gentlemen of Florence as described under their feast on February 12, but had not yet been officially recognized by the Holy See. At their principal house on Monte Senario, six miles from Florence, they lived in little cells, something like the hermits of Camaldoli, possessing nothing but in common, and professing obedience to St Buonfiglio Monaldi. The austerities which they practised were great, and they lived mostly on alms; St Buonfiglio was the first superior of this company. On the Thursday in Easter Week, 1254, Philip was in prayer at Fiesole when the figure on the crucifix seemed to say to him, " Go to the high hill where the servants of My Mother are living, and you will be doing the will of My Father." Pondering these words deeply Philip went to the chapel at Carfaggio to assist at Mass, and was strongly affected with the words of the Holy Ghost to the deacon Philip, which were read in the epistle of that day, " Go near and join thyself to this chariot." His name being Philip he applied to himself these words as an invitation to put himself under the care of the Blessed Virgin in that order, and he seemed to himself, in a dream or vision, to be in a vast wilderness (representing the world) full of precipices, rocks, flint-stones, briers, snares, and venomous serpents, so that he did not see how it was possible for him to escape so many dangers. Whilst he was thus in dread and consternation he thought he beheld our Lady approaching him in a chariot and about to speak to him, but he was recalled to his surroundings by St Alexis Falconieri who, thinking he was asleep, had shaken him by the shoulder. " God forgive you, Brother Alexis," said Philip. " You have brought me back from Paradise." But that night the vision was repeated and our Lady called him to her new order. Reflecting that great watchfulness and an extraordinary grace are requisite to discover every lurking rock or quicksand in the course of life in the world, and persuaded that God called him to this order as to a place of refuge, he went to Monte Senario and was admitted by St Buonfiglio to the habit as a lay-brother, that state being more agreeable to his humility: " I wish," he said, " to be the servant of the Servants of Mary." In consideration of the circumstances in which he had joined the order he retained his baptismal name in religion. He began his novitiate at Carfaggio but was afterwards sent back to Monte Senario, where he was made gardener and put to work at every kind of hard country labour. The saint cheerfully applied himself to it in a spirit of penance and accompanied his work with constant recollection and prayer; he lived in a little cave behind the church where, in ecstacies of divine love, he often forgot the care which he owed to his body. He concealed his learning and talents till they were at length discovered; but those who conversed with him admired the prudence and light with which he spoke on spiritual things. He was sent in 1258 to the Servite house at Siena and on the way there he undesignedly displayed his abilities in a discourse on certain controverted points, in the presence of two learned Dominicans and others, to the great astonishment of those that heard him, and especially of his companion, Brother Victor.

The matter was reported to the prior general, who examined St Philip closely and then had him promoted to holy orders, though nothing but an absolute command could extort his consent to such a step. He was ordained by the Bishop of Florence on Holy Saturday in 1259 but did not say his first Mass until the following Pentecost.

All Philip's hopes of living out his life in quiet and obscurity, serving God and his brethren as a lay-brother, were now at an end. He was appointed assistant to St Buonfiglio, who had retired from the generalate and been made colleague to his successor, which involved travelling about with him throughout Tuscany, Umbria, Emilia, and Lombardy, visiting the houses of the order. Buonfiglio died in 1261 and St Philip thereupon went to the Siena monastery as novice-master. He filled this congenial office for only eighteen months, being taken from it to be one of the four vicars appointed by the chapter to assist the prior general; soon after he became himself colleague of the prior general. In 1267 a chapter of the whole order (which had been in effect recognized by Pope Alexander IV eight years before) was held at Carfaggio; at this chapter St Manettus resigned the generalship and, in spite of his protests, St Philip Benizi was unanimously elected in his stead. During his first year of office he made a general visitation of the provinces of northern Italy, which at the time were torn and distracted by the strife of Guelf and Ghibelline. It was on this tour that his first miracle was reported of him, very similar to one attributed to St Dominic and other saints: owing to the troubles the Servites of Arezzo were unable to get food and were on the verge of starvation; when they assembled for supper there was nothing to eat until, when St Philip had exhorted them to have faith and had prayed before our Lady's image in the church, a knock was heard at the monastery door and two large baskets of good bread were found on the steps. He codified the rules and constitutions of the Servite order and this work was confirmed by the general chapter held at Pistoia in 1268; afterwards he submitted them to Pope Clement IV at Viterbo and would on the same occasion have asked leave to give up his office. But he was so warmly dissuaded by his colleague, Brother Lottaringo, that he resigned himself to holding it so long as his brethren should wish, which proved to be for the rest of his life.

Upon the death of Clement IV the conclave assembled at Viterbo early in 1269, and it was rumoured that Cardinal Ottobuoni, protector of the Servites, had proposed St Philip to succeed him, and that the suggestion was well received. When word of this came to Philip's ears he ran away and hid himself in a cave among the mountains near Radicofani, where he was looked after for three months by Brother Victor, until he deemed the danger past (the cardinals were unable to agree and it was not till September 1271 that Theobald Visconti, Archdeacon of Liège, was elected as Gregory X). During this retreat St Philip rejoiced in an opportunity of giving himself up to contemplation ; he lived chiefly on dry herbs, and drank at a fountain, since esteemed miraculous and called St Philip's bath, situate on a mountain named Montagnata. He returned from the desert glowing with zeal to kindle in the hearts of Christians the fire of divine love. After the chapter at Florence at Whitsun of the same year he appointed a vicar general there to govern his order and with two companions, St Sostenes and St Hugh, two of the seven original founders, undertook an extensive mission, preaching with great fruit at Avignon, Toulouse, Paris, and in other great cities in France, and also in Flanders, Friesland, Saxony, and Higher Germany. He left Sostenes at Paris in charge of the scattered Servite houses of France, and proceeded to establish the order in Germany, where he deputed Hugh as vicar and gave him as assistant the neophyte Bd. John of Frankfort, who became one of the saint's most loved disciples. Philip visited Germany again in 1275 and 1282, but before that he was summoned by Bd. Gregory X to be present at the second general council of Lyons. At it he made a profound impression and the gift of tongues was attributed to him, but his reputation did not serve to obtain for the Servites that formal papal approbation for which St Philip worked continually. The Council in fact reiterated the decree of the fourth Council of the Lateran forbidding new religious orders, and the Servites were more than ever in danger of suppression till the death of Bd. Innocent V in 1276 ; even then the desired confirmation did not come till 1304, nineteen years after Philip's death.

The saint announced the word of God wherever he came and had an extraordinary talent in converting sinners and in reconciling those that were at variance. Italy was still horribly divided by discords and hereditary factions. Holy men often sought to apply remedies to these quarrels, which had a happy effect upon some ; but in many these discords, like a wound ill cured, broke out again with worse symptoms than ever. Papal Guelfs and imperial Ghibellines were the worst offenders, and in 1279 Pope Nicholas III gave special faculties to Cardinal Latino to deal with them. He invoked the help of St Philip Benizi, who wonderfully pacified the factions when they were ready to tear each other to pieces at Pistoia, and other places. He succeeded at length also at Forli, but not without first exposing himself to many dangers. The seditious insulted and beat him in the city, but his patience at length disarmed their fury, and vanquished them. Peregrine Laziosi, who was their ringleader and had himself struck the saint, was so powerfully moved by the example of his meekness and sanctity that he threw himself at his feet and with tears begged his pardon and prayers. Being become a model penitent he was received by him into the order of Servites at Siena in 1283, and continued his penance till his happy death in the eightieth year of his age. So evident were his holiness and perseverance that he was canonized by Benedict XIII in 1726. St Philip made the sanctification of his religious brethren the primary object of his zeal, as it was the first part of his charge, and he attracted a number of notably good men to himself. Among them were Bd. John of Frankfort and St Peregrine, mentioned above; Bd. Joachim Piccolomini, who met Philip at Siena; Bd. Andrew Dotti, a soldier, and Bd. Jerome, both of Borgo San Sepolcro; Bd. Bonaventure of Pistoia, converted by a sermon of the saint from a life of violence and crime; Bd. Ubald of Florence, whose quarrelling had turned Florence upside down; and Bd. Francis Patrizi. In 1284 St Alexis Falconieri put his niece St Juliana under the direction of St Philip, and from his advice to her sprang the third order regular of the Servants of Mary. He was also responsible for sending the first Servite missionaries to the East, where some penetrated to Tartary and there gave their blood for Christ. Throughout his eighteen years of generalship of his order Philip had as his official colleague Lottaringo Stufa, whom he had known and loved from boyhood. They remained the closest friends and the utmost confidence subsisted between them; Philip made Lottaringo his vicar whenever he had to leave Italy, and was followed by him in the generalship. Their long association was an ideal partnership.

Four hundred years before Abbot de Rancé Philip Benizi realized that a religious community in which regular discipline is weakened and those who profess the rule are strangers to its true spirit is not a harbour or place of refuge, but a shipwreck of souls. Scarce could a saint be able to resist such example or the poison of such an air, in which everyone is confined. Though gross crimes of the world are shut out, the want of the religious spirit and a neglect of the particular duties of that state are enough to damn souls. To preserve his family from so fatal a misfortune, he never ceased to watch and pray. Judging at length by the decay of his health that the end of his life drew near, he set out in 1285 to make the visitation of the convents of his order and at Florence convened a general chapter at which he announced his approaching departure and handed over the government to Father Lottaringo. " Love one another! Love one another! Love one another!" he adjured the friars, and so left them. He went to the smallest and poorest house of the order, at Todi, where he was enthusiastically received by the citizens, and when he could escape from them he went straight to the altar of our Lady, and falling prostrate on the ground prayed with great fervour, and said, " This is the place of my rest for ever." He made a moving sermon on the glory of the blessed on the feast of the Assumption of the Mother of God, but at three o'clock in the afternoon of that day was taken seriously ill. He sent for the community, and again spoke of brotherly love : " Love one another, reverence one another, and bear with one another." Seven days later the end came ; he called for his " book," by which word he meant his crucifix, and devoutly contemplating it, calmly died at the hour of the evening *Angelus*. The *cultus* of St Philip Benizi was confirmed for the whole Church by Pope Clement X in 1671.

La Vie de Saint Philippe Benîzi (1886), by Père Soulier, O.S.M. (Eng. Trans.), must still be regarded as the standard biography of this saint. Though a long list of sources is set out in an appendix, it must be confessed that the early evidence is not quite so full as might be desired. It is often difficult to decide how large a part legend has played in the story commonly circulated. Père Soulier has, however, edited very carefully some of the most important biographical materials. See the *Monumenta Ordinis Servorum Sanctæ Mariæ*, vols. ii, iii, and iv. Of post-Reformation Lives that by Giani (1604) and that by Malaval (1672) have enjoyed the greatest vogue, and the latter has been translated into English in the Oratorian Series. In the *Acta Sanctorum*, August, vol. iv, a Life has been reproduced which is in substance a Latin rendering of the more relevant portions of Giani.

SS. CLAUDIUS, ASTERIUS, NEON, DOMNINA, AND THEONILLA, MARTYRS.

A.D. 303

Though the Emperors Diocletian and Maximian were for a great part of their reign indifferent to the Christians and passed no edicts against them, yet several martyrs suffered in the beginning of their reign in various places. This was owing to particular occasions or to the isolated action of governors of provinces, who acted by virtue of laws which had never been repealed. In this manner the above-mentioned five martyrs were crowned in Cilicia (or as the Greeks claim, at Mopsuestia in Isauria). Claudius, Asterius, and Neon were three brothers, who were impeached as Christians before the magistrate of their city, Ægea, by their mother-in-law, who hoped to possess herself of their estate. About the same time two women named Domnina and Theonilla with a little child (perhaps Domnina's) were likewise on account of their faith thrown into prison, and brought to trial before the proconsul of Cilicia, whose name was Lysias. He, when he came into his tribunal, said, " Bring before me the Christians whom the officers have delivered to the city magistrate." Euthalius, the gaoler, said, " The magistrate of this city having pursuant to your orders made the strictest inquiry after Christians, has apprehended six ; three young men, all brothers, two women, and a small child. One of them is here before you." Lysias said to him, " Well ; what is your name ? " He answered, " Claudius."

Lysias. " Do not be such a madman as to throw yourself away in youth ; sacrifice to the gods, and escape the torments prepared for you if you refuse."

Claudius. " My God requires no such sacrifices ; He delights rather in alms-deeds and holiness of life. Your gods are unclean spirits, who are pleased with such oblations whilst they are preparing eternal punishments for those who offer them."

Lysias. " Let him be bound and beaten ; there is no other way of bringing him to reason."

Claudius. " Though you inflict upon me the most cruel tortures you will not move or hurt me."

Lysias. " The Emperors have commanded that the Christians sacrifice to the gods, and that they who refuse to do it be punished ; those who obey are to be rewarded."

Claudius. " Their rewards are temporary and short-lived ; but the confession of Jesus Christ earns everlasting glory."

Then the proconsul commanded him to be put upon the rack, fire to be laid to his feet, and flesh to be cut off his heels. The martyr said, " Neither your fire nor anything else can hurt those who fear God ; it brings them to eternal life." Lysias ordered his flesh to be torn with hooks and the wounds burned, but Claudius only said, " I hold it a great benefit to suffer for God, and the greatest happiness to die for Jesus Christ."

Lysias. " Take him back to prison, and bring another."

Euthalius. " We have brought hither Asterius the second brother."

Lysias. " Take my advice and sacrifice to the gods ; you have before your eyes what is prepared for those who refuse."

Asterius. " There is one God, who dwells in the Heavens and in the greatness of His power sees the lowest things. Him my parents have taught me to love and worship. I know not those that you worship and call gods."

Lysias. " Crush his sides, tear them with hooks, and make him sacrifice to the gods."

Asterius. " I am the brother of him whom you just now questioned. We agree, and we make the same confession. My body is in your power; but my soul is out of your reach."

Lysias. " Bring the pincers and pulleys, bind his feet, squeeze and torture him to teach him I can make him suffer." And when this was done, " Put live coals under his feet, and lash him on the back and belly."

Asterius. " All I ask of you is that you will not spare any part of my body."

Lysias. " Take him away, put him with the rest, and bring the third."

When Neon was brought Lysias called him "son," and treated him with kindness, urging him to sacrifice to the gods that he might escape torment. Neon answered that his gods had no power if they were not able to defend themselves without having recourse to his authority.

Lysias. " Strike him on the neck, and bid him not blaspheme the gods."

Neon. " You think I blaspheme when I speak the truth."

Lysias. " Stretch him on the rack, put burning coals on him, and scourge his back."

Neon. " I will do what is good for my soul, and no man shall ever make me change this resolve." When therefore he had been fruitlessly tortured, Lysias dictated this sentence : " Euthalius the gaoler and Archelaus the executioner shall take these three brothers to be crucified outside the town, that the birds of the air may devour their bodies."

Then Euthalius presented Domnina; whereupon Lysias said to her, " You see, woman, the fire and torments which are prepared for you; if you would avoid them, draw near and sacrifice." Domnina replied, " I shall not do it, lest I fall into eternal fire and endless torments. I worship God and His Son Jesus Christ, who hath made Heaven and earth and all that is therein." Lysias said, " Strip her and scourge her." While this was done, Archelaus, the executioner, said to Lysias, " Sir, Domnina is dead," and Lysias replied, " Throw her body into the river and bring the next one." To Theonilla he said, " You have seen the torments with which the others have been punished. Honour the gods and sacrifice."

Theonilla. " I dread eternal torments, which will destroy both body and soul."

Lysias. " Buffet her, lay her flat and bind her; torture her to the utmost."

Theonilla. "Are you not ashamed to inflict such punishments on a woman that is free, and a stranger too? You know it to be shameful, and God sees what you do."

Lysias. "Hang her up by the hair and beat her face."

Theonilla. "Is it not enough that you have stripped me naked? It is not me only that you injure: your mother and your wife are also put to confusion in my person."

Lysias. "Are you married, or a widow?"

Theonilla. "I have been a widow these three and twenty years. It is for the love of God that I have continued in this state, in fasting, watching, and prayer, ever since I forsook your filthy idols."

Lysias. "Let her suffer the last indignity and have her head shaved. Tie brambles round her middle; stretch out her legs and arms and tie them to stakes; scourge her all over; put coals on her belly. And let her die."

When Theonilla had soon succumbed to these cruelties, Lysias said, "Sew her body up in a sack, and throw it into the water," and this was done, that the Christians might not get possession of the martyrs' relics.

This account of the passion of SS. Claudius and his companions is preserved in the form of the so-called proconsular acts of their trial, that is to say, the official report of the proceedings subsequently worked over one or more times by a Christian hand, and somewhat embellished with a view to edification, *e.g.*, by the multiplying of tortures patiently endured. The proconsul Lysias had a peculiar hatred for Christians and pursued them even before the persecution of Diocletian was ordered; among the others he tried and sentenced were SS. Cosmas and Damian, the holy moneyless physicians.

These Latin Acts will be found printed in Ruinart, and also in the *Acta Sanctorum*, August, vol. iv; while the Synaxaries (see Delehaye's edition, Oct. 30, p. 178) show that they were known in the Byzantine Church. A French translation is in Leclercq, *Les Martyrs*, vol. ii, pp. 182–190. The "Hieronymianum" duly commemorates the saints under this date, as noted in the *Acta Sanctorum*, Nov., vol. ii, part 2, p. 461. *Cf.* P. Allard, *Histoire des Persécutions*, vol. v, pp. 63 *seq.*

ST EUGENE or EOGHAN, Bp. and Conf.
Sixth Century

Eoghan (the equivalent of which name in English is Owen, not Eugene, as he is generally called) is venerated as the first bishop at Ardstraw in Tyrone, predecessor of the see of Derry. According to his Latin life, on which little reliance can be put, his father Cainnech was a Leinster man and his mother Muindecha from county Down, and he was related to St Kevin of Glendalough. While a child he was carried off with two other boys, Tighernach and Coirpre, first to Britain and then to Brittany, where they were sold into slavery and set to grind corn. One day the chieftain found the three reading, the mill meanwhile being worked by angels, and he ordered them to be released. They found their way back to Ireland, where Coirpre became a bishop at Coleraine. St Eoghan was for fifteen years a monk, with St Kevin, at Kilnamanach in county Wicklow, and then set out for the north where, after helping St Tighernach to found the monastery of Clones, he settled with his disciples at Ardstraw in the valley of Mourne in Tyrone and was made a bishop. The feast of St Eoghan is kept throughout Ireland.

The Latin life spoken of above is in the Codex Salmanticiensis and has been printed both in the *Acta Sanctorum*, August, vol. iv, and in De Smedt's edition of that Codex, pp. 915–924. St Eoghan is also mentioned on this day in the *Félire* of Oengus.

BD. JAMES OF MEVANIA, Conf.

A.D. 1301

Mevania, now called Bevagna, is a small town in Umbria, and here this James was born in the year 1220, of the family of the Bianconi, people of distinction. His future holiness was foreshadowed in his childhood, and a reconciliation of the Bianconi to the Alberti, with whom they had quarrelled, was attributed to his youthful prayers. When he was sixteen, two Dominicans came to Bevagna to preach during Lent, and the boy was attracted by what he heard of the life of the preachers and by their discourses; he considered the matter over and over and when, after his communion on Maundy Thursday, he was saying Psalm 118, the appositeness of the thirty-third verse struck him: "Set before me for a law the way of thy justifications, O Lord, and I will always seek after it." He went straight to one of the friars, and opened his mind, and was recommended to watch all that night before the Blessed Sacrament in the Easter sepulchre, asking for light, to fast during Good Friday on bread and water, and to await the will of God. This he did, and as he slept on the eve of Holy Saturday St Dominic appeared to him and said, "Do it! According to God's will I choose you, and will be ever with you." And so when the friars returned to their house at Spoleto James went with them. He was clothed, professed, and ordained, and then sent to teach theology at Orvieto until he was given permission to establish a house of his order at Bevagna, of which he became prior. The neighbourhood gave ample scope for the labours of the friars, and after the town had been sacked by the Emperor Frederick II in 1248 Bd. James more than ever endeared himself to the people by his solicitude for them in their misfortunes. This was a time of recrudescence of Manichæan errors, and a particularly pestilential sect of Antinomians was active in Umbria ; James set out to combat it with great energy, and succeeded in inducing one of its leaders to make a public repudiation of his heresy at Orte. Bd. James was very strict in his observance of his vow of poverty, and when his mother gave him some money to buy a new habit, which he badly needed, he got permission from his superior to buy a crucifix for his cell instead. When his mother saw the worn-out habit again, she remonstrated with him, but he answered with a smile, " I have done as you wished. St Paul tells us to ' put on the Lord Jesus,' and that is the habit I have bought." But that crucifix was to clothe him in a way he never thought of, for praying before it one day in great dryness and fear of spirit, almost despairing of his salvation, it is said that a spurt of blood miraculously sprang from the image over his face, and he heard a voice saying, " Behold the sign of your salvation ! " This marvel is referred to in the prayer of his office. Another miracle recorded is that after he had received the holy Viaticum on his death-bed, he blessed a vessel of water which was changed into wine, and however often consumed never decreased in volume, until it was destroyed by a man out of contempt—but the evidence for this miracle is insufficient. After his death a penitential chain was found wound around his body, and as his brethren were reciting the prayers for the dead a voice was heard, saying, " Do not pray for him, but ask him to pray for you." Another marvel reported at his death is recounted in the notice of Bd. Joan of Orvieto, under July 23. Pope Boniface IX approved the *cultus* of Bd. James of Mevania, to whom the title Saint is sometimes given, following the precedents of Popes Paul V and Clement X, who so referred to him.

The Bollandists in giving an account of this *beato* (August, vol. iv) deplore, and not without reason, the lack of any early biography. The narrative of Father Taigi is certainly full of legendary matter ; neither can one feel any more confidence in the *Vita del B. Giacomo Bianconi* by Father Piergili (1729) or in that compiled by F. Becchetti or in the summary given in Procter, *Lives of Dominican Saints*. For a fuller bibliography see Taurisano, pp. 23–24.

AUGUST 24

ST BARTHOLOMEW, Apostle
First Century

THE name given to this apostle is probably not his proper name, but his patronymic, meaning the son of Tolmai, and beyond the fact of his existence nothing is certainly known of him. Many scholars, however, take him to have been the same person as Nathanael, a native of Cana in Galilee, of whom our Lord said, " Behold ! an Israelite indeed, in whom there is no guile." Among the reasons advanced for this supposition is that, as St John never mentions Bartholomew among the Apostles, so the other three evangelists take no notice of the name of Nathanael ; and they constantly put together Philip and Bartholomew, just as St John says Philip and Nathanael came together to Christ ; moreover, Nathanael is reckoned with other apostles when Christ appeared to them at the sea of Galilee after His resurrection (John xxi, 2).

The popular traditions concerning St Bartholomew are summed up in the Roman Martyrology, which says he " preached the gospel of Christ in India ; thence he went into Greater Armenia, and when he had converted many people there to the Faith he was flayed alive by the barbarians, and by command of King Astyages fulfilled his martyrdom by beheading. . . ." The place is said to have been Albanopolis (Derbend, on the west coast of the Caspian Sea), and he is represented to have preached also in Mesopotamia, Persia, Egypt, and elsewhere. The earliest reference to India is given by Eusebius in the early fourth century, when he relates that St Pantænus, about a hundred years earlier, going into India (St Jerome adds " to preach to the Brahmins "), found there some who still retained the knowledge of Christ and showed him a copy of St Matthew's Gospel in Hebrew characters, which they assured him that St Bartholomew had brought into those parts when he planted the faith among them. But " India " was a name applied indifferently by Greek and Latin writers to Arabia, Ethiopia, Libya, Parthia, Persia, and the lands of the Medes, and it is most probable that the India visited by Pantænus was Ethiopia or Arabia Felix, or perhaps both. Another eastern legend says the Apostle met St Philip at

Hierapolis in Phrygia, and travelled into Lycaonia, where St John Chrysostom affirms that he instructed the people in the Christian faith. That he preached and died in Armenia is possible, and is an unanimous tradition among the later historians of that country; but Christianity probably first reached there from Edessa in the second to third centuries. The journeys attributed to the relics of St Bartholomew are even more bewildering than those of his living body; alleged relics are venerated at present chiefly at Benevento and in the church of St Bartholomew-in-the-Tiber, at Rome.

When we consider the labours and journeyings of the Apostles we have every reason to wonder at and deplore our own indifference, for we so often do nothing for the enlargement of God's kingdom in others, or even for the sanctification of our own souls. It is not owing to want of means or of strength through the divine grace that we do so little, but to want of courage and sincere resolution that we find no opportunities for exercising charity towards our neighbour, no time for prayer and recollection, no strength for fasting and penance. If we face the truth we shall find that we blind ourselves by pretence, and that laziness and lukewarmness provide the hindrances which fervour and resolution find ways readily to remove.

Although, in comparison with such other apostles as St Andrew, St Thomas, and St John, the name of St Bartholomew is not conspicuous in the apocryphal literature of the early centuries, still we have what professes to be an account of his preaching and " Passion," preserved to us in a Greek and several Latin copies. Max Bonnet (*Analecta Bollandiana*, xiv, 1895, 353–366) thinks the Latin was the original; Lipsius less probably argues for the priority of the Greek; but it may be that both derive from a lost Syriac archetype. The texts are in the *Acta Sanctorum*, August, vol. v; in Tischendorf, *Acta Apostolorum Apocrypha*, pp. 243–260; and also in Bonnet, *Act. Apocryph.*, vol. ii, part 1, pp. 128 seq. There are also considerable fragments of an Apocryphal Gospel of Bartholomew (on which see the *Revue Biblique* for 1913, 1921, and 1922), and traces of Coptic " Acts of Andrew and Bartholomew." The Gospel which bears the name of Bartholomew is one of the apocryphal writings condemned in the decree of Pseudo-Gelasius. The statement that St Bartholomew was flayed alive before being beheaded, though this is not mentioned in the " Passio," is contained in the so-called " Breviarium Apostolorum " prefixed to certain manuscripts of the " Hieronymianum." It is the flaying which has probably suggested the knife, often associated as an emblem with pictures of the saint; but on St Bartholomew in art see Künstle, *Ikonographie*, vol. ii, pp. 116–120. Although the later Armenian Church claimed Bartholomew as a sort of national possession, the early Armenian writers, as Tournebize points out (*Histoire politique et religieuse de l'Arménie*, p. 413 and note), make little or no reference to him as connected with their country.

THE MARTYRS OF UTICA, CALLED THE "WHITE MASS"
c. A.D. 258

In the persecution of Valerian the proconsul of Africa went from Carthage to Utica, and commanded all the Christians who were detained in the prisons of that city to be brought before him. He had ordered a great pit of burning lime to be prepared in a field, and by it an altar of idols, with salt and hog's liver placed on it ready for sacrifice. He caused his tribunal to be erected near this place in the open air, and he gave the prisoners their choice either to be thrown into this pit of burning lime, or to offer sacrifice to the idols which were set by it. They unanimously chose the first, and were all consumed together in the furnace. Their ashes were afterward taken out, and as they made up but one common mass cemented with the lime, these martyrs were called the White Mass. This is recorded in the Roman Martyrology to-day in these words: The passion "at Carthage, of three hundred holy martyrs in the time of Valerian and Gallienus. The governor, among other torments, ordered a limekiln to be lighted and charcoal and incense to be at hand near by; then he said to them, 'Choose one of these two things: either offer incense to Jupiter upon these coals, or be thrown into that lime.' They, armed with faith and confessing Christ the Son of God, on a swift impulse threw themselves into the fire and were reduced to powder in the heat of the lime. Wherefore this white-robed company of the blessed earned for itself the name of the White Mass." St Augustine says that this happened at Utica, twenty-five miles from Carthage, and that the martyrs numbered not three hundred but one hundred and fifty-three. Prudentius refers to them in one of his hymns: " Whiteness [*candor*] possesses their bodies; purity [*candor*] bears their souls to Heaven. Hence they have merited to be for ever called the White Mass [*Massa candida*]."

As Père Delehaye points out in his commentary upon the " Hieronymianum " (*Acta Sanctorum*, November, vol. ii, part 2, pp. 449–450) the poetic description of Prudentius is set aside by recent critics. " Massa Candida " is really the name of a place—the White Farm. A number of martyrs were buried there, but there is nothing to show that they suffered under Valerian. There was quite probably something in the nature of a massacre, as an early sermon, formerly without warrant attributed to St Augustine (see Migne, *P.L.*, vol. xxxix, pp. 2352–4), dwells upon the bloodshed and the readiness of the martyrs to submit their necks to the sword; but on the other hand there is no evidence that they numbered either 300 or 153, for the latter figure was merely suggested to St Augustine by a reference he had made in the same sermon to the draught of fishes in

John xxi, 11. There can be little doubt that Prudentius evolved the whole story of the lime out of the name "massa candida," which he interpreted according to his own exuberant fancy. See also P. Franchi de' Cavalieri in *Studi e Testi*, vol. ix (1902), and G. Morin in *Miscellanea Augustiniana*, vol. i (1930), p. 647. The proper day of the "White Farm" martyrs is August 18, as is attested by St Augustine and by the Carthaginian Calendar. Ado seems to have been responsible for their wrongful transference to the 24th.

ST OUEN or AUDOENUS, Abp. of Rouen, Conf.

A.D. 684

He was born at Sancy, near Soissons, about 609, of a Gallo-Roman family, his father being St Authaire. While he and his brother Ado were still children, living at Ussy-sur-Marne, their father entertained St Columban in his house. The brothers were educated well and when they were of sufficient age were put at the court of King Clothaire II, where they met St Eligius and were inspired by him to devote themselves to the service of God. St Ado executed his design some time after, and founded upon an estate which he had near the river Marne the double monastery of Jouarre, which he endowed. St Ouen was in great favour with the King and with his son and successor, Dagobert I, who made him his referendary or chancellor; in this office Ouen steadily opposed the prevalent simony and in concert with St Eligius brought about a synod at Orleans at which a Greek who had been preaching Monothelism at Autun was expelled from France. Ouen obtained of the King a grant of a piece of land situated in the forest of Brie where, in 634, he erected a monastery called Resbac, at present Rebaix. By the advice of St Faro, Bishop of Meaux, he sent for St Aile, a disciple of St Columban, and got him appointed the first abbot by a council held at Clichy in 636; but in this he was forced to make use of the King's authority, for the cities of Metz, Langres, and Besançon had at the same time requested St Aile to be their bishop. St Ouen would have retired himself to Rebaix, but King Dagobert and his nobles could not be induced to give their consent. St Ouen and St Eligius, though yet laymen, were for their zeal, piety, and learning considered as equals even of the bishops, and they promoted the cause of religion and virtue through the whole kingdom. Dagobert dying in 638, Clovis II, his son and successor, testified the same esteem for St Ouen, and kept him in the office of referendary, by virtue of which all the letters and edicts of the King were brought to him, and he put the King's seal upon them. At length Clovis was prevailed upon to give Ouen leave to receive ordination from Dieudonné, Bishop of Mâcon, and he was shortly after elected archbishop of Rouen in the room of St Romanus; at the same time his friend St Eligius was chosen bishop of Noyon and Tournai. They took a considerable time to prepare themselves for this dignity, by retreat, fasting, and prayer, and received the episcopal consecration together at Reims in 641.

St Ouen in this new office increased his humility, austerities, and charities. His zeal was indefatigable, and by his affability and patience he was truly all things to all men. He encouraged learning by the foundation of monasteries, and sent missionaries to those parts of his diocese that were still pagan; nor did he slacken his efforts for extirpating simony and other abuses; he promoted everywhere the reformation of discipline, especially in the third council of Châlons in 644. He was a trusted adviser of King Thierry III and upheld the policy of Ebroin, the mayor of the palace, without condoning his persecution of St Philibert, the abbot of Jumièges. Being sent by the King to Cologne for that purpose he arranged a peace between the French in Austrasia and Neustria, and went to carry the news to Thierry at Clichy, where an assembly of prelates and lords was held. There he fell ill and died, on August 24, 683, after having asked the King that St Ausbert, abbot of Fontenelle and the royal confessor, might succeed him at Rouen.

The earliest of the Lives of St Ouen dates from the beginning of the eighth century, and has been critically edited by W. Levinson in the *Monumenta Germaniæ, Scriptores rerum Meroving.*, vol. v, pp. 536–567. Levinson also comments (pp. 548 *seq.*) on the two ninth-century Lives, the former of which is printed with the first-named in the *Acta Sanctorum*, Aug., vol. iv, and the latter in the *Analecta Bollandiana*, vol. v, pp. 76–146. By far the best modern contribution to the history of St Ouen is that of G. Vacandard, *Vie de Saint Ouen; étude d'Histoire Mérovingienne*, Paris, 1902. He has in particular rectified in several points the chronology of previous writers and has established that St Ouen was consecrated bishop in 641 and died in 684.

AUGUST 25

ST LOUIS IX, KING OF FRANCE, CONF.
A.D. 1270

IN the person of St Louis IX were united the qualities which form a great king, a hero of romance, and a saint. He was endowed with qualifications for good government, he excelled in the arts of peace and in those of war, and his courage and greatness of mind received from his virtue the highest setting; ambition had no share in his enterprises, his only motives in them was the glory of God and the good of his subjects. Though the two crusades in which he was engaged were failures, he is certainly to be ranked among the most valiant of princes, and a perfect example of the good and great mediæval nobleman. He was son of Louis VIII and was eight years old when the death of his grandfather, Philip II Augustus, put his father in possession of the crown of France. He was born at Poissy on April 25, 1215, and, because he had been there made a Christian by the grace of baptism, he afterwards honoured that place above others; he took pleasure in bestowing charities and doing other good actions there, and in his letters and private transactions he signed himself " Louis of Poissy." His mother was Blanche, daughter of Alfonso of Castile and Eleanor of England, and to her care and attention in the education of St Louis we are indebted, under God, for the great example of his virtues. From his birth she would never suffer him to be put out to nurse, and gave all possible attention to his education and that of her other children. She appointed his tutors, from whom he became a master in the Latin tongue, learned to speak in public and to write with grace and dignity, and was instructed in the arts of war and of government, and all the accomplishments of a king. But it was his mother's first care to instil into his soul the highest regard and awe for everything that pertained to divine worship, religion and virtue, and a particular love of chastity. She used often to say to him when he was a child, " I love you, my dear son, as much as a mother can love her child; but I would rather see you dead at my feet than that you should ever commit a mortal sin." Nor did Louis forget the lesson. His friend and biographer, the Sieur de Joinville, historian of the Crusades, relates that the King once asked him, in the presence of some friars, "What is God?" Joinville replied, "That which is so good that there could be nothing better." "Well said. Now tell me, would you rather be a leper or commit a mortal sin?" "And I, who never told a lie," says Joinville, "answered, 'I would rather commit thirty mortal sins than be a leper.'" Later Louis led him apart and took him to task for his honest but misguided reply.

King Louis VIII died on November 7, 1226, and Queen Blanche was declared regent for her son, who was then only eleven years old. To prevent seditions she hastened the ceremony of his coronation, which was performed at Reims on the first Sunday of Advent by the Bishop of Soissons, the archbishopric of Reims being then vacant. The young King trembled in taking the coronation oath, begging of God resolution, light, and strength to employ his authority according to his obligations, for the divine honour, the defence of the Church, and the good of his people. Several of the feudal lords of the kingdom, thinking to take the opportunity of the King's minority, entered into a confederation, and made many extravagant demands. None of these would be present at the coronation, and they appeared in arms soon after it was over. The chief were Philip, Count of Boulogne, a natural son of Philip Augustus, Peter Mauclerc, who was Count of Brittany, Raymund of Languedoc, Hugh of Lusignan, Count of La Marche, and Thibault, Count of Champagne, afterwards King of Navarre. The whole time of the King's minority was disturbed by these ambitious barons, but Blanche by several alliances and by her courage and diligence overcame them in the field and forced their submission. Louis rejoiced in his victories chiefly because he procured by them the blessings of peace to his subjects. He was merciful even to rebels, and by his readiness to receive any proposals of agreement gave the proof that he neither sought revenge nor conquests. Never had any man a greater love for the Church, or a greater veneration for its ministers. Yet this was not blind; he opposed the injustices of bishops, when he saw them betrayed into any, and did not listen to their complaints till he had given a full hearing to the other party, as he showed in the contests of the Bishops of Beauvais and Metz with the corporations of those cities. In 1240 Pope Gregory IX, in the broils which the Emperor Frederick II had raised about the investitures of bishops, wrote to St Louis and proposed Robert, the King's brother, as emperor in Frederick's place. Louis did not accept the proposal and continued to interest himself in procuring a reconciliation of the Emperor to the Holy See. When Cardinal Fieschi, a Genoese, was elected under the name of Innocent IV these struggles were yet more bitter, and the Pope at the Council of Lyons in 1245 excommunicated Frederick II and took away his imperial crown. But St Louis would not interfere on either side; he continued to treat the Emperor as such, and bent all his energies towards peace and to diverting these energies into a crusade against the Saracens.

This good King was never so happy as when he enjoyed the conversation of holy priests or other religious men, and he often invited such to his house, but he knew how to observe seasons with a decent liberty. Once when a friar had started a grave religious topic at table, he turned the discourse to another subject, saying, " All things have their time." He celebrated feasts and rejoicings on the creation of knights and other such occasions with great magnificence, but banished from his court all diversions dangerous to morals. And he would tolerate neither vulgar obscenity nor thoughtless profanity; " I was a good twenty-two years in the holy King's company," says Joinville, " and never once did I hear him swear, either by God or His mother or His saints. I did not even hear him name the Devil, except if he met the word when reading aloud, or when discussing what had been read." And a Dominican testified that he had never heard him speak ill-naturedly of anyone. When he was urged to put to death the rebel son of Hugh de la Marche, he refused, saying, " A son cannot refuse to obey his father's orders."

When he was nineteen St Louis married Margaret, the eldest daughter of Raymund Berenger, Count of Provence, whose second daughter, Eleanor, was married to Henry III, King of England; his third, Sanchia, to his brother Richard of Cornwall, afterwards King of the Romans; and Beatrice, the youngest, to Charles, brother to St Louis. The marriage was celebrated on May 27, 1234, at Sens, and God blessed it with a happy union of hearts and eleven children, five sons, six daughters, from whose descendants kings were given to France until that January 21, 1793, when the Abbé Edgeworth said to Louis XVI as the guillotine was about to fall, " Son of St Louis, go up to Heaven ! " Two years later, having come of age, St Louis took the government of his kingdom into his own hands. But he continued to show the greatest deference to his mother, and to profit by her counsel, though Blanche was inclined to be jealous of and unkind to her daughter-in-law. The first of many religious foundations for which Louis was responsible was the abbey of Royaumont. His father had ordered in his will that the price of his jewels should be laid out in founding a monastery; St Louis very much increased that sum, and made the foundation truly royal and magnificent. This was one of those places to which he frequently retired for solitude and to attend to God with more perfect recollection. In 1239 Baldwin II, the Latin Emperor of Constantinople, made St Louis (in gratitude for his largesse to the Christians in Palestine and other parts of the East) a present of the Crown of Thorns, which was formerly kept in the imperial palace but was then in the hands of the Venetians as a pledge for a loan of money to Baldwin, which Louis had to discharge. He sent two Dominican friars to bring this treasure to France, and met it himself beyond Sens, attended with his whole court and numerous clergy. To house it he pulled down his chapel of St Nicholas and built the *Sainte Chapelle*, which is now empty of its relic.* He brought the Carthusians to Paris and endowed them with the palace of Vauvert, and helped his mother in the foundation of the convent of Maubuisson.

Several ordinances of this prince show us how much he applied himself to see justice well administered. In succeeding reigns, whenever complaints were raised among the people, the cry of those dissatisfied was to demand that abuses should be reformed and justice impartially administered as was done in the reign of St Louis. In 1230, he forbade all manner of usury, and restrained the Jews in particular from practising it. He compelled them to restore what they had exacted and, where the creditors could not be found, to give such gains towards the crusade which Gregory IX was endeavouring to set on foot. He published a law commanding all who should be guilty of blasphemy to be branded, and thus punished a rich citizen of Paris, a person of great consideration; to some of his courtiers who murmured at this severity he said that he would undergo that punishment himself if thus he might put a stop to the crime. But afterwards, on the advice of Pope Clement IV, he reduced the punishment to a fine, flogging, or imprisonment, according to the circumstances. He protected vassals from oppressive lords, and when a Flemish count had hanged three children for hunting rabbits in his woods, had him imprisoned in the Louvre and tried, not by his peers as he demanded, but by the ordinary judges, who condemned him to death. He afterwards spared his life, but subjected him to a fine which deprived him of the greater

---

* What remains of it is now in Notre Dame de Paris and is, in fact, only part of the rush foundation, with no thorns thereon. Several of these were given away by St Louis in golden reliquaries: one such is in the British Museum and appears still to contain the thorn it was made to enshrine. After the Revolution what remained of the crown, or its rush foundation, was brought to light in 1805 through the compunction of an " insufficiently apostatized " priest, the Abbé Cotterel.

part of his estates. This money the King ordered to be expended on religious and charitable works. He forbade feudal lords ever to make private war upon one another, which custom had been the occasion of continual bloodshed and disorders. The scholars and doctors of the University of Paris, upon an alleged infraction of their privileges by the execution of certain students for murder, closed the university for two years; when feeling was worked up to the highest pitch, the prudence of St Louis brought about the satisfaction of both parties. His scrupulous fidelity in keeping his word and observing treaties was notable in all negotiations, and his impartial and inflexible integrity made barons, prelates and even foreign kings ask to have him for judge and arbitrator, and put their affairs into his hands. He was extremely careful in his dealings with other princes, not to be drawn into their quarrels, and he used all possible good offices to reconcile their differences. When he had to reduce rebels he caused the damage which innocent persons had received, even by his enemy's forces, to be inquired into and full restitution to be made for them. The Count of La Marche again made trouble soon after the King's majority; his estates were a fief of Poitou and he refused to pay homage to the Count of Poitiers, the brother of St Louis. Hugh's wife, Isabel, was the widow of King John and mother of Henry III of England, who came over to support his stepfather. St Louis defeated King Henry III (who was never born to be a soldier) at Taillebourg, upon the Charente, and the city of Saintes opened its gates to him in 1242. Henry III fled to Bordeaux and the next year returned to England, having made a truce with the French. Fifteen years later Louis concluded another treaty, that of Paris, with Henry III. By it he yielded to England Limousin, Quercy, and Périgord, and the reversion of Agenais and Saintogne, King Henry III renouncing, on his side, all pretensions to Normandy, Anjou, Maine, Touraine, and Poitou. The French criticized their sovereign's concessions, and Louis replied that he hoped by them to cement a lasting peace between the two nations, and that it was very honourable to his crown to have so great a king as vassal for Guienne. But some historians are of the opinion that had Louis pushed home his advantage the Hundred Years' War would have been averted for his successors.

In December 1244 St Louis was seized at Pontoise with a violent dysentery and fever, which rapidly got worse. He became comatose and was thought to be already dead. Then a piece of the true cross and other relics that had been sent him by the Emperor Baldwin were brought, and applied to his body. Soon after this he began to move, and was heard to murmur, " The Light-bringer from on high has visited me by the grace of God, and has called me back from the dead." Then, speaking with difficulty, he announced his intention of undertaking a crusade to the East (which had been long in his mind), and calling for the Bishop of Paris he desired him to receive his vow for that expedition, and to put the badge of the cross on his shoulder. At this the two Queens, his mother and wife, fell at his feet weeping, and the Bishops of Paris and Meaux urged him not to entertain such a thought. But he was not by any means to be moved from his decision and in the beginning of the next year he renewed his vow, and by letter assured the Christians in Palestine that he would make all possible haste to their assistance against the infidels, who a few months before had retaken Jerusalem. But the opposition of his councillors and nobles, the preparation of the expedition, and the settling of his kingdom put off his departure for three and a half years. At the thirteenth general council at Lyons in 1245 all benefices were taxed a twentieth of their income for three years for the relief of the Holy Land (the English representatives strongly protested against this), and this gave encouragement to the crusaders. The Queen Mother was named regent, as the King's three brothers and the Queen Consort were to accompany him; on June 12, 1248, he took the Oriflamme of St Denis at Paris; and sailed from Aigues Mortes on August 27 for Cyprus, where he was joined by William Longsword, Earl of Salisbury, and two hundred English knights. The objective was Egypt, whose sultan, Melek Seleh, had made use of the Kharizmians, fleeing from Jenghiz Khan and the Mongols, to overrun Palestine. Damietta, in the delta of the Nile, was easily taken and St Louis made a solemn entry into the city, not with the pomp of a conqueror but with the humility of a truly Christian prince, walking barefoot with the Queen, the princes his brothers, the King of Cyprus and other great lords, preceded by the papal legate, the Latin Patriarch of Jerusalem, and all the clergy of the camp. Returning humble thanks to God, they went in this manner to the principal mosque, which the legate purified and consecrated with the usual ceremonies of the Church, dedicating it under the name of the Mother of God. The King ordered that all plundering and other crimes should be strictly inquired into and punished, and that ample restitution should be made. He forbade any infidel to be slain whom it was possible to make prisoner, and he took care that all who desired to embrace the Faith should be instructed and baptized. But notwithstanding all his watchfulness, whilst the army stayed about Damietta many, to his grief, gave themselves up to debauchery and outrageous acts of violence. Owing to the rising of the Nile and the summer heat the crusaders could not follow up their advantage, and it was not till six months had passed that they advanced to attack the Saracens, who were the other side of the river, in Mansourah. Then followed another six months of desultory fighting, in which the crusaders lost many by battle and sickness, until in April 1250 St Louis himself was taken prisoner, and his army routed with frightful slaughter.

During his captivity the King recited the Divine Office every day with two chaplains just as if he had been in perfect health in his own palace, and he also had the prayers of the Mass read (without the consecration) that he might the better join in spirit and desire with the Church in her daily sacrifice. To the insults that were sometimes offered him he opposed an air of majesty and authority which kept his guards in awe. When he was asked and refused to give up the castles in Syria he was threatened with the most ignominious treatment and with torture; to which he coolly replied that they were masters of his body, and might do with it what they pleased. The Sultan sent to him a proposal by which he demanded a million bezants of gold and the city of Damietta for his ransom and that of the other prisoners. He answered that a king of France ought not to redeem himself for money, but that he would give the city for his own release and the million bezants for that of all the other prisoners. The Sultan at that time was overthrown by the Mameluke emirs, and these eventually released the King and the other prisoners on these terms, but the sick and wounded crusaders in Damietta they treacherously slew. St Louis then sailed to Palestine with the remainder of his army. There he remained until 1254, visiting all the holy places he could, encouraging the Christians, and strengthening the defences of the Latin kingdom—such as it was. Then, news being brought to him of the death of his mother, the Queen Regent, he returned to France. He had been away almost six years, but he was oppressed by the memory of the distresses of the Christians in the East and he continued to wear the cross on his clothes to show that he intended to return to their assistance. Their position got rapidly worse: between 1263 and 1268 the Mameluke Bibars took Nazareth, Caesarea, Jaffa, and Antioch.

The Treaty of Amiens with Henry III of England in 1258 has been mentioned. Five years later Henry and his barons, having exhausted the realm by their disputes, agreed on both sides to make St Louis their judge, and engaged themselves to submit to his decision, so great was the opinion of his wisdom, equity, and uprightness. The King and Queen of England, Prince Edmund, and many bishops and lords of their party, and a great number of the confederate barons on the other side, came to

Amiens. St Louis, after both parties had pleaded, by a definitive sentence annulled all the articles granted by Henry to the barons in the "Mad Parliament," called the Provisions of Oxford, as being extorted by compulsion and as innovations injurious to the royal majesty; but he confirmed to the barons their ancient privileges. About 1257 Master Robert de Sorbon, a canon and very learned doctor of Paris, laid the foundations of that theological institute in the city which became known after him as the Sorbonne. Master Robert was a personal friend of St Louis and sometimes acted as his confessor, and the King enthusiastically seconded his project, helped to endow it, and obtained for it the approbation of Pope Clement IV. It became practically the theological faculty of the University of Paris, and until the rise of Jansenism and the Revolution it was one of the chief schools of Europe. The King also founded in Paris, for poor blind men, the hospital of Quinze-Vingt, so called because there were in it at the first foundation three hundred such patients. He likewise made provision of all kinds for the poor; in addition to thirteen special indigent guests he had daily a large number of poor folk to meals near his own palace, and in Lent and Advent all who presented themselves; and these he often served in person. He kept lists of needy people, especially *les pauvres honteux*, whom he regularly relieved in every province of his dominions. Though not personally a legislator he had a passion for justice, and he transformed the feudal "king's court" into a highly organized royal court of justice and, as has been shown, sovereign princes submitted their difficulties to his ruling; in all causes he endeavoured to substitute proof by witnesses and decision by judicial process or arbitration for appeal to arms.

Having one day stood godfather to a Jew who was baptized at Saint Denis, St Louis said to the ambassador of the Emir of Tunis, that to see his master receive that sacrament he would with joy pass the rest of his life in chains under the Saracens. Accordingly people were not surprised when in 1267 he announced another crusade: nor were they pleased. Among less worthy reasons, they feared to lose so good a king, who if only fifty-two years old was weak with toil, ill-health, and austerities. Joinville said bluntly that "those who recommended this voyage to the king sinned grievously." To prepare himself for the crusade Louis made two retreats at Maubuisson, and towards the expense the Pope granted him the tenth penny of all ecclesiastical revenues, and he levied a capitation upon his subjects. He nominated to the regency of the kingdom during his absence Matthew, Abbot of St Denis, and Simon of Clermont, persons of known probity and prudence, for the King's three eldest sons, Philip, John, and Peter, took the cross to accompany him. Joinville excused himself, urging the necessity of his staying at home to protect his vassals from the oppression of the Count of Champagne. The King embarked with his army at Aigues-Mortes on July 1, 1270, and when the fleet was over against Cagliari in Sardinia it was resolved to proceed to Tunis, where Louis had been deceived into thinking that the Emir would be converted and join him. He soon found out his mistake after landing at Carthage, and encamped there to await the arrival of the forces of his brother, the King of Sicily, before attacking Tunis. Dysentery and other sickness broke out among the crusaders, and St Louis's second son, John Tristan of Nevers, who had been born at Damietta, died. On the very same day the King himself and his eldest son Philip both sickened and it was soon seen that Louis was dying. He gave his last instructions to his sons and to his daughter, the Queen of Navarre, settled his other affairs, and composed himself for death. He prayed with many tears that God would enlighten and show mercy to infidels and sinners, and that his army might be led back into its own country without falling into the hands of the enemy and that none of them might be tempted through weakness to deny Christ. On August 24, which was Sunday, he received the last sacraments, and called for the Greek ambassadors, whom he strongly urged to union with the Roman Church. He lost his speech the next day from nine till twelve o'clock; then, recovering it and lifting up his eyes towards Heaven, he repeated aloud the words of the psalmist, " Lord, I will enter into Thine house; I will adore in Thy holy temple, and will give glory to Thy name." He spoke again at three in the afternoon, " Into Thy hands I commend my soul," and immediately after breathed his last. His bones and heart were taken back to France and enshrined in the abbey-church of St Denis, whence they were scattered at the Revolution; he was canonized by Pope Boniface VIII in 1297.

The heroic virtue of St Louis shone brighter in his afflictions than it could have done amidst the greatest triumphs. He longed to see the faith of Christ and His love reign throughout the whole world, especially in that country which He had sanctified by His bodily presence on earth; but God was pleased that he should rather glorify Him by his sufferings. Louis found his comfort in the accomplishment of His holy will: and seeing his good designs defeated, his army destroyed, and himself in the hands of infidels, he declared that he found more joy in his chains than he could have done in the conquest of the world. Nothing can show more clearly the principles upon which St Louis conducted his life, both as a man and as a king, than the written instructions which he left for his son Philip.

Authentic materials for the life of St Louis are naturally abundant. We have in the first place the charming French Memoirs of the Sieur de Joinville which have been translated into almost every European language. Then, from a more spiritual point of view, there are somewhat detailed Latin biographies by his confessors and chaplains, Geoffrey de Beaulieu and William de Chartres, both of them Dominicans. The text of these two narratives will be found in the *Acta Sanctorum*, August, vol. v, but they have been printed more than once elsewhere. Most valuable also is the copious French account of the saint, compiled by the confessor of the Queen, whose name, strangely enough, is not known to us. A Latin version of this Life, which contains a good deal of information about the canonisation, is printed by the Bollandists. From the King's own hand we have the account of his captivity, and the instructions which he drew up for his son Philip and his daughter Isabel. These instructions should not be read without reference to the comments of Paul Viollet in the *Bibliothèque de l'École des Chartres*, 1869 and 1874. There are excellent modern Lives by H. Wallon, and on a smaller scale (in the series " Les Saints ") by Marius Sepet (Eng. Trans.). *Cf.* also especially Elie Berger, *Saint Louis et Innocent IV* and the same author's *Histoire de Blanche de Castille*. Among slighter sketches, which are numerous in every language, that of W. F. Knox, *The Court of a Saint*, may be recommended.

ST GENESIUS THE COMEDIAN, Mart.

A.D. 303 (?)

The story of St Genesius is classed by the Bollandist Père Delehaye in the category of hagiographic romances, that is, a composition in which truth and fiction have been deliberately mixed in order to produce an edifying result. The *acta* are of the seventh century and it is not known how much of them is historical; it is possible that Genesius never existed at all, but is a Western version of St Gelasinus of Heliopolis, of whom (and of other martyrs) a similar tale is told. The legend of St Genesius is narrated by Alban Butler as follows.

Christ who, to show the power of His grace and the extent of His mercy, called a publican to the apostleship, honoured with the glory of martyrdom this saint drawn from the stage, then the most infamous school of vice and the just abhorrence of the holy fathers of the Church, of all zealous pastors, and all sincere lovers of virtue. The Emperor Diocletian coming to Rome, he was received with great rejoicings. Among other entertainments prepared for him, those of the stage were not neglected. In a comedy which was acted in his presence one of the players took it into his head to burlesque the ceremonies of Christian baptism, which could not fail to amuse the people, who held our religion and its mysteries in contempt and derision. This player therefore, whose name was Genesius and who had learned some things concerning Christian rites from friends who professed that religion, laid himself down on the stage, pretending to be ill, and said : " Ah ! my friends, there is a great weight upon me, and I would gladly be eased." The others answered, " What shall we do to give you ease ? Would you like us to plane you and reduce the weight that way ? " " Idiots ! " he exclaimed, " I am resolved to die a Christian, that God may receive me on this day of my death as one who seeks His salvation by turning from idolatry and superstition." Then a priest and exorcist were called, that is to say, two players who impersonated these characters. These, sitting down by his bedside, asked, " Well, my child, why did you send for us ? " But here Genesius was suddenly converted by a divine inspiration and replied, not in mockery but seriously, " Because I desire to receive the grace of Jesus Christ and to be born again, that I may be delivered from my sins." The other players then went through the whole ceremony of Baptism with him ; but he in earnest answered the usual interrogatories, and on being baptized was clothed with a white garment. After this, other players, dressed like soldiers, to carry on the jest, seized him and presented him to the Emperor, to be examined as the martyrs were wont to be. Genesius then declared himself openly and seriously, standing upon the stage, " Hear ! O Emperor, and all you that are present, officers, philosophers, senators, and people, hear what I am going to say. I never yet so much as heard the word Christian but I reviled it, and I detested my very relations because they professed that religion. I learned its rites and mysteries only that I might the better ridicule it, and inspire you with the utmost contempt for it ; but when I was to be washed with the water and examined, I had no sooner answered sincerely that I believed, than I saw a company of angels over my head, who recited out of a book all the sins I had committed from my childhood ; and having plunged the book into the water which had been poured upon me in your presence, they showed me the book whiter than snow. Wherefore I advise you, O great and mighty Emperor, and all people here present who have mocked these mysteries, to believe with me that Jesus Christ is the true Lord ; that He is the light and the truth ; and that it is through Him you may obtain the forgiveness of your sins."*

---

* Assuming the story to be true, the " baptism " administered would not be valid, for lack, on the part of the sacrilegious actor, of any intention even " to do what the Church does " when she baptizes. Genesius received the baptism, not of water, but of desire and of blood.

Diocletian, enraged at these words, ordered him to be beaten, and afterward to be put into the hands of Plautian, the prefect of the prætorium, that he might compel him to sacrifice. Plautian put him upon the rack, where he was torn with iron hooks and then burnt with torches; but the martyr persisted in crying out, " There is no other Lord beside Him whom I have seen. Him I worship and serve, and to Him I will cling, though I should suffer a thousand deaths. No torments shall remove Jesus Christ from my heart and my mouth. Bitterly do I regret that I once detested His holy name, and came so late to His service." At length his head was struck off.

For satisfactory proof that Dom Ruinart blundered in including the story of this probably mythical personage among his *Acta Sincera*, the reader must consult the *Martyrologes historiques* of Dom Quentin, especially pp. 533–541, and also the *Analecta Bollandiana*, vol. xxix (1910), pp. 258–269. The legend of the mock baptism of the comedian Genesius was no doubt in circulation before the sixth century, for " Genesius the actor " is commemorated in the calendar of Carthage. Still the text in Ruinart is certainly not the primitive form of his Acts. What Ruinart has printed is only a copy of Ado's abridgement of the longer narrative which is known to us through Surius and others. It is not disputed that in early times the Christian rites were often burlesqued upon the stage (though H. Reich in his book *Der Mimus* has greatly exaggerated the evidence for this), and early currency was given to the tradition or legend that the practice had resulted in the conversion of an actor, who was thereupon put to death ; but unfortunately what is substantially the same story is connected with four different names, Genesius, Gelasius or Gelasinus, Ardalio, and Porphyrius. We have no guarantee in any of these cases that it is not a hagiographical fiction. See further Bertha von der Lage, *Studien zur Genesiuslegende* (1898) ; Mostert and Stengel, *L'ystoire et la Vie de Saint Genis* (1895) ; and also Paul Allard, *La Persécution de Dioclétien*, i (1908), pp. 7–9, who argues in favour of the real existence of the martyr.

ST GENESIUS OF ARLES, Mart.

A.D. 303 (?)

On this day is commemorated another St Genesius (Gènes), the patron of the city of Arles. He was a catechumen and by profession a notary, one of those *notarii* who took down shorthand notes of judicial proceedings for the public archives to whom reference is several times made in the acts of the martyrs. His *acta* say that he " studied with great perseverance and exercised with much success that useful art by which he was able at a single stroke to take down words, and by the speed of his hand to equal the rapidity of the discourse of an orator, and to render word for word, with abridged notes, the pleadings of counsel, the depositions of witnesses, and the answers of the accused. . . . Now it happened one day that, while he was performing his duties as clerk of the court before the judge at Arles, there was read out an impious and sacrilegious edict which the Emperors had published throughout all the provinces [of persecution against the Christians]. The ears of the religious clerk were wounded and his hand refused to trace the words on the wax. He did more: he got up from his seat, flung his registers at the feet of the judge, and renounced for ever such a wicked occupation." He then fled secretly, seeking safety from town to town and, " as he thought that he had need to be fortified in the Faith by Baptism (for he had not yet been born again by water and the Holy Spirit), he sent his request to the bishop by some faithful persons. But whether the bishop was meanwhile arrested himself, or that he distrusted the youth of Genesius, would not risk conferring the sacrament, and put it off, he only told him that his blood shed for Jesus Christ would take the place of the baptism he so ardently wished to receive. And I think myself that it was not without a special dispensation of Providence that the bishop made difficulties: for without doubt Heaven wished alone to consecrate him and Jesus Christ had prepared for him a double baptism, that of the water and blood which flowed from the side of the divine Saviour." Genesius was at length overtaken by the persecutors and beheaded on the banks of the river Rhône, during the persecution of Maximian and Diocletian.

The mention of this martyr by Prudentius, by Fortunatus and by others, as well as his inclusion in the "Hieronymianum" on this day, can leave little doubt that the honour paid to him at Arles rested on a sound historical foundation. The brief Acts have been printed by Ruinart and again with a much fuller discussion in the *Acta Sanctorum*, August, vol. v. Père Delehaye in the second volume for November, part 2, pp. 464–465, has discussed the case of the two saints called Genesius in some detail. His conclusion is that the martyr of Arles is alone historical. He became so famous that his cult was adopted in Rome, and thence spread to Africa and other places. From the fact that a church was built to him in Rome it was rashly announced that his body was buried there and that he was a Roman martyr. In a short time a story was invented transforming him into an actor who made sport of the Christian religious rites in presence of the Emperor himself.

ST MENNAS, Patriarch of Constantinople, Conf.

A.D. 552

Mennas, a native of Alexandria, was abbot of a monastery in Constantinople until, in the year 536, he was appointed patriarch of that city and consecrated there by Pope St Agapitus, who issued an encyclical recommending the new patriarch to the Christian world. He set himself to repair the harm done by his predecessor Anthimos, who was a Monophysite, and to deal with a number of sectaries who, sheltering behind the name of Origen, were troubling the East. The Emperor Justinian who, like most Eastern emperors and with more reason than some, fancied himself as a theologian, wrote a *Book against Origen*, containing a number of impugned texts from his works and ten propositions to be condemned. He ordered Mennas to call a synod in 543 and to anathematize these propositions thereat; this was done and the condemnation was confirmed by each of the other patriarchs, including Pope Vigilius. But it has not been proved that Origen and Origenism were subsequently condemned by the fifth general council, which opened ten years later to deal with the affair of the Three Chapters. This was a condemnation of three Nestorian documents, written by Theodore of Mopsuestia, Theodoret of Cyrus, and Ibas of Edessa, which the Emperor hoped would facilitate the reconciliation of the adherents of Monophysism. All the bishops were ordered to sign it and St Mennas was the first to obey; not, however, very happily, for he expressly laid down that he signed on the understanding that no attack on the Council of Chalcedon was intended and that if the Pope of Rome did not sign it his own signature was to be withdrawn. The other Eastern patriarchs and bishops followed his example. What followed need not be traced in detail here, but the bishops of the West, although they recognized that the writings were heretical in part, objected to the condemnation because it compromised the Council of Chalcedon. The Pope, Vigilius, was first on one side, then on the other, but eventually in 551 refused to accept a re-issue of Justinian's edict, and sought refuge first in the church of St Peter at Constantinople and then in that of St Euphemia at Chalcedon, from whence he excommunicated St Mennas and others who had contrived to accept it. At once Mennas submitted, convincing Vigilius that he in no way deviated from the acts of the Council of Chalcedon and referring the matter of the Three Chapters to the decision of an œcumenical council. This council Mennas did not live to see, for he died on August 24, 552, and the fifth general council did not assemble till the following year. It then condemned the Three Chapters, as the Emperor had done, and Pope Vigilius approved and confirmed the condemnation. We thus have the curious and unusual spectacle of a Patriarch of Constantinople firmly supporting a policy which was to be eventually confirmed by a general council, as against a feeble Pope who allowed his judgement and actions to be swayed from side to side by the conflicting views of Western bishops and Eastern Emperor ; but it must be borne in mind that the matter at issue was concerned not with any definition of faith, but with the expediency and implications of the proposed condemnation. St Mennas is named in the Roman Martyrology and his feast is observed by the Latin Catholics of Constantinople.

A short Greek life with a general discussion of the saint's career is in the *Acta Sanctorum*, August, vol. v, but the story belongs rather to general ecclesiastical history. See Hefele-Leclercq, *Conciles*, vol. iv ; F. Savio, *Il Papa Vigilio* (1904) ; and especially the *Dictionnaire de Théologie Catholique*, vol. xi, cc. 1574–1588.

ST EBBA, Virg. and Abbess

A.D. 683

This St Ebba is sometimes called the Elder to distinguish her from St Ebba the Martyr, also abbess of Coldingham, said to have been put to death by the Danes about the year 870. She was sister to St Oswald and Oswy, Kings of Northumbria, and Oswy wanted her to marry the King of the Scots, but when she refused and took the monastic habit from St Finan of Lindisfarne he gave her a piece of land on the Derwent, where she founded the monastery of Ebbchester. She afterwards moved to Coldingham on the coast of Berwick, and there founded a double monastery, which both in arrangement and situation resembled that of St Hilda at Whitby ; the promontory on which it was built is still called St Abb's Head. Here she was visited by St Cuthbert and St Etheldreda was a nun under her for a year before becoming abbess of Ely. Personal sanctity, that is, ability rightly to rule oneself, by no means always involves ability to rule others well and apparently St Ebba was not a very successful abbess. For St Bede relates that St Adamnan (not he of Iona), who was a monk at Coldingham, had a vision in which he learned that the monastery would be destroyed by fire, because its monks and nuns were slack and even sinful ; " the cells that were built for prayer or reading are now turned into places for feasting, drinking, talk, and other pleasures ; the very maidens, dedicated to God, lay aside the respect due to their profession and employ their leisure in weaving fine clothes, either to adorn themselves like brides, which is dangerous to their state, or to attract the attention of strangers." Perhaps St Adamnan, being himself a holy man and seeing how things were, cast his prophecy in the form of a vision from God for motives of prudence.

For when it came to the ears of St Ebba and she asked for an explanation, he said, "I was afraid to say anything about it before, out of respect for yourself," and added tactfully, "But this calamity will not happen in your time." The chronicler goes on to say that the religious were frightened and behaved themselves better for a short time, but after the death of St Ebba they became worse than ever, and the house was in fact burned down very shortly after her death. St Ebba was buried at Coldingham, but some of her relics were afterwards put into the tomb of St Cuthbert at Durham.

A Life of Ebba by Capgrave, partly based on Reginald of Durham, is printed in the *Acta Sanctorum*, August, vol. v. See also Plummer's Bede ; the *Dictionary of Nat. Biog.*, the *Dict. of Christ. Biog.*, and Stanton's *Menology*, p. 412. Apart from the lessons in the Aberdeen Breviary, there is not much trace of *cultus*.

ST GREGORY OF UTRECHT, Abbot

c. A.D. 776

He was born in the territory of Trier about the year 707. His father Alberic's mother was a lady named Addula (who has been wrongly identified with Adela, daughter of Dagobert II, King of Austrasia) ; this lady, after the death of her husband, built the monastery of Pfalzel near Trier, and putting on the religious habit was chosen the first abbess. Gregory returning one day from school, when he was fifteen years of age, was desired by his grandmother to read to the nuns. St Boniface, who was travelling from Friesland into Hesse and Thuringia, was present. After he had finished reading, Gregory was asked by the abbess to explain what he had read for the benefit of those who did not understand Latin ; but this he said he was not able to do, probably because he was not sufficiently acquainted with the Teutonic language. Whereupon St Boniface got up and expounded the passages, and added a homily on the need and beauty of an apostolic and virtuous life by way of commentary. Gregory was so moved by his discourse that he resolved upon the spot to forsake the world and follow the holy man wherever he went. His friends do not seem to have opposed his inclination ; for St Boniface took him with him, and was himself his master and instructor. He seems to have placed him for some time in the monastery of Ordorf to finish his studies ; but he took him very young wholly to himself, made him his constant attendant, and always loved him as his son. The disciple was a faithful imitator of his spirit and virtues, assisted him in his missions, and accompanied him on his journeys, including his third visit to Rome, in 738. St Boniface a little before his death sent Gregory to Utrecht to govern a monastery lately founded there, dedicated in honour of St Martin. In 754 St Boniface received the crown of martyrdom and at the same time St Eoban, who had administered the see of Utrecht since the death of St Willibrord. Thereupon Pope Stephen III and Pepin obliged St Gregory to take upon him the care of that church. He never received the episcopal consecration, though he administered the diocese during twenty-two years, to his death ; that he never was more than priest appears from his life written by St Ludger, though he is called bishop in the Roman Martyrology and elsewhere.

The abbey of St Martin became a great missionary centre under the rule of St Gregory ; candidates came to it from all the neighbouring countries, not least from England : among its *alumni* were St Ludger, just mentioned, St Lebwin, and St Marchelm, all three associated with England, the last two as natives and Ludger being a student at York. By his preaching and care St Gregory made the diocese for which he was responsible a fitting surrounding to the abbey. St Ludger speaks particularly of his prudence, generous alms-deeds, and spirit of forgiveness. The last trait was exemplified after his two brothers had been treacherously killed. When the murderers were sent to him by the magistrate to be put to what death he should think fit, according to the barbarous custom of the country in that age which left the punishment of assassins to the direction of the relations of the deceased person, the saint gave every one of them a suit of clothes with an alms, and dismissed them with good advice. For the last three years of his life St Gregory bore with fortitude and patience a creeping paralysis, which attacked his left side and spread to the whole body. He died at Maastricht on August 25, about the year 776, and his feast is kept at Utrecht and Trier as well as by the Canons Regular of the Lateran.

As mentioned above St Ludger wrote a Life of Gregory which is our principal source of information. It has been printed by Mabillon and in the *Acta Sanctorum*, August, vol. v. Moreover it has been critically re-edited in Pertz, *Monumenta Germaniæ, Scriptores*, vol. xv. See further H. Timerding, *Die christliche Frühzeit Deutschlands*, ii, " Die angelsächsische Mission " (1929), and J. A. Coppens, *Kerkgeschiedenis van Noord-Nederland* (1902), pp. 62–70 ; with Hauck, *Kirchengeschichte Deutschlands*, vol. ii.

BD. MICHAEL CARVALHO, Mart.
a.d. 1624

The Society of Jesus commemorates on this day the martyrdom of Blessed Michael Carvalho. He was born at Braga in Portugal in 1577, entered the Jesuit novitiate in 1597, and being filled with zeal for the conversion of souls was sent at his own request to India in 1602. There, however, in the college of Goa he was found so useful as a teacher for theological and other studies, that obedience detained him for fifteen years busied in preparing others for the active missionary work for which his own soul thirsted. At last his desire was gratified, and after an incredibly toilsome journey (in the course of which he was shipwrecked at Malacca, made his way to Macao and was thence recalled to Manila in the Philippines), he succeeded in getting himself conveyed to Japan in the disguise of a soldier. During all this time of preparation he had led a life of great austerity, fasting three days in each week on bread and water and constantly keeping his body in subjection by manifold forms of penance. For two years, despite the persecution which was then raging, he ministered to the needs of the Catholics in the island of Amakusa, opposite Nagasaki. Having been summoned to hear confessions in another province, he was betrayed by a spy and captured. For more than twelve months he was kept a prisoner in irons, but managed to get letters conveyed out of prison, several of which, still preserved to us, manifest an extraordinary desire to give his life for the faith by any form of torment the persecutors might devise. His imprisonment was shared by a Dominican priest, Father Peter Vasquez, and by three Franciscans, of whom Father Louis Sotelo is best remembered. All five suffered together on August 25, 1624, being in fact roasted to death by a slow fire. After long inquiry and an examination of witnesses and documents which began in 1627, Pius IX finally in the year 1867 issued the brief *Martyrum rigata sanguine*, by which two hundred and five of those who had been put to death in Japan, including the group here in question, were declared Blessed Martyrs and worthy of the *cultus* of the faithful.

See G. Boero, *Relazione della gloriosa Morte di 205 BB. Martiri nel Giappone* (1867), pp. 110–118; and Guilhermy, *Ménologe de l'Assistance de Portugal*, vol. ii, pp. 172–174, where a full bibliography may be found. But, of course, the most reliable source of information is the body of documents printed in the Process of Beatification.

BD. JOAN ANTIDE THOURET, Virg.

a.d. 1826

Jeanne Antide Thouret was born on November 27, 1765, at Sancy-le-Long, near Besançon. Her father was a tanner, and she was the fifth child of a large family. She lost her mother when she was sixteen, and thereafter took charge of her father's household, which she managed for six years until it was made clear to her that she was called to serve God in the religious life. Her father was naturally unwilling to lose her, but he was induced to give his consent and, by the offices of her parish-priest, Mlle Thouret was accepted by the Sisters of Charity of St Vincent de Paul in Paris. During her period of postulancy and noviceship Sister Joan was twice taken very seriously ill; when the Revolution began in 1789 the Sisters of Charity were allowed to carry on their work only on sufferance and with the threat of the " constitutional oath " always over their heads (Sister Joan twice refused to take it); and so when in 1793 the religious were dispersed she had not yet made her profession. In November she made her escape from Paris and begged her way on foot to Besançon, where she was kindly received by a Madame de Vannes, and then to her home at Sancy. Her father was now dead, and to her bitter grief one of her brothers had become a revolutionary. So she went to live with her godmother and opened a free school, where in the mornings she taught reading, writing, and catechism to the village children, and spent the rest of the day, and much of the night, in visiting the sick and needy all over the large parish. She sheltered priests and enabled them to say Mass and administer the sacraments. She was denounced to the magistrates for these activities, but her disarming frankness kept her from harm. But in 1796 she took refuge in Switzerland and attached herself to the Sisters of the Christian Retreat, established by the Ven. Antony Receveur at Fribourg; she accompanied them to Germany, but after a time was advised to return to Switzerland, and again begged her way on foot, this time to Landeron, in the canton of Neufchâtel. Here she met M. de Chaffoy, vicar-general of Besançon, who invited her to come back there now conditions were improved and take charge of a school and a hospital. She at first demurred, pointing out that she had had no proper formation and training in the religious life, but M. de Chaffoy waved aside her scruples: " All that is true, but you can do it, nevertheless. Courage, virtue, and trust in God are what are required, and it seems to me that you have these qualities."

In April 1799 the school was opened at Besançon and in the following October, with four other sisters, had to move to a larger house, to which they added a soup-kitchen and a dispensary. In 1800 the community numbered twelve, they had opened a second similar house, and the sisters were allowed to take their vows. Bd. Joan was subjected to much adverse criticism for having established this new institute, it being objected that after the Concordat of 1801 she ought to have returned to her own congregation in Paris. She herself had scruples in this matter, but she was assured by M. de Chaffoy that she was under no obligation towards the community to which she had formerly belonged : she had taken no vows with them, she had been separated from them by force of the Revolution, and the community was not yet re-established. And she had established the Besançon institute purely and simply in obedience to her ecclesiastical superiors. At the request of the prefect of the city she took charge of the municipal female asylum at Belleveaux, which sheltered orphans, beggars, and criminals as well as lunatics, and her acceptance of this charge involved her in a deal of odium and persecution which for a time grievously hampered her work. But this was put on a more secure footing when in 1807 the rule of her sisters, which she had drawn up in the suppressed Visitation convent at Dol, was approved by Mgr. le Coz, Archbishop of Besançon. In the following month imperial authorization was given to her institute and it was recognized as entirely distinct from that of the Sisters of Charity of St Vincent ; it now had over one hundred members. By 1810 it had spread into Switzerland and Savoy, and in that year Joachim Murat, King of Naples, asked Bd. Joan to occupy the convent of Regina Cœli and administer a hospital in his capital city. With seven sisters she accordingly went, and remained there until 1821, laying firm foundations for the educating of girls, the care of the sick, and the spiritual and temporal welfare of her community. One of the first things to be done, and Bd. Joan did it with determination and spirit, was to get rescinded in their favour the local law which put nuns at the mercy of the civil authorities and forbade their dependence on a foreign mother general. Within six years the institute was well established and extending its activities in Naples.

In 1818 Pope Pius VII approved the institute, and confirmed it by a brief in the following year. But this, instead of giving joy and increased stability to the sisters, precipitated a schism that filled with sorrow the remaining years of life of the foundress. In its approbatory brief the Holy See made some small alterations in the rule, and decreed that for the future all the convents of the congregation of the Daughters of Charity under the protection of St Vincent de Paul (as they were to be called) were to be subject to their local bishop and not, as hitherto, to the Archbishop of Besançon. The then archbishop, Mgr. Cortois de Pressigny, a Gallican-minded prelate, announced that he refused to accept these amendments and, while he conducted a controversy with the papal nuncio at Paris, separated all the convents in his diocese from the rest of the congregation and even forbade them to receive their foundress and mother general within their walls. In 1821 she came to France and passed eighteen months in Paris, trying in vain to smooth out the difficulties and effect a re-union. As a last resort she presented herself at the mother-house in Besançon—and was refused admission. Both charity and the facts incline us to the view that this action was prompted not by partizanship but by loyal obedience to their archbishop; before the schism had hardened many of the sisters of the Besançon diocese, notably Sister Elizabeth Bouvard of Belleveaux and Sister Barbara Gauthier, openly adhered to their foundress and to the directions of the Holy See. Bd. Joan wrote of these troubles, "As for French affairs, we commit all to divine providence. With the advice of the Holy See we have done all that is possible to achieve unity; that unity has not yet been effected. We therefore leave it to the mercy of God, in whose hands we long ago placed it. May His will be done and everything be for His glory!" Then she returned to Naples and, having spent three strenuous years in founding new convents in Italy, she died peacefully at the Regina Cœli on August 24, 1826. One hundred years later, on May 23, 1926, she was beatified by Pope Pius XI, when the houses of her institute numbered over five hundred, mostly in Italy.

A biographical summary is contained in the decree of beatification printed in the *Acta Apostolicæ Sedis*, vol. xviii (1926), pp. 220–224. Other details may be found in the *Analecta Ecclesiastica* for 1901, pp. 212 and 258. See further, Kempf, *The Holiness of the Church in the Nineteenth Century* (Eng. trans.), pp. 207–209, and Blanche Anderdon, *Life of the Ven. Mother Jeanne Thouret, Foundress of the Sisters of Charity*.

BD. MARY MICHAELA OF THE BLESSED SACRAMENT, VIRG.

A.D. 1865

The full official style of this high-born Spanish lady who was formally beatified in 1925 is somewhat overwhelming. She was Mary Michaela Florez y Lopez de Dicastillo Olmeda—this at least is the name which appears in Kempf's *Heiligkeit der Kirche im*

19 *Jahrhundert*, but, curiously enough, in the decree of beatification she is called simply Maria Michaela Desmaisières, and is elsewhere designated Viscountess de Jorbalàn. Names and titles, however, signify little when we are dealing with the saints. There is abundant and unanimous testimony regarding her life of personal austerity, all-embracing charity, and extraordinary energy in promoting good works. She was born in 1809, lost her mother in childhood, resisted all attempts to persuade her to accept most eligible suitors, but none the less seems to have lived for some years with her brother while he held the post of Spanish ambassador at Paris and in Brussels. Her position necessitated her attendance at banquets, state balls, and theatrical performances, but she fortified herself against the seductions of this outwardly worldly life by daily communion and by wearing instruments of penance beneath her dress. All her interest was given to the religious instruction of the ignorant, the rescue of the unprotected and the fallen, and the relief of sickness and poverty. When she returned to Madrid she started more than one organisation for work of this kind, but she had to encounter in full measure the contradictions from without and from within which usually beset such efforts. Her most lasting achievement was the foundation of the " Congregation of Handmaids of the Blessed Sacrament and of Charity." In this she herself was enrolled, taking the simple and later the public vows of religion. The institute was approved by the Holy See for five years in the lifetime of its foundress and first superior, and shortly after her death it obtained permanent recognition. It had in the meantime spread widely and was full of promise for the future. In 1865 in connection with the business of this final approbation Mother Michaela had set out on her way to Rome, when an epidemic of cholera broke out in Valencia. Thither she hastened to the succour of her religious daughters who were attending the plague-stricken. But though she had more than once in previous outbreaks attended cholera patients, she took the infection herself and died a victim of charity, near midnight on August 24, 1865.

The brief of beatification with a biographical summary is printed in the *Acta Apostolicæ Sedis*, vol. xvii (1925), pp. 292–296. See also some earlier pronouncements of the Congregation of Rites in the *Acta Sanctæ Sedis*, xxxv (1903), p. 164 and p. 292 ; Kempf, *Holiness of the Church* (Eng. trans.), pp. 199–201 ; and Angelo Romano di S. Teresa, *La Beata Maria Michelina del Sacramento*, Rome, 1925.

AUGUST 26

ST ZEPHYRINUS, POPE AND MART.

A.D. 217

ST ZEPHYRINUS, a native of Rome, succeeded St Victor I in the pontificate in the year 199; he was a simple man, of no great theological attainments, and made his adviser the deacon St Callistus, who succeeded him as pope. Soon after he began to rule the Emperor Septimius Severus raised the fifth persecution against the Church. Under this storm the chief pastor was the support and comfort of the distressed flock of Christ, and he suffered by charity and compassion what each confessor underwent in deed. The triumphs of the martyrs were his consolation, but his heart received deep wounds from the fall of apostates and heretics, principal among whom was Tertullian, whose fall seems to have been owing partly to his pride and partly to one Proclus or Proculus, an eloquent Montanist, whom Tertullian highly praised after he became an adherent of his heresy. This Proculus was confuted at Rome by Caius, a most learned priest, under St Zephyrinus, who also had to deal with the case of Natalis. This man lived at Rome and, having confessed the Faith before the persecutors, underwent torments in defence of it; but afterward he was seduced into heresy by Asclepiodotus and Theodotus the Banker, who were both disciples of Theodotus the Tanner, whom Pope St Victor had excommunicated for reviving the heresy of the Ebionites, in the form called Monarchianism, affirming that Christ was no more than a mere man, though a prophet. These two heretics had persuaded Natalis to allow them to ordain him a bishop of their sect, promising that he should be paid monthly one hundred and fifty silver denarii. But God, having compassion on His confessor, warned him by several visions to abandon these heretics, and at last he covered himself with sackcloth and ashes, and with tears threw himself at the feet of Zephyrinus, and also before both the clergy and the laity in the assembly. Though he entreated so earnestly, and showed the marks of the stripes he had received for the Faith, it was with much difficulty that St Zephyrinus re-admitted him to the communion of the Church, granting him, in recognition of his great contrition, an indulgence or relaxation of the severity of the discipline which required a penitential delay and trial. Eusebius tells us that this holy Pope exerted his zeal so strenuously against the blasphemies of the two Theodoti that those heretics treated him in the most contumelious manner: but it was his glory that they called him the principal defender of Christ's divinity. St Zephyrinus was buried in his own cemetery in the catacomb of Callistus on the Appian Way. He is venerated as a martyr, which title he might deserve by what he suffered in the persecution, though he probably did not die by the hand of the executioner.

God has always raised up holy pastors, zealous to maintain the sacred deposit of the faith of His Church inviolable, and to watch over the purity of its morals and the sanctity of its discipline: and with what constancy, watchfulness, and courage did they stand their ground against idolatry, heresy, and the corruption of the world! We profit through their labours; and we owe to God perpetual thanksgiving and praise for all those mercies which He has afforded His Church on earth. We are bound also to recommend most earnestly to Him His own work, praying that He exalt the glory of His divine name, by extending His holy faith on earth; that He continually raise up in His Church pastors filled with His Spirit and a people disposed to submit their understandings to His revealed truths, and subject their hearts to the sweet yoke of His love and law, watchful to detect and oppose every erroneous innovation of doctrine and all assaults and artifices of vice.

We know little of St Zephyrinus beyond what may be gathered from a passage or two in Eusebius and a rather perplexing notice in the *Liber Pontificalis*. Mgr. Duchesne has striven without much success to elucidate the latter (i, pp. 139–140). For the rest see the *Acta Sanctorum*, August, vol. v. The statement that Zephyrinus was a simple man and a mere tool in the hands of Callistus can hardly be accepted on the bare authority of Hippolytus in the *Philosophoumena*. It is true that he calls him $\dot{a}\nu\dot{\eta}\rho$ $\dot{\iota}\delta\iota\dot{\omega}\tau\eta s$ $\kappa a\dot{\iota}$ $\dot{a}\gamma\rho\dot{a}\mu\mu a\tau os$, but the writer's prejudice is manifest. On the Pope's place of burial see Marucchi in the *Nuovo Bulletino di Arch. Crist.*, 1910, pp. 205–225.

SS. SECUNDUS AND ALEXANDER, MM.

c. A.D. 287

The Roman Martyrology speaks of both these martyrs as being soldiers in the Theban legion, the commemoration of whose massacre is made on September 22: Secundus is said to have been the officer commanding the legion and Alexander its standard-bearer or else a centurion, but their *acta* are contradictory and worthless. According to Ligurian tradition St Secundus fled from Agaunum but was overtaken and executed at Ventimiglia, his relics being venerated in the cathedral of Turin. St Alexander also fled and after being captured was brought before Maximian at Rome, who ordered him to be beheaded; he again escaped but was re-taken at Plotacco near Bergamo. Here he was put to death before a pagan image. His body is supposed to have been buried by St Grata, a devout widow. The relics of St Alexander are now in the cathedral of Bergamo, of which diocese he is principal patron. Neither of these martyrs had anything to do with the Theban legion. On this day another ST ALEXANDER is venerated at Brescia, alleged to have been a companion of St Lazarus at Marseilles and to have been martyred for overthrowing idols.

The fabulous Acts may be found in the *Acta Sanctorum*, August, vol. v.

ST ADRIAN, MART.

c. A.D. 320

"At Nicomedia," says the Roman Martyrology, "the passion of St Adrian, a son of the Caesar Probus, who for upbraiding Licinius for the persecution he had stirred up against the Christians was ordered by him to be slain. His uncle Domitius, Bishop of Byzantium, buried his body in a suburb of that city called Argyropolis." The Greek legend says that Domitius was Adrian's brother, not his uncle, and that they became Christians together after the death of their father, the Emperor Probus; Adrian attacked Licinius for his persecution, was beheaded in consequence, and was buried at Argyropolis, as the Roman Martyrology states. It has been suggested that this Adrian is the same as the Adrian, husband of St Natalia, who was also a martyr at Nicomedia and buried at Argyropolis and whose feast is kept on this day by the Greeks; but they have venerated the two Adrians as different persons from early times, and their historical distinctness is now generally recognized. But there are several difficulties in the traditional story, as, for example, that no such person as this Domitius, Bishop of Byzantium, is known to history: the first known bishop of Byzantium was St Metrophanes, who occupied the see at this time; he is said to have been a nephew of Probus.

See the bibliography appended to the account of St Adrian on September 8.

BD. HERLUIN, Abbot of Bec, Conf.
a.d. 1078

Was born at Brionne in Normandy in 994 and was bred to the profession of arms. About the year 1031 he left the court of Gilbert, Count of Brionne, whose knight he was, and founded a monastery on his own land at Bonneville, of which he became abbot. About 1040 the community was moved to a better neighbourhood on the banks of the little river Bec, and here the famous abbey began to grow up, the final site chosen by Herluin not long before his death being further up the valley. One of the first novices to be received at Bec was Lanfranc, afterwards to be archbishop of Canterbury, who came from the theological school at Avranches; he was appointed to assist Bd. Herluin as prior and laid the foundations of the school of Bec. Then came Anselm, of Aosta, who also became archbishop of Canterbury and was a Doctor of the Church and a canonized saint as well. Thus under the guiding hand and holy direction of Bd. Herluin was begun a monastery that was to be one of the most influential of the Middle Ages: within a few years it was "the most famous school of Christendom. It was in fact the first wave of the intellectual movement which was spreading from Italy to the ruder countries of the West. The whole mental activity of the time seemed concentrated in the group of scholars who gathered around [Lanfranc]; the fabric of the canon law and of mediaeval scholasticism, with the philosophical scepticism which first awoke under its influence, all trace their origin to Bec" (J. R. Green). And the occasion of all this was the desire to serve God under the rule of St Benedict of a rough Norman soldier, Bd. Herluin. When Lanfranc went to be abbot of Caen in 1062, St Anselm took his place as prior and succeeded as abbot when Bd. Herluin died at the age of eighty-four in 1078. The life of this holy founder was written by Gilbert, Abbot of Westminster in the middle of the twelfth century, and his name is preserved in that of the village near the ruins of his monastery, now called Bec-Hellouin.

Two Lives of Herluin have been printed by Mabillon, *Acta Sanctorum O.S.B.*, vol. vi, part 2, pp. 342–364. The earlier is by Gilbert Crispin, abbot of Westminster, a contemporary who had himself been a monk of Bec. The Bollandists have excluded Herluin from their collection on the ground that, as Mabillon himself admits, there has been no *cultus*.

BD. TIMOTHY OF MONTECCHIO, Conf.

A.D. 1504

Very little seems to be recorded concerning the life of this holy Franciscan priest, although his *cultus* was formally confirmed by Pius IX in 1870. He was, we are told, of good family and came from the neighbourhood of Aquila in the Abruzzi. He entered the Franciscan noviceship at an early age and was remarkable from the first for his austerity of life and for his scrupulous observance of the rule. What seems most of all to have impressed his contemporaries was the efficacy of the prayers which he said for those in need of help. He worked many miracles, and it is alleged that he was visited by our Blessed Lady and St Francis and that our Saviour spoke to him audibly from the Sacramental species. He died, aged 60, in the friary of St Angelo at Ocra, where his remains are still honoured.

See Mazara, *Leggendario Francescano* (1680), vol. iii, p. 540 ; and Léon, *Auréole Séraphique* (Eng. trans.), vol. iii, p. 88.

BD. THOMAS PERCY, Earl of Northumberland, Mart.

A.D. 1572

The father of this martyr was Sir Thomas Percy, brother and heir-presumptive to the sixth Earl of Northumberland, who, if not formally himself a martyr, died for the denial of the ecclesiastical supremacy of King Henry VIII in that he was one of the leaders of the Pilgrimage of Grace, and was hanged at Tyburn, with the Abbot of Jervaulx and others, in 1537. His elder son, Thomas, was then nine years old and with his brother Henry was removed from the care of his " treasonable " mother and entrusted to Sir Thomas Tempest of Tong and others. In 1549 the attainder under which they suffered as a result of their father's action was to a certain extent removed, they were " restored in blood," and eight years later Queen Mary permitted Sir Thomas Percy to succeed to the now vacant earldom of Northumberland, in consideration of his " noble descent, constancy in virtue, valour in arms, and other strong qualifications " in general, and of his capture of Scarborough castle from the rebel Sir Thomas Stafford in particular. He served the Queen well in military and civil affairs on the Scottish border, and in 1558 married Anne Somerset, daughter of the Earl of Worcester. During the years following the accession of Elizabeth, while she was consolidating her position and laying the foundations of the Anglican Church, the Earl became a suspect person, he was " considered very Catholic," and this in spite of the fact that he used considerable prudence in opposing the Queen and, partly on account of his duties in the northern marches, played only a minor part therein ; indeed, the Queen gave him the order of the Garter in 1563, and certain words of the Earl during his trial suggest that he was not satisfied with his own behaviour at this time. But he was soon to come to the forefront of affairs. The north of England was still fairly solidly Catholic: a Protestant observer said of Yorkshire that, " There were scarcely ten gentlemen of note that favour the Queen's proceedings in religion " ; and when Queen Mary of the Scots had to take refuge at Carlisle in 1568 she was soon regarded as the Catholic champion. The Earl of Northumberland espoused her cause, hoping by her liberation " to have some reformation in religion, or at the least some sufferance for men to use their conscience as they were disposed." His support of her attracted attention and he was peremptorily ordered to leave Carlisle, a " gross disrespect " at which he was very indignant. In 1569 the gentlemen of the north began to plan a rising in her favour as next heir to the throne and in order " to restore the Crown, the nobility, and the worship of God to their former estate " ; the Earl was doubtful about the project, and wished it to be clear that it was not a political one : " we are seeking, I imagine, the glory not of men but of God." He, therefore, with the Earl of Westmorland, Charles Neville, sent a letter to Pope St Pius V, asking for his advice and direction, but they were forced into action before his reply could be received.* The movement was known, and only a few days after they had written to the Pope the two Earls were summoned to appear before Elizabeth ; a hasty meeting of the leaders was called at Brancepeth Castle, they decided (against Northumberland's will and judgement) to ignore the summons, and on 14th November they marched into Durham at the head of their forces. They were welcomed by the townsmen and the cathedral was at once restored to Catholic worship. A priest named William Holmes, whose activity earned him the nickname of "the Pope's patriarch ", was put in charge, altars were set up, Protestant service-books destroyed, on St Andrew's day Mr. Robert Peirson sang High Mass in the cathedral, and on the following Sunday Mr. Holmes, who had the necessary faculties, publicly reconciled the huge congregation and

* The Pope's eventual answer was approving and encouraging, and referred to the example of St Thomas Becket. It was dated three days before his bull of deposition of Elizabeth, *Regnans in excelsis*.

absolved them from censures. However inopportune and regrettable the Rising of the North may have been, it at least shows that, after eleven years of forced apostasy, the people of northern England were Catholic at heart, for not only at Durham was the restoration of the religion received with enthusiasm. Mass was said in the parish-churches of Bishop Auckland, Darlington, Ripon, Staindrop, Stokesby, and Whitby, and a joyous revival was chronicled at many other places. Meanwhile the Earl's forces, under the banner of the Five Wounds and with Bd. Thomas Plumtree as chief chaplain, marched into Yorkshire as far as Wetherby, collecting recruits and encouraging the people, but then had to turn back north, where they captured Hartlepool and Barnard Castle. But that was the limit of their success. At the end of a month Elizabeth's troops, under the Earl of Sussex, were in control, the Earls disbanded their men at Durham, and with the other leaders fled across the border into Scotland.

The Earl of Sussex took bloody vengeance. People of substance were let off with a good fine, but the common people were hanged in hundreds : every village between the Wear and the Tyne suffered. Westmorland escaped into Flanders ; the Countess of Northumberland, who had been one of the leading spirits of the rebellion, and entirely without her husband's scruples and fears, eventually came under the protection of Lord Home ; and Northumberland himself was captured by the Scottish regent, the Earl of Moray, to whom he was betrayed. He was not willing to hand him over to Elizabeth, but his successor, the Earl of Mar, sold him for £2000—not the first nor the last time in history that a refugee in Scotland was given up for gold. Before this haggling was concluded, the Earl had been shut up for two and a half years in Lochleven castle. Dr. Nicholas Sander, a leading Catholic divine of the day, records that he bore this imprisonment and his separation from his wife and four small children with exemplary patience ; he observed all the fasts of the Church, spent much time in prayer and meditation (a book of prayers which he wrote out still exists), and resolutely refused to purchase his pardon (which was offered him) by apostasy. His keeper at Lochleven, William Douglas, was also negotiating for the sale of his prisoner—to the Countess his wife, who was scouring Scotland and the Netherlands to raise the ransom. But Elizabeth closed first ; the Earl was handed over ; and eventually conveyed to York, where he was lodged in the castle on August 21, 1572. On the Queen's instructions he had been examined on the way, at Berwick ; a last offer of release on condition of apostasy was made to him ; and when he refused he was told to prepare for death on the very next day. He spent all the night, except for a brief space when sleep overcame him, in prayer, and the next afternoon was marched to "the Pavement," where the scaffold was set up. He told the people that he died a Catholic, " as for this new Church of England, I do not acknowledge it "; and expressed sorrow that he had been the occasion of so many meeting their death in following him for the furtherance of religion, " yet I have no fear but that their souls have obtained the glory of Heaven." Then his head was struck off, and every drop of his blood was gathered up with handkerchiefs, " for throughout his life he was beyond measure dear to the whole people." He was forty-four years old. The Countess of Northumberland died in exile at Namur in 1596; two years later their youngest daughter, Mary Percy, whom her father probably never saw, founded at Brussels a monastery of Benedictine nuns (now at East Bergholt), from which derive the present convents of Stanbrook, Oulton, Colwich, Teignmouth, Kylemore, and Atherstone. Bd. Thomas Percy was equivalently beatified in 1896.

A full account of this noble martyr was contributed by Father G. E. Phillips to the second volume of *Lives of the English Martyrs* edited by Dom Bede Camm (1905), pp. 111–186. His information is largely drawn, apart from the State papers at the Record Office, from De Fonblanque's *Annals of the House of Percy* (1887), vol. ii, pp. 3–123, and from a Surtees Society publication, *Depositions and Ecclesiastical Proceedings from the Courts of Durham* (1845). A description of the martyrdom of the Earl, written by Nicholas Sander, is in Bridgewater's *Concertatio*.

AUGUST 27

ST JOSEPH CALASANCTIUS, Conf., Founder of the Piarists

a.d. 1648

JOSEPH CALASANCTIUS, called in religion "of the Mother of God" and one of the foremost figures in the educational activities of the Counter-reformation, was the youngest of five children borne by Donna Maria Gastonia to her husband Don Pedro Calasanza. He was born in his father's castle near Petralta de la Sal in Aragon in the year 1556, and in due course was sent to study the humanities at Estadilla, where his virtue and religious observances were regarded with considerable disrespect by his fellow-students. He refused to be moved by their mischievousness and ridicule, and being no less fervent in his studies he completed his course of rhetoric with distinction at the age of fifteen. He then returned home, and his father wanted him to be a soldier and start on that career at once; but Joseph had other ideas and induced Don Pedro instead to send him to the University of Lerida, where he took his doctorate in law before going on to Valencia. It is said that he left this university in order to escape the attentions of a young kinswoman, who subjected him to a temptation similar to that undergone by his namesake many centuries before at the court of Pharao; certainly he continued his theology at Alcalá, and there met Ascanio Colonna, who as a cardinal and viceroy of Aragon befriended him in after years. In 1579 Joseph's only brother died childless and Don Pedro naturally wished his surviving son to marry and perpetuate the family in the male line. Joseph temporized, for he had not only determined to be a priest but had already taken a private vow of celibacy, and, after graduating, accepted an invitation from Mgr. Gaspar della Figuera, Bishop of Jacca, to be his *socius*. After a year his father required him to return home and renewed his entreaties that Joseph should follow a secular career; these entreaties were checked by a sudden illness which brought the young man near to death, and Don Pedro was so frightened of losing him altogether that no further objections were raised to Joseph's vocation. In 1583 he was ordained priest by the Bishop of Urgel, being already twenty-eight years old, and was at once recalled to the service of Mgr. Figuera, now bishop of Albarracin. He was made the bishop's confessor and theologian, and synodal examiner and procurator of the diocese, and when shortly afterwards Mgr. Figuera was translated to the see of Lerida, Don Joseph accompanied him. Already the fame of his wisdom, learning, and goodness was spread abroad ; he was consulted by Father Aguilar about the reform of the Spanish Augustinian friars, and assisted his bishop in an apostolic visitation of the great monastery of Montserrat, which was disordered by internal disputes. During the course of this work Mgr. Figuera died and, when the charge had been handed over to the Bishop of Vich, Joseph resigned his own position in order to go to Calasanza, where his father also was nearing his end. After Don Pedro's death Joseph remained at home for a time administering the estate and helping its dependents until he was appointed by the Bishop of Urgel vicar general of the district of Trempe. He was so successful here that he was sent to deal with the Pyrenean part of the diocese, which comprises the valleys of Andorra of which the Bishop of Urgel was joint sovereign prince (he still holds the title) as well as ordinary. This lonely and inaccessible region was in a terrible state of religious and moral disorder, and St Joseph conducted a long and arduous visitation of which the first task was to bring the clergy to a sense of their responsibilities and obligations ; on its completion he returned to Trempe and remained there until he was made vicar general of the whole diocese. But for some time he had been listening to an interior call to undertake a quite different sort of work ; at length he resigned his office and benefices, divided the Calasanza patrimony between his sisters and the poor, reserving a sufficient income for himself, endowed several charitable institutions, and in 1592 left Spain for Rome.

Here Joseph met his friend of Alcalá, Ascanio Colonna, already a cardinal, and for five years he was under the direct patronage of the Colonnas. He was theologian to the aged and venerable Cardinal Marcantonio Colonna, tutor to his little nephew, Prince Filippo, and spiritual director of the whole family, to which he gave a conference every week in the church of the Apostles. During the plague of 1595 he distinguished himself by his devotion and fearlessness, and entered into a holy rivalry with his friend St Camillus of Lellis as to who should expend himself the more freely in the service of the sick and dying. He was one of the first to welcome to Rome some friars of the new Carmelite reform of St Teresa and St John-of-the-Cross, influenced Cardinal Marcantonio in their favour, and helped to obtain for them the church of our Lady *della Scala* in the Trastevere. But during these years St Joseph never lost sight of the work which had drawn him to Rome, namely, the instruction of young children, of whom there were many, neglected or homeless, in the most urgent need of interest and care. He had become a member of the Confraternity of Christian Doctrine, whose business it was to teach the Faith to both children and adults on Sundays and feast-days, and in so doing was brought home vividly to St Joseph the state of degradation and ignorance in which so many of the children of the poor lived. He was soon convinced that periodical instruction was utterly inadequate to cope with the situation, and that free day-schools for both religious and secular education were required. He therefore first of all invited the official parish-schoolmasters to admit poor pupils to their schools without payment, but they would not undertake the extra work without a rise in salary, and this the Roman senate refused to grant. He then approached the Jesuits and the Dominicans, but neither order could see a way to extending its activities, for their members were already fully engaged. St Joseph then came to the conclusion that it was God's will that he should begin the work himself, single-handed if necessary. Don Antonio Brendani, parish-priest of Santa Dorotea, offered him the use of two rooms and his own services, two more priests joined them, and in November 1597 the public free school was opened.

At the end of a week the school had a hundred pupils and before long many more, and the founder had to engage paid teachers from among the unbeneficed clergy of the city. In 1599 it was moved into new quarters and St Joseph obtained permission from Cardinal Ascanio to leave the Colonna household and take up his residence on the school premises with the other masters; they lived a quasi-community life and the founder acted as superior, with the title of Prefect of the Religious Schools. During the following couple of years the pupils increased to seven hundred, and in 1602 another move was made, to a large house adjoining the church of Sant' Andrea della Valle. While hanging a bell in the courtyard St Joseph fell from a ladder and broke his leg in two places, an accident the effects of which were a source of lameness and pain for the rest of his life; but while he was in bed he had the consolation and encouragement of receiving three valuable recruits for the school in the persons of Dr. Tomasso Vittoria, Canon Gellio Ghellini, and Gaspar Dragonetti. The last named was ninety-five years old, but had still many years of vigorous work before him, and was 120 when he died in 1628. Pope Clement VIII having made a grant of 200 scudi a year towards the rent and people of consequence having begun to send their children to the school, the parish-schoolmasters and others began to criticize it with some vehemence; complaints of its disorders were made to the Pope and he directed Cardinals Antoniani and Baronius to pay it a surprise visit of inspection. This was done and as a result of their report Clement took the institution under his immediate protection. In similar circumstances the same course was taken and the grant doubled in 1606 by Paul V, who also appointed Ludovico de Torres, Archbishop of Monreale, as cardinal protector; but these difficulties were the beginning of trials and persecutions which beset St Joseph until the end of his life. Nevertheless during the succeeding five years the work prospered and grew in spite of all opposition, and in 1611 a *palazzo* was purchased to house it near the church of San Pantaleone; there were about a thousand pupils, including a number of Jews whom the founder himself invited to attend and encouraged by his kindness.

Two years later, with the permission of the Holy See, St Joseph united his informal congregation to the recognized institute of the Clerks Regular of the Mother of God, founded by Bd. John Leonardi in 1574, but this arrangement did not work well. By the beginning of 1617 the Roman schools were in a state of decline, and Joseph was hastily recalled from Frascati where he had been inaugurating a new school. He laid the matter before the Pope, and Paul V revoked the brief of union, at the same time recognizing the priests of the Religious Schools as a separate institute, with simple vows and the obligation of teaching children gratuitously. On the feast of the Annunciation Father Joseph-of-the-Mother-of-God received the religious habit from the hands of Cardinal Giustiniani, and himself conferred it on his fourteen assistants. The Roman school under the new régime at once began to recover, another was opened near St Peter's basilica and others were called for at Sabina and Narni; the time was come for the new congregation to have definitive constitutions, and after a retreat for forty days Father Joseph began to draw them up. They were not finished before the death of Paul V but were at once submitted to his successor, Gregory XV; after some difficulty they were accepted and at the end of 1621 the congregation was recognized as a religious order under the name of the Pauline Poor Clerks Regular of the Mother of God of the Religious Schools; early in the following year it was granted the privileges of a mendicant order and St Joseph was named its superior general. The canonical novitiate was opened at Sant' Onofrio, but the requirement of new schools in Lombardy and Liguria brought an increase of novices which a few years later necessitated its transfer to bigger and healthier premises. St Joseph did not let the cares of the generalate diminish either his numerous religious observances or his care for the needy, the sick, and any to whom he could be of service. About this time there came to Rome, with his wife and family, an English gentleman, Mr. Thomas Cocket, who by abjuring Protestantism had brought himself within reach of the penal laws ; him the saint assisted, and the Pope followed his example, assigning a pension to the refugee converts. For ten years the congregation continued to prosper and extend and spread from Italy into the Empire ; at Leipsic the example of the fathers led to wholesale conversions in faith and morals, and the Lord of Strasnitz wrote to the founder : " This city, this county, and all the neighbourhood, might well be called a nest, in which an endless brood of heretical sects was continually springing into life : Calvinists, Lutherans, Picardians, Hussites, Anabaptists, Atheists, and so on. Now, on the contrary, we see almost all of them brought to the one true Faith, full of zeal and devotion, and that in a very short time."

In 1630 was admitted to the institute at Naples one Mario Sozzi, a middle-aged priest, who in due course was solemnly professed. For several years his froward and perverse behaviour made him a great nuisance to his brethren but, having by a show of burning zeal for right faith gained the good will and influence of the Holy Office, he contrived to get himself, in 1639, made provincial of the Clerks Regular of the Religious Schools in Tuscany, with extraordinary powers and independence of the superior general. He proceeded to administer the province in the most capricious and damaging way, harmed as much as he could the reputation of St Joseph with the Roman authorities, and, when his ambition had led to his banishment from Tuscany for intriguing in affairs of the state, he denounced St Joseph to the Holy Office on the false charge of having instigated the Grand Duke to that action to spite Mario and the sacred congregation. Cardinal Cesarini, as protector of the new institute and in order to vindicate Joseph, ordered Father Mario's papers and letters to be seized ; these included some documents of the Holy Office and that congregation, spurred on by Mario, straightway had St Joseph arrested and carried through the streets like a felon. He was brought before the assessors and only saved from imprisonment by the intervention of Cardinal Cesarini. But Father Mario was unpunished, and continued to plot for control of the whole institute, representing St Joseph to be too old and doddering for the responsibility ; he managed by deceit to get him suspended from the generalate and contrived that a visitor apostolic be appointed who was favourable to himself. This visitor and Father Mario became in effect in supreme command, and St Joseph was subjected by them to the most humiliating, insulting, and unjust treatment, while the order was reduced to such confusion and impotence that

Aug. 27] ST JOSEPH CALASANCTIUS

the loyal members were unable to persuade the superior authorities of the true state of affairs. Towards the end of 1643 Mario died and was succeeded by Father Cherubini, who pursued the same policy. St Joseph bore these trials with marvellous patience, urging the order to obey his persecutors for they were *de facto* in authority, and on one occasion sheltering Cherubini from the violent opposition of some of the younger fathers who were indignant at his treachery. The Holy See had some time previously set up a commission of cardinals to look into the whole matter, and at length in 1645 it ordered the reinstatement of St Joseph as superior general; this announcement was received with great joy but led at once to renewed efforts on the part of the malcontents, who now aimed at having the order reduced to the status of a congregation without vows. They were successful, and in 1646 Pope Innocent X published a brief of which the effect was to make the Clerks Regular of the Religious Schools simply a society of priests subject to their respective bishops. Thus in his ninetieth year St Joseph saw the apparent overturning of all his work by the authority to which he was so greatly devoted and the indirect disgrace of himself before the world; when the news was brought to him he simply murmured, " The Lord gave and the Lord hath taken away. Blessed be the name of the Lord."

The business of drawing up new constitutions and regulations for the shattered institute of Religious Schools was entrusted to Father Cherubini, but within a few months he was convicted by the auditors of the Rota of the maladministration of the Nazarene College, of which he was rector. He retired from Rome in disgrace, but returned in the following year to die, repentant of the part he had played and reconciled to St Joseph, who consoled him on his death-bed. A few months later, on August 25, 1648, St Joseph himself died, and was buried in the church of San Pantaleone; he was ninety-two years old. There is an obvious parallel between this history and that of St Alphonsus Liguori and the early days of the Redemptorists, and during the troubles of his young congregation St Alphonsus used to encourage and fortify himself by reading the life of St Joseph Calasanctius; he was canonized in 1767, six years before the death of Alban Butler, who only gives to him a brief notice in his *Lives*, wherein he is referred to as " a perpetual miracle of fortitude and another Job "—a comparison made by Cardinal Lambertini (afterwards Pope Benedict XIV) before the Congregation of Sacred Rites in 1728.

The failure of St Joseph's foundation was only apparent. Its suppression was strongly objected to in several places, especially Poland, Germany, and Moravia, and it was reconstituted with simple vows in 1656 and restored as a religious order in 1669. To-day the Clerks Regular of the Religious Schools (commonly called Piarists or Scolopii) number over 4000 religious with 350 schools in various parts of the world.

The documents submitted in the process of beatification and canonisation have been largely utilised by the biographers of St. Joseph Calasanctius, and this is notably the case in the Life written in Italian in the eighteenth century, a translation of which was published in the Oratorian Series edited by Father Faber (1850). The beatification decree is printed among the works of Benedict XIV, vol. xvi (1846), pp. 413–415. The earliest detailed account of Calasanctius seems to have been compiled by one of his religious sons, Father Mussesti, for the information of Pope Alexander VII, less than twenty years after the saint's death. A considerable number of biographies have since appeared in Italian, French, Spanish and German. Those by Timon-David (2 vols., Marseille, 1883), Tommaseo (Rome, 1898), Casanovas y Sanz (Saragossa, 1904) and Heidenreich (Vienna 1907) may be specially mentioned. See also Heimbucher, *Orden und Kongregationen der. Kat. Kirche*, vol. iii, pp. 287–296 ; and Pastor, *Geschichte der Päpste*, especially vol. xi, pp. 431–433.

ST MARCELLUS AND HIS COMPANIONS, MM.

A.D. 303

During the persecution of Diocletian the governor of the Egyptian Thebaïd summoned before him seventeen individuals, the whole Christian congregation of Oxyrynchus, who had been denounced to him as "the only ones in the city who oppose the imperial decree, who are impious towards the worship of the gods, and who despise your tribunal by not obeying your commands." They were the tribune Marcellus, his wife Mammæa, and their two sons, a bishop and three clerks, a soldier, seven other laymen and a woman. When they had been brought in chains before the governor at Thmuis he tried to move them to obedience, and when he failed condemned them all to the beasts. He made a last attempt to save them the next day, in the amphitheatre itself. "Are you not ashamed," he cried, " to worship a man who was put to death and buried years ago by order of Pontius Pilate, whose ' acts,' as I am told, are still in existence ? " (This is not a reference to the so-called *Gospel of Nicodemus* but to one of several earlier *acta Pilati* supposed to have been extracted from the archives of the *prætorium* at Jerusalem.) The Christians refused to be moved by this appeal, and the writer of their *acta** puts into the mouth of the

---

* Julian, a priest, who wrote them by the hand of his son Stelechius, "because of the weakness of my eyes," and gave a copy with relics of the martyrs to a deaconess, Issicia.

bishop, Miletius, a confession of faith in the divinity of Jesus Christ in words obviously inspired by the Arian controversy and the definitions of the Council of Nicæa. They were therefore put to death, the *acta* say by beheading, because the bears when let loose would not touch them and a fire could not be kindled to burn them.

The Roman Martyrology refers to these martyrs as Marcellinus and Mannea with their three sons, and puts the place of the passion at Tomis in Pontus.

Although Achelis in his book *Die Martyrologien* (1900), pp. 173-177, adopted a view substantially identical with that expressed above, more recent investigation has departed from his conclusions. Père Delehaye does not think it probable that Tomis has been substituted for Thmuis, but that the martyrs really belonged to Moesia and were transferred by the hagiographer to Egypt. See the *Analecta Bollandiana*, vol. xxxviii (1920), pp. 384-385, and P. Franchi de Cavalieri in *Nuovo Bulletino*, 1905, pp. 237-267. The text of the Acts is printed in the *Acta Sanctorum*, August, vol. vi, pp. 14-15, and *cf.* November, vol. ii, part 2, p. 471.

ST PŒMEN, Abbot

c. A.D. 450

The abbot Pœmen was one of the most celebrated of all the Fathers of the Desert. He forsook the world about the middle of the fourth century and went into the Egyptian desert of Skete, one elder and several younger brothers of his accompanying him. After some years they were driven away from their first settlement by raids of barbarians from Libya, and took refuge in the ruins of a pagan temple at Terenuth. Anubis, the eldest, and Pœmen governed the little community of hermits by turns. Of the twelve hours of the night, four were allotted to work, four to singing office, and four to sleep ; in the day they worked till noon, read till three in the afternoon, and then went to gather firing, herbs for food, and other necessaries.

St Pœmen often passed several days, sometimes a whole week, without eating, but it was his constant advice to others that their fasts should be moderate, and that they should take some sufficient nourishment every day : " We fast," he said, " to control our bodies, not to kill them." But he taught that no monk ought ever to taste wine or to seek any deliberate gratification of the senses : " for sensuality expels the spirit of penance and the holy fear of God from the heart as smoke drives away bees ; it extinguishes that grace, and deprives a soul of the comfort and presence of the Holy Ghost." In his youth he visited the older hermits and monks and received great profit from their experience and instructions. He much admired that lesson of abbot Moses, that a servant of God must keep his heart always full of sorrow and compunction and humbled at the consideration of his sins, which he must always have before his eyes; but he must never think of those of others, or judge anyone, farther than charity or authority may oblige him. St Pœmen feared the least occasion that could interrupt his solitude, or make the distractions of the world break in upon him; and on one occasion he even went so far as to refuse to see his mother, foregoing that happiness then that they might enjoy it more hereafter. He used the like severity towards the governor of the province, who never was able to draw him out of his desert to pay him a visit. Among the remarkable sayings of this abbot it is related that, when one who had committed a fault told him he would do penance for it three years, the saint, doubting his perseverance for so long, advised him to confine his penance to three days, but to be very fervent in it. A monk who was grievously molested with thoughts of blasphemy often went to him, but for a long time had not the courage to tell him the trouble. The saint, perceiving his difficulty, encouraged him to lay open his perplexity, and the brother had no sooner done it than he found himself at ease. Pœmen comforted him, and bade him confidently say to the Devil, whenever he suggested any abominable thought, " May your blasphemy fall on you; it is not mine, for my heart detests it." But to another who spoke of the Devil he said, " Devil! It's always the Devil that's blamed. I say that it's self-will." And another time, " Never try to have your own way. Those who are self-willed are their own worst tempters, and require no devil to tempt them." A person came out of Syria to consult him by what remedies a spiritual dryness and hardness of heart is best overcome. The saint answered, " By perseverance in fervent prayer and meditation on the word of God. Water is soft, and stone hard; yet drops of water often falling upon it wear it hollow; so by the divine word often falling upon our heart, though it were of adamant, it must at length yield to the impression." St Pœmen used strongly to exhort to frequent communion and to a great desire for that divine food, as the stag pants after the cool spring. " Some aver," said he, " that stags feel a violent inward heat and thirst, because in the deserts they eat serpents and their bowels are parched with the poison. Thus souls in the wilderness of this world always suck in something of its poison, and so need perpetually to approach the body and blood of Jesus Christ, which fortifies them against all such venom." To one who complained that his neighbour was a monk of whom derogatory tales were told, and gave the authority of another monk to prove their truth, he said, "There could not be worse evidence than scandalous stories told by a monk; by telling them he shows himself unworthy of credence." And to his own monks: "He that is quarrelsome, or is apt to murmur and complain, can be no monk; he that renders evil for evil can be no monk; he that is ill-tempered can be no monk." It was another saying of this abbot that "silence is no virtue when charity requires speech" that "people should not waste other people's time by asking advice when no advice is necessary or wanted"; and that "a living faith consists in thinking little of oneself and having tenderness towards others."

St Pœmen took over complete control of the community on the death of Anubis. "We lived together," he said, "in complete unity and unbroken peace till death broke up our association. We followed the rule Anubis made for us; one was appointed steward, and he had care of our meals. We ate such things as were set before us, and no one said: Give me something else; I cannot eat this." How much the support of these solitaries was valued, even in external matters, is shown by the visit of some heretical men to Pœmen, decrying the Archbishop of Alexandria; apparently they were Arians, trying to prejudice the abbot against St Athanasius. Pœmen simply said, "Prepare the table, make them eat, and let them go in peace." He returned from Terenuth to Skete but was again driven out by raids about the year 430; he was present at the death of St Arsenius on the rock of Troë, near Memphis: "Happy Arsenius!" he cried, "who had the gift of tears in this life! For he who does not weep for his sins on earth will bewail them for ever in eternity." St Pœmen himself died very soon afterwards. He is named in the Roman Martyrology and in the Byzantine liturgical books is referred to as "the lamp of the universe and pattern of monks."

A short Greek Life with other miscellaneous references will be found in the *Acta Sanctorum*, August, vol. vi; but the most convenient source of information concerning Pœmen and the other Fathers of the desert is the *Vitæ Patrum* of Father Rosweyde.

ST CÆSARIUS, ABP. OF ARLES, CONF.

A.D. 543

St Cæsarius was born in 470, in the territory of Chalon on the Saône, descended from a family of distinguished lineage and virtue. In his youth he laid a good foundation of learning and determined to become a priest, and at eighteen years of age he asked Sylvester, Bishop of Chalon, to give him the tonsure that he might enter himself in the service of the Church. This was done accordingly; but two years after Cæsarius withdrew to the monastery of Lérins, which had produced many learned and holy men, under the direction of the abbot Porcarius. In this house the abbot appointed him cellarer; but as human passions creep into places the furthest removed from the incentives of vice, some of the monks were offended at his scrupulously just administration and complained so much that the abbot with regret was forced to relieve him of his office. Cæsarius was glad to be at liberty to give himself up entirely to contemplation and penance; but his health gave way and he was sent to Arles to recover. Here his scruples about the use of pagan authors for study by Christian clerics drew the attention of the bishop, Æonus, to him; they were kinsmen, and Æonus was sufficiently attracted by the young man to write to the Abbot of Lérins, asking that he might be released for the episcopal service; to this, after some objection, Porcarius agreed. Cæsarius was then ordained deacon and priest, and put by Æonus in charge of a neighbouring monastery whose discipline was very relaxed. He gave these monks a rule, governed them for three years, and in spite of his youth and inexperience made them a model body of religious. The Bishop of Arles, on his death-bed, recommended him for his successor. The saint fled and hid himself among the Roman tombs near the city; but he was discovered and obliged to acquiesce in the election of the clergy and the city. He was then thirty years old, and he presided over that church more than forty years.

Cæsarius had not the Roman sense of order nor the sumptuous habits by which some bishops of those times supported the temporal importance of their positions, but he had a high and holy religious conscience which made him the leading prelate of Gaul. Among the first things he did was to regulate the singing of the Divine Office, which he ordered to be celebrated publicly, not only on Sundays, Saturdays, and solemn festivals as had been the custom at Arles, but every day as was done in other neighbouring churches. He induced the laity to attend and exhorted all never to fail, except in case of necessity, to assist at all the hours of the Divine Office sung in the day, and in Lent also at those of the night; he introduced into his cathedral the hours of Terce, Sext, and None. He was careful to instruct his flock in prayer, and to teach them to cry to God with earnest desires of the heart: not with their lips only, which can be no prayer but only mockery and an insult to God, for prayer is the raising of the heart and mind to God. "A man," said he, "worships that on which his mind is intent during prayer. Whoever in his prayers thinks of public affairs, or of the house he is building, adores them rather than God." In order to devote himself more assiduously to prayer, reading, and preaching, he left to stewards and deacons the care of his temporalities. Knowing that the Church puts the poor under the special protection of the bishops, he consecrated to them much of his revenue, and built many hospitals. He preached on all Sundays and holidays, and often on other days, both morning and evening, and if he was hindered he ordered the priests or deacons to read to the people some homilies of the Fathers; and he had some such homily always read after Matins and Vespers that the people might never leave church without some instruction. He was opposed to studied discourses, and his own style is plain, natural, and pleasing. He used to descend very much to particulars, and spoke chiefly against those vices which prevailed most, especially warning against a delay of repentance, and inculcating fear of Purgatory for venial sins and the necessity of effacing them by daily penance. His ordinary exhortations were on prayer, fasting, alms, the pardon of injuries, chastity, and the practice of all manner of good works. He was, in fact, the first " popular " preacher whose words have come down to us; his discourses are full of homely allusions and illustrations, and they rarely exceeded a quarter of an hour in length. At the same time he urged the value of the corporate worship which he took so much pains to have observed fittingly. " Match your behaviour to the words you sing," he said. " Let your souls be as pure as the text *Beati immaculati in via*. When you sing the verse *Confundantur superbi*, hate pride and flee from it. And so, while your ears are charmed with melody, you will realize what the Psalmist meant when he said, *Quam dulcia faucibus meis eloquia tua!*"

An early biographer refers to St Cæsarius as " another Noe, who built an ark to shelter his daughters against the perils of the times." This refers to the monastery he established to give a more permanent home to the maidens and widows of southern Gaul who wished to give themselves to God. It was first at Aliscamps, among the Roman tombs, and then removed within the city walls. This monastery was at first called St John's, but afterward took the name of St Cæsarius, who committed the government of it to his sister St Cæsaria, she having been educated and taken the veil in a nunnery at Marseilles, probably that founded by Cassian. St Cæsarius drew up a rule for these women, which was one of the principal preoccupations of his life; in it for the first time enclosure is made permanent and complete, and Pope St Hormisdas confirmed its autonomy and exemption from episcopal jurisdiction. The nuns made their own clothes, and were generally employed in weaving and needlework; they were allowed to embroider and to wash and mend clothes for persons that lived out of the convent. The ornaments of their church were only of woollen or linen cloth, and plain, without embroidery or flowers. Some of them worked at transcribing books. They all studied two hours every day, and one of them read to the rest during part of the time they were at work. Flesh meat was forbidden, except to the sick, and the rule enjoined the use of baths, but pointing out that they were for health, not for enjoyment : nor were they to be indulged in during Lent. Only the abbess and her assistant were exempt from helping in the housework.

St Cæsarius was promoted to the see of Arles when it had just succeeded in maintaining its extensive jurisdiction against the Archbishop of Vienne, and he found himself metropolitan of twenty-seven suffragan sees. As such he presided over an important synod at Agde in 506 at which many disciplinary canons were passed and a collection of statutes and decretals approved. He also presided, as delegate apostolic, at the synods of Arles and Carpentras in 527, the second of Orange and of Vaison in 529, and of Marseilles in 533. At Orange was condemned the heresy of the Semipelagians, who affirmed that the first desire or beginning of faith and good works is from the creature. This council pronounced against those who blasphemously affirm that God predestines any man to damnation; on the other side, it declared that according to the Catholic faith God inspires into our souls, by His grace, the beginning of His faith and love, or the first desire or good disposition of the soul towards it, and that He is the author of our conversion. St Cæsarius sent the decrees of this council to Rome to be confirmed by Pope Felix IV, which was done by his successor Boniface II, and from that time the Semipelagians were ranked by the whole Church among heretics.

Side by side with his ecclesiastical labours, St Cæsarius had his share in the public upheavals of the age in which he lived. The city of Arles was at that time subject to Alaric II, King of the Visigoths, who was master of the greatest part of Spain, all Languedoc, and part of Provence. It was suggested to this prince that the Archbishop, being born a subject to the King of Burgundy, did all that lay in his power to bring the territory of Arles under his dominion. This was untrue, but Alaric in 505 banished him to Bordeaux. During his brief residence in that city a fire one night broke out, and the people ran and besought him to pray for the extinction of the flames. He knelt in prayer before the fire, which was then soon got under, and he was hailed as the saviour of the city. Alaric, having

discovered his innocence, recalled him from exile and condemned
his accuser to be stoned, but pardoned him at the earnest intercession
of Cæsarius. On his return to Arles, all the people went to meet
him, singing psalms and holding tapers in their hands; and they
thought they were indebted to his prayers for plentiful rain that fell
at that time after a long drought. The French and Burgundians
laid siege to Arles in 508, during which the Archbishop saw his flock
reduced to terrible straits; in the midst of his efforts for them the
Goths threw him into prison, upon suspicion that he had attempted
to deliver up the city to the besiegers; but he was cleared, and
again set at liberty. The siege was raised and a number of prisoners
were brought into the city, and the churches filled with them. St
Cæsarius was moved exceedingly at their condition, for they were
in want both of clothes and food. He gave them both and employed
in relieving them the whole treasury of his church. He stripped off
silver and melted down and gave away the very censers, chalices,
and patens, saying, " Our Lord celebrated His last supper in earthen
dishes, not on plate, and we need not scruple to part with His vessels
for those whom He has redeemed with His own life. I should like
to know if those who censure what we do would not be glad to be
themselves helped in the same way were the same misfortune to
befall them." St Cæsarius took the utmost care of the sick, whom
he provided with a spacious house, where they might hear Mass at
their ease and where they were carefully attended. The poor always
had access to him, and his servants had a standing order to see
whether there was some poor person at the door who was afraid of
coming in. After the death of the King of the Visigoths, Theodoric
the Ostrogoth, King of Italy, seized those dominions in Languedoc
and Spain, and St Cæsarius came under his suspicion; so he was
apprehended and brought under a strong guard to Ravenna. When
the saint came into the King's presence and saluted him, Theodoric,
seeing his venerable aspect and intrepid air, rose up, took his diadem
from his head, and returned his courtesy. He then spoke kindly
with the Archbishop on the state of his city and after he had dismissed him said to those about him, " May God punish those who
have been responsible for this holy man's undertaking so long a
journey without cause. I trembled when he came in; he has the
face of an angel. I can believe no harm of such a person." He
sent to his house a silver basin, with three hundred pieces of gold,
and the message, " Receive the offering of the King, your son, and
look on it as a token of friendship." Cæsarius sold the basin publicly
and ransomed several captives with the money. When the King
was told this, and that the bishop's door was so crowded with poor

people that it was difficult to get near it, he so praised his charity that the rich and great of Ravenna thronged to offer St Cæsarius alms for his distribution. In 514 he went on to Rome, where Pope St Symmachus confirmed the metropolitan rights of Arles, recognized him as apostolic delegate in Gaul, and conferred the *pallium*, which St Cæsarius is said to have been the first bishop in western Europe to receive.

St Cæsarius then returned to Arles and continued to watch over and instruct his people for many years. When the city was taken by the Franks in 536 he retired somewhat from public life and spent much time at the convent of St John. He made a will in favour of those nuns, and in his seventy-third year began to prepare finally for the death which he knew to be near. He asked how long it was to the festival of St Augustine, saying, " I hope I shall die about that time ; you know how much I always loved his truly Catholic doctrine." He caused himself to be carried in a chair to the monastery of his nuns, whom he endeavoured to prepare and comfort for the grief which he knew his death would give them ; they were above two hundred in number, and their superior was called Cæsaria, and had succeeded his sister of the same name. Having given them his blessing, he returned to the metropolitan church, and died in the presence of several bishops and priests, on the eve of the feast of St Augustine in 543.

We possess what may be called two early biographies of St Cæsarius. Both of them, after having been printed by Mabillon and the Bollandists, have been critically edited by Bruno Krusch in the *Monumenta Germaniæ, Scrip. rerum Meroving.*, vol. iii, pp. 457–501. The authenticity of the Saint's last will and testament has been called in question by the same critic, but it has been successfully vindicated by Dom G. Morin in the *Revue Bénédictine*, vol. xvi (1899), pp. 97–112, who also provides a revised text. Two important monographs dealing with St Cæsarius were published in 1894, the first by a non-Catholic, B. F. Arnold, *Cæsarius von Arelate und die gallische kirche seiner Zeit*, the other by the Abbé A. Malnory, *Saint Césaire Évêque d'Arles*, and with these may be coupled a valuable summary by the Abbé P. Lejay in the *Dictionnaire de Théologie Catholique*, vol. ii, cc. 2168–2185. But the scholar who has admittedly the most competent knowledge of the life and writings of Cæsarius is Dom G. Morin. A list of his earlier contributions to the subject will be found in his book *Études, Textes, Découvertes* (1913), pp. 41–45. He has long been engaged upon an edition of the Saint's sermons and other works, but it has not yet seen the light. Dom Morin has proved that Cæsarius, if not himself the author, is at least the earliest writer to show familiarity with the so-called Athanasian Creed (*Quicunque vult*) ; and he was at one time inclined to identify him with the important canonical collection *Statuta Ecclesiæ antiqua*, but this attribution is much contested. A useful, but not altogether reliable, modern life of St Cæsarius is that of M. Chaillan in the series " Les Saints."

ST SYAGRIUS, Bp. of Autun, Conf.

A.D. 600

Syagrius is supposed to have been by birth a Gallo-Roman, and he was raised to the see of Autun about the year 560. He was present at almost all the synods that were held in France in his time, whether for the preservation of the Faith or of good morals, and exercised great influence both in these councils and in the training of persons in the Christian life. To his prudence was committed the difficult business of re-establishing tranquillity in the convent of the Holy Cross at Poitiers, where two nuns were in rebellion against their abbess; but the task was too much for him and the other bishops associated with him in it, and the rebels had to be excommunicated by a synod. Apparently this experience made the good bishop over-careful, for some years later we find him reproved by Pope St Gregory the Great for not preventing the marriage of a nun (named, curiously enough, Syagria) who had been abducted from her cloister. The Pope nevertheless gave distinguishing marks of the esteem he had for the virtue and capacity of Syagrius. When he sent St Augustine with missionaries into England, he recommended them to him, and they were entertained by St Syagrius on their journey. Moreover, though he was only a bishop he was granted permission to wear the *pallium* and given precedence after the metropolitan of the province of Lyons, even before those who were older in years or consecration. These privileges are still enjoyed by the Bishops of Autun. King Gontran, who also greatly appreciated his abilities, chose St Syagrius for the companion of his journey when going to Paris to be present at the baptism of Clotaire II; this took place at Nanterre in 591. St Syagrius died in the year 600 and his relics are preserved at Saint-Audoche.

See the *Acta Sanctorum*, August, vol. vi, and Duchesne, *Fastes Épiscopaux*, vol. ii, p. 173.

BD. AMADEUS, Bp. of Lausanne, Conf.

A.D. 1159

Was of the royal house of Franconia and born at the castle of Chatte in Dauphiné in 1110. When he was eight years old his father, Bd. Amadeus of Clermont, Lord of Hauterive, with other gentlemen, took the religious habit at the Cistercian abbey of Bonnevaux, his mother at the same time becoming a nun at Val-de-Bressieux.

Young Amadeus went with the others to Bonnevaux to be educated there, but after a time he and his father migrated to Cluny. Amadeus senior returned to the more austere Cistercian house (from which he founded four abbeys, Léoncel, Mazan, Montperoux, and Tamis), while Amadeus junior went for a short time into the household of the Emperor Henry V. He then received the Cistercian habit at Clairvaux, where he lived for fourteen years. In 1139 the Abbot of Hautecombe in Savoy retired and St Bernard appointed Bd. Amadeus in his place at the monks' request; the monastery had adopted the reform only four years before and its temporal affairs were in a bad way. Amadeus encouraged the community to bear these extra hardships cheerfully, and by careful administration got the monastery out of its difficulties. In 1144 he accepted, by order of Pope Lucius II, the see of Lausanne, where he was at once involved in struggles with the nobles of the diocese and a vain effort to induce the Emperor Conrad to go to the help of the Pope against Pierleoni. When Amadeus III, Duke of Savoy, went on the second Crusade, Bd. Amadeus was appointed as a sort of co-regent with his son Humbert; in the same year the Pope, Bd. Eugene III, spent twelve days with the bishop at Lausanne. Four years before his death Bd. Amadeus was made chancellor of the kingdom of Burgundy by Frederick Barbarossa. Nicholas, the secretary of St Bernard, speaks highly of the virtues of this active bishop, and his age-long *cultus* was approved by Pope Pius X in 1910. A number of sermons of Bd. Amadeus are still extant.

There seems to be no early life of Amadeus, but an account of him has been compiled from various sources in such works as the *Gallia Christiana*, vol. xv, pp. 346–348, and Manrique, *Annales Cisterciensium* under the year 1158. A more modern survey of his career will be found in the *Cistercienser-Chronik*, vol. xi (1891), pp. 50 *seq.* and vol. xxiii (1911), pp. 297 *seq.* There is also a memoir incorporated in an article by Baron de Braux in the *Bulletin Mensuel* of the Archæological Society of Lorraine, 2 ser., vol. xiv (1914), pp. 30–41.

BD. ANGELO OF FOLIGNO, Conf.

A.D. 1312

This Angelo must not be confounded with Bd. Angela of the same place. He was born at Foligno in 1226, the son of Bernard, Count of Torre and Vignole, and at the age of twenty became an Augustinian friar at Botriolo, near Cesena. In 1248 he was sent to his native town to found a house of the order there; ten years later, with Bd. Ugolino Mevainati, he established another in an abandoned Benedictine house at Gualdo Cattaneo in Umbria; and in 1275 another at Montefalco, where he remained as prior till 1292. The last twenty years of his long and arduous life were spent in holy retirement at Foligno, where he died on August 27, 1312. Bd. Angelo had as novice-master Bd. John Buono, the converted clown, and was bound in friendship to St Nicholas of Tolentino; he was himself venerated as a saint immediately after his death, and his *cultus* was approved by the Holy See in 1891.

A short biographical notice with indication of authorities will be found in the *Dictionnaire d'Histoire ecclésiastique*, vol. iii, c. 21. See also Seeböck, *Herrlichkeit der Katholischen Kirche*, p. 308; and Torelli, *Ristretto delle Vite*, etc.

ST MARGARET THE BAREFOOTED, Widow

A.D. 1395

Was born of a poor family in the March of Ancona in the middle of the fourteenth century, and was married at the age of fifteen to a husband who ill-treated her. He was particularly annoyed at the nickname which the people gave her because she went about without shoes, making herself like one of those beggars whom she delighted to help. St Margaret bore this patiently for years until the man died, and she was free to pass the rest of her life unmolested in prayer and alms-deeds. Her body is entombed in the church of St Dominic at Sanseverino, and she is named in the Roman Martyrology on this day. On the day before is commemorated in some martyrologies Bd. Margaret of Faenza, abbess of the Vallumbrosan convent of St John the Baptist at San Salvio, near Florence; she had a number of supernatural experiences, and died in 1330.

A brief, but, in view of the lack of reliable materials, a fairly exhaustive account of this saint is given in the *Acta Sanctorum* in the second volume for August under August 5. A fragment will there be found of a Life by a contemporary, Pompilio Caccialupo, but the editors were unable to obtain a copy of the complete text.

BD. GABRIEL MARY, Conf.

A.D. 1532

Gilbert Nicolas was born at Riom, near Clermont, in 1463 and at the age of sixteen sought admission among the Friars Minor at

Amboise; he was refused, because he looked a boy of very delicate health, but undeterred by the rebuff he journeyed on across Touraine and Poitou until he came to a friary near Rochelle, where he again presented himself, without hiding that he had been refused at Amboise. The father guardian liked his pluck and accepted him. His novice master " had rather to use a bridle to restrain him from excess than a goad to urge him on," and Friar Gilbert proved an exemplary Franciscan, " no more kind or charitable man could be found." He became a very proficient philosopher and theologian, was made guardian of the friary that had turned him away at Amboise, and filled various other offices among the Friars Minor of France. In 1517 he attended the general chapter of his order at Rome, where he was elected commissary general for the Observants of France, Spain, and the neighbouring territories on this side of the Alps, an office which he held till the end of his life. Long previously, before 1500, Friar Gilbert had been appointed confessor to St Joan of Valois who, after King Louis XII had obtained a declaration that his marriage with her was null, had retired to Bourges and devoted herself to founding the Order of the Annunciation (*Annonciades*). She was assisted in this by her confessor, who obtained the approbation of her rule by Pope Alexander VI in 1502. He was named visitor general of the order, which he directed for thirty years, and the Pope, struck by his love for the mystery of the Annunciation gave him the name of Gabriel Mary by which he has since been called. He revised the constitutions of the order for the confirmation of Pope Leo X, who put it under the jurisdiction of the Friars Minor, and he founded six convents of these nuns in France and the Netherlands. Throughout his life Bd. Gabriel Mary was distinguished by his devotion to our Lady, of whom he frequently preached and was never tired of speaking; he died with her *Magnificat* on his lips in the *Annonciade* convent of Rodez on August 27, 1532.

This feast does not seem to be kept liturgically by the Franciscans; and the Bollandists, when registering the name of " Gabriel ab Ave Maria " among the *prætermissi* on August 27, do not seem to have been aware in 1743 that his *cultus* was said to have been approved. A somewhat lengthy account of this servant of God is, however, to be found in Léon, *Auréole Séraphique* (Eng. trans.), vol. iii, pp. 74–87, and other memoirs by H. Nicquets, S.J., and Bishop d'Attichy are there referred to.

BD. DAVID LEWIS, Mart.

A.D. 1679

David Lewis (*alias* Charles Baker) was a Monmouthshire man, son of Morgan Lewis, a Protestant member of a recusant family, and Margaret Prichard, a Catholic. All their nine children were brought up Catholics except, curiously enough, the future martyr. He was born in 1616 and lived at Abergavenny, where he was educated at the Royal Grammar School (Father Augustine Baker, Bd. Philip Powell, and others had preceded him there); at the age of sixteen he was entered at the Middle Temple, but after three years in London went abroad as tutor to the son of Count Savage, and it is probable that he was reconciled to the Church while staying in Paris. He returned home to Abergavenny for a couple of years, during which his father was received into the Church, and in 1638 entered the *Venerabile* at Rome, with the assistance of Father Charles Browne, S.J. He was ordained priest in 1642 and two years later became a Jesuit novice; in 1646 he was simply professed and sent on the mission, but such was the impression he had left behind him that he was almost at once recalled to Sant' Andrea and made spiritual director of the English College. In 1648 the Jesuit general again sent him to Wales and he was stationed at the Cwm, an obscure hamlet on the Hereford-Monmouth border; here in a large farm-house was the College of St Francis Xavier, which from 1625 to 1678 was the Jesuit centre in the west of England and the shelter and refuge of hunted priests for miles around. When Father Lewis arrived about twenty Jesuits had their headquarters there. For the next thirty-one years he worked in this borderland, which was full of recusants: " a zealous seeker after the lost sheep, fearless in dangers, patient in labours and sufferings, and so charitable to his indigent neighbours as to be commonly called the father of the poor." Severity in applying the penal laws had by 1678 reduced the Fathers at the Cwm to seven, of whom Father Lewis was superior, and in that year Titus Oates discovered his " popish plot." When the anti-Catholic panic reached Monmouthshire the Jesuits got ready to leave the Cwm and cover up their tracks, and they did so only just in time. The Cwm was sacked by the sheriff's men, who found pictures of saints, " also crucifixes and bottles of oyle, reliques, an incense-pot, a mass-bell, surplices and other habits, boxes of white wafers, stamps with Jesuitical devices," and a number of books which are still in the cathedral library at Hereford. Father Lewis was by then safely in hiding; but there was a woman, Dorothy James, wife of a servant of Father Lewis, and now apostates both, who had tried to get some money from him on false pretences, and she was going about the streets of Caerleon saying that " she would wash her hands in Mr. Lewis's blood, and would have his head to make porridge of, as a sheep's head." James found out his refuge, denounced him, and he was taken by six dragoons early on Sunday morning, November 17, just as he was going to say Mass. John Arnold of Llanfihangel Crucorney and two other magistrates conveyed him into Abergavenny, where the recorder was wakened from his Sunday afterdinner nap, and in a room of the " Golden Lion " inn David Lewis was committed to Monmouth jail. Here he remained till the following January 13 ; " I was kept close prisoner, locked up at night and barred up by day, though indeed friends by day had access unto me, with an underkeeper's leave. " Then he was removed to Usk, " and it snowing hard on the way, we alighted at Raglan to warm and refresh ourselves. While I was there a messenger comes to the door and desires to speak to me. His business was that a very good friend of mine, one Mr. Ignatius, *alias* Walter Price [S.J.], lay dying about half a mile off thence." Being able to do no more, Father Lewis " sent him his best wishes for his soul's passage out of this turbulent world into an eternity of rest, and so went forward with his keepers to his new prison of Usk."

He was tried at the March assizes before Sir Robert Atkins, and was condemned for his priesthood, chiefly on the evidence of James and his wife ; though, on the prisoner's strong protest, the judge exonerated him from " a foul aspersion " being circulated in a pamphlet, it is said by Dr. Croft, Bishop of Hereford. The words of the sentence, as used in all such cases, have a grim interest : " David Lewis, thou shalt be led from this place to the place from whence thou camest, and shalt be put upon a hurdle and drawn with thy heels forward to the place of execution, where thou shalt be hanged by the neck and be cut down alive, thy body to be ripped open and thy bowels plucked out ; thou shalt be dismembered and thy members burnt before thy face, thy head to be divided from thy body, thy four quarters to be separated, and to be disposed of at his Majesty's will. So the Lord have mercy on thy soul ! " And so it was done. But not before this old man, together with Bd. John Kemble who was much older, had been made to ride up to London to be examined by the Privy Council touching the plot, about which they could tell them nothing because there was nothing to tell. On August 27, 1679, at some spot on or near the site of the present Catholic church at Usk, the gallows was set up by a bungling amateur (he was a convict, who thus earned his freedom), the official executioner having decamped, with his assistants. After a ringing speech from Bd. David the crowd threatened to stone the proxy hangman, who ran away, and a blacksmith was bribed to take his place—but no one would employ him after at his own trade. The body of Bd. David Lewis was buried in the neighbouring churchyard, and within a short time a handkerchief dipped in his blood had been the occasion of the cure of an epileptic child and of other miracles.

In the case of this blessed martyr we are fortunate in possessing his own account of his arrest, imprisonment, and trial; a summary of the proceedings in court, and also a copy of the speech (written out in prison beforehand) which he delivered to the assembled crowd at the time of his execution. All these have been utilised in the admirable sketch contributed to *St. Peter's Magazine* in 1923 by Mr. J. H. Canning under the general title of " The Titus Oates Plot in S. Wales and the Marches." See also Foley, *Records of the English Province, S.J.*, vol. v, pp. 912 *seq.*, and Challoner's *Memoirs of Missionary Priests* (ed. Pollen), pp. 557–561.

AUGUST 28

ST AUGUSTINE, Bishop of Hippo, Doctor of the Church
A.D. 430

SO great is the veneration which popes, councils, and the whole Church have paid to the memory of this glorious saint through every succeeding age since his time that Pope Leo X ordered that his feast should be observed with the same honours as that of an Apostle, and he is recognized as a model of true penitents, a triumphant champion of the Faith, the equal of any philosopher, and the first of theologians, supreme Doctor of Grace. He was born on 13th November, in the year 354, at Tagaste, a small town of Numidia in north Africa, not far from Hippo, but at some distance from the sea, which he had never seen till he was grown up. His parents were of good position, but not rich; his father, Patricius, was an idolater, and of a violent disposition; but by the example and prudent conduct of St Monica, his wife, he at length learned the humility and meekness of the Christian religion, and was baptized a little before his death in 371. She bore him several children; St Augustine speaks of his brother Navigius, who left a family behind him, and of a sister who died an abbess. At the wish of his mother and with the consent of his father he was entered in his infancy among the catechumens, Baptism itself being deferred, according to a common custom of the time; but in early youth he fell into grave sin and until the age of thirty-two led a life morally defiled by licence and intellectually by Manichæism. Of this time, up to his conversion and the death of St Monica, he speaks at large in his *Confessions*, a book written for "a people curious to know the lives of others, but careless to amend their own"; written not indeed to satisfy such curiosity, but to show forth to his fellows the mercy of God and His ways as exemplified in the life of one sinner, and to endeavour that no one should think of him above that which he confessed himself to be. He therefore divulged all the sins of his youth in the nine first books and, in the tenth, published the many imperfections to which he was still subject, humbly begging the intercession of all Christians on his behalf. Sending this book to Count Darius, he tells him that, "The caresses of this world are more dangerous than its persecutions. See what I am from this book: believe me who bear testimony of myself, and regard not what others say of me. Praise with me the goodness of God for the great mercy He hath shown in me, and pray for me that He will be pleased to finish what He hath begun in me, and that He never suffer me to destroy myself." By the care of his mother he was instructed in the Christian religion, and taught to pray. He was made a catechumen, by being marked with the sign of the cross and blessed salt being put in his mouth; and whilst still a child, falling dangerously ill, he desired Baptism and his mother got everything ready for it; but he suddenly grew better, and it was put off. This custom of deferring Baptism for fear of sinning under the obligations of that sacrament, St Augustine very properly condemns; but the want of a sense of its sanctity and the sacrileges of Christians in defiling it, by relapsing into sin, is an abuse which no less calls for our tears. The Church has long since forbidden the baptism of infants ever to be deferred: but it is one of the principal duties of pastors to instruct the faithful in the obligations which the sacrament lays them under, and to teach them to value and to preserve the grace which they received by it.

"And so I was put to school to learn those things in which, poor boy, I knew no profit, and yet if I was negligent in learning I was whipped: for this method was approved of by my elders, and many that had trod that life before us had chalked out unto us these wearisome ways. . . ." Augustine thanks God that, though the persons who pressed him to learn had no other end in view than "penurious riches" and "ignominious glory," yet divine Providence made a good use of their error, and forced him to learn for his great profit and manifold advantage. He accuses himself of often studying only by constraint, disobeying his parents and masters, not writing, reading, or minding his lessons so much as was required of him; and this he did, not for want of wit or memory, but out of love of play. But he prayed to God with great earnestness that he might escape punishment at school, for which dread he was laughed at by his masters and parents. Nevertheless, "we were punished for play by them that were doing no better; but the boys' play of them that are grown up is named *business*. . . . Who is he that, weighing things well, will justify my being beaten when I was a boy for playing at ball, because by that play I was hindered from learning so quickly those arts with which, when grown up, I should play far worse?"
"No one does well what he does against his will," he says, and takes notice that the master who corrected him for a small fault "if overcome in some petty dispute by a fellow-teacher, was more envious

and angry than the boy ever was when outdone by a playfellow at ball." He liked Latin very well, having learned that language from his nurses, and others with whom he conversed; but not the Latin "which the first masters teach; rather that which is taught by those who are called grammarians." Whilst he was little he hated Greek, and, for want of understanding it sufficiently, Homer was disagreeable to him; but the Latin poets became his early delight.

Augustine went to school first in his own town; then at Madaura, a neighbouring city, where he studied grammar, poetry, and rhetoric. When he was sixteen years old his father made him return to Tagaste, and kept him a whole year at home. During this time the young man fell into bad company, and gave himself up to games and diversions. His passions grew unruly and were indulged, but his father took no care of his growing up in virtue, provided he was eloquent. His mother indeed implored him to keep himself free from vice; "which," says he, "seemed to me but the admonitions of a woman, which I was ashamed to obey; whereas they were Thy admonitions, O God, and I knew it not. By her Thou didst speak to me, and I despised Thee in her."

He went to Carthage towards the end of the year 370, in the beginning of his seventeenth year. There he took the foremost place in the school of rhetoric and applied himself to his studies with eagerness and pleasure; but his motives were vanity and ambition, and to them he joined loose living, though Vincent the Rogatist, his enemy, acknowledges that he always loved decency and good manners even in his irregularities. Soon he entered into relations with a woman, irregular but stable, to whom he remained faithful until he sent her from him at Milan in 385; she bore him a son, Adeodatus, in 372. His father, Patricius, died in 371; but Augustine still continued at Carthage and, by reading the *Hortensius* of Cicero, his mind was turned from rhetoric to philosophy. He at length grew weary of the books of the heathen philosophers because Christ was not mentioned in them, whose name he had sucked in, as it were, with his mother's milk, and retained in his heart. He undertook therefore to read the Holy Scriptures; but he was offended with the simplicity of the style, and could not relish their humility or penetrate their spirit. Then it was that he fell into the error of the Manichees, that infirmity of noble mind troubled by the "problem of evil," which seeks to solve the problem by teaching a metaphysical and religious dualism, according to which there are two eternal first principles, God, the cause of all good, and matter, the cause of all evil. The darkening of the understanding and clumsiness in the use of the faculties which wait on evil-living helped to betray him into this company, which he kept till his twenty-eighth year; and pride did the rest. "I sought with pride," he says, "what only humility could make me find. Fool that I was, I left the nest, imagining myself able to fly; and I fell to the ground." His vanity was flattered by the Manichees, who claimed to try everything by the test of bare reason, and scoffed at all those who paid deference to the authority of the Catholic Church, as if they shackled reason and walked in bonds. It was by this familiar trick that he was seduced and caught in the nets of the Manichees, who promised to show him everything by demonstration, and calling faith weakness, credulity, and ignorance. "They said that, setting aside imperious authority, they would lead men to God and free them from all error by reason alone." Writing afterwards to a friend, he said, "You know, my dear Honoratus, that upon no other ground we adhered to these men. What else made me, rejecting for almost nine years together the religion which was instilled into me in my childhood, a follower and diligent hearer of these men, but their saying that we are overawed by superstition, and that faith is imposed on us without reason being given: whereas they tie none to believe, except upon the truth being first examined and cleared up? Who would not have been inveigled by such promises? Especially a young man desirous of truth and, by reputation among learned men in the schools, already proud and talkative. They derided the simplicity of the Catholic faith, which commanded men to believe before they were taught by evident reason what was truth." St Augustine frequently teaches, in his other works, that this is the general method of false teachers and a usual cause of wreck of faith.

For nine years Augustine had his own schools of rhetoric and grammar at Tagaste and Carthage, while his devoted mother, spurred on by the assurance of a holy bishop that "the son of so many tears could not perish," never ceased by prayer and gentle persuasion to try to bring him to conversion and reform. After meeting the leading Manichæan teacher, Faustus, he began to be disillusioned about that sect, and in 383 departed to Rome, secretly, lest his mother should prevent him. After a serious illness he opened a school of rhetoric there, but finding the scholars were accustomed frequently to change their masters in order to cheat them of their salary for teaching, he grew weary of the place; and it happening that orders were sent from Milan to Symmachus, prefect of Rome, requiring him to send thither some able master of rhetoric, Augustine applied for the post; and, having given Symmachus proofs of his capacity, was chosen by him and sent. At Milan he was well received and the bishop, St Ambrose, gave him marks of his respect. Augustine was very desirous of knowing him, not as a teacher of the truth, but as a person of great learning and reputation. He often went to his sermons, not so much with any expectation of profiting by them as to gratify his curiosity and to enjoy the eloquence; but he found the discourses more learned than those of the heretic Faustus and they began to make impression on his heart and mind; at the same time he read Plato and Plotinus: " Plato gave me knowledge of the true God, Jesus Christ showed me the way." St Monica, having followed him to Milan, wished to see him married, and the mother of Adeodatus returned to Africa, leaving the boy behind; but neither marriage nor single continence followed. And so the struggle, spiritual, moral, intellectual, went on. He found the writings of the Platonic philosophers bred pride in his soul, making him have a mind to seem wise and leaving him full of his punishment, instead of teaching him to bewail his own misery. Finding nothing in them about the mystery of man's redemption or Christ's incarnation, he with great eagerness betook himself to read the New Testament, especially the writings of St Paul, in which he then began to take great delight. Here he found the testimonies of the Old Testament illustrated, the glory of Heaven displayed, and the way clearly pointed out which leads thither; here he learned that which he had long felt, that he had a law in his members warring against the law in his mind, and that nothing could deliver him from this body of death but the grace of Jesus Christ. He perceived an infinite difference between the doctrine of him who styled himself the last of the apostles, and that of those proud philosophers who esteemed themselves the greatest of men. Augustine himself was now convinced of the truth and excellence of that virtue which the divine law prescribes in the Catholic Church, but was haunted with an apprehension of insuperable difficulties in its practice, that kept him from resolutely entering upon it. And so, by listening to St Ambrose and reading the Bible he was convinced of the truth of Christianity, but there was still wanting the will to accept the grace of God. He says of himself: " I sighed and longed to be delivered, but was kept fast bound, not with exterior chains but with my own iron will. The Enemy held my will, and of it he had made a chain with which he had fettered me fast; for from a perverse will was created wicked desire or lust, and the serving this lust produced custom, and custom not resisted produced a kind of necessity, with which as with links fastened one to another, I was kept close shackled in this cruel slavery. I had no excuse as I pretended formerly when I delayed to serve Thee, because I had not yet certainly discovered Thy truth: now I knew it, yet I was still fettered. . . . I had nothing now to reply to Thee when Thou saidst to me, 'Rise, thou that sleepest, and rise up from the dead, and Christ shall enlighten thee.' . . . I had nothing, I say, at all to reply, being now convinced by Thy faith, except lazy and drowsy words, 'Presently, by and by, let me alone a little while longer'; but this 'presently' did not presently come; these delays had no bounds, and this 'little while' stretched out to a long time." He had been greatly impressed by hearing the conversion of the Roman neo-Platonist professor, Victorinus, related by St Simplician, and soon after Pontitian, an African who had employment in the Emperor's court, came one day to pay a visit to Augustine and his friend Alipius. Finding a book of St Paul's epistles lying on the table, he took occasion to speak of the life of St Antony, and was surprised to find that his name was unknown to them. They were astonished to hear of miracles so well attested done so lately in the Catholic Church, and did not know before Pontitian mentioned it that there was a monastery full of fervent religious outside the walls of the very city in which they lived, under the care of St Ambrose. Pontitian then went on to speak of two gentlemen who had been suddenly turned to the service of God by reading a life of St Antony. His words had a powerful influence on the mind of Augustine, and he saw, as it were in a glass, his own filthiness and deformity. In his former half desires of conversion he had been accustomed to beg of God the grace of continence, but was at the same time in some measure afraid of being heard too soon. "In the first dawning of my youth," says he, "I had begged of Thee chastity, but by halves, miserable wretch that I am; and I said, 'Give me chastity, but not yet awhile'; for I was afraid lest Thou shouldst hear me too soon, and heal me of the disease which I rather wished to have satisfied than extinguished." He was ashamed and grieved to find his will had been so weak, and directly Pontitian had gone he turned to Alipius with these words: "What are we doing to let the unlearned start up and seize Heaven by force, whilst we with all our knowledge remain behind, cowardly and heartless, wallowing in our sins? Because they have outstripped us and gone on before, are we ashamed to follow them? Is it not more shameful not even to follow them?" He got up and went into the garden. Alipius, astonished at his manner and emotion, followed, and they sat down as far as they could from the house, Augustine undergoing a violent inward conflict. He was torn between the voice of the Holy Ghost calling him to chastity and the seductive memory of his former sins, and going alone further into the garden he threw himself to the ground below a fig-tree, crying out, "How long, O Lord? Wilt Thou be angry for ever?

Remember not my past iniquities!" And seeing himself still held back, he reproached himself, miserably: "How long? How long? To-morrow, to-morrow? Why not now? Why does not this hour put an end to my filthiness?" As he spoke these things and wept with bitter contrition of heart, on a sudden he heard as it were the voice of a child singing from a neighbouring house, which frequently repeated these words, *Tolle lege! Tolle lege!* "Take up and read! Take up and read!" And he began to consider whether in any game children were wont to sing any such words; and he could not call to mind that he had ever heard them. Whereupon he rose up, suppressing his tears, and interpreted the voice to be a divine admonition, remembering that St Antony was converted from the world by hearing a particular passage of the gospel read. He returned to where Alipius was sitting with the book of St Paul's epistles, opened it, and read in silence the words on which he first cast his eyes: "Not in rioting and drunkenness; not in chambering and impurities; not in contention and envy; but put ye on the Lord Jesus Christ, and make not provision for the flesh in its concupiscences." All the darkness of his former hesitation was gone. He shut the book, and with a serene countenance told Alipius what had passed. Alipius asked to see the passage he had read, and found the next words to be: "Him that is weak in faith, take unto you"; which he applied to himself, and joined his friend in his resolution. They immediately went in, and told their good news to St Monica, who rejoiced and praised God, "who is able to do all things more abundantly than we desire or understand." This was in September 386, and Augustine was thirty-two.

He at once gave up his school and retired to a country house at Cassiciacum, near Milan, which his friend Verecundus lent to him; he was accompanied by his mother St Monica, his brother Navigius, his son Adeodatus, St Alipius, two cousins, and several other friends, and they lived a community life together under the direction of St Monica. Augustine wholly employed himself in prayer and study, and his study was a kind of prayer by the devotion of his mind therein. Here he sought by austere penance, by the strictest watchfulness over his heart and senses, and by humble prayer, to control his passions, and to prepare himself for the grace of leading a new life in Christ and becoming in Him a new creature. "Too late," he prayed, "have I loved thee, O Beauty so ancient and so new, too late have I loved thee! Thou wast with me, and I was not with thee; I was abroad, running after those beauties which thou hast made; those things which could have no being but in thee kept me far from thee. Thou hast called, thou hast cried out, and hast pierced my deafness. Thou hast enlightened, thou hast shone forth, and my blindness is dispelled. I have tasted thee, and am hungry for thee. Thou hast touched me, and I am afire with the desire of thy embraces." From the conferences and conversations which took place during these seven months St Augustine drew up his three dialogues, *Against the Academicians, Of the Happy Life,* and *Of Order*. Among the bad habits he had contracted was that of swearing. Later, urging others to refrain from it, he set before them how he had overcome that habit. " We also were formerly given to that low and vicious custom : we once swore ; but from the time that we began to serve God, and understood the evil of that sin, we were seized with great fear, and by fear we restrained it. You say you do it by habit ; but above all things watch over yourselves that you may never swear. A more inveterate habit requires the greater attention. The tongue is a slippery member, and is easily moved. Be then the more watchful to curb it. If you refrain to-day, you will find it more easy to refrain to-morrow. I speak from experience. If your victory be not complete to-morrow, it will at least be more easy by the victory of the day before. The mischief dies in three days. And we shall rejoice in our advantage and in our deliverance from such an evil." In another sermon he says, " I know it is difficult to break your habit ; it is what I found myself ; but by fearing God we broke our custom of swearing. When I read His law I was struck with fear ; I strove against my habit, I invoked God my helper, and He helped me. Now nothing is more easy to me than not to swear." During the early days of his conversion, God as he tells us, " by His grace brought down the pride of his spirit, and laid low the lofty mountains of his vain thoughts, by bringing him daily to a greater sense of that misery and bondage from which he was delivered."

He was baptized by St Ambrose on Easter-eve in 387, together with Alipius and his dearly loved son Adeodatus, who was about fifteen years of age and was to die not long afterwards. He was still at Milan when the relics of SS. Gervase and Protase were discovered, and was witness to certain miracles that were wrought on persons touching them, but in the autumn he resolved to return to Africa. Accordingly he went on to Ostia with his mother and several friends, and there St Monica died in November 387. To her life and last days Augustine devotes six moving chapters of his *Confessions*. He returned for a short while to Rome, refuting Manichæism there, and went on to Africa in September 388, where he hastened with his friends to his house at Tagaste. There he lived almost three years, disengaged from all temporal concerns, serving God in fasting, prayer, good works, meditating upon His law and instructing others by his discourses and books. All things were in common and were distributed according to everyone's needs; St Augustine himself reserved nothing which he could call his own, having alienated the very house in which they lived. He had no idea of becoming a priest, but had good reason to fear that attempts would be made to make him a bishop. He therefore carefully avoided going to any cities in which the sees were vacant, for fear of being chosen; but in 391, having occasion to go to Hippo, there being then a bishop there, he went thither. Valerius, bishop of the city, had mentioned to his people the necessity of ordaining a priest for the service of his church, and so, when St Augustine came into the church, they presented him to Valerius, desiring with great earnestness that he might be forthwith ordained priest. St Augustine burst into tears, considering the great dangers that threatened him in that charge, but was obliged in the end to acquiesce, and was ordained. By this time he was a new man, even more conspicuous for his piety than for his great learning, and he now employed his friends to beg of Valerius some respite, in order to prepare himself in solitude for the exercise of his office. He made the same request himself, by a letter which tacitly condemns the presumption of those who without a holy fear and true vocation intrude themselves into the ministry. Valerius seems to have granted him this respite till the following Easter, for his first sermons coincide with that time. Augustine removed to Hippo and in a house adjoining the church established a sort of monastery, modelled on his household at Tagaste, living there with St Alipius, St Evodius, St Possidius, and others " according to the rule of the holy Apostles." Valerius, who was a Greek, and had, moreover, an impediment in speaking, appointed him to preach to the people in his own presence, as was customary for bishops to do in the East, but till that time was unusual in the West; more unusual still, he was given permission to preach " on his own "; knowing that the instruction of the flock was a principal duty of the pastoral charge, he from that time never interrupted the course of his sermons till his death. We have nearly four hundred extant, though many were not written by him but taken down by others as he delivered them. During these early days he vigorously opposed the Manichæans and the beginnings of Donatism, as well as effected such domestic reforms as the abolition of feasting in the chapels of the martyrs (a debased survival of the primitive love-feast) and of family fights as a public amusement : " I used appeal and persuasion to the utmost of my ability to extirpate such a cruel custom from their minds and manners. I thought I had done nothing while I only heard their acclamations and raised their delight and admiration. They were not persuaded so long as they could amuse themselves with giving applause to the discourse which they heard. But their tears gave me some hope, and showed that their minds were changed. When I saw them weep, I believed this horrible custom would be abolished. It is now eight years ago and upwards and, by the grace of God, they have been restrained from attempting any such practice." In the sermons which fill the fifth volume of his works this father inculcates assiduous meditation on the last things; for "if the Lord's day (or last judgement) may be at some distance, is your day (or death) far off?" He enforces the necessity of doing penance; "For sin must be punished either by the penitent sinner or by God, his judge; and God, who has promised pardon to the penitent sinner, has nowhere promised him who delays his conversion a to-morrow to do penance in." He frequently speaks of almsdeeds, and claims that the neglect of them is the cause of the loss of the greatest number that perish, seeing Christ mentions only this crime in the sentence both of the elect and the reprobate at the last day. He often mentions Purgatory, and recommends prayer and the Sacrifice for the repose of the faithful departed. He speaks of holy images and of the respect due to the sign of the cross. He relates miracles wrought by it, and by the relics of martyrs. He often speaks of the honour due to the martyrs, as in most of his sixty-nine sermons *On the Saints*, but he remarks that we build altars and offer sacrifice to God alone, not to any martyrs. He addresses himself to St Cyprian and others to implore their intercession. "All the martyrs," he says, "that are with Christ intercede for us. Their prayers never cease, so long as we continue our sighs." St Augustine preached always in Latin, though among the peasants of the country in certain parts of his diocese some understood only the Punic tongue, and these he found it difficult to furnish with priests.

In 395 he was consecrated bishop as coadjutor to Valerius, and succeeded him in the see of Hippo on his death soon after. He established regular and common life in his episcopal residence, and required all the priests, deacons, and subdeacons that lived with him to renounce property and to embrace the rule he established there; nor did he admit any to holy orders who did not bind themselves to the same manner of life. His biographer, St Possidius, tells us that the clothes and furniture were modest but decent, and not slovenly. No silver was used in his house, except spoons; dishes were of earthenware, wood, or stone. He exercised hospitality, but his table was frugal; nor was wine wanting, but the quantity was regulated, which no guest was ever allowed to exceed. At meals he preferred reading or literary conferences to secular conversation. All his clerks who lived with him ate at the same table and were clothed out of the common stock. Thus, in the words of Pope Paschal II, " The regular mode of life recognized in the early Church as instituted by the Apostles was earnestly adopted by the blessed Augustine, who provided it with new regulations." He also founded a community of religious women among whom, on the death of his sister, the first abbess, there was a dispute about the succession ; in dealing with this he addressed to them a letter on the general ascetic principles of the religious life. This letter, together with two sermons on the subject, constitutes the so-called rule of St Augustine, which is the basis of the constitutions of many canons regular, friars, and nuns. St Augustine committed to overseers among his clergy the entire care of his temporalities, and took their accounts at the end of the year, and he entrusted to the management of others the building of the hospitals and churches which he erected. He never would receive for the poor any estate or present when the donation seemed a prejudice to an heir. He employed the revenues of his church in relieving the poor, as he had before given his own patrimony, and Possidius says that he sometimes melted down part of the sacred vessels to redeem captives : in which he was authorized by the example of St Ambrose. In several of his letters and sermons mention is made of the custom he had got his flock to establish, of clothing all the poor of each parish once a year, and he was not afraid sometimes to contract considerable debts to help the distressed. Nor did his zeal and charity for the spiritual welfare of others have bounds. " I do not wish to be saved without you," said he to his people, like another Moses or St Paul. " What shall I desire ? What shall I say ? Why am I a bishop ? Why am I in the world ? Only to live in Jesus Christ : but to live in Him with you. This is my passion, my honour, my glory, my joy, and my riches."

There were few men endowed by nature with a more affectionate and friendly soul than St Augustine ; but his tender and benevolent disposition was heightened by the supernatural motive and powerful influence of charity and religion, of which his letters and the history of his life furnish many examples. He conversed freely with infidels, and often invited them to his table ; but generally refused to eat with Christians whose conduct was publicly scandalous and disorderly, and was severe in subjecting them to canonical penance and to the censures of the Church. He never lacked courage to oppose iniquity without respect of persons, though he never forgot the rules of charity, meekness, and good manners. He complains that some sins were by custom become so common that, though he condemned them, he dare not oppose them too violently for fear of doing much harm and no good should he attempt to extirpate them by excommunication; yet he trembled lest he should be guilty of remissness. He scarcely ever made any visits other than to orphans, widows, the sick, and other distressed persons, and he observed the three rules of St Ambrose : never to make matches for any persons, lest they should prove unhappy; never to persuade any to be soldiers; and never to dine out in his own city, lest invitations should become frequent and he should be drawn into intemperance and much loss of precious time. The letters of great men are generally interesting both for illustrating their history and throwing light on their minds. Those of St Augustine are particularly so. Several are so many excellent and learned treatises, and contain admirable instructions. In his fifty-fourth to Januarius he says that they do well who communicate daily, provided it be done worthily and with the humility of Zaccheus when he received Christ under his roof; but that they are also to be commended who sometimes imitate the humble centurion and set apart only Sundays and Saturdays or other days for communicating, in order to do it with greater devotion. He explains the duties of a wife towards her husband in his letter to Ecdicia, telling her that she ought not to wear black clothes, seeing this gave him offence, and she might be humble in mind in rich and gay dress if he should insist upon her wearing such. He tells her she ought, in all things reasonable, to agree with her husband as to the manner of educating their son, and leave to him the chief care of it. He severely chides her for having given goods and money to the poor without his tacit consent, and obliges her to ask his pardon for it, whether his unwillingness to allow her extraordinary charities proceeded from a prudent care to provide for their son, or from an imperfect motive. In like manner did he impress upon husbands the respect, tender affection, and consideration which they owe to their wives. There is a good example of St Augustine's modesty and humility in his discussion with St Jerome over the interpretation of a text of Galatians. Owing to the miscarriage of a letter Jerome, not an easily patient man, deemed himself publicly attacked. Augustine wrote to him : " I entreat you again and again to correct me confidently when you perceive me to stand in need of it ; for though the office of a bishop be greater than that of a priest, yet in many things Augustine is inferior to Jerome." He grieved at the violence with which the controversy between St Jerome and Rufinus was carried on, and wrote concerning it : " Could I meet you both together in any place I would fall down at your feet, I would weep as long as I were able, I would beseech as much as I love you, sometimes each for himself, then each one for the other, and for many others, especially the weak for whom Christ died." He always feared the deceit of vain-glory in such disputes, in which men love an opinion, as he says, " Not because it is true, but because it is their own, and they dispute, not for the truth, but for the victory."

Throughout his thirty-five years as bishop of Hippo St Augustine had to defend the Catholic faith against one heresy or another. First it was Manichæism, in which the most spectacular event was the public conference in 404 with one of their leaders, Felix. He was not so learned as Fortunatus, whom St Augustine had formerly confuted, but he had more cunning; nevertheless he closed the discussion by publicly professing the Catholic faith, and anathematizing Manes and his blasphemies. The heresy of the Priscillianists was akin to some of the Manichæan principles, and at that time infected several parts of Spain. Paul Orosius, a Spanish priest, made a voyage into Africa in 415 to see St Augustine, and gave occasion to the saint's work *Against the Priscillianists and Origenists*, in which he condemns the errors of those who taught the human soul to be of a divine nature, and sent into the body in punishment of former transgressions. The Jews he confuted by a treatise in which he shows the Mosaic law was to have an end, and to be changed into the new law. The neighbouring city of Madaura was full of idolaters. Their good will he gained by rendering them important public service and doing them good offices. Their grateful feelings towards him he improved to their advantage, and induced them to embrace the faith of Christ. When Rome was plundered by Alaric the Goth in 410 the Pagans renewed their blasphemies against the Christian religion, to which they imputed the calamities of the Empire. To answer their slanders, St Augustine began his great work *Of the City of God* in 413, though he only finished it in 426. More serious trouble was given by the Donatists, whose chief errors were that the Catholic Church by holding communion with sinners had ceased to be the Church of Christ, this being confined within the limits of their sect, and that no sacraments can be validly conferred by those that are not in the true Church. These Donatists were exceedingly numerous in Africa, and reckoned five hundred bishops. At Hippo the number of Catholics was very small, and the Donatists had such sway there that, a little before St Augustine came thither, Faustinus their bishop had forbidden any bread to be baked in that city for the use of Catholics and was obeyed, even by servants who lived in Catholic families. Indeed, the majority of Christians in Africa were at that time infected with the errors of the Donatists, and they carried their fury to the greatest excesses, murdering many Catholics and committing all sorts of violence. By the learning and indefatigable zeal of St Augustine, supported by the sanctity of his life, the Catholics began to gain ground; at which the Donatists were so exasperated that some preached publicly that to kill him would be doing the greatest service to their religion, and highly meritorious before God. Augustine was obliged in 405 to invoke the civil power to restrain the Donatists about Hippo from the outrages which they perpetrated there, and in the same year the Emperor Honorius published severe laws against them. Augustine at first disapproved such measures, though he afterwards changed his opinion, except that he would not countenance a death-penalty. A great conference between the two parties at Carthage in 411 marked the beginning of the decline of these heretics, but almost at once the Pelagian controversy began.

Pelagius is commonly called a Briton, but as St Jerome refers to him as "big and fat, a fellow bloated with Scots porridge," he has been claimed for Ireland; he rejected the doctrine of original sin and taught therefore that Baptism was simply a title of admission to Heaven and death not a result of the fall, and that grace is not necessary to salvation. In 411 he left Rome for Africa with his friend Celestius, and during the very next year their doctrines were for the first time condemned by a synod at Carthage. St Augustine was not at this council, but from that time he began to oppose these errors in his sermons and letters. Before the end of that year he was persuaded by the tribune St Marcellinus to write his first treatises against them. This, however, he did without naming the authors of the heresy, hoping thus more easily to gain them; he even praised Pelagius by name. "As I hear, he is a holy man, well exercised in Christian virtue : a good man, and worthy of praise." But he was fixed in his errors and throughout the series of disputations, condemnations, and subterfuges that followed, St Augustine pressed him relentlessly. Through the corruption of human nature by sin, pride being motive-power of our heart, men are born with a propensity to Pelagianism, of principles which flatter our own strength, merit, and self-sufficiency. It is not therefore to be wondered at that this heresy found many advocates : and the wound which Pelagius caused would certainly have been much deeper had not God raised up this Doctor of Grace to be the defence of the truth. He was a trumpet to call up the other pastors, and the soul of their deliberations, councils, and endeavours to extinguish the rising flame. To him is the Church indebted as the chief instrument of God in overthrowing this heresy. From it sprang Semi-pelagianism, against which St Augustine wrote two books, one entitled *On the Predestination of the Saints*, the other *On the gift of Perseverance*, showing that the authors of this doctrine did not really recede from the principles of Pelagius himself.

In his *Confessions* St Augustine, with the most sincere humility and contrition, lays open the errors of his conduct; in his seventy-second year he began to do the like for his judgement. In this work, his *Retractations*, he reviewed his writings, which were very numerous, and corrected with candour and severity the mistakes he had made, without seeking the least gloss or excuse to extenuate them. To have more leisure to finish this and his other writings, and to provide against a troublesome election after his death, he proposed to his clergy and people to choose for his coadjutor Heraclius, the youngest among his deacons, but a person of great virtue and prudence, and his election was confirmed with great acclamation in 426. But in spite of this precaution Augustine's last years were full of turmoil. Count Boniface, who had been the imperial general in Africa, having unjustly incurred the suspicion of the regent Placidia and being in disgrace, incited Genseric, King of the Vandals, to invade the African provinces. Augustine wrote a wonderful letter to Boniface, recalling him to his duty, and the Count sought a reconciliation with Placidia, but could not stay the Vandal invasion. St Possidius, now Bishop of Calama, describes the dreadful ravages by which they scattered horror and desolation as they marched. He saw the cities in ruin and the houses in the country razed to the ground, the inhabitants being either slain or fled. Some had perished by the sword; others had become slaves. The praises of God had ceased in the churches, which had in many places been burnt. Mass was said in private houses, or not at all, for in many parts there were none left to demand the sacraments, nor was it easy elsewhere to find any to administer to those who required them. The bishops and the rest of the clergy who had escaped were stripped of everything, and reduced to beggary; and of the great number of churches in Africa, there were hardly three remaining (namely, Carthage, Hippo, and Cirta) whose cities were yet standing. Amidst this desolation St Augustine was consulted by a bishop named Quodvultdeus, and afterwards by Honoratus, Bishop of Tabenna, whether it was lawful for bishops or other clergy to fly upon the approach of the barbarians. St Augustine's answer to Quodvultdeus is lost; but in that to Honoratus he refers to it, and affirms that it is lawful for a bishop or priest to fly and forsake the flock when he alone is aimed at by name, and the people are threatened with no danger, but left quiet; or when the people are all fled, so that the pastor has none left who have need of his ministry; or when the same ministry may be better performed by others who have no need of flight. In all other cases, he says, pastors are obliged to watch over their flock, which Christ has committed to them, nor can they forsake it without crime. He more than any mourned the miseries of his country, when he considered not only the outward calamities of the people, but also the ruin of a multitude of souls that was likely to ensue, for the invading Vandals were Arians as well as barbarians. Count Boniface fled to Hippo, which was the strongest fortress in Africa, and St Possidius and several neighbouring bishops took refuge in the same place. The Vandals appeared before it about the end of May 430, and the siege continued fourteen months. In the third month St Augustine was seized with a fever, and from the first moment of his illness knew that it was a summons of God to Himself. Ever since he retired, death had been the chief subject of his meditations; and in his last illness he spoke of it with great cheerfulness, saying, " We have a merciful God." He often spoke of the joy of St Ambrose in his last moments, and of the saying of Christ to a certain bishop in a vision mentioned by St Cyprian. " You are afraid to suffer here, and unwilling to go hence: what shall I do with you ? " " What love of Christ can that be," he wrote, " to fear lest He, whom you say you love, shall come ? Brethren, are we not ashamed to say we love, when we add that we are afraid lest He come ? " In this last illness he asked for the penitential psalms of David to be written out and hung in tablets upon the wall by his bed; and as he there lay he read them with tears. The strength of his body daily and hourly declined, yet his senses and intellectual faculties continued sound to the last, and he calmly resigned his spirit into the hands of God on August 28, 430, after having lived seventy-six years and spent almost forty of them in the labours of the ministry. St Possidius adds, " We being present, the Sacrifice was offered to God for his recommendation, and so he was buried," in the same manner as St Augustine says was done for his mother. Whilst the saint lay sick in bed, by the imposition of his hands he restored to health a sick man, and Possidius says, " I know, both when he was priest and when he was bishop, that being asked to pray for certain persons that were possessed, he poured out supplications to our Lord, and the evil spirits departed from them."

The height of the sanctity of this illustrious doctor was derived from the deep foundation of his humility, according to what he himself lays down : " Do not attempt to attain true wisdom by any other way than that which God has enjoined. This is, in the first, second, and third place, humility; and thus would I answer so often as you ask me. Not that there are not other precepts; but unless humility go before, accompany, and follow after, all that we do well is snatched out of our hands by pride. As Demosthenes, the prince of orators, is said to have replied when asked which of the rules of eloquence was to be observed first: The manner of address, in other words, the delivery. Which second? Delivery. Which third? Nothing else but Delivery. So, if you should ask me about the precepts of the Christian religion, I should answer you, Nothing but humility. Our Lord Jesus Christ was made so low in order to teach us this humility—which certain most ignorant science opposes."

It is from St Augustine's own writings, more particularly from his *Confessions*, his *De Civitate Dei*, his correspondence, and his sermons, that we obtain the fullest insight into his life and character. All these are readily accessible both in the original and in translations. The text of the Vienna *Corpus Scriptorum Ecclesiasticorum Latinorum* is generally reliable so far as it is available, but for the *Confessions* that of Pierre de Labriolle, published in 1926 with an excellent French translation, may be preferred. The best English translation of this last work, among many, is probably that of Gibb and Montgomery (1927). A convenient edition of the *De Civitate Dei* with English notes has been published by Dean Welldon (1924). Another Anglican, W. J. Sparrow Simpson, has produced a good translation of the *Letters* (1919), as well as a sympathetic study, *St. Augustine's Conversion* (1920). Some points of importance relating to the Saint's correspondence have recently been discussed by H. Lietzmann in a paper in the *Ab. handlungen* of the Prussian Academy (1930). But of all modern contributions to Augustinian literature the most outstanding is the publication, the merit of which mainly rests with Dom Germain Morin, of a revised and much enlarged collection of the Sermons. This forms the first volume of the *Miscellanea Agostiniana* (1931) brought out to commemorate the fifteenth centenary of the Saint's death. The early Life of Augustine by his disciple St Possidius has also been re-edited and translated into German by Adolf Hamack (1930). But the whole literature is too vast for detailed discussion. To quote only the titles of books produced in view of the recent centenary would fill more than a page. It must suffice here to mention *A Monument to St Augustine* (1930), a volume of essays by well-known English Catholic writers. For a general account of both life and writings, the article by Père Portalié in the *Dictionnaire de Théologie catholique*, vol. i, cc. 2208–2472, may be specially recommended; as also Bardenhewer's *Geschichte der altkirch. Literatur*, vol. iv, pp. 435–511. There are Lives of a more popular character in English by Bertrand and by Hatzfeld, and Miss Mary Allies has brought out two or three volumes of selections and translations from St Augustine's various works.

ST HERMES, Mart.

A.D. 132

On August 28 a commemoration is made in the Roman liturgy of St Hermes, said to have been " an illustrious man who, as may be read in the acts of the holy Pope Alexander I, was first imprisoned and then with many others fell by the sword, ending his martyrdom under the judge Aurelian " in the reign of Hadrian (Roman Martyrology). He was buried in the catacomb of St Basilla, which is also called after him, on the Old Salarian Way, where a large subterranean basilica of the fourth century was found over his tomb ; Pope Pelagius II (578–590) renovated and ornamented this tomb, and Pope Adrian I removed the relics into the city at the end of the eighth century. Two other martyrs of the name of Hermes are commemorated this month : one on the 24th, at Ostia with St Aurea, about the year 250 ; the other on the 25th, with St Rufina and her companions at Capua. They are duplicates of the same saint.

For the martyrdom of St Hermes at Rome and for his early *cultus* there and elsewhere, we have the fullest evidence. He is mentioned in the " Depositio Martyrum " of 354. His name occurs in the " Hieronymianum " and in the itineraries of the pilgrims. See the *Acta Sanctorum*, November, vol. ii, part 2, pp. 472–473. But upon the " Passio S. Hermetis," which forms part of the " Acta " of Pope Alexander, no reliance can be placed. See also Leclercq in the *Dictionnaire d'Archéologie*, etc., vol. vi, cc. 2303 *seq.*

ST JULIAN OF BRIOUDE, Mart.

A.D. 304

This Julian was one of the most famous martyrs of Gaul ; he is sometimes called Julian of Auvergne, and was born at Vienne in Dauphiné. He served with the tribune Ferreolus (who also became a martyr), and knew how to reconcile the profession of arms with the teaching of the Gospel. Crispin, governor of the province of Vienne, having declared himself against the Christians, Julian withdrew to Auvergne, not that he dreaded the persecution, but that he might be at hand to be of service to the faithful there ; afterwards, learning that he was sought after by the persecutors, of his own accord he presented himself before them, saying, " I have been too long in this bad world ; I would be with Jesus." He had scarce uttered these words, when they fell upon him and cut his throat. It was near Brioude ; but which of three bodies later found at the place of his burial was his, was unknown, until God revealed it to St Germanus of Auxerre, when he passed by on his return from Arles, about the year 431. A church was then built at Brioude (near Clermont-Ferrand) to shelter the relics, and it became a great place of pilgrimage. St Gregory of Tours relates a number of miracles wrought by St Julian's intercession ; he also mentions a church dedicated at Paris under the invocation of the holy martyr ; it is that which is now known as St Julian-le-Pauvre, used by the Catholic Melkites of the city.

Apollinaris Sidonius, Gregory of Tours, and the " Hieronymianum " sufficiently attest the early *cultus* of this martyr, but Gregory also lets us know that they were at first in doubt on what day he ought to be venerated. See Delehaye *Les Origines du Culte des Martyrs*, pp. 390–392. The " Passio ", printed in the *Acta Sanctorum*, August, vol. vi, and also by E. Munding (1918), is of little value, but E. C. Babut in the *Revue d'Histoire et de Littérature religieuses*, 1914, pp. 96–116, has tried to turn it to historical account.

SS. ALEXANDER, JOHN III, AND PAUL IV, CONFS.
PATRIARCHS OF CONSTANTINOPLE
A.D. 340, 577, 784

Alexander of Byzantium was already seventy-three years old when he was elected to the episcopal throne of Constantinople, and he filled the office for twenty-three years in the troubled days of the heresiarch Arius. Soon after his election the Emperor Constantine ordered a conference between the Christian theologians and a number of pagan philosophers, and the discussion was thrown into confusion by all the philosophers trying to talk at the same time. On St Alexander's suggestion they then chose the most learned among them to voice their views, and while one of them was speaking Alexander suddenly exclaimed, " In the name of Jesus Christ, I command you to be silent ! " Whereupon, it is said, the unfortunate man found his tongue was paralysed and his mouth unable to utter a word until Alexander gave him leave, and by this manifestation of divine power the Christian cause made more impression than by the most solid arguments. On account of his age St Alexander was unable to be present at the Council of Nicæa, sending to represent him a priest of his own name ; after the council, he enforced its decrees, protecting his flock against the spread of Arianism and supporting St Athanasius in his refusal to admit Arius to communion, even though threatened with deposition and banishment. In 336 Arius arrived in triumph at Constantinople, with an order from the Emperor that

St Alexander should give him communion in his cathedral. Exactly what happened is not known. Some say that St Alexander was deceived by the professions of the heretic and was going to comply with the Emperor's order ; others, that, with St James of Nisibis, he prayed earnestly to God that He would remove either himself or Arius. In either case, on the night before the day appointed for his solemn reception, Arius suddenly died. It was natural that Christians should look on this as a divine intervention at the intercession of St Alexander, and this view is expressed by the Roman Martyrology, which refers to him as, " a glorious old man, on account of whose prayers Arius, condemned by the judgement of God, brake in the middle and his bowels poured out."

The Byzantine Catholics join in one commemoration with St Alexander two other holy archbishops of Constantinople, John III and Paul IV, called " the Young." John was born near Antioch, and had been a lawyer before he was ordained. He was sent as patriarchal legate from Antioch to Constantinople, where his great learning caused him to be known as " the Scholastic " ; he had already made a collection of canons of ecclesiastical law, which recommended him to the Emperor Justinian I, and in the year 565 he was made patriarch of the imperial city. While he held that office he revised and enlarged his collection of canons, which was the first to be made systematically, adding to it a number of chapters from the fourth part (*Novellae*) of Justinian's *Corpus iuris civilis :* this work grew eventually into the compendium of Eastern Church law called the *Nomocanon* of Photius. St John the Scholastic died in 577. St Paul the Young was a native of Salamis who became patriarch of Constantinople in 780, during the last months of the Emperor Leo IV. Directly the Empress Irene became regent he advocated and practised the restoration of holy images and their veneration ; in 784 he withdrew to the monastery of Florus, avowedly as an act of penance for his compromises and lack of boldness during the Iconoclast regime. Until his death shortly afterwards he encouraged the assembling of the second council of Nicæa for the condemnation of Iconoclasm ; it eventually met in the year 787.

The not entirely concordant stories of St Athanasius and the Church historians concerning St Alexander will be found sufficiently illustrated in the *Acta Sanctorum*, August, vol. vi.

ST MOSES THE BLACK, Mart.
End of Fourth Century

This Moses was an Ethiopian and the most picturesque figure among those remarkable men who are known as the Fathers of the Desert. At first he was a servant, or slave, in the house of an Egyptian government official; the general immorality of his life, but particularly his continual thefts, caused his dismissal—in those days he was lucky to have got off with his life—and he took to brigandage. He was a man of huge stature, with corresponding strength and ferocity, and he soon gathered a gang about him that was a terror to the district. Once some contemplated villainy was spoiled by the barking of a sheep-dog giving the alarm, and Moses swore to kill the shepherd. To get at him he had to swim across the Nile with his sword in his teeth, but the shepherd had hidden himself by burrowing into the sand; Moses could not find him, so he made up for it by killing four rams, tying them together, and towing them back across the river. Then he flayed the rams, cooked and ate the best parts, sold the skins for wine, and walked fifty miles to join his fellows. That was the sort of man Moses was. Unfortunately the circumstances of his conversion are not known; it is possible that he hid himself among the solitaries to avoid the law and was touched and conquered by their example, for when next heard of he was at the monastery of Petra in the desert of Skete. Here he was attacked in his cell by four robbers. Moses fought and overpowered them, then tied them together, slung them across his back, and went to the church, where he dumped them on the floor, saying to the astonished monks, " I am not allowed to hurt anybody, so what do you want me to do with these ? " They are said to have reformed their ways and become monks themselves. But Moses did not become well-behaved in a day and, despairing of overcoming his violent passions, he consulted St Isidore. The abbot took him up to the roof of the house at dawn : " See ! " he said, " the light only gradually drives away the darkness. So it is with the soul." Eventually by hard physical labour, especially in waiting on his brethren, hard physical mortification, and persevering prayer he so conquered himself that Theophilus, Archbishop of Alexandria, heard of his virtues and ordained him priest. Afterwards as he stood in the basilica, anointed and vested in white, the archbishop said, " Now, Amba Moses, the black man is made white." St Moses smiled ruefully. " Only outside ! God knows that inwardly I am yet dark," he replied. When a raid on the monastery was threatened by some Bedu Arabs, he refused to allow his monks to defend themselves but made them run away before it was too late : " All that take the sword shall perish with the sword." He remained, and seven with him, and all save one were murdered by the infidels. St Moses was then seventy-five years old and he left seventy disciples to mourn him.

A Greek life, said to have been written by Laurence, a monk in Calabria, is printed in the *Acta Sanctorum*, August, vol. vi, with a commentary. But St Moses also figures in Palladius' *Historia Lausiaca* and in some of the early church historians.

ST RUMON or RUAN, Conf.
Sixth Century

Before the dissolution of the monasteries the Benedictine abbey of Tavistock claimed to possess the relics of St Rumon, who in the beginning of the fifteenth century was referred to by one of the monks of Glastonbury as a brother of St Tudwal, bishop of Tréguier in 552. In the twelfth century William of Malmesbury wrote of Tavistock that, " There Rumon is venerated as a saint, and lies buried as a bishop in a beautiful shrine. Want of all written evidence concerning him confirms the belief that not only in this but in many parts of England you will find all knowledge of events swept away by the violence of warfare, the names of saints left bare, miracles unrecorded." This Rumon, who gave their names to Ruan Lanihorne, Romansleigh, and other places in Devon and Cornwall, has been believed to be the St Ronan venerated in Brittany. He was an Irishman and a disciple of St Senan on Scattery Island and, whether or no he visited the west of England, he went over into Armorica and landed near Léon. Of his life and apostolate there nothing is known, but there is a story that he had to defend himself from the charge of being a werewolf and carrying off and eating a child ; this charge was made by a young woman who feared that the missionary would make her husband a monk. Ronan's humanness was demonstrated by the chief's wolf-hounds, which refused to touch him. He founded the church of Locronan, where his feast is now kept on the second Sunday in July, and died at Hillian in Lower Brittany about the year 540. There is no very convincing reason why this St Ronan should be identified with the English Rumon, especially as his relics are (or were) claimed by the cathedral of Quimper (though this does not necessarily prove anything). The Rev. G. H. Doble, who has put in so much good work on the history of the saints of Cornwall, has recently pointed out that the St Rumon place-names are found in Devon and Cornwall side by side with those of St Kea and that an arm of St Rumon was formerly venerated at Glastonbury; he has shown that St Kea was the founder of a monastery or hermitage at Street, near Glastonbury; and makes the reasonable suggestion that both Rumon and Kea were native monks of the British Glastonbury who went to make settlements in the Dumnonian peninsula. St Rumon died on August 28 in an unknown year and was buried on the 30th, on which day his feast was sometimes observed; the translation of his relics to their shrine in his abbey-church at Tavistock, finished by Earl Ordulf, was made on January 5, 981.

This saint, who is elsewhere apparently honoured on June 1, has a biography which is printed in the Bollandist catalogue of Paris hagiographical Latin manuscripts, vol. i, pp. 438-458. M. Ernest Renan, as he told the Cambrian Archæological Association in 1889, claimed him as a patron: " Vous connaissez mon patron Saint Renan sous sa vraie forme Ronan (Locronan, les eaux de Saint Renan, etc.). C'était un Irlandais, un grand original." By William of Malmesbury he is mentioned in the *Gesta Pontificum* (Rolls Series, p. 202), under the form " Rumonus." Probably the best attempt to disentangle the threads of this complicated problem is that of Canon Doble in his brochure *Four Saints of the Fal*. But see also Baring Gould and Fisher, *Lives of the British Saints*, vol. iv, pp. 120 seq.; Stanton's *Menology*, p. 427 (under August 30); Duine, *Origines Bretonnes;* Gougaud, *Gaelic Pioneers*, pp. 137-138; and A. Thomas, *Saint Ronan et la Troménie* (1893).

THE LONDON MARTYRS OF 1588

Whatever the attitude of those on the continent, English Catholics at home did not lag behind in opposition to the Great Armada of Spain or in preparation for defence against it; nationalistic patriotism as we know it to-day was not then matured, but, even though one of Philip's admitted objects was to re-establish the Faith, Catholics no more than anybody else wanted a Spanish invasion of England: the Queen persecuted them, but she was still the Queen, and had full claim on their civil allegiance. But in spite of this the defeat of the Armada at the end of July 1588 was followed at once by a more severe persecution, of which the first victims suffered in London on August 28 and 30. Six new gallows were set up in various parts of the city, and each of these received its hallowing of innocent blood. At Mile End Green was hanged BD. WILLIAM DEAN, a Yorkshire man born at Linton in Craven. He was a convert minister, who had been ordained at Rheims and already banished once on pain of

Aug. 28] THE LONDON MARTYRS OF 1588

death if he returned to the country; but come back he did, and was the first victim after the Armada. At the place of execution he began to speak to the people, " but his mouth was stopped by some that were in the cart, in such a violent manner that they were like to have prevented the hangman of his wages." With this remarkably grave and learned man died the Ven. Henry Webley, a layman who had befriended him. A short distance away, at Shoreditch, was hanged BD. WILLIAM GUNTER, a Welshman from Raglan in Monmouthshire. He also was a priest from Rheims and had been ordained only the previous year. BD. ROBERT MORTON and BD. HUGH MORE were both hanged in Lincoln's Inn Fields. Mr. Morton was born at Bawtry in Yorkshire, educated and ordained at Rheims and Rome, and sent on the mission in 1587. Mr. More was condemned for being reconciled to the Church by Father Thomas Stephenson, S.J. He was born at Grantham in 1563 and educated at Broadgates Hall, Oxford; after his conversion he studied for a time at the Rheims seminary and upon returning home resolutely refused to conform to the law of attending the Protestant church. BD. THOMAS HOLFORD (*alias* Acton and Bude) was the son of a minister of Aston in Cheshire. He became tutor in the household of Sir James Scudamore at Holme Lacy in Herefordshire, where he was converted by Mr. Davis, a very zealous priest in those parts, who wrote an account of him. From it we learn that he was ordained at Rheims (in 1583) and worked in Cheshire and London, having many narrow escapes, till he was seen coming out of the house of Bd. Swithin Wells after saying Mass there, when the pursuivant " dogged him into his tailor's house, and there apprehended him." He was hanged at Clerkenwell. BD. JAMES CLAXTON (or Clarkson) was sent on the English mission from Rheims in 1582; he was banished in 1585 but returned, and was hanged at Isleworth, together with BD. THOMAS FELTON. Bd. Thomas was a Minim friar, the son of Bd. John Felton, only twenty years old and not yet a priest, and of him there is an account from the hand of his sister, Mrs. Frances Salisbury. She tells us that he came into England to recover his health and was about to return to his monastery when he was arrested and imprisoned for two years. He was twice released and re-arrested, and in Bridewell was confined in the " little ease," put to labour at the mill, and finally tortured, in order to make him betray the names of priests. When brought up at Newgate after the Armada and asked whether he would have taken the Queen's side or that of the Pope and the Spaniards, he replied, " I would have taken part with God and my country." According to Mrs. Salisbury he was condemned for denying the Queen's supremacy: "I have read divers chronicles, but never read that God ordained a woman should be supreme head of the Church"; but other accounts say it was for being reconciled, and, as Mrs. Salisbury certainly fell away from the Faith for a time, her brother may have done so too, in spite of their martyred father.

On August 30 six more martyrs were hanged, all at Tyburn. One only was a priest, BD. RICHARD LEIGH (*alias* Garth), a Londoner, who had made his studies at Rheims and Rome, been sent to England in 1586, banished in the same year, returned almost at once, and was committed for offering to answer questions put to a Catholic gentleman on his examination by the Protestant Bishop of London. Mr. Leigh and all the priests mentioned above were condemned for their priesthood. BD. EDWARD SHELLEY, BD. RICHARD MARTIN, and the Ven. Richard Flower (*vere* Lloyd) all suffered for harbouring or relieving priests. Mr. Shelley was a gentleman of Warminghurst in Sussex, son of that Edward Shelley whose name is familiar to men-of-law from "the rule in Shelley's case"; Mr. Martin, born in Shropshire and educated at Broadgates Hall, Oxford, had had the infamy to pay sixpence for a supper for Bd. Robert Morton; Flower was from Anglesey. The other two victims at Tyburn on this day were BD. MARGARET WARD and BD. JOHN ROCHE (*alias* Neale). Bd. Margaret was a gentlewoman, born at Congleton in Cheshire, in the service of another gentlewoman, Mrs. Whitall, in London. She had visited in the Bridewell prison Mr. Richard Watson, a secular priest who under duress of torture had once attended Protestant service, publicly repudiated his act, and been re-imprisoned; to him she smuggled in a rope, but in making use of it to escape Watson had fallen and broken an arm and a leg. He was got away by a waterman and Bd. Margaret's young Irish serving-man, John Roche, who, to assist the priest's escape, changed clothes with him, and so was himself arrested. When charged, both Bd. Margaret and Bd. John refused to disclose Mr. Watson's whereabouts; they were offered their liberty if they would ask the Queen's pardon and promise to go to church: to which they replied that they had done nothing that could reasonably offend her Majesty, and that it was against their conscience to attend a Protestant church. And so they were condemned. Father Ribadeneira, S.J., wrote that all these martyrs, who suffered with such firm constancy and patience, were forbidden to speak to the people from the scaffold because their persecutors were afraid of the impression they would make; "but the very death of so many saint-like innocent men (whose lives were unimpeachable), and of several young gentlemen, which they endured with so much joy, strongly pleaded for the cause for which they died."

See Challoner, *Memoirs of Missionary Priests* (ed. Pollen), pp. 133–145; Burton and Pollen, *Lives of the English Martyrs*, second series, vol. i, pp. 351–430; and *Catholic Record Society Publications*, vol. v, *passim*, but especially pp. 150–159.

BD. EDMUND ARROWSMITH, MART.
A.D. 1628

Was born in 1585 at Haydock, near Saint Helens, the son of Robert Arrowsmith, a yeoman farmer, and his wife Margery, a Gerard of Bryn, both of Catholic families which had already suffered for the Faith. He was baptized Brian, but took the name of Edmund at Confirmation and ever after used it. The recusant Arrowsmiths were subjected to a good deal of persecution (on one occasion their house was searched for priests at night and the father and mother taken off to Lancaster jail, leaving four small children shivering in their shirts), and at last Robert and his brother Peter went abroad, and visited their other brother, Dr. Edmund Arrowsmith, who was a professor in the college at Douay. After some years Robert returned and died in England and his widow confided young Edmund to the care of an old priest who had him educated. The youth was of an unquestionably religious disposition, and he managed to make his way out of the country to Douay in December 1605. His studies there were interrupted by ill-health, and he was not ordained till 1612, and sent to Lancashire in the following year. For ten years he worked there fruitfully and without mishap, in spite of the fact that his enthusiasm for controversy made him indifferent to its dangers. "Though his presence was very mean, yet he was both zealous, witty, and fervent, and so forward in disputing with heretics that I often wished him merrily to carry salt in his pocket to season his actions, lest too much zeal without discretion might bring him too soon into danger, considering the vehement and sudden storms of persecution that often assailed us." "He was a man," says another contemporary, "of great innocency in his life, of great sincerity in his nature, of great sweetness in his conversation, and of great industry in his function. And he was ever of a cheerful countenance—a most probable sign of an upright and unspotted conscience." He had several times to exorcise the possessed, and never without effect. About 1622–3 Bd. Edmund was taken up and examined before the Protestant Bishop of Chester, but, King James being at that time interested in a Spanish match for his son, all priests in custody were ordered to be released in order to make a good impression on his Most Catholic Majesty. Dr. Bridgman, the bishop, a kindly old man, was at supper with several ministers when he was brought in, and apologised for eating meat on a Friday because of his age and infirmity. " But who has dispensed these lusty gentlemen ? " inquired Bd. Edmund. Immediately afterwards he decided to offer himself to the Jesuits, and after a retreat of several months in Essex in lieu of a novitiate abroad he was admitted to the order. Five years later he was betrayed to a magistrate by a young man whom he had reproved for his irregular life, and at Lancaster assizes in August 1628 he was indicted before Sir Henry Yelverton on charges of being a priest and a Jesuit and of persuading the King's subjects to join the Church of Rome. The charges, of course, were true, but he was convicted on grossly insufficient evidence and sentenced to death. At the express command of the judge he was heavily manacled and put into a cell so small that he could not lie down ; here he was left from two o'clock on Tuesday afternoon till midday on Thursday, apparently without food and with no one allowed to speak to him except a Protestant minister. When he was passing through the courtyard on his way to execution, there was standing at a window Bd. John Southworth, who had been (temporarily) reprieved ; Bd. Edmund lifted up his hands to him as a sign of humble contrition, and Bd. John gave him absolution before all the people, who had assembled in great numbers. Up to the last moment before he was thrown off the ladder he was pestered with offers of life and liberty if he would conform, that is apostatize. " Tempt me no more," he replied, " I will not do it, in no case, on no condition." He was allowed to die before the rest of the sentence was carried out ; his last audible words were " Bone Iesu ! "

A relic of this martyr, known as the Holy Hand, is preserved in the church of St Oswald at Ashton-in-Makerfield and is greatly venerated ; it has been and is the occasion of remarkable cures of sickness and disease and of the granting of spiritual requests. Bd. Edmund Arrowsmith was beatified in 1929.

    The fullest account of this holy martyr is probably that preserved in a booklet entitled *A Full and Exact Relation of the Death of Two Catholicks who suffered for their Religion at Lancaster in* 1628 (London, 1737). It is taken in large part from Henry More, S.J., *Historia Provinciæ Anglicanæ* (1630). See also Challoner, *Memoirs of Missionary Priests* (ed. Pollen), pp. 362-373 ; and Bede Camm, *Forgotten Shrines*, pp. 183-201.

AUGUST 29

THE BEHEADING OF ST JOHN THE BAPTIST

c. A.D. 30

JOHN THE BAPTIST, the preparation of whom for his unique office of forerunner of the Messias has already been referred to on the feast of his birthday (June 24), began to fulfil it in the desert of Judæa, upon the banks of the Jordan, towards Jericho. Clothed in skins, he announced to all men the obligation of washing away their sins with the tears of sincere penitence, and proclaimed the Messias, who was about to make his appearance among them. He was received by the people as the herald of the most high God, his voice as a trumpet sounding from Heaven to summon all men to avert the divine judgement and to prepare themselves for the mercy that was offered them. All ranks of people listened to him and amongst others came many Pharisees, whose pride and hypocrisy he sharply reproved. The very soldiers and tax-gatherers, who were generally hardened in immorality, violence, and injustice, came to him. He exhorted all to charity and to a reformation of their lives, and those who came to him in these dispositions he baptized in the river. The Jews practised religious washings of the body as legal purifications, but no baptism before this of John had so great and mystical a signification. It chiefly represented the manner in which the souls of men must be cleansed from all sin to be made partakers of Christ's spiritual kingdom, and it was an emblem of the interior effects of sincere repentance ; a type of that sacrament of Baptism which was to come with our Lord. So noteworthy was this rite in St John's ministrations that it earned for him even in his own life the name of " the Baptist," *i.e.*, the baptizer. When he had already preached and baptized for some time our Redeemer went from Nazareth and presented Himself among the others to be baptized by him. The Baptist knew Him by a divine revelation and at first excused himself, but at length acquiesced out of obedience. The Saviour of sinners was pleased to be baptized among sinners, not to be cleansed himself but to sanctify the waters, says St Ambrose, that is, to give them the virtue to cleanse away the sins of men.

The solemn admonitions of the Baptist, added to his sanctity and the marks of his divine commission, gained for him a mighty veneration and authority among the Jews, and some began to look upon him as the Messias Himself. But he openly declared that he only baptized sinners with water to confirm them in repentance and a new life : that there was One ready to appear among them who would baptize them with the Holy Ghost, and who so far exceeded him in power and excellence that he was not worthy to untie His shoes. Nevertheless, so strong was the impression which the preaching and behaviour of John made upon the minds of the Jews that they sent priests and levites from Jerusalem to inquire of him if he was not the Christ. And St John " confessed, and did not deny ; and he confessed, I am not the Christ," neither Elias, nor a prophet. He was indeed Elias in spirit, being the great herald of the Son of God, and excelled in dignity the ancient Elias, who was a type of John. He was likewise a prophet, and more than a prophet, it being his office, not to foretell Christ at a distance, but to point Him out present among men. So, because he was not Elias in person, nor a prophet in the strict sense of the word, he answers " no " to these questions and calls himself " the voice of one crying in the wilderness " ; he will not have men have the least regard for him, but turns their attention to the summons which God has sent them by his mouth. The Baptist proclaimed Jesus to be the Messias at His baptism ; and the day after the Jews consulted him from Jerusalem, seeing Him come towards him, he called Him, " the Lamb of God " ; also when his disciples consulted him about the baptism of Jesus, and on other occasions. He baptized first in the Jordan ; afterwards on the other side of that river, at a place called Bethania ; at Ennon in Galilee, and elsewhere. Like an angel of the Lord " he was neither moved by blessing nor cursing," having only God and His will in view. He preached not himself, but Christ. His tenderness and charity won the hearts, and his zeal gave him a commanding influence over the minds of his hearers. He reproved vice with impartial freedom and undaunted authority ; the hypocrisy of the Pharisees, the profaneness of the Sadducees, the extortion of the publicans, the rapine and licentiousness of the soldiers, and the incestuous adultery of Herod himself.

This Herod Antipas, Tetrarch of Galilee, had put away his wife and was living with Herodias, who was both his niece and the wife of his half-brother Philip. St John Baptist boldly reprehended the tetrarch and his accomplice for so scandalous a crime, and said to that prince, " It is not lawful for thee to have thy brother's wife." Herod feared and reverenced John, knowing him to be a holy man and he did many things by his advice; but on the other hand, he could not bear that his worst sore should be touched, and was highly offended at the liberty which the preacher took. Whilst he respected him as a saint he hated him as a censor, and felt a violent struggle between his veneration for the sanctity of the prophet and the reproach of his own conduct. His anger got the better of him and was nourished by the clamour and artifices of Herodias. Herod, to content her, and perhaps somewhat because he feared John's influence over the people, cast the saint into prison, in the castle of Machærus, near the Dead Sea; and our Lord during the time of his imprisonment spoke of him, saying, "What went you out to see? A prophet? Yea, I say to you, and more than a prophet. This is he of whom it is written: Behold I send my angel before thy face, who shall prepare thy way before thee. For I say to you, amongst those that are born of women there is not a greater prophet than John the Baptist."

Herod continued still to respect the man of God, listened to what he had to say, and sometimes acted on his advice; but he was troubled when he was admonished by him for his sins. Herodias, on the other hand, never ceased to endeavour to exasperate him against John and to seek an opportunity for his destruction. Her chance at length came when Herod on his birthday gave a feast to the chief men of Galilee. At this entertainment Salome, a daughter of Herodias by her lawful husband, pleased Herod by her dancing so much that he promised her with an oath to grant her whatever she asked, though it amounted to half of his dominions. Herodias thereupon told her daughter to demand the death of John the Baptist and, for fear the tyrant might relent if he had time to think it over, instructed the girl to add that the head of the prisoner should be forthwith brought to her in a dish. This strange request startled Herod; as Alban Butler says, "The very mention of such a thing by a lady, in the midst of a feast and solemn rejoicing, was enough to shock even a man of uncommon barbarity." But because of his oath, a double sin, rashly taken and criminally kept, as St Augustine says, he would not refuse the request. Without so much as the formality of a trial he sent a soldier of his guard to behead John in prison, with an order to bring his head in a dish and present it to Salome. This being done, the girl was not afraid to take that present into her hands, and deliver it to her mother. Thus died the great forerunner of our blessed Saviour, the greatest prophet " amongst those that are born of women." His disciples so soon as they heard of his death came and took his body and laid it in a tomb, and came and told Jesus. "Which when Jesus had heard, He retired . . . into a desert place apart." Josephus gives remarkable testimony to the sanctity of John, and says, " He was indeed a man endued with all virtue, who exhorted the Jews to the practice of justice towards men and piety towards God ; and also to baptism, preaching that they would become acceptable to God if they renounced their sins and to the cleanness of their bodies added purity of soul." He adds that the Jews ascribed to the murder of John the misfortunes into which Herod fell.

This glorious saint was a martyr, a virgin, a doctor, a prophet, and more than a prophet. He was declared by Christ Himself to be greater than all the saints of the old law, the greatest of all that had been born of women. And the grace with which he was endowed all sprang from his humility : in this all his other virtues were founded. If we desire to form ourselves upon so great a model, we must, above all things, labour to lay the same deep foundation. We must never cease to purge our souls more and more from all leaven of pride, by earnestly begging grace of God, by studying with St John truly to know ourselves, and by exercising continual acts of sincere humility. Meditation on our own nothingness and wretchedness will help to fill us with this saving knowledge ; and repeated humiliations will ground and improve our souls in a sense of our feebleness and a sincere contempt of ourselves.

Although this feast does not seem to have been adopted in Rome until a comparatively late period, we can trace it at an early date in other parts of the Western Church. We find it mentioned not only in the " Hieronymianum " and in the Gelasian sacramentaries of both types, but it occurs in the " Liber Comicus " of Toledo belonging to the middle of the seventh century. Moreover, either then or even sooner it had probably established itself firmly at Monte Cassino (Morin in the *Revue Bénédictine*, 1908, p. 494) ; and indeed we may assume that its observance was introduced into England from Naples as early as 668 (*Rev. Bénédictine*, 1891, p. 487). As we find this special feast, as distinct from that of the Nativity of the Baptist, kept on the same day (August 20) in the Synaxaries of Constantinople, it is quite likely that it was of Palestinian origin. In the " Hieronymianum " it is associated with a commemoration of the Prophet Eliseus, the link being that both Eliseus and St John Baptist were believed in St Jerome's time to have been buried at Sebaste, a day's journey from Jerusalem. Now the gospel-book of Würzburg, dating from about 700, has an entry " Depositio Helisei et santi Johannis Baptistæ " (Morin in *Rev. Bénédictine*, 1893, p. 120 n.), and there are other gospel-books which couple the two in the same way. See also Cabrol in the *Dictionnaire d'Archéologie*, etc., vol. v, c. 1431, and Duchesne, *Christian Worship*, p. 270.

ST SABINA, Mart.

c. A.D. 126

She was the widow of one Valentinus, and lived near Terni, in the province of Umbria. According to her *acta*, which are not worthy of credence, she had a servant called Serapia, a native of Antioch in Syria, who was a Christian, and the life of this virtuous maiden had such an influence over the mistress that she was converted to the Faith, and so powerfully did our holy religion operate in her soul that her fervour and piety soon made her name illustrious among the lights of the Church in the beginning of the second century. The persecution beginning under Hadrian, Beryllus, governor of the province, caused Sabina and Serapia to be arrested, and the latter to be beaten to death with clubs. Sabina was discharged in consideration of her rank and friends; but she received the crown of martyrdom the year following, at Rome. St Serapia also is honoured on this day and again on September 3, because on that day the relics of both were translated to a church on the Aventine, dedicated to God under the patronage of these two saints, in 430. It at present bears only the name of St Sabina, and in it was kept the first among the stations in Lent, on Ash Wednesday. St Sabina is named in the canon of the Ambrosian Mass.

It would seem that we can have no assurance even of the existence of any such martyr. As we hear first of the "titulus Sabinæ," and later always of "titulus Sanctæ Sabinæ" it remains possible that this was one of the cases in which the founder of a church whose memory was annually commemorated there, was subsequently mistaken for the patron under whose invocation the church had been built, an appropriate story being invented to do him honour. In the *Acta Sanctorum*, November, vol. ii, part 2, pp. 475–476 Père Delehaye discusses the case of St Sabina, quoting the divergent opinions of De Rossi, J. P. Kirsch, Lanzoni, and others.

ST SEBBE, King of the East Saxons, Conf.

c. A.D. 694

This prince was the son of Seward, and in the year 664, which was remarkable for a terrible pestilence, began to reign over the East Saxons, who inhabited the country which now comprises Essex, Middlesex, and part of Hertfordshire; he was co-king of this region with Sighere, under Wulfhere, King of Mercia, and this Sighere, fearing that the plague was a token of the wrath of the pagan gods whom he had abandoned, apostatized to their worship again, with many of his people. Thereupon a bishop, Jaruman, came from Mercia to show these the error of their ways. On the authority of a priest that was with him, St Bede says he was a very discreet, religious, and good man, and was successful in his mission. In it the bishop had the support of Sebbe, who was by his wise government the father of his people and a model of virtue, who on the throne sanctified his soul by penance, alms-deeds, and prayer, so that many said he was more suited by disposition to be a bishop than a king. When he had reigned happily for thirty years, he resigned his crown to his two sons, which he had long desired to do in order to be more at liberty to prepare himself for his last hour; but his queen had resolutely refused to agree to a separation and was only won over at last by the ill-health of her husband, which presaged that his death was not far off. St Sebbe received the monastic habit from the hands of Waldhere, successor of St Erconwald in the bishopric of London, whom he charged with the distribution of all his personal estate among the poor. " When the aforesaid sickness increased upon him," says St Bede, " and he perceived the day of his death to be drawing near, being a man of royal disposition he began to apprehend lest, when under pain and the approach of death, he might be guilty of anything unworthy of his person, either in words or any movement of his limbs. Wherefore, calling to him the said Bishop of London, in which city he then was, he asked him that none might be present at his death besides the bishop himself and two attendants." Shortly after this truly royal man died, and was buried against the north wall of old St Paul's. He is named in the Roman Martyrology, having been added thereto by Cardinal Baronius in the sixteenth century.

All that we know of St Sebbe is derived from Bede, *Ecc. Hist.*, iii, ch. 30, and iv, ch. 11. From Mr. Edmund Bishop's study of the calendars, incorporated in Stanton's *Menology*, there would seem to be no trace of *cultus*.

ST MEDERICUS OR MERRY, ABBOT

A.D. 700

He was born at Autun, in the seventh century, and from an early age realized that the great end of human life is the sanctification and salvation of the soul. That he might wholly give himself to God, when he was but thirteen years old he so earnestly desired to embrace a monastic life that his parents presented him to the abbot of St Martin's in Autun. In that monastery then lived fifty-four fervent monks, whose penitential and regular lives were an object of sanctity to the whole country. Merry in this company grew up in the exercise and habits of every virtue, and a scrupulous observance of the rule. Being chosen abbot much against his own inclination, he pointed out to his brethren the narrow path of true virtue by example, walking before them in every duty ; and the great reputation of his sanctity drew the eyes of all men upon him. The distractions which continual consultations from all parts gave him, and a fear of the dangers of forgetting himself and falling into vanity, made him resign his office and retire into a forest four miles from Autun, where he lay hid some time in a place called to this day St Merry's Cell. He earned himself all necessaries of life by the labour of his hands, and found this solitude sweet by the liberty it gave him of employing his time in heavenly contemplation, prayer, and work. The place of his retreat at length becoming public, and being struck down by sickness, he was obliged to return to the monastery of Champeaux and then to his own ; after having edified his brethren and strengthened them in religious perfection, he again left them in order to make a pilgrimage to the shrine of St Germanus of Paris (also a native of Autun) in that city. There with one companion, St Frou or Frodulph, he chose his abode in a small cell adjoining a chapel dedicated in honour of St Peter, in the north suburb of the city; and, after two years and nine months during which he bore with patience a painful lingering illness, he died happily about the year 700.

There is a Latin Life printed by Mabillon and in the *Acta Sanctorum*, August, vol. vi. It manifests a relative sobriety in the matter of miracles.

BD. RICHARD HERST, Mart.
A.D. 1628

On the day following the martyrdom of Bd. Edmund Arrowsmith at Lancaster there suffered in the same town Bd. Richard Herst, whose story is one of the most remarkable in the histories of the English and Welsh martyrs. He was hanged, ostensibly for wilful murder. Richard Herst (Hurst, Hayhurst) was born in a year unknown, near Preston, probably at Broughton, and was a yeoman farmer, comfortably off. Being a recusant, on a day in 1628 the Bishop of Chester sent a pursuivant, Norcross, with two men, Wilkinson and Dewhurst, to arrest him. They found him plowing, and as Norcross handed him the warrant, Wilkinson struck at him with a stick. A girl at work in another part of the field, seeing this, ran to summon her mistress, who came running out with a farm-servant and another man. The process-servers turned to meet this diversion and Wilkinson knocked the two men down, whereat the girl (unfortunately the name of this spirited young woman is not known) hit Dewhurst over the head. The pursuivant's men then ran away, but Dewhurst, "partly on occasion of the blow, partly also to apply himself close to Wilkinson, made more haste than good speed, and ran so disorderly over the hard ploughed lands, as that he fell down and broke his leg." The fracture mortified and thirteen days later Dewhurst died of it, after declaring that his fall had been quite accidental. Nevertheless Herst was indicted for murder before Sir Henry Yelverton and convicted, in defiance of all the evidence, the known facts of the case, and the finding of the coroner's jury; the criminal jury was unwilling to bring in a verdict of guilty, but the judge told the foreman in private that it must be done "for an example." A petition of reprieve was sent to the King, Charles I, supported by Queen Henrietta Maria, but the contrary influence was too strong; his life was offered him if he would take the oath which had been condemned by the Holy See, which fact alone shows the wicked humbug of the murder charge. Three short letters are extant from Bd. Richard to his confessor. In one he says, "I pray you remember my poor children, and encourage my friends about my debts; and let it appear that my greatest worldly care is to satisfy them as far as my means will extend"; in another, "Although my flesh be timorous and fearful, I yet find great comfort in spirit in casting myself upon my sweet Saviour with a most fervent love, when I consider what He hath done and suffered for me, and my greatest desire is to suffer with Him. And I had rather choose to die a thousand deaths than to possess a kingdom and live in mortal sin; for there is nothing so hateful to me as sin, and that only for the love of my Saviour." On his way to the gallows, he looked up to where Bd. Edmund Arrowsmith's head was displayed above the castle; "I look," he said, "at the head of that blessed martyr whom you have sent before to prepare the way for us," and then turned to the minister who was questioning him, and said, "I believe according to the Faith of the Holy Catholic Church." He spent some time in prayer at the foot of the scaffold and then, seeing that the hangman was fumbling over fixing the rope, called up to him, "Tom, I think I must come up and help thee." He left behind him in the world six young children, and one yet unborn. Bd. Richard Herst was beatified in 1929, three hundred years and four months after his death.

The printed account of Blessed Edmund Arrowsmith mentioned under August 28 supplies in addition full details regarding Richard Herst; and in Challoner also the two martyrs are noticed together.

AUGUST 30

ST ROSE OF LIMA, Virg.

A.D. 1617

ASIA, Europe, and Africa had been watered with the blood of many martyrs and adorned for ages with the shining example of innumerable saints, whilst the vast regions of America lay barren till the faith of Christ began to enlighten them in the sixteenth century, and this maiden appeared in that land like a rose amidst thorns, the first-fruits of its canonized saints. She was of Spanish extraction, born at Lima, the capital of Peru, in 1586, her parents, Gaspar de Florez and Maria del Oliva, being decent folk of moderate means. She was christened Isabel but was commonly called Rose, on account of her complexion, and she was confirmed by St Toribio, Archbishop of Lima, in that name only. As a child her patience in suffering was extraordinary; she ate no fruit, and fasted three days a week, allowing herself on them only bread and water. When she was grown up, she seems to have taken St Catharine of Siena for her model, in spite of the objections and ridicule of her parents and friends. One day her mother having put on her head a garland of flowers, to show her off before some visitors, she stuck in it a pin so deeply that she could not take off the garland without some difficulty. Hearing others frequently commend her beauty, and fearing lest it should be an occasion of temptation to anyone, she used to rub her face and hands with pepper, in order to disfigure her skin with blotches. A woman happening one day to admire the fineness of the skin of her hands and her shapely fingers, she rubbed them with lime, and was unable to dress herself for a month in consequence. By these and other even more surprising austerities she armed herself against external enemies and against the insurgence of her own senses. But she knew that this would avail her little unless she banished from her heart inordinate self-love, which is the source of pride and seeks itself even in fasting and prayer. Rose triumphed over this enemy by humility, obedience, and denial of her own will. She did not scruple to oppose her parents when she thought they were mistaken, but she never wilfully disobeyed them or departed from scrupulous obedience and patience under all trouble and contradictions, of which she experienced more than enough from those who did not understand her.

Her parents having been reduced to straitened circumstances by an unsuccessful mining venture at Guanca, Rose by working all day in the garden, and late at night with her needle, relieved their necessities. These employments were agreeable to her penitential spirit, and she probably would never have entertained any thoughts of a different life if her parents had not tried to induce her to marry. She had to struggle with them over this for ten years, and to strengthen herself in her resolution she took a vow of virginity. Then, having joined the Third Order of St Dominic, she chose for her dwelling a little lonely cell in the garden, where she became practically a recluse. She wore upon her head a thin circlet of silver, studded on the inside with little sharp prickles, like a crown of thorns. So ardent was her love of God that as often as she spoke of Him the tone of her voice and the fire which sparkled in her face showed the flame which consumed her soul. This appeared most openly when she was in presence of the Blessed Sacrament and when in receiving It she united her heart to her beloved in that fountain of His love. God favoured her with many great graces, but she also suffered during fifteen years persecution from her friends and others, and the even more severe trial of interior desolation and anguish in her soul. The Devil also assaulted her with violent temptations, but the only help she got from those she consulted was the recommendation to eat and sleep more ; at length she was examined by a commission of priests and physicians, who decided that her experiences, good and bad, were supernatural. But it is permissible to think that some of them, if correctly reported, were due to natural physical and psychological causes. The last three years of her life were spent under the roof of Don Gonzalo de Massa, a government official, and his wife, who was fond of Rose. In their house she was stricken by her last illness, and under long and painful sickness it was her prayer, " Lord, increase my sufferings, and with them increase Thy love in my heart." She died on August 24, 1617, thirty-one years old. The chapter, senate, and other honourable corporations of the city carried her body by turns to the grave. She was canonized by Clement X in 1671, and was declared patroness of South America and the Philippines in 1669, being the first canonized saint of the New World.

The mode of life and ascetical practices of St Rose of Lima are suitable only for those few whom God calls to them ; the ordinary Christian may not seek to copy them, but must look to the universal spirit of heroic sanctity behind them, for all the saints, whether in the world, in the desert, or in the cloister, studied to live every moment to God. If we have a pure intention of always doing His will, as the governing principle of our whole lives, we thus consecrate to Him all our time, even our meals, our rest, our conversation, and whatever else we do : all our works will thus be *full*. To attain to this we must crucify in our hearts all inordinate self-love, or it will creep into our actions and rob God of them. We must remove every obstacle that can hinder the reign of divine love in our souls, and must pray and labour with all our strength that this love be continually increased. If true charity animate our souls, it will sanctify all our actions. By it we shall endeavour to glorify God in all our works, and sincerely offer and refer ourselves and all we do to this end, repeating in the beginning of every action, " Hallowed be thy name," both by me with all my powers and strength, and by all Thy creatures, now and for ever. Or, " Thy will be done on earth as it is in Heaven " : may it be always fulfilled by me, and in me, and all others, as it is by the blessed angels above, O God of my heart, my God, and my all !

The Bollandists in the *Acta Sanctorum*, August, vol. v, after referring to one or two earlier lives of St. Rose, in particular that of John de Vargas Machuca in Spanish, and that of D. M. Marchese in Italian, elected to print entire the Latin biography of the saint by Father Leonard Hansen, O.P. This has been the backbone of nearly all that has been subsequently written about the holy virgin. Moreover it is supplemented in the *Acta Sanctorum* by the text of Clement X's very ample bull of canonisation which gives full details both of the life of the saint and of her miracles. No very notable study of the subject seems to have been undertaken in the last two centuries. There is a German Life by Ott (1863) and one in French by A. E. Masson (1898). In English we have in the Oratorian series a translation of a seventeenth-century French life by J. B. Feuillet, and an attractive sketch by F. M. Capes, *The Flower of the New World* (1899). See also Viscomte de Bussière, *Le Pérou et Ste Rose de Lima* (1863) ; Mortier, *Maîtres Généraux O.P.*, vol. vii, pp. 76 *seq.*, and the *Monumenta O.P. Historica*, xiii, pp. 22 *seq.*

SS. FELIX AND ADAUCTUS, MM.

A.D. 304

St Felix was a holy priest in Rome, no less happy in his life and virtue than in his name. Being apprehended in the beginning of Diocletian's persecution, he was put to the torture, which he suffered with constancy, and was condemned to lose his head. As he was going to execution he was met by a stranger, who, being a Christian, was so moved at the sight of the martyr and the glory to which he was hastening, that he cried out aloud, " I confess the same law which this man professes; I confess the same Jesus Christ; and I also will lay down my life in His cause." The magistrates hearing this, caused him forthwith to be seized, and the martyrs were both beheaded together. The name of this stranger not being known, he was called by the Christians Adauctus, *i.e.*, the one added, because he was joined to Felix in martyrdom.

This story, with sundry legendary embellishments, is derived from an inscription of Pope St Damasus (d. 384), which ran: " O how truly and rightly named Felix, happy, you who, with faith untouched and despising the prince of this world, have confessed Christ and sought the heavenly kingdom. Know ye also, brethren, the truly precious faith by which Adauctus too hastened, a victor, to Heaven. The priest Verus, at the command of his ruler Damasus, restored the tomb, adorning the thresholds of the saints." SS. Felix and Adauctus were buried in the cemetery of Commodilla on the Ostian Way, where a church built over their tomb was uncovered in 1905. Their relics are said to have been removed by Pope Leo IV, about 850.

As " Felix and Adauctus, in the cemetery of Commodilla on the Ostian way " are registered in the *Depositio Martyrum* of 354, we have a solid guarantee for their early *cultus*, which is further confirmed by the Leonine sacramentary and many other records. See the *Analecta Bollandiana*, vol. xvi (1897), pp. 17–43, and the discussions by De Rossi, Wilpert, Marucchi, Bonavenia, etc., to which Père Delehaye gives references in the *Acta Sanctorum*, November, vol. ii, part 2, p. 477.

ST PAMMACHIUS, Conf.

A.D. 410

Pammachius was distinguished alike as a saint, a Roman citizen, a man of learning, and a friend of St Jerome, with whom he had studied in his youth and maintained correspondence all his life. He belonged to the house of the Furii, was a senator, and in the year 370 proconsul; in 385 he married Pauline, the second daughter of St Paula, that other great friend of St Jerome. Pammachius was probably one of the religious men who denounced to Pope St Siricius a certain Jovinian, who maintained among other errors that all sins and their punishments are equal; he certainly sent copies of the heretic's writings to Jerome, who replied to them in a long treatise. This reply did not meet with the entire approval of St Pammachius: he found its language too strong (a failing to which Jerome was very inclined) and that it contained exaggerated praise of virginity and depreciation of marriage; so he wrote and told him so, and St Jerome replied in two letters, thanking him and explaining and defending what he had written. Jovinian was condemned by the Pope in a synod at Rome and by St Ambrose at Milan, and nothing more is heard of him; St Jerome wrote a few years later that he had " belched rather than breathed out his life amidst pheasants and pork." In 397 the wife of St Pammachius died, and in a letter of sympathy St Paulinus of Nola wrote to him : " Your wife is now a pledge and an intercessor for you with Jesus Christ. She now obtains for you as many blessings in Heaven as you have offered her treasures from hence : not honouring her memory with fruitless tears only, but making her a partner of your charities. She is honoured by your virtues ; she is fed by the bread you have given to the poor. . . ." St Jerome wrote in the same strain. Pammachius devoted the rest of his life to study and works of charity. Together with St Fabiola he built at Porto a large hospice to shelter pilgrims coming to Rome, especially the poor and the sick ; this was the first institution of its kind, technically called a *xenodochium*, in the west, and received the hearty praise of St Jerome ; Pammachius and Fabiola spent much time thereat, personally looking after their guests. The site of this building has been discovered and its plan laid bare. In his devotion to the suffering Pammachius was following in the footsteps of his dead wife Pauline, and the blind, the incapacitated and the moneyless were declared by St Jerome to be her heirs ; he never went out into the streets but they flocked around him, knowing well that they would not be turned away. St Pammachius was greatly disturbed by the bitter controversy between Jerome and Rufinus ; he wrote to him urging that he should undertake the translation of Origen's *de Principiis*, and gave Jerome very useful help in his controversial writings : but abate the imprudence of expression of much of them he could not. He also wrote to the people living on his estates in Numidia urging them to abandon the Donatist schism and return to the Church, and this action drew a letter of thanks from St Augustine at Hippo in 401. Pammachius, or his father Byzantius, turned their house on the Cælian hill into a church, consequently called *titulus Byzantii* or *Pammachii :* its site is now occupied by the Passionist church of SS. Giovanni e Paolo, beneath which remains of the original house have been found. St Pammachius died in 410 while Alaric and the Goths were on their way to plunder Rome ; he is often stated to have been a priest but this does not seem to have been so.

A fairly complete account of Pammachius, compiled by Father Jean Pien, is printed in the *Acta Sanctorum*, August, vol. vi. See also Cavallera, *Saint Jérome sa Vie et son Œuvre* (1922).

ST FIACRE, Hermit
c. A.D. 670

He was born in Ireland, and had his education under the care of St Cuanna at Kilcoone; he became a hermit at Kilfiachra on the river Nore in county Kilkenny. Looking upon all worldly ties as nought to gain Christ, he left his country and friends in his prime, and sailed over into France in quest of some closer solitude, in which he might devote himself to God, unknown to the rest of the world. He arrived at Meaux, where one conducted him to St Faro, who was the bishop of that city and eminent for sanctity. The prelate, charmed with the virtue and abilities which he discovered in this stranger, and having in mind the kindness of another Irishman, St Columban, to himself, gave him a solitary dwelling in a forest which was his own patrimony, called Breüil, in the province of Brie. There is a legend that St Faro offered him as much land as he could turn up in a day, and that St Fiacre instead of driving his furrow with a plow turned the top of the soil with the point of his staff! In this place the anchorite cleared the ground of trees and briers, made himself a cell with a small garden, built an oratory in honour of the Blessed Virgin, and made a hospice for travellers which developed into the village of Saint-Fiacre in Seine-et-Marne. He tilled his garden and laboured with his hands for his subsistence. The life he led was most austere, and only necessity or charity ever interrupted his contemplation. Many resorted to him for advice, and the poor for relief. His charity for all moved him to attend cheerfully those that came to consult him; and in his hospice he entertained all comers, serving them with his own hands, and he sometimes miraculously restored to health those that were sick. He never suffered any woman to enter the enclosure of his hermitage, which was an inviolable rule among the Irish monks, and indeed of all monks; but St Fiacre extended the prohibition even to his chapel, and several rather ill-natured legends profess to account for it. Others tell us that those who attempted to transgress were punished by visible judgements, and that, for example, in 1620 a lady of Paris, who claimed to be above this law, going into the oratory, became distracted upon the spot and never recovered her senses; whereas Anne of Austria, Queen of France, out of a religious deference, was content to offer up her prayers in this place outside the door, amongst the other pilgrims. St Chillen, or Kilian, on his return from Rome, visited St Fiacre, who was his kinsman, and having passed some time under his discipline was directed by his advice and with the authority of St Faro to preach in that diocese. St Fiacre had a sister called Syra, who died in the diocese of Meaux, and is honoured there among the holy virgins; some writers mention a letter of spiritual advice which her brother wrote to her.

Hector Boece and other Scottish chroniclers state that Fiacre was son of Eugene IV, King of the Scots, and in the reign of Clothaire II of France was invited by ambassadors sent by his nation to come and take possession of that kingdom; and that he answered that for the inheritance of an eternal crown he had renounced all earthly claims. But this account of him is quite apocryphal. The fame of St Fiacre's miracles of healing continued after his death and crowds visited his shrine for centuries. Du Plessis singles out the following cures for mention. Mgr. Seguier, Bishop of Meaux in 1649, and John de Chatillon, Count of Blois, give testimony of their own relief. Anne of Austria attributed to the mediation of this saint the recovery of Louis XIII at Lyons, where he had been dangerously ill: in thanksgiving for which she made on foot a pilgrimage to the shrine in 1641. She acknowledged herself indebted to St Fiacre's intercession for the cure of a dangerous disease which neither surgeons nor physicians had been able to relieve, and she also sent to this saint's shrine a token in acknowledgement of his intervention in the birth of her son Louis XIV. Before that king underwent a severe operation, Bossuet, Bishop of Meaux, began a novena of prayers at St Fiacre's to ask the divine blessing. His relics at Meaux are still resorted to and he is invoked against all sorts of physical ills, including venereal disease. He is also a patron saint of gardeners and of the cab-drivers of Paris. French cabs are called *fiacres* because the first establishment to let coaches on hire, in the middle of the seventeenth century, was in the rue Saint-Martin, near the hotel Saint-Fiacre, in Paris. St Fiacre's feast is kept in some dioceses of France and throughout Ireland.

There is a Latin Life of some length printed in the *Acta Sanctorum*, August, vol. vi, but it is difficult to judge of its historical value. See also Gougaud, *Gaelic Pioneers of Christianity*, pp. 135–137; L. Phleger in *Zeitschrift f. die Geschichte des Oberrheins*, 1918, pp. 153–173; J. F. Kenney, *Sources for the Early History of Ireland*, i, p. 493; Bächtold-Stäubli, *Handwörterbuch des deutschen Aberglaubens*, vol. iii.

ST FANTINUS, Abbot and Conf.

End of the Tenth Century

This Fantinus is sometimes called "the Younger" to distinguish him from St Fantinus of Syracuse who lived at the time of Diocletian's persecution. He was abbot of the Greek monastery of St Mercury in Calabria, and had among his subjects St Nilus, afterwards founder of Grottaferrata, with whom he was on terms of close friendship. After some years Fantinus claimed that the voice of God was telling him to leave the monastery and he accordingly did so, wandering about the countryside from place to place, sleeping in the open, and living on fruit and herbs. When he came to a church or monastery he lamented and prophesied woe; when he met a monk he wept over him as though he were a dead man. Nilus was much upset by this strange behaviour and tried to induce him to return to the monastery, but he only replied that there would soon be no monastery to return to and that he would die in a foreign land. And in fact about the year 980 the Saracens from Sicily devastated Calabria and the monastery of St Mercury was destroyed. St Nilus and other monks fled to Monte Cassino, but St Fantinus with two disciples, Vitus and Nicephorus, went overseas and landed in the Peloponnesus. He lived for a time at Corinth and at Larissa in Thessaly, and then moved to Salonika, where his miracles and virtues made him famous. He died either at that place or at Constantinople. He is named in the Roman Martyrology and is titular of a church near Reggio.

Not much that is reliable is known of this saint, though the Bollandists have devoted a few pages to him in the *Acta Sanctorum*, August, vol. vi. It is apparently this Fantinus who figures in the Constantinople Synaxaries on November 14; though in an Italo-Greek synaxary he is assigned to August 30. See J. Rendel Harris, *Further Researches into the Ferrar Group* (1900), with Père Delehaye's comments in the *Analecta Bollandiana*, vol. xxi (1902), pp. 23–28. The story seems to be nothing but legend and confusion.

BD. BRONISLAVA, Virg.

A.D. 1259

Bd. Bronislava was a cousin of St Hyacinth, and was born in Upper Silesia about the year 1203. Moved by his example she joined the Norbertine nuns at Zwierzyniec when she was about twenty-five years old, and for some time led the ordinary life of her order. But her gift of contemplation and consequent love of solitude were so great that she was allowed to withdraw for long periods to a cell in a cave on Mount Sikonik, not far from the monastery, and was eventually permitted to live there permanently as a solitary. After her death on January 18, 1259, her body was buried in the convent church, and when the buildings were destroyed by warfare it was lost; but in the seventeenth century the relics were discovered again, and carried from church to church throughout Poland for the veneration of the people, who invoke her intercession against cholera. The *cultus* of Bd. Bronislava was confirmed by Pope Gregory XVI in 1839; her feast is observed in England by the Premonstratensian canons regular.

Most of the accounts of this rather obscure *beata* seem to be written either in Polish or in Flemish (Brabant being at present the stronghold of the Premonstratensian Order); but there are short Lives published in French by Flambeau (1897) and Van Spielbeeck (1886). Bronislava is also one of the three holy people whose story is told by J. Chrzaszcz in *Drei schlesische Laudesheilige* (Breslau, 1897).

AUGUST 31

ST RAYMUND NONNATUS, Cardinal and Conf.

A.D. 1240

ACCORDING to the words of our divine Redeemer, that Christian proves himself His most faithful disciple and gives the surest and greatest proof of his love of God, who most perfectly loves his neighbour for God's sake. By this test of sanctity we are to form our judgement of the saint whom the Church honours on this day. St Raymund was brought into the world at Portel in Catalonia in the year 1204, and was called *non natus*, " not born," because he was taken out of the body of his mother after her death in labour. In his childhood he seemed to find no other pleasure than in his devotions and his grammar studies. His father took him from school, and sent him to take care of a farm which he had in the country. Raymund readily obeyed, and enjoyed the opportunity of solitude. He was pressed by his friends to go to the court of Arragon, where by his prudence and abilities he could not fail to better himself, especially as he was related to the illustrious houses of Foix and Cardona. Instead of doing this, he made a resolution of taking the religious habit in the new order of Our Lady of Mercy for the redemption of captives. He could say with holy Job that compassion for the poor and distressed had grown up with him from his childhood. The sufferings of the Christians who in the neighbouring provinces, almost under his eyes, groaned in slavery under the Moors, particularly afflicted his heart ; by compassion he already bore their burdens and felt the weight of their chains. But if he was moved at their bodily sufferings, and desired to devote himself and all that he possessed to procure them comfort and relief, he was much more troubled by their spiritual danger of sinking under their calamities and losing their souls by impatience or apostasy from Christ. Against this he never ceased to pray, entreating the God of mercy to be Himself the comfort and support of the weak and of the strong ; and he wished with St Paul to spend and be spent himself for their souls. He obtained of his father, through the mediation of the Count of Cardona, leave to enter the Mercedarian order ; and was accordingly admitted to his profession at Barcelona by St Peter Nolasco.

So swift was the progress that he made in the perfection of his institute that within two or three years after his profession he was judged the best qualified to discharge the office of ransomer, in which he succeeded St Peter. Being sent into Barbary with a considerable sum of money he purchased at Algiers the liberty of a number of slaves. When all other resources were exhausted, he voluntarily gave himself up as a hostage for the ransom of certain others, whose situation was desperate and whose faith was exposed to imminent danger. The sacrifice which the saint had made of his own liberty served only to exasperate the Algerians, who treated him with barbarity till, fearing lest if he died in their hands they would lose the ransom which was stipulated to be paid for the slaves for whom he remained a hostage, the magistrate of the city gave orders that he should be treated with more humanity. He was permitted to go about the streets and he made use of this liberty to comfort and encourage the Christians, and he converted and baptized some Mohammedans. When the governor heard of this he condemned him to be impaled, this being a barbarous manner of executing criminals much in use among those infidels. However, the persons who were interested in the ransom of the captives prevailed that his life should be spared lest they should be losers; and, by a commutation of his punishment, he was made to run the gauntlet. This did not daunt his courage. So long as he saw souls in danger, he thought he had yet done nothing; nor could he let slip any opportunity of ministering to them. He considered that, as St John Chrysostom says, " Though a person shall have given away a large fortune in alms he has done nothing equal to him who has contributed to the salvation of a soul. This is a greater alms than ten thousand pounds—than this whole world, how great soever it appears to the eye—for a man is more precious than the whole world." St Raymund had, on one side, no more money to employ in releasing poor captives; and, on the other, to speak to a Mohammedan upon the subject of religion was by the Islamic law to court death. He could, however, still exert his endeavours with hope of some success or of dying a martyr of charity. He therefore resumed his former method of instructing and exhorting both Christians and infidels. The governor, who was immediately told of his behaviour, was enraged and commanded the servant of Christ to be whipped at the corners of all the streets in the city, his lips to be bored with a red-hot iron in the market-place, and his mouth shut up with a padlock, the key of which he kept himself and only gave to the gaoler when the prisoner was to eat. In this condition he was kept in a dungeon, where he lay full eight months, till his ransom was brought by some religious men of his order, who were sent with it by St Peter. Raymund was unwilling to leave the country of the infidels, where he wanted to remain to assist the slaves ; but he acquiesced in obedience to the orders of his general, begging God to accept his tears, seeing he was not worthy to shed his blood for the souls of his neighbours.

Upon his return to Spain in 1239 he was nominated cardinal by Pope Gregory IX. But so little was he affected by the unlooked-for honour that he neither changed his dress, nor his poor cell in the convent at Barcelona, nor his manner of living. The Pope, being desirous to have so holy a man about his person and to employ him in the public affairs of the Church, called him to Rome. He obeyed, but could not be persuaded to travel otherwise than as a poor religious. He got no farther than Cardona (Cerdagne), which is only six miles from Barcelona ; he was seized with a violent fever and died there, being only about thirty-six years old. He was buried in the chapel of St Nicholas, near the farm in which he had formerly lived at Portello. The life of St Raymund Nonnatus was not written down till some hundreds of years after his death, and it is a task of great difficulty to separate truth from fiction in the document that has come down to us ; it is adorned with numerous miracles and other marvels of very doubtful worth. He is the patron saint of midwives.

Raymund gave not only his substance but also his liberty, and exposed himself to cruel torments and death, for the redemption of captives and the salvation of souls. But how cold is charity in *our* breasts, though it be the essential characteristic of true Christians ! Do we not, merely to gratify our desire for pleasure or out of vanity or avarice, refuse to give the superfluous part of our possessions to the poor, who for want of it suffer from cold and hunger ? Are not we slothful and backward in visiting unfortunate or sick persons, and in doing our best to get some relief for the distressed ? Are we not so insensible to their miseries as to be without feeling for them, and to neglect even to commend them to God with sufficient earnestness ? Do we not fail to remonstrate with sinners according to our circumstances and with regard for prudence, and neglect to instruct, by ourselves and others, those under our care ? Is it not manifest that self-love, and not the love of God and our neighbour, reigns in our hearts, when we pursue so inordinately our own worldly interest ? If we sound our own hearts and take an impartial view of our lives we shall soon know whether this test of Christ, or that of Satan, which is self-love, be uppermost in our souls, and the governing principle of our actions.

Aug. 31]   ST RAYMUND NONNATUS

It has already been pointed out in the January volume of this series (pp. 395–396) how extremely unreliable are the accounts supplied from Mercedarian sources of the beginnings and early developments of the order of our Lady of Ransom. The Bollandists, unable to discover any trustworthy materials for the story of St Raymond Nonnatus, fell back in despair upon the account given by a sixteenth-century writer (Ciacconius) in his series of biographies of the Roman Cardinals. This penury of information has lasted to the present day, and no confidence can be placed in the accuracy of the details furnished by Butler in the above notice. All that can be said is that in the seventeenth and eighteenth centuries a number of books were printed, mostly of small bulk, by Father Dathia, Echeverez y Eyto, Juan de la Presentacion, P. E. Menendez, F. T. de Miranda, M. Ulate, etc., purporting to recount the life and miracles of St Raymund Nonnatus, that they repeat with slight variations the story told above, adding, however, numberless miracles, and that they were published with all necessary ecclesiastical sanctions. See also Gams, *Kirchengeschichte von Spanien*, vol. iii, part 1.

ST PAULINUS, Bp. of Trier, Conf.

A.D. 358

This Paulinus, called by St Athanasius " a truly apostolic man," and referred to by St Jerome as " happy in his sufferings " for the Faith, was educated in the cathedral-school of Poitiers, and was a disciple of St Maximinus whom he succeeded in the see of Trier. During the exile of St Athanasius at Trier Paulinus had become one of his most fervent supporters, and at the Arianizing synod of Arles in 353 he stood out boldly for the faith of Nicæa and opposed the papal legates who were prepared to condemn Athanasius. In the same cause he withstood the intimidation and violence of the Emperor Constantius at the synod of Milan in 355, and was banished from his see with St Dionysius of Milan, St Eusebius of Vercelli, and St Lucifer of Cagliari ; he was sent into Phrygia, to places so remote that Christians had hardly been heard of, and died in exile in the year 358 : as expressed in the Roman Martyrology, " wearied even to death by the changes and chances of exile far beyond Christian lands, he received from the Lord the crown of a blessed passion, dying at length in Phrygia." His body was brought back to Trier by its bishop St Felix in 396 and enshrined in 1402 in the church of St Paulinus, amid the ruins of which his tomb was found in 1738.

See the *Acta Sanctorum*, August, vol. vi, where a Latin Life is printed dating from the ninth or tenth century. Great interest attaches to St Paulinus from the fact that his skeleton, still wrapped in oriental silk-stuffs with fragments of the wooden coffin in which it had been brought from Phrygia, was in 1883 taken out of the sarcophagus in which it lay and minutely investigated by a committee of archæologists and experts. The scientists referred to pronounced the relics to be unquestionably authentic, and satisfied themselves that the saint had not, as some stories alleged, been decapitated. See Father Schneider in the *Jahrbüchern des Vereins für Alterthumsfreunden im Rheinlande*, vol. 78 (1884), pp. 167 *seq*. On the life of Paulinus *cf.* Ph. Diel, *Der hl. Maximinus und der hl. Paulinus*, 1875.

ST AIDAN, Bp. of Lindisfarne, Conf.

A.D. 651

When St Oswald had come to the throne of Northumbria in the year 634, and wished to spread the Faith among his people, he asked the monks of Iona to send him a bishop to preach to his pagan subjects and plant the Church among them. The first person who came was of a rough, austere temper, and therefore could do little good; being soon forced to return home again, he laid the fault on the rude character and indocile disposition of the English. The monks called a synod to deliberate what was best to be done, and Aidan, who was present, told the prelate, on his blaming the obstinacy of the English, that the fault lay rather in him: that he had been too harsh and severe to an ignorant people, who ought first to be fed with the milk of milder doctrine till they should be able to digest more solid food. At this the whole assembly turned their thoughts to him, as one endued with prudence, and he was appointed to the arduous mission. Aidan was a native of Ireland, and is said to have been a disciple of St Senan on Scattery Island, but nothing else at all is known with certainty of his early life, before he became a monk of Iona. He was graciously received by King Oswald, who bestowed on him for his episcopal seat the isle of Lindisfarne. Of his humility and piety St Bede gives a glowing account. He obliged all those who travelled with him to use their spare time either in reading the Scriptures or in learning the psalms by heart, and he did all his missionary journeys on foot. By his actions he showed that he neither sought nor loved the good things of this world; the presents which were made him by the King, or by other rich men, he distributed among the poor, as we see in the " life " of St Oswald. He rarely would go to the King's table, and never without taking with him one or two of his clergy, and always afterwards made haste away to get on with his work, to read or pray in the church, or in his cell. From his example even the laity took up the custom of fasting till three in the afternoon on all Wednesdays and Fridays, except during the fifty days of Easter time. Bede mentions his apostolic liberty in reproving the proud and the great, and the love of peace, charity, continence, and all other virtues which by his spirit and example he communicated to a rough and barbarous nation. " He was a pontiff inspired with a passionate love of goodness, but at the same time a man of remarkable gentleness and moderation : zealous in God's cause, though not altogether according to knowledge " (Bede refers to the fact that St Aidan naturally followed the Celtic customs with regard to the date of Easter, etc.). And such a man was wanted for the task in hand, for Penda and Caedwalla had effectually undone much of the work of St Paulinus. St Aidan supported his preaching with miracles, three of which Bede relates and, in speaking of the state of the country thirty years later, testifies to the effectiveness of his apostolate : " Wheresoever any cleric or monk came, he was received by all with joy as a servant of God ; and when one was met travelling, they would run up to him and bow, glad to be signed by his hand, or blessed by his prayer. They gave diligent attention to the words of exhortation which they heard, and on Sundays flocked to the churches or monasteries to hear the word of God. If any priest happened to come into a village, the inhabitants gathered together, solicitous to hear from him the words of life, nor did the clergy frequent the villages on any other account but to preach, visit the sick, and take care of souls ; and so free were they from avarice that no one would receive lands or possessions for building monasteries unless compelled to by the secular power."

The centre of St Aidan's activity was the island of Lindisfarne, now generally called Holy Isle, off the coast of Northumberland, between Berwick and Bamborough. Here he had his see and established a monastery under the Celtic rule of St Colmcille ; it has not improperly been called the English Iona, for from it the paganism of Northumbria was gradually dispelled and barbarian customs undermined. After the seventeen years of Aidan's rule there was a succession of sixteen bishops of Lindisfarne, of whom St Cuthbert was the greatest, but by no means the only saint connected with the island. St Aidan took to this monastery twelve English boys to be brought up there (of whom one, Eata, became bishop of Hexham and is venerated as a saint), and he was indefatigable in caring for the welfare of children and of slaves, for the manumission of many of whom he paid from alms bestowed on him. The great king St Oswald assisted his bishop in every possible way, as did St Oswin his successor, and when in 651 Oswin was murdered at Gilling, Aidan survived him only eleven days. He died at the royal castle at Bamborough, which he used as a mission centre, leaning against a wall of the church where a tent had been set up to shelter him.

He was first buried in the cemetery of Lindisfarne, but when the new church of St Peter was built there his body was translated into the sanctuary. St Aidan is named in the Roman Martyrology, and his feast is kept in several English dioceses.

We know little of St Aidan except what we learn from the third book of Bede's *Ecclesiastical History* ; but the notes of C. Plummer are also valuable. On points connected with archæology there is much illustrative matter in Sir Henry Howorth's *The Golden Days of the Early English Church*, vol. i. See also Father Sydney Smith, " Was St Aidan an Anglican ? " in *The Month*, February 1892.

ST CUTHBURGA, Queen and Abbess

c. A.D. 725

This saint was sister to the great King Ina of Wessex and was married to Aldfrid, who was crowned king of Northumbria in 688. At her suit he allowed her to retire to the monastery of Barking in Essex, where she was a novice under St Hildelitha. Sometime after the year 705 she founded, together with her sister St Quenburga, the abbey of Wimborne in Dorset, of which the rule of enclosure was so strict that not even prelates on their lawful occasions were allowed to enter it ; this may have been due to its having been a double monastery, for men and women in adjoining houses. This abbey St Cuthburga governed, giving herself up totally to fasting and prayer ; humble both to God and man, meek and tender to others, but always austere to herself. Under her successor, St Tetta, Wimborne contributed to the conversion of Germany by sending to assist St Boniface his kinswomen, St Lioba and St Thecla. The feast of SS. Cuthburga and Hildelitha together is kept in the diocese of Brentwood on September 3.

There is no early Life, but the summary by Capgrave is printed in the *Acta Sanctorum*, August, vol. vi, with the usual prolegomena. See also Stanton's *Menology*, pp. 431–432.

THE SERVITE MARTYRS OF PRAGUE

A.D. 1420

Among the heresies which John Hus preached in Bohemia in the early part of the fifteenth century was that holy Communion in both kinds is necessary to salvation ; this doctrine became the distinguishing mark of his followers, who in consequence were known as

Utraquists or Calixtines. In 1419 a former Premonstratensian canon, Johann, stirred up the citizens of Prague to clamour for the release of certain Utraquists who had been imprisoned for their disorderly behaviour; carrying the Blessed Sacrament in procession he led them to make their demand of the magistrates, and when it was refused urged the mob on to break into the municipal hall and murder all whom they found therein, blasphemously and sacrilegiously using the presence of the Blessed Sacrament as an incentive to fury and bloody revenge. For the next twelve months there was civil war and horrible outrages on both sides, and in March 1420 Pope Martin V called on Christendom to undertake a crusade against the Hussites and Wycliffites. He also sent into Bohemia a number of preachers, among them four Servite friars, all of noble Tuscan families, namely, Lawrence Nerucci, Augustine Cennini, Bartholomew Donati, and John-Baptist Petrucci. Shortly after they arrived the monastery in which they were staying at Prague was attacked and set on fire by Hussites, and these four with sixty other friars were burned to death as they were singing the *Te Deum* in church. The popular *cultus* of these martyrs was approved by Pope Benedict XV in 1918.

See Giani in his *Annales Ordinis Servorum B.M.V.*, vol. i, pp. 396–400, where some contemporary documents will be found printed. There was presumably a decree promulgating the *confirmatio cultus* alleged to have taken place in 1918, but it does not seem to have been published in the *Acta Apostolicæ Sedis*.

BD. JUVENAL ANCINA, BP. OF SALUZZO, CONF.

A.D. 1604

On October 19, 1545, was born at Fossano in Piedmont the first child of Durando Ancina, of a distinguished family of Spain, and his wife Lucy degl' Araudini. The boy was baptized John Juvenal, in honour of St Juvenal of Narni, patron of Fossano, to whose intercession was attributed his recovery from the weakness which threatened his life at birth. He was a pious child and in his youth increased his habits of virtue and devotion, but at first he had no intention of entering upon other than a secular career; his father proposed that he should be a physician and sent Juvenal at the age of fourteen to begin his studies at the University of Montpellier. He did not stay there long, for the Duke of Savoy, Emmanuel Philibert, alarmed by both the religious and political implications of the spread of Calvinism in France, ordered his subjects to return to their own country.

So Juvenal went to the school of Mondovi in Savoy and, after his father's death, to the University of Padua; he was a brilliant student, and when only about twenty-four took his doctorate both in philosophy and medicine at Turin. Here he was appointed to the chair of medicine in 1569; and he soon had an extensive private practice, especially among the poor, because he treated them free of charge. It was noticed that Juvenal never took part in games or recreations; the only relaxations that he allowed himself from his strenuous service of God and his sick neighbours were chess and the writing of verses in Latin and Italian: he liked to deal with the great affairs of Church and State and publicly declaimed his own ode on the death of Pope St Pius V in 1572. He continued to write verses and hymns all through his life, and composed two epigrams on Bd. Thomas More. About this same year he was assisting at a solemn Mass of requiem in the church of the Augustinian friars at Savigliano, when he was suddenly overwhelmed by the tremendous message of the *Dies irae*: he must have heard the hymn often before and as a physician he was very familiar with death, but now he realized as never before that after death comes the judgement. Hitherto his life had been blameless, but now he saw that this was not enough; God required something more of him, though what it was he did not yet know. He gave himself more than ever to prayer and meditation on the sacred Scriptures, trained himself in detachment from temporal things, and accepted the first opportunity that came along to relinquish his post at the University of Turin. This was when Count Frederick Madrucci, ambassador of the Duke of Savoy to the Holy See, asked him to become his personal private physician.

Juvenal arrived in Rome in the Holy Year of Jubilee 1575, and took a lodging near the church of *Ara Cœli*, in a beautiful spot which appealed to him because it was " close to the prisons, the hospital, a multitude of the poor, and the prison for young criminals." His official work was not arduous and he set himself to the serious study of theology, having for his master no less an one than St Robert Bellarmine himself; he became acquainted with Don Cæsar Baronius, and by him was introduced to St Philip Neri, and so frequented the most learned and most devout society of Rome. Thus he lived for three years, becoming ever more attracted to the formal religious life, but uncertain what definite step to take. He received minor orders, attended regularly the exercises at the Oratory, and put himself under the direction of St Philip, on whose advice he accepted a benefice at Cherasco in Piedmont; but almost at once legal proceedings were taken to dispossess him and he relinquished it without contesting the suit. The fact was that he was disturbed in mind by the example of a leading lawyer at Turin, who had become a Carthusian monk at Pavia, and thought he saw in that an indication of what he must do. His brother, John Matthew, with whom Juvenal kept up an intimate correspondence from Rome, was of one mind with him, and eventually they together consulted St Philip Neri. He unhesitatingly dissuaded them from the Carthusian life, as being unsuited to their temperament and needs, and recommended them to the newly founded Congregation of the Oratory, over which he himself presided. Juvenal at first dissented, wanting more austerity and solitude, but submitted to his director and on October 1, 1578, was admitted with his brother into the Congregation. Baronius said it had that day received a " second St Basil."

When Blessed Juvenal had lived four years at the Oratory he was ordained priest, and in 1586 he was sent to the Oratory at Naples, the first house of his congregation to be founded outside Rome and then in course of establishment by Father Tarugi. He was appointed to preach at once, and after a few sermons wrote to his brother, " These Neapolitans require very beautiful things, and they must be substantial as well. Ordinary things are no use here, where even the cobblers can compose sermons, and make a profession of it. One has to keep one's wits about one." But Bd. Juvenal succeeded in pleasing even the fastidious Neapolitans, and they remembered the nickname that had been given him by some wit in Rome, " the son of thunder "; " By the grace of God the people are satisfied with me," he writes. One of his most sensational conversions was that of Giovannella Sanchia, a singer who was known in the city as " the Siren "—and not solely on account of her singing. She was so touched by hearing him speak of the beauty of holiness that she made a vow never again to sing any vain, improper, or profane song, whether in Italian or Spanish, but only sacred songs. Bd. Juvenal was very fond of music ; we are told that " he wished Vespers to be sung with the best music, or if that were not attainable, with Gregorian chant faultlessly executed "—a critical distinction that is not acceptable to everybody. He therefore took a great deal of care with the music at the Naples Oratory, not simply from the point of view of the decencies of Christian worship and the honour due to Almighty God, but also because he had a firm belief in its good effect on the soul ; he got hold of all the latest popular airs and wrote devout words to them (whether or not to be sung in the Oratory church does not appear) and published a hymn-book with tunes, called the *Temple of Harmony*. One of the Oratorians, Father Borla, took up his quarters at the Hospital for Incurables, which for long had been grossly neglected.

Bd. Juvenal supported him and enlisted the interest and assistance of the Neapolitan ladies, whom he formed into a confraternity of "Benevolent Dames"; to ensure that the object for which they were banded together should not be lost sight of, it had its headquarters not at a church but in the hospital itself. His own material charity was boundless; its most unusual manifestation (but a very useful one) was to have a deposit account with a barber, to whom he sent any poor man whom he saw with unkempt hair or beard; and the barber was under orders when he met any such to use his skill on them and "put it down to Father Juvenal." How much he was respected and loved by the whole city he betrays himself in a letter written to St Philip, when convalescent from a serious illness. He obediently accepted the comforts that were provided for him by his brethren and took a reasonable delight in them.

About the year 1595, when he had been in Naples nearly ten years, Bd. Juvenal was tormented on the one hand by a desire for the cloistered and contemplative life, and on the other by the sight of so much wretchedness and wickedness around him which he could do relatively little to alleviate and reform. But in 1596 Baronius was made a cardinal and, doubtless not to miss an opportunity of settling him permanently in his vocation, the fathers of the Roman Oratory recalled Bd. Juvenal from Naples to fill the vacant place in their community. Greatly fearing what responsible dignities might be thrust on him in Rome, he obeyed at once, to the great grief of the Neapolitans; he carried on quietly for a year and then suddenly three episcopal sees fell vacant. Bd. Juvenal had good reason to think that he would be preferred to one of them; he went out from the Oratory one day and did not return, and after hiding for a time in the city fled from Rome. He spent the next five months wandering from place to place, going to Narni, San Severino, Macerata, Fermo, Loretto, and back to the Oratory at San Severino. Here he received an imperative order to come back to Rome, and found when he got there that the danger of his being made a bishop was, for the moment, over. During the next four years he worked with great energy on behalf of the Piedmontese, especially such as were in danger from or had been seduced by the teaching of the Calvinists, and met and entered into intimate friendship with St Francis de Sales.

In 1602 the Duke of Savoy asked Clement VIII to fill the two vacant sees in his dominions, and the Pope personally charged Bd. Juvenal to accept the charge of one of them. "It is time to obey and not to fly," said the saint, and on September 1 was consecrated bishop of Saluzzo by Cardinal Borghese. His troubles began at once. When he went to take possession of his see he found that, owing to certain actions of the Duke of Savoy, he could do so only either by compromising the rights of the Church or breaking with his prince. So he withdrew to Fossano, wrote a pastoral letter for his diocese, and devoted himself to good works for the benefit of his native town; supernatural gifts and the performance of miracles were, not for the first time, freely attributed to him. After four months he was able to enter his episcopal city and take possession of his cathedral, and one of his first acts was to observe the " Forty Hours " therein, for the first time in Piedmont. Towards the end of 1603 Bd. Juvenal set out on a visitation of his diocese, to extend the reforms he had inaugurated in his cathedral city. Supernatural happenings again attended his progress, especially by way of healing and prophecy—Bd. Juvenal had at all times a disconcerting habit of correctly foretelling people's approaching death! Both before and during this visitation he had foretold his own, and he had only been back in Saluzzo a few weeks when his prophecy came true. There was in the town a certain friar who was carrying on an intrigue with a nun; this came to the ears of Bd. Juvenal, who reasoned gently with them both but warned them that if their conduct was continued he would use strong measures to stop it. On the feast of St Bernard he went to officiate for and to dine with the Conventual Franciscans, it being the name-day of their church, and the criminal friar took the opportunity to poison the bishop's wine. Before Vespers he was taken ill; four days later he had to retire to bed; and by the dawn of August 31 Bd. Juvenal Ancina was dead. " He died," wrote a Carthusian monk, " for virtue, for religion, for Christ, and therefore a martyr's death "; like St John the Baptist, he " received martyrdom as the reward of fearless speech." Marvels attended his lying-in-state and burial, Masses of the Holy Ghost were celebrated rather than requiems, and the cause of his beatification was introduced at Rome in 1624; this received several set-backs and postponements and was not finally achieved till 1869, when the Vatican Council had just assembled.

A full *Life of Blessed John Juvenal Ancina*, with an admirable portrait, was published by Father Charles Bowden in 1891. The author in his preface refers to the Life by F. Bacci (1671) as his principal authority. There are other modern Lives, in French, by Ingold (1890), Richard (1891), and Duver (1905). See also F. Savio, *Marchesato e diocesi di Saluzzo* (1915). In a review of Père Duver's book in the *Analecta Bollandiana*, vol. xxviii (1909), p. 243, it is pointed out that some of the most valuable sources for the history of the *beato* have never been utilised. This is notably the case with a memoir written by Fr. B. Scaraggi, who had his work revised by Father G. M. Ancina, a brother of the holy bishop, who was also an Oratorian.

INDEX TO VOLUME VIII

(*The numbers in brackets indicate date of death*)

A

Adauctus, St (304), 383.
Addai, St (c. 150), 62.
Adrian, St (c. 320), 318.
Afra, St (304), 65.
Agapitus, St (274), 199.
Agapitus, St (with Sixtus) (258), 71.
Agapius, St (304), 220.
Agathangelo, Bd. (1638), 87.
Aidan, St (651), 394.
Aimo Taparelli, Bd. (1495), 211.
Albert of Trapini, St (1306), 86.
Alexander, St (c. 287), 317.
Alexander the Charcoal-Burner, St (250), 132.
Alexander of Constantinople, St (340), 364.
Alipius, St (c. 430), 205.
Alphonsus Liguori, St (1787), 11.
Altmann, Bd. (1091), 97.
Amadeus of Lausanne, Bd. (1159), 339.
Amadeus of Portugal, Bd. (1482), 126.
Amadour, St (n.d.), 247.
Anastasius Cornicularius, St (274), 258.
Ancina, *see* Juvenal.
Andrew, St (ninth century), 271.
Andrew the Tribune, St (c. 303), 219.
Angelo of Foligno, Bd. (1312), 340.
Angelo A. Mazzinghi, Bd. (1438), 209.
Antony Primaldi, Bd. (1480), 176.
Apollinaris, *see* Sidonius.
Araght, *see* Attracta.
Armel, St (c. 570), 189.
Arnulfus, or Arnoul, St (1087), 184.
Arrowsmith, *see* Edmund.
Arsacius, St (358), 188.
Assumption, The, *see* Blessed Virgin Mary.
Asterius, St (303), 283.
Athanasia, St (860), 174.
Attracta, St (? fifth century), 134.
Audoenus, *see* Owen.
Augustine Gazotich, Bd. (1323), 36.
Augustine of Hippo, St (430), 346.

B

Bartholomew, St (first century), 289.
Beatrice da Silva, Bd. (1490), 210.
Benizi, *see* Philip.
Benno, Bd. (940), 35.
Bernard, St (1153), 230.
Bernard Tolomeo, Bd. (1348), 266.
Bertulf, St (640), 223.
Bicchieri, *see* Emily.
Blaan, or Blane, St (? 590), 136.
Blessed Virgin Mary, The (first century), 177.
Bonosus, St (363), 260.
Bronislava, Bd. (1259), 388.

C

Cæsarius of Arles, St (543), 333.
Cajetan, St (1547), 77.
Calasanctius, *see* Joseph.
Camerinus, St (303), 259.
Carvalho, *see* Michael.
Cassian, St (? 304), 155.
Cassian of Nantes, Bd. (1638), 87.
Cecco, Bd., *see* Francis of Pesaro.
Chantal, de, *see* Jane F.
Charity, St (second century), 8.
Chromatius, St (c. 288), 128.
Cisellus, St (303), 259.
Clare, St (1253), 142.

Clare of Montefalco, St (1308), 197.
Claudia, St (first century), 83.
Claudius, St (303), 283.
Curé of Ars, see John M. B.
Cuthburga, St (c. 725), 396.
Cyriacus, St (304), 94.

D

David Lewis, Bd. (1679), 343.
Dedication of St Mary Major, see Our Lady of the Snow.
Dometius, St (362), 83.
Dominic, St (1221), 43.
Domnina, St (303), 283.

E

Ebba, St (683), 308.
Eberhard, Bd. (958), 175.
Edmund Arrowsmith, Bd. (1628), 371.
Emily Bicchieri, Bd. (1314), 228.
Equitius, St (540), 135.
Ethelwold, St (984), 8.
Eudes, see John.
Eugene, or Eoghan, St (sixth century), 286.
Euplius, St (304), 149.
Eusebius, St, conf. (fourth century), 169.
Eusebius, St, mart. (third century), 170.
Eymard, see Peter J.

F

Faber, see Peter.
Fachanan, St (sixth century), 173.
Faith, St (? second century), 8.
Fantinus, St (tenth century), 388.
Felicissimus, St (258), 71.
Felix, St (304), 383.
Felton, see John.
Fiacre, St (c. 670), 386.
Florus, St (second century), 199.
Fourteen Holy Helpers, The, 96.
Francis of Pesaro, Bd. (1350), 166.
Freeman, see William.

G

Gabriel-Mary, Bd. (1532), 341.
Gaetano, see Cajetan.
Gaugericus (625), 137.
Gazotich, see Augustine.
Genesius the Comedian, St (? 303), 303.
Genesius of Arles, St (? 303), 305.
Gertrude of Altenberg, Bd. (1297), 165.
Gery, see Gaugericus.
Gregory of Utrecht, St (c. 776), 309.
Grimaldi, see Antony Primaldi.

H

Helen, St (330), 201.
Helpers, Holy, see Fourteen.
Herluin, Bd. (1078), 319.
Hermes, St (132), 363
Herst, see Richard.
Hippolytus, St (258), 152
Hippolytus, St (with Timothy), 268.
Hope, St (? second century), 8.
Hormisdas, St, pope (523), 74.
Hormisdas, St, mart (420), 95.
Hugh, Little, St (1255), 208.
Humbeline, Bd. (1135), 265.
Hyacinth, St (1257), 192.

I

Ia, St (360), 55.

J

Jane-F. de Chantal, St (1641), 251.
James of Mevania, Bd. (1301), 287.
Joachim, St (first century), 186.
Joan of Aza, Bd. (twelfth century), 99.
Joan A. Thouret, Bd. (1826), 314.
John of Alvernia, Bd. (1322), 120.
John the Baptist, Beheading of St, 373.
John III of Constantinople, St (577), 364.
John Eudes, St (1680), 213.
John Felton, Bd. (1570), 100.
John Kemble, Bd. (1679), 275.
John of Rieti, Bd. (c. 1350), 121.

INDEX TO VOLUME VIII

John of Salerno, Bd. (1242), 118.
John M. B. Vianney, St (1859), 103.
John Wall, Bd. (1679), 274.
Joseph Calasanctius, St (1648), 324.
Julian of Brioude, St (304), 363.
Justus, St (304), 73.
Juvenal Ancina, Bd. (1604), 397.

K

Kemble, *see* John.
Kirkman, *see* Richard.

L

Lacey, *see* William.
Largus, St (304), 94.
Laurence, St (258), 123.
Laurence Loricatus, St (1243), 189.
Lewis, *see* David.
Liberatus, St (483), 196.
London Martyrs of 1588, 368.
Loricatus, *see* Laurence.
Lorus, St (second century), 199.
Louis IX, St (1270), 294.
Louis of Anjou, St (1297), 225.
Lughaedh, *see* Molua.
Luxorius, St (303), 259.

M

Machabees, The Holy (166 B.C.), 3.
Mamas, St (c. 275), 195.
Marcellus, St (303), 330.
Marcellus of Apamæa, St (389), 172.
Margaret the Barefooted, St (1395), 341.
Mari, St (c. 150), 62.
Mary-Michaela, Bd. (1865), 312.
Mary the Virgin, St, *see* Blessed Virgin Mary.
Maximian, St (363), 260.
Maximus Homologetes, St (662), 161.
Mazzinghi, *see* Augustine.
Medericus, or Merry, St (700), 378.
Mennas, St (552), 306.
Michael Carvalho, Bd. (1624), 311.
Mochta, St (sixth century), 222.
Molua, St (605), 56.

Moses the Black, St (fourth century), 366.
Muredach, or Murtagh, St (? sixth century), 150.

N

Nathy, St (sixth century), 114.
Neon, St (303), 283.
Nerses Glaiëtsi, St (1173), 164.
Nonna, St (374), 67.
Nonnatus, *see* Raymund.

O

Oswald, St (642), 115.
Oswin, St (651), 248.
Ouen, St (684), 292.
Our Lady St Mary, *see* Blessed Virgin Mary.
Our Lady of the Snows (c. 435), 61.

P

Pammachius, St (410), 384.
Pastor, St (304), 73.
Paul IV of Constantinople, St (784), 364.
Paulinus of Trier, St (358), 393.
Percy, *see* Thomas.
Peter-in-Chains, St (c. 42), 1.
Peter J. Eymard, Bd. (1868), 38.
Peter Faber, Bd. (1546), 138.
Phelim, St (sixth century), 114.
Philibert, St (684), 249.
Philip Benizi, St (1285), 278.
Philomena, St (n.d.), 129.
Pœmen, St (c. 450), 331.
Portiuncula Indulgence, The, 28.
Porcarius, St (c. 732), 151.
Prague, Servite Martyrs of (1420), 396.
Primaldi, *see* Antony.

R

Radegunde, St (587), 157.
Raymund Nonnatus, St (1240), 390.
Richard Herst, Bd. (1628), 379.

405

Richard Kirkman, Bd. (1582), 271.
Roch, St (fourteenth century), 190.
Romanus, St (258), 113.
Rose of Lima, St (1617), 381.
Rumon, or Ruan, St (sixth century), 367.

S

Sabina, St (*c.* 126), 377.
Saviour, St, *see* Transfiguration.
Sebald, St (? eighth century), 224.
Sebbe, St (*c.* 694), 377.
Servite Martyrs, *see* Prague.
Secundus, St (*c.* 287), 317.
Sidonius Apollinaris, St (*c.* 488), 261.
Sigfrid, St (689), 270.
Silva, da, *see* Beatrice.
Simplician, St (400), 156.
Sixtus II, St (258), 71.
Sixtus III, St (440), 221.
Smaragdus, St (304), 94.
Sophia, *see* Wisdom.
Stephen I, St (257), 24.
Stephen, St, Finding of (415), 32.
Susanna, St (295), 133.
Syagrius, St (600), 339.
Symphorian, St (second century), 268.

T

Taparelli, *see* Aimo.
Tarsicius, St (third to fourth century), 183.
Thecla, St (304), 220.
Theodota, St (304), 27.
Theonilla, St (303), 283.
Thomas of Dover, St (1295), 68.
Thomas Percy, Bd. (1572), 320.

Thouret, *see* Joan A.
Tiburtius, St (*c.* 288), 128.
Timothy, St (304), 220.
Timothy, St (with Hippolytus) (fourth century), 268.
Timothy of Montecchio, Bd. (1504), 320.
Tolomeo, *see* Bernard.
Transfiguration of our Lord, The, 69.

U

Utica, Martyrs of (*c.* 258), 291.

V

Vianney, *see* John M. B.
Victricius, St (*c.* 409), 84.

W

Wall, *see* John.
Waltheof, or Walthen, St (1160), 57.
White Mass, The, *see* Utica.
Wigbert, St (*c.* 746), 163.
William Freeman, Bd. (1595), 167.
William Lacey, Bd. (1582), 271.
Wisdom, St (? second century), 8.

X

Xystus, *see* Sixtus.

Z

Zephyrinus, St (217), 316.

The Mayflower Press, Plymouth. William Brendon & Son, Ltd.